Market and Plan Under Socialism

Market and Plan Under Socialism:

THE BIRD IN THE CAGE

Jan S. Prybyla

HOOVER INSTITUTION PRESS
Stanford University • Stanford, California

The Hoover Institution on War, Revolution and Peace, founded at Stanford University in 1919 by the late President Herbert Hoover, is an interdisciplinary research center for advanced study on domestic and international affairs in the twentieth century. The views expressed in its publications are entirely those of the authors and do not necessarily reflect the views of the staff, officers, or Board of Overseers of the Hoover Institution.

Hoover Press Publication 335

Manufactured in the United States of America
91 90 89   9 8 7 6 5 4 3 2

Library of Congress Cataloging in Publication Data

Prybyla, Jan S.
  Market and plan under socialism.

  Bibliography: p.
  Includes index.
  1. Central planning—Communist countries.
2. Communist countries—Economic policy.   I. Title.
HC704.P8   1987   338.9'009171'7   86-10391
ISBN 0-8179-8351-1 (alk. paper)
ISBN 0-8179-8352-X (pbk.: alk. paper)

Stimulating the economy is to be done within the framework of the state plan. The relationship between the two is like a bird in the cage. A bird should be allowed to fly, but within the framework of the cage. Otherwise it will fly away.

CHEN YÜN, Chinese economist, member of the Standing Committee of the Politburo of the Communist Party of China, and leading architect of China's First Five-Year Plan (1953–1957), in the *Beijing Review* (1983)

CONTENTS

LIST OF TABLES AND FIGURES

TABLES

FIGURES

ACKNOWLEDGMENTS

The substance of Part I ("Concepts"), Chapters 1–6, was first presented at the Twelfth Sino-American Conference on Mainland China (Airlie House, Virginia, June 1983). It was subsequently included in a collection of the conference papers. This material is included by permission of Westview Press and is drawn from *Mainland China's Development*, edited by King-yuh Chang (Boulder, Colo.: Westview Press, 1984). It has since been significantly expanded and modified.

The description of Jaroslav Vanek's model of the labor-managed market economy in Chapter 1 appeared earlier in my *Issues in Socialist Economic Modernization* (New York: Praeger, 1980), pp. 89–94. It is reproduced here by permission of the Center for Strategic and International Studies at Georgetown University. Direct citations from Vanek's *The Participatory Economy* are made by permission of Cornell University Press.

Most of Chapter 9, "China: Stalinplan, Maoplan, Neoclassical Conservative Plan, and Beyond," appeared earlier under the title "The Economic System of the People's Republic of China" in *Asian Thought and Society* 9, no. 25 (March 1984). It is reprinted here, with additions and modifications, by permission of the journal editor. A portion of Chapter 12, "Summary and Conclusions," first appeared as "The Chinese Economy" in *Asian Survey* 25, no. 5 (May 1985). It is reprinted here by permission of the Regents of the University of California.

Appendix B, the Novosibirsk Document (*New York Times*, August 5, 1983), is reprinted here by permission of the New York Times Company, copyright 1983.

I acknowledge with thanks a grant from the Hoover Institution that has been helpful in the preparation of this book.

INTRODUCTION

All centrally planned state socialist economies derive—conceptually and in practice—from a common source: the Stalinplan, introduced in Russia in the late 1920s. The institutional arrangements and goals of the Stalinplan were transplanted to other countries and used in faithful imitation of the original after World War II and, with the exception of Yugoslavia, well into the 1950s. In its Soviet Stalinist form, the plan produced rapid growth of heavy industry. It also, however, produced chaotic inefficiencies, which in time began to affect the growth itself. Not much was done about this problem, however, until Stalin's death in 1953. Shortly thereafter, various attempts to change the plan began to be made in the Soviet Union, in Eastern Europe, and, after 1957, in China. Such attempts have continued to this day.

Basically, changes in the plan are of two kinds: intrasystemic adjustments and intersystemic reforms. The former are concerned with repairs and renovations to the existing institutional structure of information, coordination, property, and motivation. Their purpose is to make the status quo work better. Reforms, on the other hand, involve replacement of existing institutions, changes in the economic system itself. The only plan reform currently feasible requires the marketization of information, coordination, and motivation, and the privatization of property rights. Marketization and privatization must become dominant in the system to constitute an effective remedy for the plan's ills. Naturally, such drastic surgery, involving as it does fundamental changes in economic society, meets with resolute opposition from several threatened quarters. First and foremost among these is the planning (but also managerial) bureaucracy, the plan's surrogate for the market mechanism.

Because of this opposition—and the political, ideological, and psychological repercussions of economic reform—so far changes in the

Stalinplan have been of the adjustment variety. With the exception of radical leftist adjustments in China from 1958 to 1960 and 1966 to 1976, these intrasystemic revisions have involved partial, truncated marketization and circumscribed privatization. The form, rather than the substance, of the market and of private property has been used. In some instances (for example, Yugoslavia between 1965 and 1975, and China today), adjustments have skirted reform, but so far systemic borders have not been crossed—not even by maverick Yugoslavia at the height of its affair with the market.

Some plan adjustments have been very modest. I categorize these timid departures from the classical Stalinplan as the "neoclassical conservative plan." As of 1985, most state socialist countries—including the Soviet Union—fell into this category of dynamic immobilism. Other rightward adjustments have been more venturesome. These are represented by Hungary's on-again, off-again New Economic Mechanism. China, which began with fairly conservative changes after the death of Mao Tse-tung, has made significantly bolder adjustments in the past few years in marketization and the privatization of property rights; in the absence of sudden reversals, it may yet move into the category of the "neoclassical liberal plan," currently occupied only by Hungary. Because of its distinct property and motivational arrangements, and, lately, because of its unique system of information and coordination, Yugoslavia stands alone. I call its plan variant the "neomarket Yugoplan." Mao's leftist adjustments of the periods from 1958 to 1960 and 1966 to 1976, now no longer in vogue anywhere, stand in contradiction to the liberal plan. I designate them as the "radical Maoplan."

This book consists of two parts. In Part I, the concepts underlying each category of the plan are examined in terms of how they affect the institutions of information, coordination, property, motivation, and societal goals. In Part II, case illustrations of each conceptual category are provided: the Soviet Union's collective farm property arrangements under the Stalinplan and, together with other institutional arrangements, under the Soviet neoclassical conservative plan; China's experience with the Stalinplan, Maoplan, and neoclassical conservative plan; China's movement beyond neoclassical conservatism; Hungary's neoclassical liberal plan; and Yugoslavia's strange neomarket Yugoplan.

For the sake of intellectual propriety (because these things are much made of in the literature), in Chapter 1 I have reviewed three impractical theoretical constructs: the model of perfectly centralized planning, the supplemented market model (also known as market socialism), and the labor-managed market economy model.

The book is, in effect, a comparative analysis of centrally planned, state socialist economies: their common parentage in the Stalinplan, their diverse (but not very divergent) evolution through adjustment, and their apparent inability or unwillingness, thus far, to apply systemic reform measures to their structural problems.

I
CONCEPTS

CHAPTER ONE

Market and Plan:
Typology of Plan Models

Market and Plan

The purpose of an economy is to apportion the scarce resources of land, labor, capital, and entrepreneurship among competing alternative uses, both private and public.[1] The institutional structure of the economy should be such that it produces a set of goals to be achieved and allocates resources to the chosen goals. This structure is comprised of four major institutions: information, coordination, property, and motivation.[2]

Information is the continuous generation, transmittal, and processing of intelligence about resources and goals, supply and demand (costs and utilities), in the economy. Coordination is the reconciliation and harmonization of disparate pieces of information into a coherent system of production, exchange, and distribution. Property is a socially enforced group of economically valuable rights to the acquisition, use, and disposal of assets. It has important implications for the apportionment of wealth, income, and power in the economy and for incentives (relationships among economic agents). Motivation is the provision of incentives to economic units to engage in wealth-producing activities.

Economic institutions (agreed-upon ways of doing things) constitute the organizational core of an economy.[3] They affect the manner in which resources are used (that is, how things are produced) and the ends toward which they are employed (that is, toward which alternative goals and for whose benefit resources are allocated). They do this by the way in which they distribute the power of decision over resources and goals. Institutions may be designed either to diffuse decision-making power among the economy's producing and consuming units and the government, or to concentrate that power in governmental hands.

Ideally, economic institutions should possess five attributes: coherence, economy, accuracy, flexibility, and acceptability. Coherence means that economic institutions work in concert rather than being at odds with each other. For example, if private property is to provide incentives to individual farm families, it cannot be restricted and neutralized by information in the form of administrative orders that limit the size of the farm and its sale, number of nonfamily workers that can be hired, acquisition of nonlabor inputs, credit, and marketing of produce. Economy means that in fulfilling their functions, economic institutions should use the least amount of resources possible: ideally, the institutions would be costless.[4] Accuracy means that the institutions should indicate precisely what needs to be done in the economy and the opportunity costs of alternative courses of action. Flexibility means that the institutions should be capable of instant adaptation to changes in resource (cost) and goal (utility) conditions. Acceptability means that the economy's organizational structure should not raise opposition from those who use it: ideally, acceptance should be given freely, rather than obtained by resorting to administrative constraint.[5]

Conceptually, using two workable extremes, the job of goal selection and attainment can be done either by the competitive market or by the central administrative command plan. *Market* is taken to mean voluntary, contractual, competitive, horizontal transactions carried out by individual, autonomous, property-owning buying and selling units for utility or profit-maximizing purposes, by consulting spontaneously generated price signals, through the disbursement of money votes.[6] *Plan* is taken to mean the setting of mandatory general and specific goals by government officials regarding production, exchange, and distribution, as well as the outlining of procedures for attaining those goals (the goals and procedures being expressed in physical-technical and financial terms, and enforced primarily by administrative means). All significant means of production are government-owned, either directly (nationalization) or indirectly (nominal cooperativization).

The decentralized voluntary market and the centralized imperative plan are both market and plan systems, because in the process of goal selection and attainment, they harmonize (or claim to) individual and social interests. The market, by means of Bernard de Mandeville's and Adam Smith's Invisible Hand, is said to transform individual rational decisions into social rational ones (decentralized general equilibrium).

Similarly, the plan, through Jean-Jacques Rousseau's general will or Lenin's all-knowing vanguard proletarian party (the Visible Hand), is said to separate social rational decisions into individual rational ones (centralized general equilibrium).

In reality, the Invisible Hand is stayed by externalities, increasing returns, monopolies, problems with public goods, complementarities, indivisibilities, less than full employment, and the "prisoners' dilemma."[7] The Visible Hand demonstrably fails to bring about the congruence of social and private interest and to eliminate class conflict.[8] The practical compromise emerging from this twin failure is the "mixed" economy, which combines elements of both market and plan. The market-plan mix varies considerably among real-life national economies, as does the mix of different market structures within market economies and the mix of indicative and imperative planning and planning levels (macro, micro) within planned economies. The proportions in which the ingredients of market and plan are mixed are of critical importance.[9]

At some point in the market-plan mix, a systemic transition occurs: plan becomes market, and market becomes plan. This crossing of systemic borders is brought about by the marketization and privatization of major plan institutions (to use Chen Yün's simile in the epigraph to this book, the bird flies away), or, conversely, by the bureaucratization by the plan and socialization of the major market institutions. Marketization and privatization of the plan require decentralizing resource-use decisions and broad ownership rights over assets to the economy's basic producing and consuming units: individual firms and consumers (with consumers in the lead). In this condition, therefore, market demand determines the allocation of investment resources, and therefore, the pattern of production. Marketization and privatization of the plan presuppose a qualitative change in the plan's economic and legal philosophy: recognizing that the right of allocative decision originates in the private unit, rather than in "society" as manifested by government. More simply, the starting point of economic and legal reasoning is that the individual knows best what is good for him. Supplanting the market by the plan and socializing it involve a movement in the opposite direction, both in terms of ownership rights and the locus of resource-use decisions. Changes in economic institutions that result in a change of system we will call "reforms." Changes that do not bring about such a result (intrasystemic changes) we will call "adjustments."[10] Put another way, reforms involve the manipulation of institutional-systemic variables; adjustment is confined to the use of policy variables within an established or slightly renovated institutional edifice.[11]

Pure and Operational Plan Models

The selection and attainment of goals and the harmonization of private and public interests (the "allocative problem") ideally require internal consistency and optimality of decisions. Consistency is a physical problem of the correct fit of inputs and outputs, a concordance that hinges on technical coefficients.[12] Optimality is an economic problem of cost minimization or output maximization (allocative or static efficiency); it requires scarcity (opportunity cost) prices for its determination. These prices, which reflect the marginal costs of goods and the marginal productivities of factors, may emerge spontaneously through the operation of competitive markets, or they may have to be deliberately constructed (made shadow prices) through linear programming.

Just as there are actual market models (imperfect competition, oligopoly) operating between the polar abstractions of perfect competition and pure monopoly, so too are there actual or operational plan models operating between the polar abstractions of perfectly centralized (electronic) planning and the supplemented market model (market socialism) and its close relative, the model of a labor-managed market economy.[13]

Pure Plan Models

The model of perfectly centralized planning. This model, associated with Soviet mathematical economists L. V. Kantorovich, N. S. Nemchinov, and V. V. Novozhilov envisages the construction by the central planners of an internally consistent, optimal plan variant through use of a computer-assisted solution of very large numbers of simultaneous equations. The idea is to construct many variants of the plan based on different resource allotments and alternative technologies, the optimization criterion in a given period being (a) the minimization of resource outlays costs to obtain a given level and composition of output, or (b) the maximization of output for a given quantity and composition of inputs. The optimal plan can then be the basis for inputting rational (programming, opportunity cost, shadow) prices. Once the shadow prices are found, as they can be, all the planners need do is leave it up to all economic agents to reduce costs and increase output in accordance with those prices.[14]

The model is impracticable at the present time for four easons: (1) the very high computational cost involved in collecting and processing all the information needed from all the agents; (2) the probability that much of the information obtained will be inaccurate (this because in the absence of a foolproof system of incentives or a perfect *Gleichschaltung* of people [universal presence of the "socialist man"], people will play games with each other in the course of information exchange); (3) the planned system's demonstrated obsession with secrecy; and (4) the shortage of appropriate computer hardware. *Planometrics*, as the perfectly centralized plan is sometimes called, requires the diffusion of information through the system. In actual practice, however, plan directors regard information not as a right, but as a privilege; they release it on a need-to-know basis, the need being determined by themselves in very narrow terms. For these reasons, the quest for optimality through mathematical modeling assisted by high-memory computers has so far been limited in practice to determining the effectiveness of investment projects, foreign trade, and industrial location.[15]

It might be added that, translated into actuality, the model of perfectly centralized optimal planning would perfectly serve the purposes of political autocracy.[16]

The supplemented market model. This plan model is associated with Polish economist Oskar Lange.[17] Its essence is that in a setting of relative scarcity of means to ends, consumers have freedom of choice, and planners must respect that choice. Consumer goods prices are free to fluctuate in the market, and consumers base their choices on those prices. Producing firms are guided by prices and profitabilities (that is, they equate marginal revenue with marginal cost). The planners are responsible for investment goods and industrial materials (for which there is no market), regulating stocks by raising and lowering prices in response to threatened shortages and abundance in a process of continuous *tâtonnement.*

This model is impracticable for six reasons: (1) the high computational cost of fixing producer goods and industrial materials prices; (2) the impermissible separation of the market for consumer goods from the apportionment of producer goods and materials ("a market for ends is unworkable unless there is a market also for means");[18] (3) the failure to take growth into account; (4) the absence of a credible discussion of motivation; (5) the assuming-away of externalities, complementarities, indivisibilities, and the like; and (6) the assumption that planners will always respond to threatened shortages and surpluses by raising and lowering prices, and that they will not try to foist their output preferences on consumers by determining the volume and assortment of consumer goods and by fixing appropriate prices to clear the shelves.[19]

The model of the labor-managed market economy. This model has been elaborated by the American economist Jaroslav Vanek.[20] It is said by its inventor to be of special applicability to the neomarket Yugoplan, and has the following major characteristics:

1. *Participation.* "The labor-managed economy is one based on, or composed of, firms controlled and managed by those working in them. This participation in management is by all and on the basis of equality, that is, on the principle of one-man one-vote" [pp. 8–9]. Alternatively, each voter is given the same number of points and is allowed to assign different weights to alternative issues to be decided upon simultaneously. This participation is to be carried out through elected representative bodies and officers: a workers' council, an executive board, and the director of the firm. It should be noted that participation in control and management derives exclusively from work in the enterprise, not from participation in ownership.

2. *Income Sharing.* After paying for all operational costs (expenditures for supplies, interest on capital, turnover tax, and other obligations), worker-participants share equitably in the net income (total profit) of the enterprise. Equity requires that payment be equal for labor of equal intensity and quality, and that it be governed by a democratically agreed-upon income distribution schedule. A collectively agreed-upon share of net income can be channeled into reserve funds, collective consumption funds, and investment funds. In the latter case, "it may be preferable to recognize the contributions of savings to the firm's capital formation as individual claims of each participant, and express them in the form of fixed interest-bearing financial obligations of the firm" [p. 10], such financial claims carrying, however, no right of control or management of the firm.

3. *Property Structure.* Worker-managers do not have full ownership of the capital assets they use. They can enjoy the fruits of production in which the assets were used, but must pay a rental fee for this, and they cannot destroy or sell the real assets and distribute the proceeds as current income. In turn, lenders of financial capital and lessors of physical assets to the firm have no right of control over the assets as long as the enterprise meets its debt-servicing obligations to them.

4. *Other Institutional Arrangements.* The labor-managed economy must be a fully decentralized market economy. In addition to the labor-managed firms, other decision-making units in the system (individuals, households, associations, the government) "decide freely and to their best advantage on actions they take, without direct interference from the outside. Economic planning and policy may be implemented through use of indirect policy instruments, discussion, improved infor-

mation, or moral suasion, but never through a direct order to a firm or a group of firms" [p. 11]. Transactions among the various decision-making units are made through markets, which are perfectly free whenever there are many buyers and sellers relative to the total volume of transactions. Where monopolistic and monopsonistic situations occur, the government may intervene, but this intervention is limited to rendering the market structure more competitive by stimulating entry or opening up the market to international competition. The government may also fix minimum or maximum prices in such situations. The social preference function that emerges from such uninhibited market interaction among participants may be modified, but only through the use of "legitimate" instruments of economic policy, such as taxes.

5. *Employment.* The labor-managed economy is characterized by freedom of employment. This means that the individual is free to take, refuse, or leave a particular job, and enterprises are free to hire or not hire a particular worker. "However, the firms can, as a matter of their collective and democratic decision, limit in various ways their own capacity to expel a member of the community even where strictly economic considerations might call for doing so" [p. 12].

The advantages claimed for the theoretical model of a labor-managed economy are the following:

1. Economic self-determination by all who work reduces the worker's alienation from the product he produces and the exploitation by managers and owners of capital. Each employee becomes part worker, part manager. He is able to control both the product he makes and the conditions of work under which he produces his share of the product. In Vanek's words, the model has the merit of avoiding the "mutilation of men when used exclusively as mechanical factors of production" [p. 119].

2. Labor management (or worker dominance) eliminates class distinctions that beset other systems. There is no tyranny of capitalists, corporation managers, or state bureaucrats.

3. A labor-managed economy, according to the model's proponents, will tend to coexist with political self-determination (democratically elected government) since workers' democracy and political democracy are mutually reinforcing. In fact, the implanting of workers' economic self-determination will, through its salutary democratic training, promote the emergence of political democracy where such is lacking.

4. It is also argued that "under the scrutiny of economic theory the participatory economy appears in a very favorable light, both in comparison to an absolute standard of efficiency and in comparison with other economic systems" [p. 38]. This theoretical assessment is said to

be confirmed by the empirical record of the Yugoslav worker-managed economy's performance.

The theoretical model of a labor-managed economy has been criticized on the following grounds:

1. Assuming that "the quest of men to participate in the determination and decision-making of the activities in which they are personally and directly involved" is really "one of the most important sociopolitical phenomena of our times" [p.1], alienation in the Marxian sense of exploitation, coupled with the divorce of the worker from his product, may indeed be attenuated in a worker-managed firm. Presumably this participation would make workers more productive. One could argue, however, that alienation in the Marxian sense is not the only form of alienation. Analytically it is possible, for any firm in the setting of competitive markets, to make a distinction between the firm as an entrepreneurial economic unit and the employees of the firm as suppliers of labor. As an entrepreneurial economic unit, the firm presumably will seek to maximize, increase, or simply retain its revenue. To achieve this goal, it will exert internal pressure on production costs; such pressure will include an attempt on the part of the unit to increase output per worker by, for example, intensification of work.[21] Where workers and managers are one, it is conceivable that a conflict between the two welded roles may arise. In that event, alienation will simply have been redefined. A subtle attempt to shift the entrepreneurial function of the firm to the director would tend to undo much of the original cooperative idea.

2. Concerning the objective of classlessness, three related difficulties are likely to present themselves. First, there will be a tendency for worker-managed firms to erect job entry barriers in both the short and the long run. The firm may be expected to try to maximize average long-run profits per worker rather than total long-run profits, sales, or growth. Thus, there will tend to be built-in reluctance to spread profits over more employees; one way of ensuring that long-run profits per worker are not spread too thinly is by keeping potential job entrants out of the firm. In fact, it can be shown that the worker-managed firm's short-run reaction to a price increase in its product is to reduce the amount of the product supplied and to increase output of the product when the price falls.[22] The propensity of worker-managed firms to keep their doors closed may result in the firms' becoming exclusive social clubs, making the system a conglomerate of such clubs. In the long run, this tendency will be strengthened by the role of the firm as a social and recreational center for its employees, as well as by a "social constraint" that works against putting club members out to pasture

(Vanek's power of the firm to "limit in various ways [its] own capacity to expel a member of the community even where strictly economic considerations might call for doing so").[23] Second, within the firm, rules of seniority may well encourage the emergence of hierarchic worker structures. Such seniority rules are more likely to exist where the length of workers' tenure is considerable, as it is likely to be in worker-managed enterprises. Third, worker-managed firms are presumed to operate in a competitive market setting. It is reasonable to suppose that differences in material well-being among the firms will develop, some firms doing much better than others. In fact, in a small country (such as Yugoslavia), it is conceivable that monopolistic firms will flourish in a number of sectors. Therefore, in addition to the class nature of the firms and the class structure within each firm, there will be class ranking among firms in the system. As with alienation, the class nature of society simply will be redefined.

3. The contention that economic self-determination will promote political democracy is questionable. The coexistence of economic self-determination with benevolent or not-so-benevolent dictatorship cannot be ruled out.

4. The absolute and relative efficiency of the model remains a matter of debate. We will mention only one problem: "If technology," writes one critic of the model, "moves in the direction of substantially increasing externalities [the model's contention that only the market is consistent with efficiency], is clearly false within the neoclassical framework which [the model] accepts."[24]

5. It has been suggested that the nearest thing to a fallacy of composition is to imply that a national economic system, the component enterprises of which are employee-managed, is itself thereby labor-managed. "A general economic system has its own organization, structure, regulation, properties, and operating characteristics distinct from such attributes of the entities it comprises."[25] A market economy tends to be endogenously self-regulating, not exogenously managed by, for example, workers' collectives.

6. Some critics have asked to what extent workers (or anyone else, for that matter) are genuinely anxious to participate. Direct participation in allocative power connotes material risks as well as benefits and "higher" (nonmaterial) gratifications. To be directly involved takes time away from consumption and requires a significant amount of technical expertise; it increases self-esteem but also entails a great deal of heartbreak, disappointment, disillusion, and possible financial loss. The assumption that men are inherently democratic and involved, that they possess a developed sense of social responsibility by

virtue of being workers, and that they have the ability to grapple with complex technical questions (or even undemanding repetitive administrative chores) may be quite simply the projection onto others of the idiosyncratic temper of those who make the assumption. The history of humanity is in large part a record of individuals submitting, with varying degrees of assent, to autocratic authority: surrendering or delegating their decision-making power and, as often as not, liking it. It is argued that the phenomenon of widespread flight from choice is as true of Soviet consumers and enterprise managers as it is of stockholders and "manipulated" consumers and citizens in the West. And, the argument continues, this is not all due to the dark machinations of power-hungry elites. The qualities of individual self-assertion and social consciousness, fair play and toleration of opposing views, democratic coordination through reasoned discussion and the instinct for equity—all these cannot simply be postulated.

Operational Plan Models

In real life, things are not as straightforward as the transcendental theories suggest. Figure 1.1 gives a taxonomy of real-life plans that have been operational at different times and indicates the country membership in those plans.

The classical plan is the original Soviet administrative command system installed in the USSR by Stalin in the late 1920s, which was adopted by all Eastern European countries in the late 1940s and by China in the early 1950s. By 1955, Stalin's "socialism in one country" had become "one socialism in all countries." Only Yugoslavia managed to break away; for a time it proceeded along a path indicated by the model of labor-managed market. The Stalinplan was, in every case, unrelated and irrelevant to either the national and cultural experience or the geopolitical and economic realities of the individual countries adopting it (most often with the help of Soviet arms).

After 1955, a process of adjusting the Stalinist plan began in the USSR and Eastern Europe. This resulted in the emergence of a neoclassical plan in two variants: conservative and liberal, the former by far the more common. China began its adjustment in 1958, swinging first toward a radical Maoist variant of the classical plan, then toward a conservative variant in the early 1960s, then back to the radical plan from 1966 to 1976, then again to conservatism, and from 1979 to the mid-1980s toward ever-greater marketization and privatization.[26] There has been an occasional mild flirtation with the Yugoplan, but nothing has come of it so far. The radical neoclassical plan (Maoism), applied in

China from 1958 to 1960 (the Great Leap Forward) and again, off and on, during the Cultural Revolution from 1966 to 1976, tried to democratize allocation by "mass planning," in the process vandalizing much of the classical plan's formal structure. The Maoplan had been found wanting, and has now been discarded everywhere.

In contrast to Yugoslavia, which at times came close to crossing the systemic border through reform (1965–1975) but always stopped short, all other state socialist countries have kept well within the systemic frontiers. Most have readjusted a great deal, but reformed not at all. The cage has been expanded to let the bird fly around a bit, but has not been dismantled.[27]

The expansion, however, has not been uniform. Within the neoclassical conservative plan some economies are more conservative than others (for example, those of Romania and Bulgaria). The differences are defined by the relative distance traveled toward marketization of the institutional structure of information, coordination, and motivation and toward the privatization of property. The countries of the neoclassical conservative plan cover differing distances toward legitimizing a range of economic activities undertaken by individuals (as consumers, workers, and managers), initiatives that are legally prohibited and morally condemned under the classical plan. Overall, measured by the yardstick of market economies, the distance traveled has not been great.

National cultural traits also intrude to make some equally conservative neoclassical economies unequal. For instance, the East German economy seems to be located at the liberal end of the conservative spectrum. This comes as a surprise, because the Germans take their Marxism-Leninism seriously; they have a well-developed sense of discipline, and regimentation, though not savored, comes more easily to them than, for example, to the Romanians. And so the East German economy appears more conservative than some others, when, in fact, the opposite is probably true. The perception, however, is not altogether wrong: the in-depth seriousness with which the tiny bit of liberalism is taken in East Germany shrivels the roots of liberalism and blights what little fruit manages to mature.

The Reason for Adjustment, Possibly Even Reform

The old Stalinist classical plan was, like Stalin himself, crude in character. It set for itself two prime objectives: the preservation and consolidation of monopolistic state power, and product growth. The quality of that growth—its cost in human lives and values, and in material resources—was discounted in its pursuit. Growth was generated primarily through the addition of factors (especially labor and capital) and through the diffusion of production technologies from a given technological base—by "extensive" means, rather than by the improved performance of factors (rising factor productivity—"intensive" means). The classical plan was allocatively inefficient, that is, wasteful.[28] It was also internally inconsistent, a condition manifested in chronic shortages of wanted goods and surpluses of unwanted ones. The combination of quantitative inconsistency and qualitative inefficiency became worse as the economy expanded and its complexity increased. It was not so much the brutality of the classical plan as its progressively adverse impact on planner control and growth rate that persuaded

FIGURE 1.1

Operational Plans in Different Countries, Selected Years

COUNTRIES		USSR			China			E. Germany			Romania		
	YEARS	'55	'68	'84	'55	'68	'84	'55	'68	'84	'55	'68	'84
CLASSICAL *(Stalinplan)*		X			X			X			X		
NEOCLASSICAL Conservative			X	X					X	X		X	X
Liberal						X							
Radical (Maoplan)							X						
NEOMARKET *(Yugoplan)*													

TYPE OF PLAN

(with a little prodding from the Poles and Hungarians in 1956) post-Stalin leaders to try their hand at adjustment and, conceivably, even reform. In a curious twist of Adam Smith's dictum of *The Wealth of Nations*, it was not from the benevolence of the planners that the people expected relief, but from the planners' regard for their own self-interest: "We address ourselves not to their humanity but to their self-love, and never talk to them of our necessities but of their own advantage."[29]

Let us now look at the main features of the classical, neoclassical, and neomarket plans. This we will do by referring to the institutions of information, coordination, property, and motivation, with a quick glance at some of the plans' goals.

Bulgaria			*Poland*			*Czecho-slovakia*			*Albania*			*Hungary*			*Yugoslavia*		
'55	'68	'84	'55	'68	'84	'55	'68	'84	'55	'68	'84	'55	'68	'84	'55	'68	'84
X			X			X			X	X	X	X					
	X	X		X	X		X	X									
													X	X			
															X	X	X

CHAPTER TWO

The Classical Plan: Stalinplan

The classical plan is highly centralized and bureaucratized. Decisions, both macro and micro, are taken at a high level of the single-party state bureaucracy, and rely heavily upon administrative (physical-technical) criteria.

Information

Information in the plan takes two forms. The dominant form is physical-technical information (tons, meters, British thermal units). The secondary and subsidiary form is planner-set prices. Both forms are mandatory for the producers and significantly constrain the free choice of consumers and workers. The information is conveyed to specific addressee firms in annual and quarterly physical and financial norms for inputs and outputs within the context of longer-term (five-year) plans. It is conveyed to consumers either in designated physical rations or, more commonly, in state-determined quantities and assortments of consumer goods offered at state-fixed prices. It is conveyed to workers in the form of administrative job assignments (as in China) or, more often, in differentiated state-set basic wage schedules to which the addressees respond (as in the USSR and Eastern Europe).[1]

Physical-Technical Indicators

The primacy of physical indicators and technical coefficients in the classical plan must be insisted upon (the Germans call this *Tonnenideologie*). In socialism's more innocent days, it was thought that planned prices would be allocatively neutral and that eventually, under full communism, they could be dispensed with, along with money and all its works. As we shall see in a moment, in the classical plan prices do play a limited allocative role, but they are still envisaged as simple translations into monetary terms of the quantities specified in the physical-technical orders where it is inconvenient or impossible to express plan magnitudes in physical-technical notations.[2] (In the radical neoclassical plan—Mao's Great Leap Forward and the Khmer Rouge's genocidal economics of the period from 1975 to 1978—financial transactions were tightly compressed. In Cambodia, money was abolished.) The important point is that at the very foundation of classical plan thinking is the idea that prices should not be autonomous nodes of allocative power, independent of single-party state preferences expressed in the planners' physical commands.

The issuance of physical commands requires that three types of information be available to the planners: (1) the economy's physical capacity to produce; (2) the production function for each commodity, that is, the amount and assortment of inputs needed to produce each output (direct technical coefficient) and the substitutability of inputs for each other; and (3) a leadership ("planners' ") preference function for all intermediate and final goods.

Prices

A good summary conceptualization of the nature and role of prices in a planned economy of the Soviet type has been devised by American economist Gregory Grossman. It is reproduced in Figure 2.1 to help us understand both the limited function of prices (and markets) in the classical version of the plan and the plan's limited marketization carried out in the USSR and Eastern Europe in the 1960s and early 1970s, and in mainland China in the late 1970s and early 1980s.

Quadrant IV represents the pure classical case: the greatest limitation on the choice of both buyers and sellers. It is the heart of the classical plan. The job of allocation is done here primarily by physical commands, while prices are used for firm economic self-accounting (*khozraschet*), plan control, and anti-inflationary purposes. The use of money is sectorally restricted. The situation applies to goods—especially producer goods—transferred by state bank book entries within the state sector, and to compulsory quota deliveries of collective farm produce. Prices consist of state-set wholesale and quota agricultural procurement prices, the first set on the basis of a rough calculation of average cost plus normal profit, the latter set in essence as a confiscatory tax. State demand is given and its satisfaction by the sellers is compulsory, that is, subject to central physical rationing by the material-technical supply network (known in China as the State Bureau of Supplies). Theoretically, the "law of value" is suspended as planners cause goods to be supplied in response to their demand and move the goods around by allocation certificates (prices are allocatively passive). Practically, things are a bit different. Whenever (which means almost always) the interests of the planners ("society") and the enterprise are not reconciled by the planner-set price, "regulator games" will be played between the central planning organs and the enterprises the planners are trying to regulate. Two situations may be envisaged. Where an enterprise produces a single product or a narrow range of standardized products, the quality of which can be unequivocally defined, the pricing authority can enforce its will and, without much trouble, check on the relationship between costs and prices (for example, basic materials, primary energy). Where, however, an enter-

FIGURE 2.1

Price Formation in a Soviet-Type Economy

Buyer

		Free Choice	Constrained or No Choice
Seller	*Free Choice*	I Formed freely by D & S in the market	II Set by the state to equate S to D (plus some "drift")[a]
	Constrained or No Choice	III Set by the state to equate D to S	IV Set by the state chiefly on the basis of cost; little attention to equating S & D

SOURCE: Gregory Grossman, *Economic Systems*, Foundations of Modern Economics Series, 2nd ed. (Englewood Cliffs, N.J.: Prentice-Hall, 1974), p. 108. Reprinted by permission of the publisher.

NOTE: D = demand; S = supply.

[a]Because of labor shortage, officially set wage rates are often ignored by firm managers, while the planners look the other way.

prise produces many differentiated products and sells them in diverse markets, it becomes very difficult for the planners to enforce their prices.

> We have to put up with the fact that it is the relatively smaller part of production where real administrative prices can be set or the method of price calculations can be prescribed in an administrative manner. With the greater part of production this is sheer illusion, only pseudo-administrative prices come about.[3]

Quadrants II and III represent compromise and an accommodation of the plan with constrained market. In Quadrant III, the planners cannot physically dictate—except at prohibitively high cost in consumer goods rationing—everything consumers should and should not demand. What the planners do is decide on a given volume and assortment of consumer goods (that is, fix the supply, S) and then set retail prices at shelf-clearing levels for each commodity. This is a most difficult task given the number of commodities involved, the changeability of consumer wants, and the retarded state of demand studies in all state socialist countries. The raising and lowering of state retail prices is done manually by administrative authorities located high in the state bureaucracy.[4] This means that price adjustments are carried out infrequently, with sizable time lags behind changes in consumer demand. Consequently, the consumer goods economy is in endemic disequilibrium, with shortages of wanted goods here and surpluses of unwanted goods there. The situation is aggravated by the low opinion in which consumer want satisfaction is held in classical planning circles. Misallocations occurring in Quadrant IV, expecially shortages of key inputs, are relegated for solution to the semimarket of Quadrant III. If there is a shortage of cotton, army uniforms will not suffer, but civilian suits and dresses will. Quadrant III also applies to the sale of consumer and producer goods by state sector firms to collective farms.

Quadrant II represents a situation in which the seller has free choice (meaning, "take it or leave it"), but the buyer does not. The wages of labor in the USSR and Eastern Europe are a good example of prices in this quadrant. To make a worker move from Moscow to a Siberian construction site these days requires a price. This was true even under Stalin, but much less so (see Aleksandr Solzhenitsyn's *The Gulag Archipelago*). It has not been true of China, where most wages belonged until recently to Quadrant IV. In Quadrant II, the demand for labor (or for above-quota, noncompulsory collective farm sales to the state) is determined by the planners; the supply needed to meet the demand at some rough equilibrium level must be coaxed out by varying the supply price. Here, too, the magnitude of the task is forbidding, and other considerations enter to immobilize the wage level over long periods of time—more than twenty years at a stretch in both Russia and China. These considerations have to do largely with the planners' desire to prevent inflationary wage drifts (cost-push inflation) in a setting of almost permanent labor shortage caused by ambitious output growth targets ("taut planning"). So here, too, as in Quadrant III, the partial and highly circumscribed operation of markets inevitably gives rise to the coexistence of shortages and surpluses, plus behavioral distortion (labor hoarding) by firm managers.[5] The failure of wages to approximate the value of the workers' marginal product (that is, to reflect with a fair degree of accuracy the underlying forces of supply and demand in the labor market), combined with both the classical plan's "law" of rational low wages (which ordains that wages should be kept low to restrict consumption in the interest of state investment) and the social desideratum of lifelong employment, weakens motivation (that is, plays havoc with labor incentives).

Quadrant I represents the market. In the classical Soviet-type plan, it consists of legal free peasant markets, illegal markets, and those in between. The structure of these markets is not uniform locationally, statically (at a given time), and dynamically (over time). American economists Aron Katsenelinboigen and Herbert S. Levine identify three types of legal markets, one type of semilegal market, and two types of illegal markets.[6]

Reform of the classical plan means movement from Quadrant IV to Quadrant I: it involves marketization, the freeing of prices, and the liberation of choice. Reform (not shown in Figure 2.1) may also consist of substantially altering the ingredients of Quadrants II and III (and even IV) in favor of the market. Adjustment of plan means movement from Quadrant IV to Quandrants II and III: it involves caged marketization, "contractual" and "limit" prices, and constrained free choice, but no sovereignty of individual choice (See Figure 2.2).

In sum, information in the classical plan is primarily physical, vertical, prepared manually and deliberately, mandatory, and recipient-specific (that is, addressed to identifiable units, rather than being general, "pure" information addressed to no one in particular, as with competitive market prices).

Because physical and nonscarcity price information is unidimensional (nonsynthetic in terms of opportunities foregone), any one piece of information must be clarified by additional pieces to prevent its willful misreading by the recipient. (A good example is the target for nail production expressed in tons. The easiest way for the nail factory is to produce one big, heavy nail, which does not happen to be in the social interest. Hence, the tonnage target must be supplemented by many other physical indicators: assortment, size, and so on.) State socialist economies are noted for information inflation, the greater part of it being trivial and, in the last analysis, dysfunctional. The classical First Five-Year Plan (1947–1951) document for the rather rudimentary Yugoslav economy weighed 1½ tons.

In the absence of mathematical modeling backed by computers, physical information and its classical nonscarcity plan price expressions are of no help in arriving at allocative efficiency, which must be counted as a systemic cost. Moreover, domestic planned prices ⸱re divorced from and cannot be compared with world market prices to help the planned economy determine the commodities in which it has a comparative cost advantage. (Even where such advantage can be pinpointed, it might not be followed in practice if the internationally cost-advantageous commodities are low on the planners' scale of goal priorities.) Soviet economist R. I. Shniper estimates that, using world market prices, Soviet Siberia had a 1975 export surplus of 8–9 billion rubles in contrast to an import deficit of 3 billion rubles at official prices.[7]

Because plan information is compulsory for the recipient, certainly

FIGURE 2.2

Adjustment and Reform in the Classical Plan

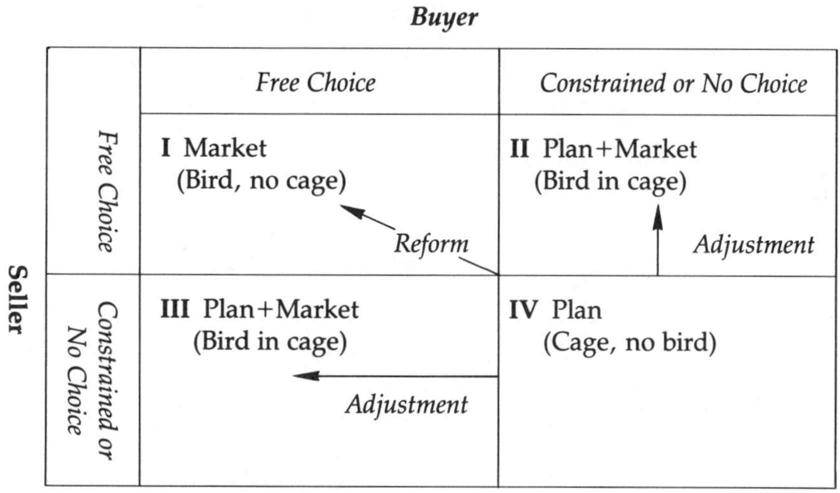

Buyer

		Free Choice	Constrained or No Choice
Seller	*Free Choice*	I Market (Bird, no cage)	II Plan+Market (Bird in cage)
	Constrained or No Choice	III Plan+Market (Bird in cage)	IV Plan (Cage, no bird)

Reform (arrow from II to I)

Adjustment (arrow from IV to II)

Adjustment (arrow from IV to III)

with regard to firms and partly with regard to workers and consumers, there is a tendency to prevaricate. This is so because the social interest (as formulated by the planners) and the individual interest of economic units are identical only by the rarest of accidents. A system that generates, as an integral part of its organic logic, an abundance of erroneous information that must be acted upon, creates legions of people whose sole reason for professional existence is to check up on others (and these people in turn must be checked up on by still others). All of this is costly not only in the economic sense, but in the psychological as well.[8]

In the original Soviet Stalinplan, consumer goods prices were high compared with the prices of producer goods; that is, consumer goods (food included) carried high rates of turnover tax, while producer goods were tax-free. The purpose of these "price scissors" was to impart an additional informational bias to the industrial structure in favor of producer goods production—additional to the administrative physical commands in the form of key input and output targets. In 1948, the prices of Soviet producer goods (weighted by quantity) were two times their 1927–28 level (the final year before the Stalinplan). Weighted consumer goods prices in 1949 were thirty times their 1927–28 level. The low producer goods prices were arrived at by adding a very small profit margin to average production cost (3–5 percent).[9] This meant that a large segment of Soviet producer goods industries was operating at a financial loss, and was being kept alive by budgetary subsidies. China's classical plan departed from this pattern of pricing (see Chapter 9).

Similarly, in the Soviet Stalinplan, state purchase prices of agricultural products (procurement prices) were kept low relative to industrial prices, thus strengthening the industrial bias of the plan's physical commands. In China, these price scissors were narrowed during the classical plan period (1953–1957), and the antiagriculture terms of trade were probably reversed after 1958 (see Chapter 9).

Coordination: The Visible Hand

The pieces of information transmitted through the economic system must be coordinated into a coherent and, if possible, allocatively optimal input-output whole. In the absence of markets, this is done administratively by the planners. It means, first, that a planned economy requires a formal organization staffed with officials who are paid salaries for doing the coordinating work of the market. Although Marx and

Lenin were convinced of the ultimate feasibility—indeed, inevitability—of bureaucrat-free socialism, it is clear intuitively and has been demonstrated historically that planning is synonymous with and inseparable from bureaucracy. The bureaucracy can be computerized, but it cannot be abolished without abolishing the plan.

The important points to be made are (a) prior to 1956, the organizational chart of the Stalinist classical model was adopted and implemented with only minor changes by all state socialist countries; and (b) the behavioral traits of the Soviet bureaucracy were duplicated in all the client states with results similar to those in the USSR.

Formal Organization

The formal organization of the classical plan consists of a pyramid-like structure comprised of about six major layers of authority in hierarchically descending order (see Figure 2.3).[10] The national system is reproduced at the republic/province and lower administrative echelons. Although territorial divisions are not without significance (especially in China), the principle governing the classical plan is that of the nationwide product "branch" directed by a ministry (represented in Figure 2.3 by the several columns). The state pyramid interacts with and is dominated by a territorially organized party pyramid.

In the classical plan, decision-making power and control are concentrated at the first four levels, operationally (a) at the level of the Council of Ministers/State Council commissions, which includes the Central Planning Commission (*Gosplan*) and bodies dealing with the physical rationing of key materials and capital goods (material-technical supply network), wages and price determination, banking, capital construction, science and technology policy, and statistics; and (b) at the level of the national ("branch") ministries. It should be noted that at the height of the Soviet Stalinplan, many of the functions listed under (a) were either concentrated in the *Gosplan* (or its equivalent) or distributed among industrial ministries. For example, before 1957, every Soviet branch ministry had its own material-technical supply network for acquiring and allocating supplies (except for the most important "funded" commodities, which were allocated by *Gosplan*).

Control over state-owned firms (and though not always in the same way, over cooperatives) is exercised by the superior state organs in a variety of ways. These include having the firms surrender the bulk of their profits and depreciation funds to the state treasury; allocating capital out of the state budget; rationing key inputs; determining output and assortment (product mix) targets, an aggregate wages fund, job grades and a wage coefficient; elaborating rules governing the formation and distribution of bonuses; fixing input and output prices; establishing a monopoly over bank credit; monitoring all interfirm transactions by the state bank (all such transactions to take place by means of entries in the bank's account books); determining the volume and composition of key investments; establishing a tax policy; setting agricultural procurement quotas and prices; and stipulating minimal rates of formation for collective farm accumulation and social funds. At the lowest level, state firms operate on "economic self-accounting" (*khozraschet*), which is another means of central control and is comprised of two elements: separate financial accounts kept by the firms, and the meeting of firm expenses from the firm's sales revenue (the whole expressed in planner-set prices).

FIGURE 2.3

Organization of the Plan

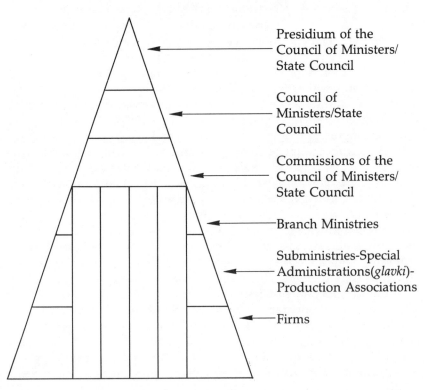

Presidium of the Council of Ministers/ State Council

Council of Ministers/State Council

Commissions of the Council of Ministers/ State Council

Branch Ministries

Subministries-Special Administrations(*glavki*)- Production Associations

Firms

Bureaucratic Behavior

The bureaucrats in charge of the plan, especially those above the subministry level, are an elite group (*klan*) despite their huge numbers. They are appointed from a patronage list (*nomenklatura*) for which the party's Politburo, Central Committee, or lesser committees are responsible, depending on the importance of the appointment. These people exercise enormous power over the citizenry, not only because of their grip on administrative and economic levers, but because of their party affiliation. Among their behavioral characteristics are aversion to risk, preference for routine, a tendency to blur the locus of personal responsibility for decisions, ability to recognize class interest, skill at eroding professional competence through time-consuming administrative duties, arrogance, and a propensity to be corrupted.[11]

Physical Coordination

The chief tool for achieving classical plan cohesion is the material balances method. In this method, output targets are equated with constraining resource supply by a process of administrative iteration on the basis of input coefficients based on past experience and adjusted for expected technical advance.[12] This bureaucratic iteration process is fairly similar to, but more flexible than, the method of solving an input-output matrix through iteration techniques. The balances relate to major commodity groups for the economy as a whole and for its major branches. They do not add up to a complete input-output table for the economy; that is, not all commodities are covered, and those that are covered are commodity groups rather than individual goods (see Table 2.1). The balances are disaggregated as they make their way down the planning pyramid until they end up as the individual firm physical and financial plans (see Figure 2.4). At the level of the firm, the disaggregated plan takes the form of several managerial "success indicators," that is, payoff formulae for fulfilling and exceeding input, output (of principal products), and profit or sales (financial) norms. The most important norm is the gross value of output (*val*).

From the planners' standpoint, there are three principal drawbacks of the material balances method of coordination:

1. At the macro planning level (the top three tiers in Figure 2.3) the balances are, as has just been noted, input-output statements for broad

TABLE 2.1
ANNUAL MATERIAL BALANCE FOR STEEL IN THE CLASSICAL PLAN
(in physical or financial units)

Supply	Uses
I. Amount in storage at the beginning of the year	I. Amount in storage at the end of the year
+	+
II. Production	II. Amount consumed in
	1) steel industry itself
	+
	2) the construction industry
	+
=	3) the machinery industry
	+
	4) the making of trucks
	+
	5) personal uses (for example, refrigerators)
	+
	6) government uses (for example, weapons)
	(and so on)
+	+
III. Imports	III. Exports

SOURCE: Harry Schwartz, *Russia's Soviet Economy*, 2nd ed. (Englewood Cliffs, N.J.: Prentice-Hall, 1982), pp.152–55. Adapted by permission of the publisher.

NOTE: The equation above can be written:

$$S_0 + P + I = Se + C_1 + C_2 + C_3 + C_4 + C_5 + C_6 + \ldots C_n + E$$

where S_0 is amount in storage at the beginning of the year; P is production; I is imports; E is exports; Se is amount in storage at the end of the year; and $C_1, C_2, C_3, C_4 \ldots C_n$ is the amount consumed in different industries (n is the number of different industries using steel).

In actuality, each term will be composed of various terms: S_0 might read $S_0' + S_0'' + S_0''' \ldots {}_0^n$ for as many terms (n) as there are storage facilities.

To obtain a fuller picture in a monetized economy using prices, a set of financial balances is required.

Example. The freight car industry produces q freight cars during the year and sells them at the (same) price p per unit. Yearly income is pq.

Let c_8 be the amount of various commodities going into the manufacture of freight cars and primes denote the different materials. Thus, c_8' is amount of coal, c_8'' is amount of steel, c_8''' is amount of wood, and so on. The prices of these commodities are $p', p'', p''' \ldots p^k$, where p^k is the price of the last commodity (c_8^k) purchased. D is the difference between income and cost. Thus,

$$pq = p'c_8' + p''c_8'' + p'''c_8''' \ldots p^k c_8^k + D$$

Where D is zero, income = cost. Where D is positive, income > cost; there is a profit. Where D is negative, income < cost; there is a loss.

For capital construction projects, replace the income term pq by the amount allocated to each project.

categories of goods and factors lacking detailed specifications within each category. Despite disaggregation at lower levels of the planning pyramid, this leaves the precise determination of the details (which, after all, are the practical usable components of each category) to a varying extent up to managerial interpretation, which may be (and usually is) at odds with the planners' intent. Moreover, as has also been noted, not all categories are captured by the balances, which leaves unplanned, uncoordinated gaps in the economy. To an important extent, an underground barter-cum-market economy fills this coordination void. The result is that actual outcomes deviate from planned outcomes, the deviation being particularly pronounced in areas of the economy located at the lower end of the scale of planners' priorities— over much of the civilian consumer economy, for example.

2. The disaggregated plan norms at the micro level of the firm (managerial success indicators) still leave room for informal maneuver by the manager, especially with respect to quality and assortment.[13] This is for two reasons: (a) it is not possible to define every detail of every input and output of the firm, so that even in their (ministerial and subministerial) specificity, the indicators leave discretionary gaps; and (b) because the indicators are primarily physical-technical or expressed in one-dimensional, cost-plus prices, there is a tendency for the planners to multiply the number of indicators for cross-checking purposes. This indicator inflation makes it almost certain that there will be lack of coherence among the prescribed norms. Most often, they cannot all be carried out; some will be sacrificed by firm managers, usually those least consonant with the micro interest of the firm as perceived by management. In addition to the high cost of the operation, chances are good that actual outcomes will again depart from planners' preferences. This cat-and-mouse game of plan execution, supported by frequently misleading statistical information on firm output capacity and input requirements as communicated by the producing units to their supervisory authorities and ultimately to the central planners in the course of plan formulation, represents the "countervailing allocative power of the weak," or distorted (being illegal and demoralizing) "market creep" within the formally planned system. Realistically, much of the business of the classical plan is transacted informally and illegally, within the interstices of the plan.

3. The third problem with material balances is that they are static with respect to technology. The input-output relationships they express reflect technological coefficients as of a given point in time (the time at which the balances are constructed). The balances do not, by their very nature, indicate the dynamics of technical progress. These

FIGURE 2.4

The Plan at the Level of the Firm

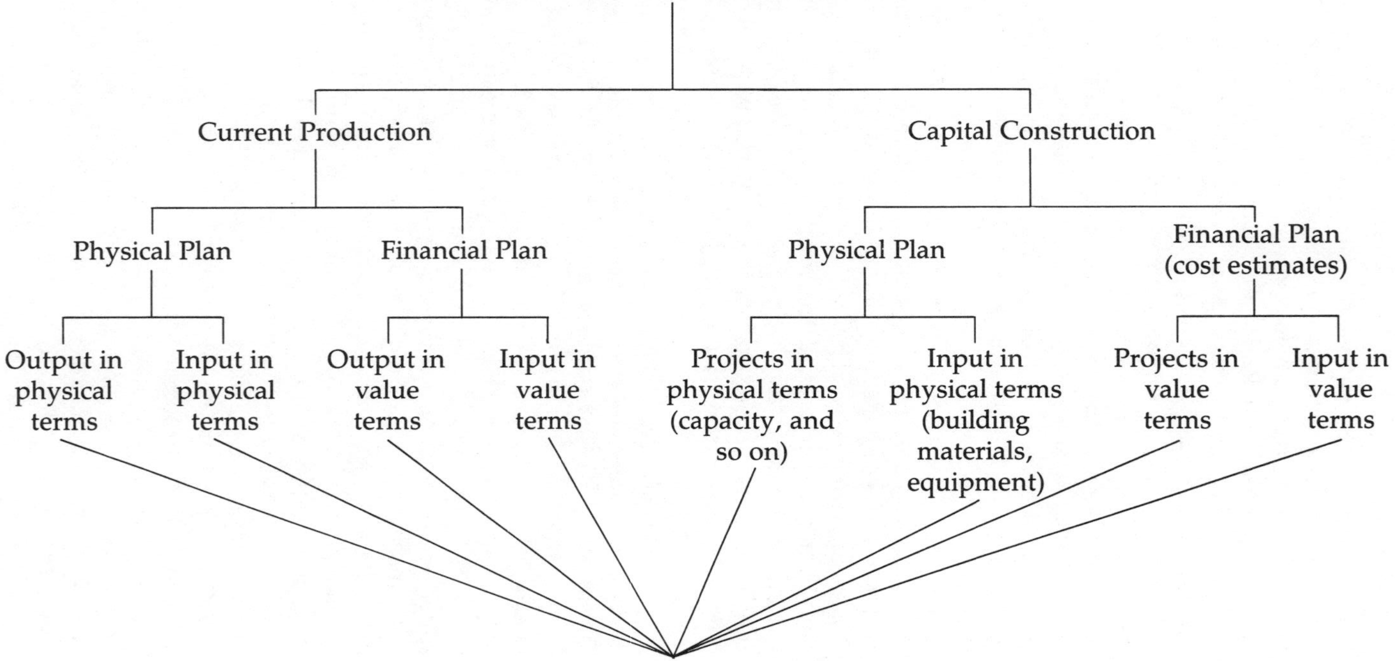

Specific Success Indicators of the Firm

1. Volume and gross value of output of principal products (*val*)
2. Assortment of output of principal products
3. Volume and schedule of sales (deliveries) of principal products with specifications of principal buyers
4. Other goods produced
5. Supply of key materials and equipment by superior agencies; that is, central funding of key material-technical supplies with specification of principal suppliers
6. Prices of outputs and inputs of principal products
7. Aggregate profits or losses and profitability rates
8. Total cost targets
9. Norms for materials costs
10. Budgetary grants and levies
11. Aggregate wages fund based on *val* and/or average wage; job categories and rates; regional differentials in compensation; bonus rules; total labor force
12. Volume of investment from central funds with specification of fixed capital construction
13. Labor productivity norms and targets for increases of labor productivity
14. Production techniques and targets for assimilation of new products and technology
15. Key managerial and technical appointments
16. Rules governing labor relations
17. Improvements in utilization of capacity
(and so on)

NOTE: See also Alec Nove, "The Problem of 'Success Indicators' in Soviet Industry," *Economica*, n.s. 25, no. 97 (February 1958): 1–13.

are factored in largely on the basis of guesswork about future capacity changes resulting from the introduction of more progressive technology and more advanced equipment. The technological statics implicit in the use of material balances as coordinating tools injects an anti-innovation bias into the system.

Physical coordination through material balances (including labor balances expressed in man-hours) is supplemented by "value" coordination through financial balances based on state-determined prices.

Financial Coordination

In addition to the Central Planning Commission (*Gosplan*), several other agencies are involved in the preparation and implementation of the financial plan. These include the State Bank (*Gosbank*, or People's Bank), which monitors domestic transactions among economic agents; the Foreign Trade Bank, which deals with foreign exchange transactions; and the Ministry of Finance, which prepares the state budget.

The financial plan consists of a cash and credit plan (see Tables 2.2

TABLE 2.2
CASH PLAN
(Stalinplan)

Cash Income
(withdrawal of cash from circulation)

(1) Monies received from sale of goods to the public by state and collective commerce
(2) Savings deposits by the public
(3) Charges for public services
(4) Taxes on individuals

Cash Expenditure
(injection of cash into circulation)

(1) Wages and other compensation paid to workers and employees
(2) State procurement of farm and sideline products
(3) Purchases of industrial goods, handicraft products, mining goods, gold and silver
(4) Administrative expenses of government agencies and business expenses of government units
(5) Withdrawals of savings deposits by the public in urban areas

TABLE 2.3
CREDIT PLAN
(Stalinplan)

Sources of Funds

(1) Budgetary deposits of the Ministry of Finance and deposit accounts of other government departments and institutions, military units, enterprises, rural collectives, and individuals
(2) Money in transit (for example, capital construction funds earmarked, but not yet allocated, to enterprises by the relevant authorities)
(3) Currency in circulation
(4) Self-owned funds of the State Bank from accumulated profits
(5) Foreign deposits and loans

Uses of Funds

(1) Loans to industry, commerce, agriculture, and the state budget
(2) Cash in the hands of the public
(3) Foreign exchange requirements

SOURCE: International Monetary Fund, *Recent Economic Developments in the People's Republic of China* (Washington, D.C.: I.M.F., 1981).

and 2.3). An important component of the overall financial plan is the state budget (*gosbiudzhet*), which is comprised of key policy variables (see Table 2.4). The budget shown here is consolidated; that is, it is an amalgam of central, provincial, municipal, and local government budgets.

As noted, in addition to the formal organization and tools, coordination in the classical plan is accomplished by legal and illegal markets. This officially sanctioned and unregistered market coordination both helps the planned economy out of its frequent mismatchings and produces outcomes not desired by the planners.

Planning Sequence

The planning process unfolds in roughly the following sequence. The Central Planning Commission (*Gosplan*) prepares preliminary output and input targets for the annual plan in physical and financial terms. These "control figures" are passed down to the branch ministries (and provincial-republican authorities) where they are disaggregated and allotted to individual production units. At this point, the production

TABLE 2.4
CONSOLIDATED STATE BUDGET
(Stalinplan)

Revenues

---

(1) Tax receipts (sales taxes on goods and services [in the USSR, turnover tax], taxes on profits of state enterprises, income taxes on collectives and individuals, social insurance taxes, customs duties, excise taxes, local taxes, other taxes [for example, in China, agricultural tax])

(2) Transfers of net profits from state enterprises (in some countries)

(3) Depreciation fund (transfers of depreciation allowances from state enterprises)

(4) Income from machine tractor stations (abolished in the USSR in 1958)

(5) Treasury bonds (primarily loans forced from economic units and individual wage earners)

(6) Rental income on property of local governments, forestry income, and miscellaneous

---

Expenditures

---

(1) Financing the national economy:
    a) fixed capital investment in state enterprises
    b) planned increases of working capital for state enterprises in industry, agriculture, commerce, transportation, communications, municipalities, housing

(2) Financing social-cultural measures:
    a) education
    b) culture
    c) science
    d) health (including physical culture)
    e) social insurance, social security, social welfare

(3) Defense

(4) Administration

(5) Reserve funds

NOTE: See also Chapter 8.

---

units suggest changes in the control figures ("counterplan"), which are aggregated by the ministries and reconciled by the Central Planning Commission. Discussion and some bargaining ensue between planners, ministries, firms, and localities. Modified control figures may be sent down and up again. Finally, a decision is reached by the Central

Planning Commission; it is approved by the appropriate higher governmental and party bodies, and becomes the law of the land. The plan bargaining process is known as "democratic centralism": discussion during plan formulation; unquestioning obedience once a decision is reached. Two qualifications should be noted: (a) the discussion is not between equals but between superiors and subordinates; (b) superior authorities (sometimes the supreme leader himself) often intervene with commands that take no account of the discussion. Moreover, once approved, the plan may be modified by the planners without consultation. In fact, frequent "undemocratic" changes in the plan during its execution are the rule. The usual direction of the changes is for output targets to rise and input allocations to decrease.

Because of the immensity of the planning job, the annual and longer-term plans (usually five-year plans) are invariably late. For example, the Chinese First Five-Year Plan (1953–1957) was not published until June 1955.

Property

The classical plan prescribes the nationalization of all foreign trade, of banking and financial services, and of the bulk of industry, services, commerce, transport, and communications. It also prescribes the collectivization of the bulk of agriculture, the collectives being "advanced" on the model of the Soviet *kolkhoz* (that is, no individual identification of capital shares, and income distribution only by labor contribution). All means of production bigger than a hammer are socialized. Private property is limited to peasant housing and de facto private use of small plots of land for family subsidiary cultivation. The existence of the legally sanctioned private sector is unwelcome, regarded as transitory by the authorities, and tolerated only out of necessity.

Property rights granted the user and custodian of socialized fixed assets (the factory director, or collective farm chairman) are extremely narrow, being limited to a very restricted interpretation of *usus* ("right of use"). In other words, the actual users of assets—the firms—have little formally recognized autonomous initiative regarding the assets they employ. Their rights over profit and working capital are close to zero.

Those in charge of socialized assets are party nominees answerable only to the single-party state—to the party first, to the state second—for the management of the assets under their control. Within the restricted parameters of their rights, they are fully in charge of the firms under their direction (embodying the principle of one-man management, or *edinochalie*).

Motivation

The classical plan approaches the crucial problem of incentives in several ways. Managers of enterprises are evaluated on the basis of their fulfillment of the major plan indicators (first and foremost, the gross output plan). This, together with the autarkic propensities of the Stalinplan (to be discussed in the next section), means that little (if any) interenterprise comparison is made. There is no selection mechanism.

> Under the traditional Soviet-type planning where performance of enterprises and even [industrial] branches is evaluated according to plan fulfillment, comparative evaluation is neither possible nor necessary. Autarky requires proportional development of all sectors and branches regardless of the efficiency of their production. There would be, therefore, no need for a selection mechanism; there are no good or bad enterprises or branches.[14]

The level of workers' money and real wages is kept low (the "law" of rational low wages). This "self-exploitation of the working class," as Leon Trotsky termed it, is implemented to enable the state to sustain high levels of investment (finance its accumulation), to keep inflationary pressures in check in the setting of the low priority assigned to the production of consumer goods, and to extract high labor participation ratios in the context of a tight labor supply.[15] In many Soviet industries, real wages were lower at the time of Stalin's death (in 1953) than they had been before the classical plan (in 1928). Rational low wages have been described graphically in China as "eight people eating five people's meals." The obverse of which, of course, is "eight people doing five people's work," resulting in three jobs without work. The "law" has been rightly diagnosed as exerting a bad incentive effect on labor productivity. To relieve pressures on urban consumers, the low basic money wage is supplemented by bonuses scaled to overfulfillment of the output plan and some subsidized services (for example, housing and medical care). Inexpensive cultural diversions and moral inducements (medals, citations, honorific titles) to groups and individuals are provided.

The plan puts much emphasis on negative incentives—that is, on imprisonment, deportation, demotion, and fines—to keep labor discipline. Such punishments are directed democratically at both workers and managers. Generous use of force to elicit fear is the plan's ultimate means of bringing about social cohesion. Behavior modification is highly discretionary and particularistic. The Stalinplan is characterized by personal rule by men rather than the impersonal rule of laws.

Occupational choice and labor mobility are restricted by administrative means. These include labor books, internal passports, registration permits (*propiski*), state feudalism (the effective tying down of the collective farm population to the farms), and—for the long-run supply of labor—state control over the educational system. The obverse of restriction on labor mobility and occupational choice is labor allocation by administrative means. Although not as comprehensive as in pre-1976 China, administrative allocation of labor was significant in the Stalinist Soviet plan.

The classical plan requires that, together with urban consumers and workers (but more so) collectivized peasants be used for the benefit of heavy industrialization. An important function of the collective farm is to act as a forced savings device rather than an efficient unit of agricultural production. The compression of peasant incomes is accomplished by low agricultural procurement prices combined with high delivery quotas, and by the work-points system of compensation (*trudodni*), whereby the peasants become the residual claimants on the farms' net income. Between 1928 and 1937, the net income of Soviet peasants declined by 40 percent. The greater part of the work payment to peasants (sometimes all of it) is made in goods, not cash, thus further reducing the peasants' choice discretion (demonetization of the countryside). In 1952 (more than two decades after collectivization), the cash paid per *trudoden* in the USSR came to 0.14 rubles (in new rubles)—the equivalent of roughly 15 U.S. cents.[16] In China, the per capita annual rural income from the collective sector in 1977 was 47.5 yuan (28 U.S. dollars), 7.5 yuan more than in 1957.[17] The result of this approach to *kolkhoz* incentives is peasant destitution and farm inefficiency. In the classical plan nothing comes from the side of society to relieve the bleakness of peasant earnings. Social benefits for the peasantry are derisory.

The thesis according to which the Stalinplan accomplishes a net transfer of real resources from agriculture to (heavy) industry through the agency of the collective farm has been questioned by American economist James R. Millar. On the basis of post-Stalin Soviet data, Millar argues that during the Soviet First Five-Year Plan (1928–1933), there was a net outflow of resources from the nonagricultural sectors to agriculture, not the other way around. According to Millar, "collectivization was an economic policy mistake in the short run, and the evi-

dence we have on the long run suggests the same. Mass collectivization produced losses without anyone, including the state, deriving a
benefit."[18]

In this interpretation, collective agriculture was not—through its
"nonequivalent" exchange with industry—the crucial contributor to industrial development under the Stalinplan that Soviet economist Evgenii Preobrazhenskii had envisaged in his *The New Economics* (1926) and
that Stalin implicitly accepted in 1928. Real resources for industrialization came from elsewhere—from the increased effectiveness of resource
utilization in general, from the concentration of resources on heavy
industry and the construction of productive facilities, and from the borrowing of new production techniques—while financial resources came
into the state budget from (a) the turnover tax, applied mainly to food
products (this tax was partly a tax on urban consumers, and, because of
the very low state procurement prices for farm produce, partly a tax on
rural producers); (b) the enterprise profits taxes; and (c) the compulsory
bond issues (affecting mainly the urban population).

Selectively sharp money and real income differentials to reflect
state preferences are sanctioned. Most earnings are related to production (rather than time worked) through various individual and group
bonus schemes and piecework rates. The emphasis is on piece rates
(approximately 70 percent of wages under the Soviet Stalinplan). Most
job grades and wage-salary rates are determined at a very high level of
the planning hierarchy (the level of Council of Ministers commissions
[see figure 2.3]). Money income differentials are open and unabashed,
whereas differences in real incomes—especially as they turn on less
tangible perquisites of party and state office—are somewhat better hidden but also very significant. In 1946, the earnings of the top 10 percent of Soviet urban workers and employees were ten times those of
the bottom 10 percent. Collective farmers are not included in this calculation. Their inclusion would make the spread much greater.[19] Egalitarianism in the distribution of income is decreed to be a counterrevolutionary offense.

Competition among workers for employment, capitalism's "reserve
army of the unemployed," and collective wage bargaining between
employers and independent labor unions are replaced by Stakhanov-
ism, that is, rate-busting. Market competition among managers and
planners is replaced by the purge that forcibly retires some incumbents
while opening up to survivors opportunities for upward mobility.
Since the Stalinist purge was most often politically motivated, being
frequently driven by paranoia, it is questionable whether it had any
significant positive economic effect.[20]

Plan discipline is also sought and managers kept alert by the method of strained balances or plan tautness: asking for more than can be delivered, and then some. This is discussed more fully in the next section.

Goal Priorities

The first priority of the classical plan is growth of output—gross, extensive growth with little regard to cost. Extensive growth means growth largely generated by the addition of resource inputs (primarily labor and capital based on already-mastered techniques rather than obtained from more productive—innovative—use of resource inputs). Between 1950 and 1962, only 29 percent of the Soviet national income's annual growth rate was attributable to growth of total factor productivity. In most Western market economies, the contribution of factor productivity improvement to national income growth was between 40 percent (in the United States) and 75 percent (in France).[21] In practice, because of the rudimentary and problem-ridden condition of information and coordination in the Stalinplan, annual growth targets for output are set by the planners in accordance with the "ratchet principle": the previous year's growth performance is taken as the base and a percentage is tacked on for the coming year. In line with the planners' well-founded suspicion that they are not in command of full and accurate information about resource availabilities and output potential at the base of the economy (both of which are understated by managers in search of a "soft"—easily fulfillable—plan), the planned percentage output increase will typically be such as to put substantial strain on the firms' supply of inputs. The Stalinplan is a "taut" (*naprazhenniy*) plan, a condition of chronic scarcity, an all-absorbing search for inputs, and a lining-up for outputs.[22] Another way of putting this is that the Stalinplan is "teleological" in the sense given that term in the 1920s during the Soviet philosophical discussion on the limits of planning. Planning goals are not constrained by any objective economic conditions, laws of value, relative resource scarcities, relative factor endowments, levels of literacy and technology, levels of national income, and the like. If failures occur in the carrying-out of the plan's objectives, they must be due to a deficiency of socialist consciousness, "wreckism" by class enemies, lax labor discipline, inadequate vigilance by the security apparatus, and so on. The teleological approach to planning is given its clearest "voluntaristic" expression in the neoclassical radical plan (Maoplan), but it is present in the Stalinplan. (The opposite of planning

teleology is planning "geneticism," exhibited in the neoclassical conservative and liberal plans—an awareness of the limits placed on planners' goals by fixed economic regularities. Liberal neoclassical planners
pay more heed to these regularities, expecially to the "law of value,"
than do conservative neoclassicists.)

In the Stalinplan, investment is favored over consumption (the
former constituting 35–40 percent of gross national product). In fact,
consumption postponement becomes a permanent feature of the plan.
Investment funds come from forced savings raised by taxation. The
taxation is more or less disguised. A major element of less-disguised
(but for the paying consumer, still not precisely identifiable) taxation is
the turnover tax levied almost exclusively on consumer goods (see note
4). The tax is buried in the retail price. More disguised taxation takes
the form of low procurement prices paid by the state to collective farms
for compulsory deliveries of produce as compared with relatively high
prices charged by the state for farm inputs and industrial goods consumed by the farmers. It is also implicit in the residual-claimant nature
of the farmers' income derived from work for the collective.[23]

Investment and the best ministrations are showered on a very narrow sector of the economy: heavy industry—specifically power, metal-
lurgy, and machine building (even more specifically, the defense and
public security subsectors).[24] Light industries are neglected. So too is
agriculture, to an even greater degree. Such investment as is made in
agriculture is largely wasted, because the socialized property and motivational structures militate against investment's efficient use. In contrast to the favored heavy industry sector (particularly its military–
public security subsectors), light industry, agriculture, housing, and
consumer services absorb planning shortfalls, especially the critical
shortages of inputs. They are, by design, the buffer sectors—shock and
schlock absorbers of the plan. The supply of social overhead capital
(roads, railroads, schools, hospitals, telecommunications, harbors, municipal facilities) lags well behind demand.

The plan is inward-oriented. Self-reliance and a closed economy
are preferred over foreign involvement (economic espionage excepted).
The level and structure of domestic prices are divorced from world
market prices by arbitrary foreign exchange rates, the differences between the two sets of prices being handled by taxes and subsidies
anchored in a price stabilization fund. There is no direct contact between domestic firms and foreign buyers and sellers. Foreign sales and
purchases are handled for the firms by the Ministry of Foreign Trade
through commodity-specialized foreign trade corporations.

The classical plan claims to put an end to economic cycles and to inaugurate an era of price and employment stability. This claim does not stand up to evidence, especially if the definition of instability is not restricted to overt phenomena captured by statistics, but is extended to include statistically elusive fluctuations in substandard and useless output, suppressed inflation, and hidden unemployment.[25] The Stalinplan is noted for its sudden introduction of huge structural changes and for an impatient uprooting of inherited institutions (for example, the accelerated forced collectivization of agriculture). This has been one source of instability. The political system's lack of a mechanism for predictable and orderly transition is also, though to a lesser extent, a source of economic instability. Most important, the classical plan, in the normal course of its operation and for reasons endogenous to the system's logic (see items 1 through 8 below), gives rise to statistically discrete output cycles, suppressed inflation, and fluctuating underemployment of capital, land, and labor. The deficiencies of information and coordination in the classical plan ensure that growth will be bumpy, marked by shortages and surpluses the size and location of which vary over time as the planners intermittently come to grips with isolated parts of the problem.

The classical plan's deficiencies of information and coordination include the following:

1. Since plan balances are strained, any maladjustment in supply and demand will cause big disruptions in the path of growth. Information on maladjustments percolates through the planning apparatus rather slowly and its accuracy is imperfect. Corrective action by the planners will take time, both for reasons of bureaucratic inertia and because it is not easy to persuade the planning authorities that they were wrong—or to admit that the information they recieved was incorrect, but now, at last, is correct. In these circumstances, disequilibria will last longer and corrective action, when finally taken, will be more heavy-handed and overcompensatory, becoming itself a cause of new disequilibria.[26]

2. The deficiencies of motivation, as they relate to the behavior of firm managers, contribute to economic cycles in the sensitive area of capital investment. Under the plan, managers are required, as a minimum condition, to fulfill their output targets 100 percent—99.9 percent fulfillment is fraught with grave personal consequences. One of the easier ways of making sure of 100 percent plan fulfillment is to have plenty of capital on hand, more than is reasonably needed—just in case. Hence, managers are prone to inflate their capital requests to the state, all the more so since capital allocations from the state budget are free grants and budget constraints are soft: the state firm will not be

allowed to go bankrupt, and once it starts its investments projects, the projects will somehow have to be completed—if need be, with additional infusions of capital, even if this serves no identifiable purpose. From time to time, the planners make a show of rolling back their investments, but without much success. Lower-level authorities always undertake extrabudgetary investment in the cracks of the plan. Long construction cycles, unfinished investment projects, and considerable duplication and underutilization of capital are the results of this expansionary drive.

3. Duplication and underutilization are further spurred by the attempts of each branch and firm to integrate vertically ("universalism") so as to assure themselves of the needed inputs and spare parts in a world of shortages and supply uncertainties. Here too, the intensity of the effort will fluctuate over time, as the planners detect waste through insufficient specialization and address themselves to it, usually through a reorganization either of the firm or its supervisory authorities. When the backs of the planners are turned, the vertical integration process begins anew.[27]

4. Annual activity cycles within firms are induced by the requirement that the plan be fulfilled 100 percent on December 31 of the calendar year. During the first three quarters, the firm looks around for the needed inputs and production proceeds at a leisurely cadence. In the last quarter, there is a big push ("storming," or *shturmovshschina*) to fulfill the plan. This is normally achieved by cutting down on quality and violating planned output assortment. (There are also quarterly and monthly activity cycles within the yearly plan.) According to the planners' ability to police the quality of production, greater or smaller amounts of substandard or useless output are turned out over the planning periods.

5. There is a bunching-up of investment in the early years of the longer-term (five-year) plan. This is usually followed by a slackening-off as supply bottlenecks develop and capital construction projects are cut back. Toward the end of the five-year period, as toward the end of the one-year control cycle, average wages tend to surge upward as workers are put on overtime and various bonus schemes go into effect aimed at fulfilling the plan output norms.

6. More visible output fluctuations are induced by agriculture's great sensitivity to changes in the weather. This sensitivity is primarily due to systemic reasons: in particular, to the size and rigidity of collective and state farm property and to deficiencies of the motivational system.

7. Although the price level can be held constant by definition (the

planners being the price determiners), the tautness of the classical plan and the producers' insatiable demand mean that there is chronic suppressed or masked (*maskirovannaia*) inflation in the system.[28] This is true of both consumer and producer goods. This inflation manifests itself in lines outside retail stores (the length of the queue being indicative of the degree of inflation at any given time), in black markets in consumer and producer commodities (most black markets in producer goods take the form of barter or exchange of favors, so as to lessen the chance of detection by financial audit), and in bribery. The clearing price of officials fluctuates according to supply and demand conditions on the corruption market and according to the changing estimates of risk. It involves greater and lesser diversions of socialized property into unplanned channels.

8. The "law" of rational low wages, combined with a no-firing policy and labor reserves hidden by managers in anticipation of unannounced upward changes in the output plan, results—as has already been noted—in considerable overstaffing (hidden unemployment) that fluctuates over time.

In sum, instability of output, price, and employment, especially (but not exclusively) in statistically elusive terms, is a characteristic of the classical plan.

CHAPTER THREE

The Neoclassical Plan: Conservative and Liberal

The neoclassical plan is less centralized and bureaucratized than the classical plan: very marginally so in the conservative Stalinist version; visibly so in the liberal version. Some decisions (primarily micro) are taken at lower levels of the single-party state bureaucracy (the level of the firm in the liberal plan) and rely more on financial criteria (profit, sales, value added).

Timing and Coverage of Change

The conservative neoclassical plan has been introduced in phases and by carefully selected firms and sectors. The liberal plan in Hungary was introduced all at once and covered the whole economy. Initial forward motion of the conservative neoclassical plan is usually followed by a freezing of positions and partial retreat.

Opposition to Change

Opposition to adjustment (and even more so to reform) comes from several quarters. Even very limited marketization meets with resistance from the planning bureaucracy, which rightly sees itself threatened in its jobs and privileges by the move. In a single-party state economy, it is this bureaucracy that must originate the move: it must liquidate itself. But, as the Chinese say, "the sickle cannot trim its own handle." Bureaucracy's reluctance to liquidate itself is not all self-interest, however. The structure of supply under the Stalinplan is bound to be out of tune with the structure of demand under any—even a conservative—version of the neoclassical plan. Hence, adjustment (and even more so reform) means shocks to the existing productive capacity administered by the new pattern of demand, and shocks to the new demand coming from supply inelasticities of the Stalinist productive arrangements. Chances are very good that new disequilibria will be piled up on top of the old as a result of adjustment, not to mention reform.[1]

A quite persuasive case can be made on economic grounds alone to justify a do-nothing attitude. There are also ideological obstacles to marketization. Unreconstructed Stalinists and radical zealots wait in the wings, ready to pounce on reformers in the name of doctrinal purity. In addition, many managers of firms are opposed to changes in the way things are done. Marketization and privatization mean not just having more authority to make decisions, but taking market punishment for wrong decisions, that is, bankruptcy. Workers like the security of employment provided by the classical plan. (One of the by-products of the Yugoslav neomarket has been a high level of unemployment.) Many workers have found ways of idling on the job and getting paid for it in a general climate of overstaffing. Expansion of private sector activities opens up possibilities for some workers to make quite a bit of extra money, which is resented by others. This problem was one of the reasons for the backtracking on the Hungarian adjustment, and it threatens the relatively liberal "production responsibility" changes introduced in China's agriculture after 1978. Consumers gripe about shortages and queues, but they like the stability of planned consumer goods prices and government subsidies for essentials. They accept the money illusion disseminated by the classical plan and resent price hikes intended to put the supply and demand for particular goods into some sort of rational relationship. Thus, powerful and quite disparate forces are allied in opposition to even relatively innocuous changes in the status quo. Opposition to basic reform of the system is almost insuperable. Advocating reform can be dangerous: "The gun shoots the bird that sticks its neck out," as the Chinese say.

Fear of radical change and the need for caution, both to lessen the shocks to the existing productive capacity and to neutralize the bureaucratic and ideological opposition, have typically resulted in an "incremental" tackling of system defects. This consists of choosing a few relatively small areas in which modest changes are made in the balance of costs and benefits facing the manager (or whoever is being targeted), and is done in a way that may be expected to improve the targeted agent's choice making. Experiments are restricted to a selected number of factories, industries, and geographical locations, and are subsequently generalized or terminated.

The incremental solution is essentially a gradualist adjustment—a selective upgrading of parts of the system. It has been found to have five drawbacks:[2] (1) The elements targeted for adjustment are normally components of a larger system. It is unlikely that improvement in one part of a complex system will result in a significant improvement in the performance of the system as a whole. (2) It is difficult to determine exactly what size the change in the single element should be to produce the desired effect of the preferred size. (3) Every change in a single element involves costs, some incurred by agents not directly involved in the adjustment. The total cost of the adjustment to the system may exceed the benefit derived from it by the targeted component. (The opposite may also hold: the benefit to the system may exceed that directly derived by the component.) (4) The adjustment is likely to have negative side effects that may outweigh its direct positive effects. (5) Wherever substitution possibilities are present, a measure intended to produce a given choice that is costly to the choice maker will induce the choice maker (for example, the manager) to choose a less costly substitute or to simulate a substitute. This is known as "formalism."

On an international level, within the Soviet sphere of influence in Eastern Europe, the pace of reform is also (perhaps mainly) a function of the Soviet Union's visceral fear of pluralism and of Russia's Byzantine identification of diversity with anarchy. The neoclassical liberal plan is about as bold and far-reaching a system-maintenance-and-repair undertaking as the Kremlin's ossified reformist spirit will tolerate.

Change in the opposite direction—the mathematization and computerization of the economy—has progressed, albeit with caution and in patches by enclaves (see Chapter 8). The conceptual and technical difficulties attendant on installing and operating a nationwide integrated computer system are not the sole causes for this. In an interesting dialectical twist, it has been found that the centralizing technique prima facie has decentralizing effects. The theoretical objective of constructing "an internally consistent and optimal plan variant through the computer-assisted solution of very large numbers of simultaneous equations" (see Chapter 1) requires that information be de-Stalinized, that it freely circulate through the system, and that the equipment necessary for its storage and processing be available to many. There are few problems technically: electronic information is housed in a technology that makes its broad diffusion quite easy. The opposition to such dispersal comes, not suprisingly, from the police mentality that sees in information sharing a threat to the exclusive privilege of the ruling party elite. The vision of Hungarian planometrician Tibor Vamos—of a future electronic socialist commonwealth in which "decisions and regulations will be accessible to and can be reviewed by everyone"—is probably an illusion, a fantasy.[3] But the decentralizing implications of what was originally thought of as a centralizing technique are nevertheless worth noting.

Information

Three developments should be noted: (1) There has occurred a shift from primary reliance on physical-technical information toward more financial-price information (increased reliance on "economic" levers, and less on "administrative" ones.) This is true of all countries (except Albania and North Korea), and is a common feature of both the conservative and liberal versions of the neoclassical plan. (2) Price information has been the subject of scrutiny. In the conservative plan, this has involved a more accurate accounting of production costs and profit markups that comprise state-set, cost-plus (supply-side) prices, but no siginificant movement toward the marketization of state-set prices, that is, toward making prices the synthetic expressions of both cost to producer and utility to user. The majority of state prices (especially, but by no means exclusively, producer goods and materials prices) are not scarcity prices in the conservative plan and cannot be used directly as indicators of allocative efficiency. In other words, the economic (allocative) base of the new accounting remains flawed.[4] In the liberal version of the neoclassical plan, concern with efficiency prices is more marked, particularly (but not exclusively) with more realistic producer prices and foreign exchange rates. Although many state-set prices of the cost-plus variety remain, others are allowed various degrees of room to express both the cost of things to producers and the worth of those things to users. (3) Some decision-making power has been transferred from the top to the lower levels of the planning/managerial pyramid (see Figure 2.3). In the conservative plan, the process has been one of administrative decentralization: it stops short of the producing firm and has barely increased the influence of consumers, managers, and workers on allocative choice. In the liberal plan, decentralization of decision-making power has been in part economic; that is, it has given firms significant (but still constrained) powers to make allocative decisions. It has also discreetly increased the influence of consumers on allocative choice, but not that of workers (there are no representative workers' councils or independent unions).

Physical-Technical Indicators and Contracts

In all countries that have adopted the conservative variant of the neo-classical plan, the number of mandatory targets communicated to firms by the planners has been reduced—in the USSR, from several dozen to a dozen or so. Within the remaining indicators, the formerly dominant gross value of output (*val*) has been demonopolized, but not de-throned. It is now rivaled by net output value (value added), and even more, by sales and profit-profitability targets. Output assortment tar-gets are now sometimes set at lower echelons of the hierarchy (in the USSR, East Germany, Poland, and Romania at a new "association" of firms level [see upcoming section, "Coordination"]). But whatever the organizational arrangement, the top planners make fewer assortment specifications than formerly, except in high-priority areas. Input norms for key materials and producer goods continue to be centrally rationed in all countries of the conservative plan.

The reduction in the number of enterprise plan indicators, how-ever, has been offset in part by indicator creep. In a system of discon-tinuous, largely unidimensional goal priorities (goal discontinuities), any reduction in the number of plan indicators means (in practice) that enterprise managers will neglect, when they do not altogether ignore, those dimensions of production expressed by the indicators dropped. So, soon after the indicators are dropped, they must be put back again in the plan.

Under the liberal variant of the neoclassical plan, profit expressed in competitive market prices is to become the only criterion of enter-prise success. To that end, a uniform taxation system is introduced to enable comparisons to be made of interenterprise and interindustry performance, and competitive prices are introduced gradually through simulation. At the same time, selective financial measures are used in the form of differentiated taxes and subsidies to soften the transitional shocks. These measures move the liberal plan only a short distance beyond its conservative counterpart on this crucial issue. However, some proponents of the liberal plan adjustment argue that the intro-duction of the uniform tax and of simulated competitive prices at least establishes a rule from which exemptions (taxes, subsidies) may be made. Nevertheless, the liberal plan is not exempt from the phenomenon of indicator creep.

In the conservative plan, compulsory collective farm delivery quotas for produce continue to be set by the planners, together with indicators of sown acreage and yield, although in less detail than previously. The quotas are also more reasonable, less confiscatory, and more in line with the capacity of farms to produce. Within the collective farm, several "production responsibility" arrangements are implemented. These are designed to decentralize some production activities, and consist of contracts entered into by the farm and its component collective units (in the USSR, the *zveno*—"link," or group—of between six and twenty-four workers). The contract specifies both the amount and kind of produce the small groups are to deliver to the farm management and the delivery prices. Anything over the quota can be sold to the farm at higher prices or disposed of on the free market. The actual implementation of the production contract is left to the discretion of the group. The land worked by the group, as well as the farm equipment, are owned by the collective farm (in the USSR, the land is nominally owned by the state); most current inputs come from the state via the collective farm, as do bank credit and the bulk of industrial consumer goods. The group distributes its income according to some work-point system. A similar (but more advanced) form of the contract, widely practiced in China after 1978, is the devolution of production responsibility (as well as income distribution) to individual farm families. Like other contractual arrangements, the Chinese system of production responsibility to households (*baogan daohu*), really a system of disguised family tenancy, is contingent on the households first fulfilling a contracted-for output quota delivered to the state at state-set prices.[5] The exception to quota setting is Poland, where the bulk of agriculture is private and the government (the main buyer) negotiates the prices of its purchases with the farmers. The government, of course, influences the outcome of the negotiations by its monopolistic control of industrial farm inputs and credit. Since early 1985, China has been moving in the same direction.

Production responsibility contracts have also been introduced in industry, commerce, transportation, and other areas, especially in China after 1978. Overfulfillment of the contracted-for norm is rewarded with bonuses. In the Soviet Union, the contract system is used in research and development work: research institutes contract with their industrial and other clients to deliver specified services. The idea is to increase the clients' interest in, and influence over, the work of research and development organizations. I agree with American economist Joseph S. Berliner that the changeover to contract financing from a management system in which firms operate under a plan and report to their ministries, though not negligible, is not a fundamental reform of the plan:

The nature of the dependence of a market economy firm on its contracts and that of a Soviet firm on its contracts are of different orders of magnitude. In that sense, this act of formal decentralization, like so many others, is more a matter of detail than of critical importance in the decisionmaking process.[6]

The contracts are in the plan—they are part of the plan, not an arrangement aimed at superseding the plan.

In the conservative neoclassical plan, new physical-technical indicators are worked out dealing with scientific developments, labor productivity, consumer spending patterns, and so on. In sum, central control over information conveyed to firms, consumers, and workers is not significantly relaxed. In fact, administrative decentralization is aimed at making such control more effective by taking some of the petty burdens off the shoulders of the central planners.

By contrast, in the liberal version of the neoclassical plan (as in Hungary), the system of mandatory output and input indicators to firms (collective farms included) is dismantled; firms are left to determine the level and assortment of output and to procure commercially the needed inputs by themselves in response to user demand, profit, and costs expressed in scarcity-oriented prices. Were this scheme actually applied, it would amount to a genuine systemic reform, a transition from planning-from-above to planning-from-below, from the base. However, in practice, the change has been more cautious. Some output targets were fixed for firms by the state (for example, output targets for exports to hard currency areas), and an increasing number of key inputs in short supply continued to be centrally rationed. Both output setting and input rationing were more informal than in the conservative plan, but not thereby significantly less constraining on the firms' choice-making discretion.[7] Jawboning in a single-party state can be extremely persuasive. The branch ministries were not dismantled, only their functions were redefined. Administratively merged, they became "advisers" to the firms formerly under their command and, as the Chinese would put it, engaged in "heart-to-heart chats" with their former subordinates.

In the neoclassical liberal plan, compulsory procurement targets for collective farms are abolished and replaced by contractual supply quotas and overquota sales at prices that closely follow market trends. A considerable increase in the element of voluntariness with regard to membership in collective farms occurs, and the farms' de facto property rights in land and other assets are significantly extended. Many flexible organizational forms (including leasing of cooperative land to individual households) are experimented with (see Chapter 10). The state's attitude toward the private sector in agriculture is supportive, and a mutually satisfactory relationship is established between socialized and private farming activities.

Prices

Adjustments of the price information system in the neoclassical plan take three forms: specific, general, and flexible.

Specific, or ad hoc, adjustments consist of raising some producer goods and agricultural procurement prices and wages, as well as several consumer goods prices. Raising producer goods and compulsory quota procurement prices is intended to make prices reflect existing production costs more accurately; to render firms and collective farms reasonably profitable on the average (that is, to reduce the burden of subsidies on the state); and, in the case of collective farms, to provide incentives for a badly needed shape-up through improvement in the farms' financial position. This is, in essence, an operation within Grossman's Quadrant IV (see Figure 2.1)—a reduction in the discrepancy between state prices and average production costs. The increasing of wages and raising of above-quota procurement prices amount to an improvement in the operation of Quadrant II: the higher wages and prices are needed to make the supply of different kinds of labor and of above-quota produce better satisfy the state's demand for them. The hikes in consumer goods prices, often very steep and involving some mass consumption commodities, represent an adjustment in Quadrant III: compressing consumer demand to the state-determined supply of consumer goods, shortening lines outside retail stores, and lessening state subsidies on at least some necessities.[8] (However, there is a contradiction in all this. Money wages are raised, often across the board, without a concurrent and proportionately correct—in terms of demand elasticities—increase in consumer goods. The effect of an across-the-board money wage increase is that people must queue longer.)

A general revision of (primarily) industrial producer prices was carried out in the 1960s by all state socialist countries except China. It was a monumental feat of bureaucratic zeal involving, in the USSR alone, several million prices and extraordinarily huge numbers of price interdependencies. As soon as the new prices were put into effect, they were obsolete.[9] From then on, general price adjustments were to take place every five to eight years, with ad hoc adjustments in between. The important point is that the general price revisions did not represent a marketization of prices: they did not bring the demand side into serious consideration but merely concentrated on a more accurate accounting of branch average production costs. The vast effort concentrated on what should and should not go into the cost-plus formula—into "prime cost" (*sebestoimost'*) and the profit markup.

Specifically, the following measures were taken in most countries (in mainland China, only in the late 1970s): Regarding production cost, (a) depreciation rates on fixed capital were raised somewhat; (b) a "capital charge" was introduced, that is, an annual tax of between 1 and 9 percent paid to the state on the value of the firms' fixed—sometimes also circulating—assets;[10] (c) increasingly the financing of the state firms' fixed capital needs was to come from repayable bank credits rather than free budgetary grants, and this—like the capital charge—had to be taken into account in the calculation of planned profitability; (d) the differential rent element was recognized and appropriated by the state (insofar as it was the result of natural differences in land fertility, location, and so forth); and (e) the expenses of geological prospecting were included in cost calculations. The cost, as before, is average for the industrial branch, and hence the profitability of the same product varies widely among firms in the same branch according to the individual firms' high or low production costs. Regarding profit and profitability (*rentabel'-nost'*), (a) output is now counted as output actually sold, not just produced; and (b) the basis for computing the rate of profit has been changed (though not uniformly, and with some backsliding) from cost to the firms' total (fixed and circulating) capital. Profit, profitability, and sales are now the chief indicators of a firm's success in the eyes of the planners; these indicators are linked to bonuses that impact primarily on managerial personnel.

It is important to bear in mind that by neglecting demand, the new prices reflect neither the utility of outputs nor the scarcity of inputs. The fact that two sets of goods cost the same to produce and use the same amount of capital does not mean that their value to the user is the same. By neglecting the use-value of the goods, the relative scarcities of the two goods are not mirrored in the (cost-plus) price; that is, the price does not reveal which of the two goods is more advantageous (profitable) to produce (that is, which good is in greater demand).[11] To rely on the new prices and profitabilities (which these prices underlie) as indicators of the congruence of the firms' and society's interests is to be seriously in error. As demonstrated in the USSR and elsewhere (most recently in China), profit expressed in cost-plus prices will pile new distortions on top of old; this will inevitably be used as an argument against further change and in favor of a return to the (at least known) inconveniences of the classical plan. It should be noted that the separation of the levels and structures of wholesale prices from those of retail prices by taxes and subsidies continues. Thus, the consumer, as before, has little or no institutionally sanctioned say in determining the level and composition of output. Cost reductions are supposed to be passed to the consumer in the form of lower retail prices, but the decision to do this rests with the planners. In short, general price adjustments leave the locus of price-setting power unchanged.

A theoretically more progressive and flexible price system adjustment, one that—at least in its conception—proposes in some instances to shift the locus of price formation from the top to the buying-selling level of the producer and his customer, is the multicategory pricing scheme discussed in the 1960s and partially implemented in all countries (except Bulgaria and Czechoslovakia), most boldly in Hungary. This scheme envisages the coexistence of four kinds of prices: (1) state-set (that is, cost-plus–based) prices for the most important products (key raw materials and capital goods inputs); (2) maxima prices, where the state sets a ceiling above which prices cannot be pushed by demand-supply forces (primarily for "less essential" consumer goods); (3) limit prices, which can fluctuate in response to supply and demand between floors and ceilings set by the state ("semiluxuries"); and (4) free market prices, entirely determined by the interplay of demand and supply ("luxury" consumer goods and some agricultural products, as well as black market prices). The state reserves for itself the right of suasion to both keep profits within ideologically healthy boundaries, even when the prices are inside the floor-ceiling parameters, and to intervene whenever inflationary pressures or monopolistic pricing by firms threaten to get out of hand. Another wrinkle consists of introducing "negotiated" prices for certain products (in China, for example). Here, the government purchaser negotiates the price of (primarily farm) products with the selling unit. Although the deals are not perfectly horizontal, they do represent a departure from the principle of unconditional planner command. Yet another situation is that in which the manufacturer is allowed to set the price of a new product (one produced for the first time in the country), subject to later "confirmation" by superior authorities. (This gives rise to cheating—putting old wine in new bottles and setting a high price on the newly packaged old product.)

The intention of Hungary's liberal New Economic Mechanism was to move the economy gradually toward the realm of free prices, that is, toward Quadrant I (Figure 2.2). It was even proposed to "commercialize" Quadrant IV by restricting, and eventually abolishing altogether, the rationing of materials and producer goods and replacing this rationing with lateral transactions among firms carried out at free, maxima, and limit prices with help from bank credits acquired at commercial rates. Steps were first taken in that direction in the late 1960s, but there has been some retreat since then.

This is what has happened. Many prices, especially in the producers' goods sector, were decontrolled. Most machinery, semimanufactures, and materials prices are free or maxima. A few remain fixed by the center. Those domestic producer goods prices that concern firms working for the capitalist export market and/or using a large proportion of imported (Western) inputs have been aligned with world market prices for similar goods. However, the state still intervenes with price subsidies (20 percent of gross domestic product in the late 1970s), export taxes, and import quotas to protect its industries from "excessive" foreign competition. Consumer prices (primarily, but not exclusively, of non-necessities) have been aligned with producer prices via a fairly uniform sales tax on non-necessities.

In comparison with the conservative variant of the neoclassical plan, the role of the banking system in investment decisions is more important in the liberal plan. In Hungary, about half the investment decisions are made by firms partly in response to information provided by free, maxima, and limit prices. However, the role of the center in investment policy is more influential than is suggested by this ratio for the following reasons: (a) the center decides on the establishment of new firms, key projects, and social infrastructure investment; (b) "free" investments by firms must be approved by the firms' "advisory" ministries (or, since the early 1980s, by the Boards of Supervision), must be officially inserted into the national plan, and must have their materialization depend on the availability of funds provided either by the state in the form of budgetary grants or by loans through the banking system (whichever way, the state has the means to fit these investments into its macro policy); (c) many key firms are very large—being, in fact, in the nature of "associations"—and are led by managers who made their way through the state bureaucracy in the days of the classical plan, and who continue to be hired and fired by the state apparat; these managers are very preoccupied with maintaining good administrative relations with their advisory superior bureaucracies and are not spontaneously inclined to run their businesses according to market rules.

In sum, the proposed transition to Quadrant I, accompanied by some marketization of Quadrants II, III, and IV, has occurred more markedly in the liberal than in the conservative plan. However, everywhere in the world of the neoclassical plan, from China to East Germany, the center continues to retain control over wage determination, prices of key materials and producer goods, purchase prices of the main agricultural products, and prices of items of mass consumption.[12]

Differences in control among countries over these strategic variables are differences of degree only. These degree differences can make much difference to the consumers' well-being. However, by and large, the price system of the neoclassical plan remains vertically inclined— less so in the liberal than in the conservative variant—and most prices are not indicators of the relative scarcities and utilities in the system. The bird flies around in the cage, but doesn't sing.

As was the case under the classical plan, black markets in consumer goods, producer goods, apartments, influence, and foreign currencies are rampant, constituting in effect a second, "shadow" or underground, economy of large proportions, which both undermines the legitimacy of the plan and helps the plan survive.[13]

Coordination

Formal Organization

There has been a great deal of organizational readjustment. Territorial reorganization of the old ministerial branch system was tried and dropped. Within the branch system, the major change has been the addition of a layer between the ministry-subministry level and the firm. This "association" is really a merger of firms—either within the ministerial branch or across branches (sometimes also, as in China, embracing collectives). The association was put on economic self-accounting and is the beneficiary of greater (but still constrained) decision-making power. American economist Vaclav Holesovsky aptly calls this administrative reshuffle "decentralizing centralization."[14] The associations take over some of the functions formerly exercised by higher authorities, but their independence is not much greater than that of the old firms. From the standpoint of central control, the net effect is more, not less, centralization. Unlike the former subministries (*glavki*) they often replace, the administrations work on *khozraschet*. Hungarian firms in key sectors are also of that nature; they are, in effect, trusts that antedate the New Economic Mechanism adjustments. However, in the neoclassical liberal plan an attempt is made to reduce the planning and supervisory bureaucracy by ministry consolidation and other means. Informal command-advice replaces formal orders.

Bureaucratic Behavior

Not much has changed in this area. The bureaucracy continues to expand exponentially, and its moral fiber has not shown any improvement: the bureaucracy remains entrenched, insensitive, self-seeking, and prone to the *vziatka* ("the take"). Its members continue to be centrally nominated and removed (*nomenklatura*), the power of appointment and dismissal being vested in the party's Central Committee, the Politburo (in exalted cases), or lesser party committees (for less important appointments). Compared with the Stalinplan, there is in the neoclassical plan (especially in its liberal incarnation) much talk about the separation of powers between state and party in matters of the economy, and occasional attempts are made to keep the party out of day-to-day economic management. Since everyone who is anyone in the government belongs to the party, the attempts are not very effective, and the effects are not lasting.[15] As in the Stalinplan, much informal coordination is done by means of personal contacts (*po znakomstvu*).

The neoclassical plan, especially in its conservative version, shows no diminution (rather the opposite) in the military and security apparats' intervention in the economy. In some countries (for example, Poland after 1982, China from 1969 to 1971, and Afghanistan), the politicized military takes over.[16] The emergence of the military–public security complex as an important economic decision maker in the neoclassical plan had been heralded by the Stalinplan's goals, which were tilted toward the enhancement of military and police powers.

Finally, in the neoclassical plan there is greater stress than before on engineering-scientific expertise, professional attainments, and formally certified educational qualifications. Political and ideological loyalty are demanded as a matter of course, but personal attitudes of new generation bureaucrats toward redness range from skepticism to demoralizing cynicism.

Physical Coordination

To arrive at internal consistency of input and output decisions, the neoclassical conservative plan tries to shift from material balances to the more reliable method of economy-wide input-output tables (or "interbranch balances"). These tables show the technical interrelationships between the various branches of the economy, the net material production created and distributed by the branches to the final recipients, the incomes generated in the branches, and the personal and state budgetary expenditures. The number of branches included in the tables has grown over time and progress has been made toward expressing the matrices in value terms. The as yet far from complete transition from material balances to input-output analysis has been made possible in large part by the application of high-memory computers to planning.[17]

A less ambitious project has been the "centralized decentralization" of materials balance construction. Some balances are now constructed by the central planners, some by ministries, and some by "associations." Such administrative decentralization of balances-building into multiple tiers was attempted in China during some of the less turbulent years of the Cultural Revolution (that is, under the radical plan).

Attention has also been given to plan optimization through the use of mathematical techniques, including linear and dynamic programming. Attempts have been made to optimize parts of the plan, especially investment (to get planning away from simple recoupment period formulae), transportation, industrial location, and foreign trade.[18] Even in this narrower sphere, numerous conceptual and practical problems remain unresolved, including the number of computers available for nonmilitary uses.[19] Both partial and more comprehensive attempts at plan optimization through the use of mathematical models and the computerization of economic administration peaked in the 1970s. There has been much disappointment with this approach since that time. Three reasons for this disappointment have been advanced: (1) the computer systems were used as mere techniques adapted to prevailing methods of economic administration, rather than as levers for improving the quality of those methods or for breaking out of them altogether; (2) economic administrators were reluctant to yield power to mathematical economists and other specialists conversant with the new techniques; and (3) designers of the models and computerized systems were not given sufficient information by the planners on the actual operational "concrete" problems of the economy and thus underestimated the complexity of the real-life problems to which their models were addressed. This last difficulty does not derive solely from (2), that is, from the planners' self-defense, but more generally from the system's propensity to treat most information as privileged. In any event, the result was that the models proposed by the technocrats, though technically complex, were operationally too simplistic relative to the problems they proposed to solve. They were in danger of committing huge errors and so were rejected, after which disillusionment set in.

In the neoclassical liberal plan, an attempt is made (with some recoiling) to progressively replace central physical plan coordination by lateral contractual linkages among firms through the agency of increasingly free market prices. Large parts of the material-technical supply network (the arrangement for input rationing) are dismantled and re-placed by commercial wholesale transactions. In short, coordination under the neoclassical liberal plan is made to rely more on the price mechanism—the prices themselves being, to a greater extent than before, the expression of allocative decisions made by decentralized buying and selling units. The market, however, is not fully liberated: it is simulated in large part by—as one Hungarian economist put it—a "rather peculiar pricing procedure."[20]

Financial Coordination

As noted earlier in the chapter (see "Information"), the neoclassical plan relies more than the Stalinplan on financial expressions, prices, and "economic" rather than administrative levers. Financial planning, especially the credit plan and the banking system, assumes new impor-tance and gains in sophistication.

Regarding state budgetary revenues (see Table 2.4), there are some nex taxes (for example, on foreign joint ventures [as in Hungary and China] and foreign employees of such ventures, as well as on private businesses); and some other taxes gain in relative importance (for ex-ample, taxes on state enterprise profits instead of profit transfers [as in China]). Within each tax category, there is quite a bit of adjustment of rates, incidence, coverage, and so on, and a general trend toward a more definite, less ambiguous legal definition of tax liabilities and procedures. Domestic government borrowing, too, is given legal garb and made less arbitrary. In general, the trend is against mandatory bond subscriptions by the public (a favorite anti-inflationary weapon of the Stalinplan). However, state enterprises and institutions are not fully exempt from mandatory subscription to government bond issues (for example, as in China). This practice continues as a way of siphon-ing out of the economy a portion of provincial, municipal, and local governments' revenues, which these governments derive from extra-budgetary sources and spend on extrabudgetary fixed capital invest-ments. Retiring domestic debt becomes a regular budgetary expendi-ture item. Under the Stalinplan most bonds (forced on the public) were simply not redeemed.

Slowly, painfully, and reluctantly in the case of some neoclassical plan countries (Poland, Romania), promptly in the case of others (Chi-na, USSR), foreign exchange loans are retired. Foreign aid (grants and loans) is extended for civilian and military purposes, the latter on a gen-erous scale. Defense expenditures (both overt and hidden under differ-ent headings) grow absolutely and relatively to gross domestic product.

Aid is given to collective farms for fixed and working capital purposes and for relief. This is a budget line shift in state goal priorities
compared with the neglect of collective agriculture by the Stalinplan.
However, there is more to this changed attitude toward agriculture
than is revealed by budget entries. In most neoclassical–conservative
plan countries, state purchase prices for collective farm quota and
above-quota produce deliveries are raised sharply, while (as part of a
social contract between the party and the citizenry) state retail prices
for goods, derived from that produce and sold to urban consumers in
state retail stores, are not raised correspondingly. This results in large
agricultural subsidies (some industrial and housing ones as well) that
do not show up as a direct budget line item, but are implicit in losses of
state revenues from commodity taxes (most basic foods carry a negative tax), profits taxes, and profit remittances. In China in 1982, consumer subsidies on grain, cotton, housing, and social welfare came to
almost 17 billion yuan (9 billion dollars), an amount roughly equal to
total state budgetary expenditures on culture, education, science, and
health (see Table 3.1).

Social insurance, security, and welfare are broadened to include
the collective farmers in national state coverage. As under the Stalinplan, "democratic centralism" guides the formulation of the neoclassical conservative plan. The difference is that there is marginally more
democracy and less centralism—but not much.

Last but not least, in addition to these various formal means, informal coordination is carried out—as always—by the illicit market mechanism of a vast underground economy. There is reason to believe that
the size and sophistication of this operation have grown faster than the
size and sophistication of the formal plan institutions.[21] As in the classical plan, the neoclassical plan's unregistered economy helps the plan
over its many inconsistencies (including the underground economy's
function as a consumption safety valve), but also depletes it of scarce
resources and redistributes goods and income in ways unintended by
the planners—ways often diametrically opposed to the planners' intent. One of the unregistered economy's effects is to reduce the disincentive effects of suppressed inflation. Another is to make a sham of
state socialism.

In both variants of the neoclassical plan, a vibrant cultural life
thrives underground. It includes a vast, innovative, and imaginative
samizdat literature written "for the drawer," but in fact widely distributed from hand to hand and occasionally published abroad. This helps
to relieve the boredom and mediocrity of the official culture: hack party
writing, socialist realism, and endless performances of *Swan Lake*. Al-

TABLE 3.1
CHINA: STATE BUDGETARY SUBSIDIES, SELECTED YEARS

	1978	1979	1980	1981	1982
Price subsidies (billion yuan)	6.57	14.05	18.43	25[a]	
Agricultural subsidies					
(1) agricultural price subsidies (billion yuan)		8.3	16.8	19.1	
of which: cereals, cotton, oilseeds		8.3	11.9	16.3	16.8
(2) Agricultural price subsidies (as percent of total price subsidies)		59.0	91.1	76[a]	
(3) Reduction in and exemption from taxes (billion yuan)		2.0	2.5	3.3	
(4) Total agricultural subsidies in billion yuan		10.3	19.3	22.4	
as percentage of budgetary expenditures		8.0	15.9	20.6	
Total subsidies as percentage of budgetary revenues	14.3	25.9	32.7	42.7	
Budgetary revenues as percentage of national income	37.2	32.9	29.9	27.3	

SOURCE: Thierry Pairault, *Politique industrielle et industrialisation en Chine* (Paris: La Documentation française, Notes et Études documentaires, nos. 4735–736, October 12, 1983), p.119. Based on Chinese sources. (See also Chapter 9 of this book.)
[a]Approximation.

though the culture of the neoclassical plan is merely sclerotic, the culture of the Stalinplan and the radical Maoplan is in a state of rigor mortis.

Property

The neoclassical plan in both versions accommodates itself to a quite significant extension of private ownership in the means of production, especially land, both legally recognized (as in Poland) and, de facto, in terms of broader rights to the production means by the actual user of those means (as in post-1978 China). A similar accommodation applies also to retail distribution and to the provision of some consumer services (for example, repairs, housing construction in the countryside).

In all cases, explicit quantitative limits are placed on private property in the form of maximum acreage that may be legally owned, number of draft animals, size of tools of trade, number of employees, and so on. More influential are the restrictions on input supplies and output marketing arising from the state's far-reaching command over resources and from the distribution network. Although private property is ideologically accommodated, it remains under a cloud. Unable to reap economies of scale and discriminated against in fact, if not in words, the private sector offers conditions of employment and security that are inferior to those of the state sector, and the social prestige derived from work in the private sector is low. Private property is viewed by the planners as a necessary nuisance.

The neoclassical conservative plan does not expand by much the rights granted to the actual users of socially owned fixed assets. (The only important exceptions are Polish, and the greater part of Chinese, farming.) As a rule, directors of firms do not have the legal right to buy, sell, rent, or alter in any way the quality of their assets without approval of higher state supervisory authorities. Their property rights to profits and working capital remain residual.[22] In the liberal plan variant, managerial property rights are comparatively broader.

In both versions of the neoclassical plan, the managers of socialized assets (factory directors, chairmen of collectives) are not in any meaningful sense subject to control by representative employee organs or by independent labor unions. Their primary reponsibility continues to be to party state authorities. The neoclassical plan does, however, make legal provision for the creation of such nominally supervisory bodies from below. Their effective supervisory power, however, is modest. Moreover, though one of the objectives of the neoclassical plan is to bring about a separation of party and state jurisdictions (that is, to get the party out of day-to-day economic policy), this, as has been argued, does not really happen.

Motivation

The neoclassical "reformers" give much thought to the motivational system, which they believe to be one of the major causes of the planned economy's apparent inability to tap the reservoir of individual entrepreneurial and managerial initiative and ingenuity. (Another cause, ideologically more delicate, is the system of property, which is characterized by the very narrow rights granted to the user-custodian of the socialized assets.) The reservoir is assumed to be there, although it is a good question whether it has not, after decades of planning, in fact evaporated. The ingenuity displayed by individuals in the underground economy falls, by and large, under the rubric of cunning: it is overwhelmingly of a redistributional quality, reshuffling the pattern of income and procuring things that are already there, rather than inventing and producing new goods. Some Westerners who have lived in the Soviet system speak of a "reverse Darwinism" in this regard. On the other hand, from time to time, the Soviet and East European press publicizes instances of creative entrepreneurial spirit, drawn from the criminal docket, that boggle the imagination.

In line with changes in the information system, the neoclassical plan in both versions relies more heavily than its predecessor on "economic levers"—wages, bonuses, interest, profits, procurement prices— to motivate workers and managers. The reliance is more pronounced in the plan's liberal than conservative version.

The "law" of rational low wages is repealed (presenting no problem), tariff money wages are raised, and an attempt is made to match the increase with a more generous flow of consumer goods.[23] In the conservative plan, the volume and composition of that flow are still determined by the planners, whereas in the liberal plan consumers do have some say in this through free and flexible prices. Little wonder that the Hungarian likes his goods better than does the Czech—and the goods are actually there much of the time (two important facts not captured by statistics).[24] Although the rates of increase of consumer goods output are not strikingly different in the conservative and liberal plans (with the possible exception being in Poland), in the liberal plan "consumption costs" (as British economist Alec Nove calls the time wasted queueing for inferior products in a rude sellers' market) are much lower in Hungary than in Poland, for example, or Romania. In the conservative plan, one buys a broom when one wants meat, because the broom is there and the meat is not, and one has the money. This situation does not occur frequently in Hungary.

It has been argued in some quarters that many consumption costs of the classical and neoclassical plans—shortages next to surpluses, queueing, rudeness, and wear and tear—are attributable to (a) the small number of people working in commerce, (b) the small number of retail outlets in the cities (both relative to the situation in market economies), and (c) defective organization of retail trade (poor "office procedures," bad store layouts, and the like). These defects, goes the argument, are separable from the system of economic organization and can be taken care of by fairly simple adjustments (for example, by opening more stores, training more store clerks, and presumably paying them better). Although (a), (b), and (c) are true, it is neither appropriate nor sufficient to divorce them from the system. For instance, the small number of retail outlets is due in large part to the socialization of private commerce (property) and to the planners' wish to control the socialized stores more effectively by consolidating them into a relatively small number of large units (coordination). The inconvenience to customers is dismissed because consumer goods and services are not ranked high by the planners in their goals, and normally receive attention only when they adversely affect work motivation. Technically, the easiest way to reduce the store shortage would be for the planners to allow private individuals to set themselves up in business (which would mean owning several stores, not just one per individual trader). This, however, touches the core of the system's property arrangements and is very hard for the planners to do, even in Hungary. In any event, shortages and poor quality of consumer goods, as well as associated consumption costs, unfavorably affect the supply of labor—primarily through absenteeism, slack performance on the job, drunkenness, and high rates of job-related accidents. All these factors in turn adversely affect the quantity and quality of output, thus raising consumption costs.

One thing the two plan variants have in common is that they do not devolve the wage-fixing function to the level of the firm. Even in liberal Hungary, the center determines (informally, but persuasively) wage categories, skill grades, and rules for bonus payments, and tries to contain sub-rosa wage drifts through progressive punitive taxes levied on firms that exceed centrally defined average wage levels. In the conservative plan, centrally determined wage funds for firms are the rule, as are the fixing of wage categories, skill grades, and complex rules for payment of profits into and out of the firms' bonus funds. The center's reluctance to let go of wage control is due as much to the desire to keep inflation in check as to the socialist state's interest in the pattern of income distribution. The preoccupation with income distribution also explains the state's continued holding-down of the prices of goods for mass consumption below market-clearing levels. This is both true of Hungary (though to a lesser degree) and of other countries. When prices of necessities are raised, they are almost invariably accompanied by increases in money wages, the latter usually substantially less than the former.

Bonuses to managers of firms and, to a lesser extent, other executive personnel (least of all, to workers) are paid from special firm "production incentive funds" (or "sharing funds") formed out of a portion of net profits. Formulae for payments into and out of the funds are established and controlled by superior authorities.[25] They are, as a rule, complex and related to various performance indicators, of which profit-ability is one—the most important, in Hungary. (Other performance indicators may include value added; sales, including hard currency sales; technical innovations; cost reduction; and increases in labor pro-ductivity.) Because the system—especially in its conservative version—has serious problems generating consumer goods flows in the right (demand and supply equilibrium) quantities and qualities, the end re-sult of money wage hikes combined with consumer goods shortages is inflation. As we have seen, suppressed inflation is a chronic condition of the Stalinplan. Additionally, in the neoclassical plan, open inflation frequently makes its appearance as the state tries to mop up the excess consumer purchasing power it has created and to lighten its burden of subsidies by selective (often very sharp) increases in its own retail prices.[26] Inflation was fairly well contained in Hungary until the late 1970s, but only at the expense of the plan's original intent to bring producer and consumer price ratios and foreign and domestic prices more in line—that is, at the expense of reform and, ultimately, of efficiency.[27]

Negative incentives are relatively de-emphasized, softened, and subjected to the rule of law. An example of softening is the changeover from criminal to civil penalties for such things as absenteeism, chronic lateness for work, and plan underfulfillment. The arbitrariness of the classical plan's penalties is attenuated by inserting punishments into the framework of "socialist legality." But the law remains arbitrary. The scope of individual initiative is not significantly enlarged, but is now explicitly defined in legal texts. An article of the Russian Repub-lic's Criminal Code states that it is illegal for store managers to repeat-edly sell poor quality goods. In Czechoslovakia, eighty-four laws and ordinances on quality control were passed in 1978 alone. If the bird were let go, there would be no need for this legal effort, because the market would take care of the problem through the lure of profit and its bankruptcy-inducing powers. Instead of being tackled as an issue in the motivational economics of the system, the managers' persistent sale of the poor quality goods constantly produced is treated as a departure from socialist morality. The normative legal remedy is alloca-tively irrelevant. The law and the economic forces that motivate indi-vidual behavior pull in opposite directions.

Curious as it may seem, some laws under the neoclassical plan are secret. An article in the *China Business Review* (an organ of the National Council for U.S.-China Trade) has this advice for prospective U.S. inves-tors in the People's Republic of China: "Because so many Chinese laws are kept secret and out of the hands of foreigners, it is very important that investors understand that their enterprises in China may come under laws they do not know about and are not allowed to see."[28]

Occupational choice and labor mobility are greater in the neoclassical plan than under its predecessor, but the freedom to choose one's jobs and move where one pleases remains restricted by administrative regulations (though less in Hungary than elsewhere). The scope of administrative allocation of labor is reduced, albeit not significantly, in China.

In both versions of the neoclassical plan, peasants are no longer used as sources of capital accumulation for heavy industry. In most countries using the conservative plan variant, an effort is made to improve the peasants' material condition by many different means, including: increases of agricultural procurement prices; greater resort to (higher) above-quota procurement prices; use of negotiated prices for local produce deliveries; improved supply of industrial inputs to farms; lower delivery quotas; fewer detailed output and input specifications for farms; more liberal attitudes toward private plots, household subsidiary activities, and free marketing; restraint in the pricing of goods of industrial origin sold to farms; reduction or removal of the "rural surcharge" (sel'skaia nadbavka) on consumer goods sold in the countryside; expansion of government grants given to farms in difficulties; lowering of agricultural taxes or tax remission in hardship cases; more generous extension of bank credit; enlargement of the share of cash in total payments to collective farmers; extension of the national system of social security to collective farmers; (in some cases) abolition of work points and changeover of collective farm remuneration to a contractual wage system; and experimentation with "production responsibility"— essentially the renting of collective farmland to peasant families under specified conditions of planned delivery (de facto family tenant farming, as in post-1978 China). In Poland (conservative), private farmers sell to the state their output—one they decide upon in a neomonopsonistic market setting—at negotiated prices. In Hungary (liberal), there are likewise no quotas, and collective farms negotiate prices with the state (the major buyer) also in a constrained setting. The policy of favoring the farmers has caused a great deal of complaint on the part of industrial, and more generally urban, workers about "unfair" and unproletarian peasant-slanted income biases, and has generated a fair amount of urban-rural class tensions. China is the latest to be hit by this problem.

In the neoclassical plan, income differentials are adjusted with a view to maximizing individual incentives. In some cases (the USSR, Eastern Europe), this means narrowing formerly very wide money income gaps (especially, as just noted, between industrial and farm workers, but also between blue- and white-collar workers, and between the lowest-paid and more-skilled industrial workers). In post-Maoplan China, it has also involved a widening of money income differentials (combating "equalitarianism") within given occupations. Simultaneous attempts are made to improve the crucial institutional links between input of effort and reward; a frequent criticism of the conservative plan is that plan norms with respect to worker compensation are "unscientific." This is important, since most production workers continue to have their pay linked in some manner to production norms rather than being paid according to time rates; that is, the classical plan's predilection for bonuses and piecework is lessened, but not fundamentally changed. (Movement toward time rates has been more notable in post-Stalinplan Russia than in post-Maoplan China.) The lowering of the rural income distribution unit in some countries, that is, its vesting in a comparatively small group of households (or even the household itself in Poland and under the family tenancy system in China) is designed to end the divorce between individual labor input and individual gain. More generally, the aim is to improve the quality of success indicators applied to workers and managers of firms so that the price of labor (wages, salaries) automatically evokes the quantity and quality (productivity) of labor desired by the planners. The liberal plan, by tying firm success to profit, and profit level to managerial bonus rewards (much more than to worker bonus rewards), as well as by providing the opportunity to engage in all kinds of private sector, income-earning activities (with their accompanying windfall earnings), has resulted at one stage in fairly sharp income differentials between white- and blue-collar workers, provoking a backlash against further liberalizing changes. As is occurring in China today, the "individualist spirit of profit seeking" was roundly criticized by socialist purists, contributing to considerable retreats from positions initially secured by the adjustment and reform offensive.

Nonmonetary income differentials (in-kind perquisites and bribes attached to job, rank, and—above all—political standing) are as important as ever: very important.[29] Corruption is pervasive, constituting, in effect, a system of crony socialism.

Compared with the Stalinplan, upward mobility of executive personnel at lower and central levels of the neoclassical plan is more sluggish as the sweep of the purge recedes. There is a tendency for old-timers to cling to their positions and perquisites, and for the average age of leading personnel to rise. In China, as in Brezhnev's Russia, this propensity toward gerontocracy tends to lower the average level of executive ability.

Job security is maintained in the state sector. State firms are not allowed to go bankrupt except in the most hair-raising cases—they are, in effect, immortal unlimited liability companies. Workers are not, as a rule, fired except for cause, and the cause tends to be political rather than economic in nature. This constraint, caused by full employment and the immortality of state firms, is important in all state socialist countries. Although understandable from the workers' standpoint, it makes nonsense of competition and militates against the socialist state's quest for improvement in the quality of economic performance.[30]

Experiments are made to stimulate technological innovation at all levels of the economy and to translate theoretical inventions into output. In the conservative plan, the means used to accomplish this are primarily administrative (for example, transferring separate research organizations to production firms or associations; putting them on *khozraschet* and on contract financing, that is, having the organizations get paid by their clients according to contracted-for results). Externally, the Stalin-plan's efforts to procure foreign technologies illegally are stepped up. Not much is done, however, to overcome the classical systemic obstacles to innovation or to accelerate the rate of equipment replacement. This occurs for four major reasons. First, in the scientific and technological "creative processes," the type and magnitude of uncertainty are different and greater than in "routine processes" of production:

> In creative processes, the prominent role of uncertainty calls for the pursuit of parallel independent approaches, the extension of competitive elements in horizontal relations. Soviet leaders have not been very successful in fostering creative activities in science and technology despite the investment of substantial resources in these areas. One reason for this is the use of vertical organizations in Soviet science and technology.[31]

This organization is related to the vertical arrangement of "branch" ministries (see Figure 2.3), that is, to administrative divisions that overlap, duplicate, and are not, as a rule, consonant with economic or technical and scientific divisions. The relationship among the ministries is generally uncooperative. The problem is compounded by administrative fragmentation at the next higher level, that of commissions of the Council of Ministers, to which the ministries appeal for resolution of their differences. Thus, the *Gosplan* is concerned with series production and technological diffusion, while the State Committee for Science and Technology (of equal nominal rank) deals with research and development up to the prototype stage. The success indicators of each commission and the horizontal relations among these two bodies are not such as to smoothly transform prototypes into mass-produced, technologically superior products.[32] Second, the neoclassical plan (in both versions) being a resource-constrained economy of demand-surplus (a chronic sellers' market), the impulse to innovate is almost absent at the firm level.[33] Third, the gradual replacement of material balances by more sophisticated methods of coordination (input-output tables for the economy) does not remove the technical innovation problems attendant on this type of coordinating technique. At the same time, the comprehensive use of linear programming techniques (which would permit the planners to consider various technologies of production and different production constraints) is hindered by (a) the task's magnitude in a complex economy characterized by many goods and technologies (high computational costs), (b) the persistent imperfections of information exchange (games playing), and (c) the system's continued obsession with secrecy. Fourth, continued plan tautness forces the firm to give all its attention to short-run performance and, by the same token, discourages managers from technical experimentation that would in any way (for example, as with downtime for retooling) interfere with the fulfillment of the short-term output plan (*otchet*).[34] One might ask, Why not build a little slack into the plan? Apart from the fact that tautness gives the planners much of their power over enterprises, the practical reason is because it is difficult for the planners to determine what "a little" is, that is, what constitutes optimal tautness.[35] The planners know that managements of firms overstate their needs and understate their capacities to obtain a "soft" plan, but don't know by precisely how much the input needs are padded and the output potential is underreported. So if the planners relax too much, underemployment of labor and capital will grow worse and the motivational structure will be further distorted by paying people extra for overfulfilling a snap plan. The best counsel is to keep raising output targets while retaining a tight grip on inputs. And thus, the administrative contradiction between production and innovation persists.

The one important exception to this is in the military sector, in which such parallel competitive research is carried on within a vertical organization. But, with the exception of the machine tools sector, spillovers from the military to the civilian economy are modest. One reason for this is the broad interpretation given to the secrecy of military research and development.[36]

In the neoclassical liberal plan, the formal organizational structure of the original Stalinplan and the neoclassical conservative plans is partially dismantled. However, informal lines of authority persist, with effects on innovation not too dissimilar to those under the more formal conservative arrangement.

Goal Priorities

In both variants of the neoclassical plan, growth is still considered to be a high-priority objective, but is to be achieved primarily through factor productivity improvements based on the adoption and diffusion of new technological processes. Less importance is attached to the pace of growth, and more to its quality (embodying the principle, as put by the Chinese, of "better less, but better"). Because of the persistence of administrative organizational structures and authoritarian habits of mind, the attainment of quality (a reduction in producer and consumer real costs in the process of growth) remains elusive in all countries (though somewhat less so in Hungary).[37]

Although investment continues to take a sizable (25–30 percent) proportion of national income, more attention is paid to improving consumption understood to be a key to productivity gains.[38] The classical plan's chronic propensity toward investment inflation persists in the neoclassical versions. In the conservative plan, this is due in large part to bad old habits. Capital being still quasi-"free" (the capital charge is quite ineffective in curbing the firm directors' appetite for extra capital), generated by forced savings rather than by the competitive bidding of users, almost risk-free, and obviously helpful in the firms' drive to fulfill output plans, there is little reason for restraint in formulating applications for capital grants or special government loans. Where firms are given greater investment discretion and importing latitude, as in the liberal plan (and, for a while, in China), there is the tendency to go on a buying spree, which results in deleterious effects on the balance of payments. Conservative and liberal readjustments have also failed to resolve the problem of investment cycles.[39]

In the Stalinplan, there was hardly any consideration of the efficiency of investment decisions measured in rates of return or some other capital-profitability ways. Such considerations were, in fact, decreed as being contrary to the interests of the proletarian state, subversive throwbacks to capitalism. Investment became a matter of political decision. The neoclassical plan in both versions pays attention to the costs and benefits associated with alternative investment projects. The notion of rates of return and capital profitability is quietly introduced into investment criteria. The two most common rules for evaluating the relative effectiveness of investment projects have been the coefficient of relative effectiveness and its later development, the comparative economic effectiveness of capital investments. The Hungarians, who have done much work in this area, for a time used an index of economic efficiency, also known as the g_n index.[40]

In the conservative neoclassical plan, suppressed inflation continues and, in addition, comes to the surface of the planned economy in big spurts. This happens (a) whenever the planners raise producer goods prices that had been held down unrealistically compared with costs (for example, coal prices in the USSR before 1967), the purpose of the upward manual price adjustment being to enable the producing firms to function on a self-accounting (profit-loss) system and allow the "average" firm to make profits (that is, not to be dependent on state budgetary subsidies); and (b) whenever the planners raise the prices of basic consumer goods (grain products, meat, vegetables, dairy products, sugar, cotton textiles, leather products) by large margins in order to lighten the state's burden of subsidies by bringing supply and demand more nearly into equilibrium (as exemplified by the price adjustment in Grossman's Quadrant III, Figure 2.1). Massive hoarding of goods whose prices are to be raised takes place in anticipation of the rise. Part of the hoarded goods is then redistributed through the underground market economy. At the same time, inflated prices on the legal free markets persist, as they did under the classical plan. In short, price stability in the conservative neoclassical plan is more elusive than in the Stalinplan. The instability, however, is less well disguised as consumers repeatedly become aware that their perception of low state consumer goods prices for basics and of comparatively high money incomes (no longer constrained by the now-repealed "law" of rational low wages) is just an illusion. Inflationary pressures, both open and suppressed, and price fluctuations are also present in the neoclassical liberal plan. This tends to be especially true where some domestic prices have been aligned with world market prices for similar goods.

Inflation in the neoclassical plan is statistically underreported for several reasons: (a) official price data (especially the cost of living index) are among the scarcer and more shoddy items produced by the plan; (b) the few prices included in the index are typically those that are kept stable, whereas many other prices (not included in the index) rise, sometimes very sharply; (c) lower-priced varieties of a particular good (for example, cheese in the USSR) disappear from the stores and only the higher-priced, higher-quality variety remains (although the higher quality may be purely nominal); consumers are forced to buy the remaining variety, but the quality change is not captured by the quantity index.[41] The cost of living index is tampered with in many other ways.[42]

Since in the conservative neoclassical plan quasi-guaranteed life-long employment and the immortality of state sector firms (soft budget constraint) have not been fundamentally changed, suppressed unemployment of labor and underemployment of capital (in the midst of capital shortage) persist and fluctuate over time. They are accompanied (for example, in post-1976 China, and Poland in the early 1980s) by instances of fluctuating open unemployment.[43]

The systemic causes that give rise to output cycles in the classical plan (see Chapter 2) are present in the neoclassical plan, especially in the conservative version. For example, the tendency of firms to maximize in-house production of hard-to-get inputs (which includes almost everything) is not eliminated.[44] It simply now emerges in the newly organized production associations. This practice not only reduces the system's economies of specialization, but contributes to output fluctuations as authorities break up these intra-association feudal fiefdoms, thereby disrupting (for a while) the associations' flow of secure inputs, and hence, their output performance (this shows up primarily in varying reductions of the quality of output and in fluctuating product assortment violations). Output cycles, in their turn, tend to lengthen construction periods through supply delays in crucial investment goods, and ultimately depress capital productivity.

The stress on the development of heavy industry is less than in the classical plan; light industry, residential housing and social overhead capital construction are raised on the planners' priority scale. The announced intent to step up the supply of consumer goods is not always carried out precisely in the terms promised, but at least effort is expended in this cause. (In 1975, Brezhnev promised to "saturate the market with consumer goods" over five years. This saturation had not materialized by 1980, but there was some slight improvement.) Agriculture, which has become a drag on the growth rate and an obstacle to the economy's qualitative improvement, is highly prized and catered to. Although some of this pampering of agriculture is limited to rhetoric, nevertheless a striking shift of official attitude toward farming and the peasantry does occur. Growth is more balanced than before, but inter- and intrasectoral imbalances persist; because of the importance attached to defense, the position of heavy industry remains dominant and heavy metal advocates are influential in party and state councils.[45]

The neoclassical plan in its liberal and conservative versions is comparatively more open to the outside world. In both the conservative and liberal plans, trade with ideologically repugnant partners is promoted because of the recognized need to import both advanced technology (cashing in on one's technological lag) and food. (Grain imports are especially important for the USSR and, until 1983, were crucial for China. Czechoslovakia and Hungary are basically self-sufficient in food.) For each country, foreign trade falls into two categories: trade with other centrally planned economies (many of them associated in the Council of Mutual Economic Assistance [CMEA]), and trade with market economies. Except in China and Hungary, a significant part of the trade of state socialist countries is carried on with one another primarily by means of bilateral (and some multilateral) trade agreements and protocols, coordinated *tant bien que mal* with the longer-term domestic plans of each country.[46] These are essentially barter deals among increasingly specialized partners. Although they represent fairly stable sources of supply and markets for the trading countries, they are rigid arrangements with fairly narrow ranges of commodity choice. Trade with market economies (70 percent for China, 50 percent for Hungary) is conducted on different principles. The relevant factors here are "world" demand for the products of state socialist economies and the ability of those economies to cater to that demand in competition with others on the world market.

In contrast to the classical plan, the neoclassical plan tries to eliminate (or at least reduce) the arbitrariness of foreign exchange rates through the use of shadow exchange rates (variously known as "coefficients of foreign trade effectiveness," "foreign trade equivalents," or "foreign trade multipliers") and to incorporate these in the domestic firms' financial accounts, that is, to express the firm's foreign transactions in shadow world market prices rather than in domestic ones. There are normally two sets of such shadow prices, one each for trade with the capitalist (dollar) and socialist (ruble) markets. The practice was taken quite seriously at one point in Hungary, but not for long. The incorporation of shadow pricing into the firms' accounts was intended not only to arrive at a fairly precise notion of the real cost of foreign trade to the plan, but also to stimulate the efficiency of domestic firms by opening them up to foreign competition. However, if this were done, and if the price messages were strictly adhered to, many domestic firms would have to fold—a politically and socially unthinkable step—while a few others would do very well. The result was the almost immediate reintroduction of subsidies and taxes differentiated by commodities, and a growing reluctance to adjust shadow exchange rates in line with changes in the conditions of world demand and supply. In effect, therefore, in Hungary as elsewhere, domestic firms remain by and large insulated from foreign competition by an array of exchange stabilization funds, and the calculation of the costs and benefits of foreign trade is hampered by both arbitrary official and obsolete shadow exchange rates. Direct access to foreign buyers and sellers is limited to associations of firms, but even here the conglomerates' decision-making discretion with respect to volume, assortment, and pricing is very restricted. By and large, the firms still have to deal through the Foreign Trade Ministry's foreign trade corporations, as is the case in the conservative plan.[47]

The neoclassical plan is involved in heavy international borrowing. It extends credit to select Third World countries, engages in compensation trade, joint ventures with foreign capitalists, and accepts foreign capitalist investments.[48] For all their glitter, these activities remain firmly controlled and, in most countries, subsidiary to both self-help and barter-type exchanges with other state socialist countries.

Although the differences between the conservative and liberal variants of the neoclassical plan remain differences of degree, there is at their root a difference in kind. This difference concerns the fundamental assumption about the relationship between the bird and the cage. There is more room for the market bird to fly around in the liberal than in the conservative plan cage. The conservative plan posits that the individual economic unit may do only that which is expressly allowed by the state. This is the quintessence of totalitarian modes of thought, and is not very different from the sort of thinking that underlies the dictatorial classical model. In the liberal variant, however, the underlying assumption is merely authoritarian: individual economic units can do everything that is not expressly forbidden. The difference between the two is not small. I agree with Nove that

> there is all the difference in the world between not being allowed to decide and having that right, even though from time to time one's superiors interfere with its exercise. Thus a Soviet firm cannot obtain inputs without an allocation certificate, and it always has an output and delivery plan imposed from above. The Hungarian firm, in principle, can choose what to purchase and from whom, and has no imposed output and delivery plan as a rule. True, ministries and party officials may issue orders: buy this, produce more of that. But the central authorities have neither the time nor the personnel to do so continuously and systematically, and so the management can act autonomously, by reference to economic criteria, most of the time. This is decisive and, despite modifications and backslidings, this is still an essential difference from the Soviet centralized model.[49]

CHAPTER FOUR

The Neoclassical Plan: Radical Maoplan

A left radical version of the classical plan was implemented in China on two occasions: between 1958 and 1960 (the Great Leap Forward), and again between 1966 and 1969 (part of the Cultural Revolution's peak phase). Although these were clearly identifiable manifestations of the Maoplan, elements of the radical neoclassical approach were present in China at other times: for example, in the course of the retreat from the Great Leap Forward (1961–1965, and especially after 1962), and during the aftershocks phase of the Cultural Revolution (1970–1976). Pieces of Maoist wreckage surfaced between 1977 and 1978 after the death of Mao, and before Teng Hsiao-p'ing took charge at the helm of party and state. In other words, although the Maoplan in its model form had a comparatively brief run of around seven years, the radical plan's lifespan in a diluted form was longer—some twenty years.

The radical Maoplan was sharply criticized by a coalition of Chinese leaders (spearheaded by Defense Minister P'eng Têh-huai) even as the Leap was collapsing (1959), and again, more conclusively, after the passing of Mao and the political death of his heir-apparent, Hua Kuo-feng. By the end of the 1970s, the radical plan had been theoretically discredited and dismantled as a policy instrument. The reasons given for its rejection were that it had inhibited growth, caused disruptive activity cycles, and worked against economic modernization (that is, intensive growth)—all true. It had also caused many deaths. As a direct result of the Great Leap Forward, China's population declined by 1.5 percent in 1960 and 0.5 percent in 1961, which translates into an absolute drop of 13 million people.[1] According to a restricted official circular disseminated among high cadres in China (in 1983), the number of unnatural deaths during the decade of the Cultural Revolution

(1966–1976) is believed to have been 20 million—"like a world war," or a holocaust.[2] In Cambodia, from 1975 to 1978, an even more radical and insane version of the Maoplan was enforced by the Khmer Rouge. The loss of life during those years is put at 3 million, or 40 percent of the country's population.[3] This bloody aberration was halted by Vietnamese armed intervention and replaced by war.

Maoist economic principles had their greatest intellectual impact not on state socialist planners and economists (least of all on Chinese planners and economists), but on a section of the West's leftist intelligentsia, who, belatedly, disheartened by the savage harvest of the Stalinplan and disenchanted with the "revisionism" of the neoclassical plan (in both its conservative and liberal versions), looked for a more promising model of socialist development and found it in Mao's China.[4]

In the sense of conventional organizational structures, the Maoist model can be described as economic nihilism: there is no market, no plan; no bird, no cage. Inevitably, the applied model has, on every occasion, produced chaos and disaster.[5] The depression that followed the Great Leap Forward was "almost unprecedented in the history of any country in peace time."[6] Although smaller by comparison, the dislocations of the turmoil phase of the Cultural Revolution (1966–1969) will have long-lasting adverse effects on China's effort to modernize its economy.

We will now look at Maoism's institutional arrangements and goals in their unadulterated form.

Information

Information is hortatory and political. Vast mobilization campaigns (*yundong*), their duration uncertain, are launched unexpectedly to accomplish (in a highly labor-intensive manner and with the help of native low-level technology) specific tasks targeted by the oracular source of wisdom in very general slogans (Mao's instructions). These bypass the (shattered) planning bureaucracy and are translated into mandatory workaday procedures ("study materials") directly for the benefit of ground-level cadres gathered in ad hoc committees.[7] The targets of mass assault are usually described with aphoristic concision (for example, "grow grain first!," or "make steel!"), and it is expected that these targets will be unerringly understood by the masses through heightened class consciousness ("redness"). It is supposed that there is no need to read books; Maoism posits the existence of such consciousness in the ranks of the correct classes (poor and lower-middle peasants, workers, soldiers, revolutionary cadres), who act as the principal carriers and spreaders of the message. In response to broad instructions from the ultimate doctrinal authority, these groups map out tasks with proletarian zeal, determination, and inborn class sagacity; they also set the pace, which is frenetic. There is fascination with movement for its own sake, with the very process of endless dialectical churning. The cryptic information is repeated over and over in easy-to-remember slogans and simple arithmetical formulae. Those who misinterpret the message have their thoughts reformed through ideological "struggle" and menial labor. For people not blessed with correct class lineage, true understanding comes from this combination of mental trauma and forced labor.

Markets and market information are abolished. Formal planning and organizational structures are done away with as planners and statisticians join workers and peasants in manual labor in factories and fields. The State Statistical Bureau, the classical and neoclassical plans' data-gathering and processing agency, was first taken apart in 1958 (the launch year of the first Maoplan), as were the organs of central planning. Both were put together after the Leap's collapse, and then reduced to ruins in 1966 (the initial year of the second Maoplan, the Cultural Revolution). At the nadir of the Cultural Revolution, the State Statistical Bureau had a staff of 13 people.[8] No statisticians were trained during the decade from 1966 to 1976. By 1981, the number of statistical workers at the State Statistical Bureau had risen to 280. Their expertise had rusted away through lengthy stints in the paddy fields and their computational equipment was equally eroded. It should come as no surprise that under such circumstances (compounded by the absence of markets), comprehensive economic planning is not possible. As late as 1980, it was officially conceded that five-year planning was "out of the question," and that not even annual plans could be constructed.[9]

The ideal to be striven for and applied (for example, in the early stages of the Great Leap Forward) is to shrink drastically the money nexus and to reduce the number of financial expressions. Compensation, for example, takes the form of "free supply" of goods and services by the collectivity: the provision of meals, dormitory space, laundry, haircuts, child care, clothing, mending services, and so on, to members of the collective in return for work done. However, even during the most agonizing convulsions of the Leap and the Cultural Revolution, state-set prices as carriers of information did not vanish from China (although they did disappear from Cambodia). State pricing (including wage-setting) under the radical plan was, when not neglected, based on revolutionary ethics rather than on any detectable calculation of economic costs. Neglect was the more common: tariff wages, for example, remained basically unchanged for twenty years, despite profound shifts in the underlying cost, technical, and labor supply patterns and conditions. (The neglect was not altogether accidental: it was connected with the Maoplan's already-mentioned adherence to the Stalinist "law" of rational low wages). The ethical element of Maoist price policy took two forms: (a) with regard to the pricing of consumer goods, there was a shift in favor of low-income groups; and (b) with respect to wage-fixing, there was a trend toward compression of income differentials at the expense of the upper brackets. Thus, "basic necessities" were priced below market equilibrium, often below average production cost of the commodity, the low prices being backed by physical rationing (for example, of grain, cooking oil, and cotton cloth). Less-necesary goods of everyday use (as defined by the radical plan's ethical rank ordering) were priced roughly at cost. Any reduction of production cost was to be passed to the consumers in lower retail prices after a fairly long interval during which the cost savings were appropriated by the state treasury and used to offset some of the state's loss on basic necessities. By contrast, "luxuries" (for example, bicycles, radios, wristwatches, electric fans) were sold at high prices, the difference between production cost and retail price being a tax fully appropriated by the state. Reductions of the production costs of luxuries could be passed in part to the consumers, but normally this was not done, in conformity with the Maoplan's belief in the character-building power of personal self-denial.

Most of the information issuing from the doctrinal fount being bulky, vague, and ambiguous,[10] there was quite a bit of variety in the way instructions were actually carried out at the base, despite campaign guidelines distributed to grassroots-level cadres and the transnational application of each mass movement. The Maoplan's information system is tense, as the "line" shifts erratically and unexpectedly assumes its own opposite (a phenomenon illustrating the concept of the dialectical relativity of truth). The system is held together by self-policing, mutual supervision, and fear. The preference is for head-on confrontation, and the emphasis is on struggle. Everyone must be sensitive to discreet changes and subtleties of the information flow (the all-important hidden meaning behind the platitude), for the personal consequences of being caught napping in the swirls of the class struggle can be calamitous. Not the least of the many problems of information retrieval is being certain that the retrieved information originates in a doctrinally unimpeachable source, for enemies and scabs abound and clog the information channels with all sorts of false-hoods. The practical difficulty is to identify the scabs, because appearances are deceiving; party rank does not invariably mean that the holder of the rank is ipso facto the possessor of the genuine goods.

Coordination

In the radical Maoplan, there is no market coordination, and coordination by material and financial planning balances is reduced to the minimum—in fact, to rubble. The Maoplan is set against bureaucratic structures that, of course, are the indispensable core and essence of the classical and neoclassical plans. So the question arises, How is the information coordinated? The answer is, Not very well. The result is breakdown, euphemistically known to the profession as "the trough." Two not-altogether detached observers of the Maoplan allow, in their sympathetic study of the radical plan (published in 1970), that they "had difficulty finding out a great deal about planning techniques and their adequacy." But, they add, "it should be emphasized that in a country which is still economically underdeveloped, strategy and discipline are as important as planning techniques."[11] Whatever the strategy and discipline were, they did not prevent the Maoplan from sliding into spasmodic discombobulations, not to mention the retarding long-term effects of economic revivalism on China's tiny pool of scientific and technical expertise.

Even at the most tempestuous moments of the Leap and the Cultural Revolution, there was some economic coordination, as there is during any civil war. No doubt discipline, although factionalized, had something to do with it, as did the individuals' and individual work units' instinct of survival: life went on locally, despite the chaos. Numerous meetings were held by harried officials to "exchange experiences," arrive at mutual accommodations, and barter surpluses against things in short supply. There was also in place, especially during the Cultural Revolution (1966–1976), an elaborate web of shifting personal-patronage connections (*guanxi*) linking the factionalized leaders at the top to their adherents at the provincial and lower levels all the way down to the basic work units, the *danwei*.[12]

Officially, coordination was to be achieved through a kind of utopian socialist Invisible Hand: a commonly shared political faith enshrined in the doctrinal godhead; the internalization by everyone of proletarian revolutionary values that made the Visible Hand of the planners superfluous (indeed, interfering and spoiling). Things allegedly fell into place because people were animated by the same lofty spirit. When that happens, as it used to occasionally in old-fashioned monasteries and some early *kibbutzim*, there is no need to promulgate elaborate rules of conduct. In what Saint Thomas Aquinas calls the "higher state of perfection," everyone knows intuitively what to do and does perfectly what is required in concert with others. The Maoplan posited that the new socialist man (the opposite of the economic man of bourgeois literature, and of the Hong Kong man of pre-1997 actuality) had emerged in China, and the plan put its trust in him as the principal agent of coordination. The socialist man had resolved within himself the contradiction between social good and private interest by dissolving the self in the collective mass (unselfish economics). The poor peasants and other members of class-correct categories had done this naturally at birth, while others accomplished it through being struggled against by the masses, through self-criticism, and through hard labor. Multiplied by several million, this transformation gave rise to a new economic, political, social, and cultural harmony in the midst of the tempering struggles that were the new China. An intangible, diaphanous cage was built out of spiritual substance, replacing the crude steel contraption of the Stalinplan. Many Western visitors to China in the early 1970s believed this; the Chinese, however, did not. People were simply compelled, by local cadres and the security people, to engage in action, much of it uncoordinated and ultimately useless. This is what the dictatorship of the proletariat really means: "authority without laws, unrestricted by any rules, and based on violence."

It has since been conceded that in matters of coordination, unity of thought through terror is no substitute for material balances and input-output tables, imperfect as these are.

Property

In the radical Maoplan, the stress is on bigness and "higher" socialist property relations—for example, on huge rural communes rather than on smaller collective farms. The final objective is "ownership by the whole people" (in fact, state ownership, provided the correct people are in control of the state). The transition from lower to higher socialist property and from small to big units is accomplished very rapidly by massive assault in response to a single instruction.[13]

In practice, this bigness and highness of property are not sustainable (partly because of diminishing returns to large organizations, but for other reasons as well). The Maoplan settles, albeit reluctantly, for three levels of ownership (in the countryside): commune, production brigade, and production team. But the pressures to lift and enlarge the property units are always present. The impracticability of "big and high" property is due to organizational problems (span of control), economic difficulties (economies of scale are less evident in agriculture than industry), and distributional handicaps (separation of the input of individual effort from individual reward, since the income distribution function is vested in a very large and distant unit).

The Maoplan attempts to "mass democratize" control of assets by the actual users of the assets. The plan's radicalism leads it to view with hostility the classical plan's principle of one-man management (*edinochalie*) and the privileges attendant on the directorial position. It regards the directorial method of firm management as a bureaucratic trick pulled by revisionists to hoodwink the masses, an elitist conspiracy that must be curbed. Ideally, in a way that is not clear and, one suspects, has not been thought through, the Maoplan wants the mass of workers and class-correct peasants to exercise spontaneous but disciplined control over the means of production, with no set organizational lines of command and no hierarchical administrative structures. One detects elements of anarcho-syndicalism in this striving directly by the workers for the exercise of power over the workplace. But once the workers have the power and have appropriately "hatted" the director and "put him on the wall" in denunciatory posters, just how are they to run the enterprise? To say that they will do this through mass democratic consultations does not advance the understanding of the problem by very much. So here, too, the Maoplan reluctantly settles for a compromise. The director is retained, but his powers of decision are restricted, shared in a three-in-one combination with class-pure cadres and thought-reformed technicians in a new managerial formation known as the revolutionary committee. The three-in-one revolutionary committee was at times interpreted to mean the combination of revolutionary cadres, army people, and representatives of the working rank-and-file "elected" at mass meetings. In fact, two of the three groups comprising the revolutionary committees (sometimes also the army representative) were local appointees of the ruling faction in the party central (Mao, his wife, Chiang Ch'ing, and her cohorts during the purer stages of the Maoplan).

Because of its troubles with nationwide economic coordination, the Maoplan shows a strong propensity to vest a good deal of power over property in regional authorities, especially in the provinces and municipalities. In this sense, the Maoplan is administratively decentralized by default. Added to the importance attached by the plan to the self-reliance of producing units and localities ("all-round" production by all-round socialists), this strengthened the centrifugal forces latent in Chinese society and made coordination of the national economic chessboard more difficult.

All private property in the means of production and distribution is extinguished.[14] Family plots are abolished and household subsidiary activities are prohibited. Rural free fairs are eliminated. Private ownership of consumer goods is restricted to indispensable items of everyday use, any excess (however slight) being equated with bourgeois conspicuous consumption.

Motivation

Motivation is the focal preoccupation of Maoist economic lore and the institutional kingpin of the Maoplan. The functioning of all other institutions and the attainment of the economy's goals hinge on successfully meeting the motivational challenge.

Motivation to "serve the people" and engage in (preferably manual) labor should be endogenous to the worker. In the proper socialist institutional environment, untouched by right and left deviations and freed of feudal and capitalist remnants, the worker will experience innately the need to serve society through unstinting labor in any location, for any purpose, and for any duration of time needed by society (which translates into comprehensive administrative assignment of labor—no freedom of occupational choice). In that happy state, there will be no need for exogenous prods of any kind. Work, like breathing, will be a necessity of life.

The path to work as a felt necessity of life lies through exogenous incentives, primarily (and increasingly) collective, cooperative, and nonmaterial (that is, moral, or normative). Material self-interest (including family interest), personal gain "at the expense of others" (or, as we would say, competitive gain), the individual desire to maximize income and accumulate wealth (the private property mentality), are inimical to the Maoplan's conception of motivation. Selflessness, total immersion of the individual in the labor and aspirations of the community, correct ideological "redness" rather than expertise, and personal asceticism (low consumption with a smile) are the foundations of the Maoist motivational edifice. Hence, a moral dimension is added to the Stalinplan's cold rationalization of low wages and lower peasant incomes.

Material poverty is more virtuous when equitably (that is, equally) shared. (Some people in China have called it the "law of equality of bitterness.") So in addition to the disparagement of material reward, the motivational system of the Maoplan shows a strong bias in favor of egalitarian modes of income sharing, or interpersonal equality of results. Less tangible perquisites of office abound about the godhead, but their enjoyment is circumspect, carefully hidden from the eyes of the masses.[15]

Cooperative incentives—the advanced helping and pulling up of laggards—are preferred over competitive incentives in which those behind in the race get stomped into bankruptcy by onrushing winners. This is nice but not efficient.

Negative incentives are a part of the system, dwindling in importance and cruelty as more people are brought up in the ethics of collective service. Punishments, like rewards, are preferably nonmaterial. Unlike the Stalinplan, which uses the execution squad as a major disincentive to deviant action, the Maoplan prefers, in theory if not always in deed, re-education of the mind conducted in public sessions of self-abasement and personal humiliation. (In practice, however, as the number of "unnatural" deaths shows, physical liquidation is far from being a minor appurtenance of the Maoplan's motivational armory.)

In sum, the motivational revolution envisaged by the radical Maoplan is the transubstantiation of individual selfishness into the ethic of disinterested public service, the rewards accruing in the form of moral satisfaction derived from this service and being equally shared by the collectivity.[16]

Goal Priorities

The two top priorities of the radical plan are growth of output and equity in the distribution of the fruits of growth. Growth is to be achieved by extensive means, that is, by additions of raw labor, ideologically inspired and politically mobilized, and by changes in the system's institutions (particularly motivation and property). Equity means rough equality of income distribution. Because of the presumed high level of political consciousness on the part of workers and reformed managerial personnel, the probability that egalitarianism might undermine labor incentives and productivity is rejected. Egalitarianism among the masses is promoted by means of "open-door" procedures for determining the distribution of income: orchestrated general meetings of commune peasants at which work-point allocations are communally determined in open (if predetermined) discussion, and knowledge by all of everyone's wage in industry. The motivational philosophy of the Maoplan combines with Maoism's egalitarian drift to rid the system of differentiated bonuses, premiums, and piecework payments.

On the rhetorical and emotional levels, the Maoplan (unlike the Stalinplan) extols agriculture and the peasantry, especially the peasantry's revolutionary lower-middle and poor-peasant foundation. To improve the well-being of the peasants is the radical plan's avowed objective, one moreover that conveys an attitude of distrust verging on hostility toward city life. Yet, despite Maoism's rural slant, the record of the operational Maoplan shows that agriculture is not the favored sector, nor is peasant welfare advanced in any tangible way. Post-Mao revelations show that heavy industry continued to be the prime beneficiary of state ministrations under the Maoplan, as it had been during the classical plan; light industry was well behind (this one would expect in line with the Maoplan's low opinion of material consumer satisfactions); and agriculture, despite official plaudits, was left to its own primitive devices. Although not so brazenly used as in the Soviet Stalinplan, Chinese agriculture under the radical Maoplan was neglected and badly mismanaged. Over the entire period from 1950 to 1979, state investment in agriculture was 11 percent of total state investment. In 1958 (during the Maoplan), it was 10 percent. During the classical Stalinplan (1953–1957), heavy industry received 8½ times the state investment in light industry. From 1958 to 1962 (largely during the Maoplan), heavy industry received 11 times as much state investment as light industry. During the turbulent Mao phase of the Cultural Revolution (1966–67) heavy industry received 14 times the state investment channeled into light industry.[17]

The radical plan's investment rates are high—higher, in fact, than those of the Stalinplan. During the classical plan (1953–1957), the share of accumulation in national income (net material product) was 24 percent. From 1958 to 1962 (largely during the Maoplan), it was 31 percent. From 1966 to 1970 (in the Second Maoplan), it was 26 percent. In the neo-Maoplan of 1971–1975 (the aftershocks phase of the Cultural Revolution), it bounced up to 33 percent.[18]

Self-reliance is highly prized: national, regional, and intrafirm self-help verging on autarky. Most often the self-reliant units are administratively defined. The Stalinplan's propensities of this kind are carried to extremes, as interregional and foreign trade is squeezed to the minimum. (During the Great Leap Forward, local self-sufficiency in cereals became an important policy goal. In 1978, after a decade of local self-sufficiency, domestic trade in grain was less than one-tenth of 1 percent of domestic output.) Resort to foreign loans, especially to longer-term developmental credits, is shunned. Foreign trade and payments should be balanced or show a surplus. The world outside is divided into socialist revisionists and capitalist imperialists, both of whom wish the Maoplan no good. Even in its acute form, which entailed sacrificing the benefits that could be derived from comparative advantage, this stance was widely praised in the West as an example of spunk, backbone, and determination (rare among poor nations) of depending on one's own resources to do the job of development. The emphasis on self-sufficiency is paralleled by disregard for specialization.

Scientific and technical invention and innovation are expected to burst forth and spread in a lava-like flow from the revolutionary enthusiasm and collective wisdom of poor and lower–middle peasants and workers. There is no need for trained and certified experts. In fact, a characteristic of the Maoplan (that it shares with the Stalinplan but, again, in greater extreme) is virulent anti-intellectualism. The intellectuals are put into the "stinking ninth" category, the pits of society— below landlords, rich peasants, capitalists, rightists, counterrevolutionary black hands, and other ghosts and monsters that inhabit the model. This is Maoism's fatal weakness, more burdened with negative consequences than the disparagement of formal organization and the experiments in equalitarianism.

Instability is not only tolerated, but actively sought. Revolutionary upheaval, institutional destabilization, and leaping over intermediate stages in any process are seen as the essence of development. Dialectical contradictions and confrontations are extended into the final phase of full communism in violation of historical materialism as elaborated by Marx. A distinguished victim of this churning, former Head of State Liu Shao-ch'i, was made to say in May 1958 that China had entered "a great period in the history of [the] country, the period of development by leaps and bounds."[19] The leaping and bounding which involved millions of largely uncoordinated people and impulsive goals, was given stature by a little noticed "theory" of U-shaped development that had once been pushed by the Maoists (both convinced and sham). The theory states that the mighty surge toward a communist society is U-shaped. Disproportionalities and an occasional absence of internal consistency and balance in economic construction are the necessary ingredients of the dialectical movement forward and upward. Ideologically, periods of tension alternate with periods of relative relaxation. The building of socialism and communism proceeds by twists and turns. This is normal and necessary.[20] The theory has been deactivated, but the effects of its past application on the growth path of China's economy are evident (see Figure 4.1). Notice the two major troughs in the figure (1960–1962, 1966–1969), both coinciding with the adoption of the Maoplan in China.

What Future for the Maoplan?

From the postmortem of the radical Maoplan, a consensus has emerged: the plan is not a viable instrument of economic modernization, not even of economic management without modernization. The contributors to this consensus are (a) the winners in China's "struggle between the two lines"—a loose and unstable conglomerate of old-time adherents of the Stalinplan, proponents of cautious readjustment leading to the emergence of a conservative neoclassical plan, bolder advocates of transition to a liberal neoclassical plan, and neomarket socialists for whom the Yugoslav model (appropriately revised to fit the conditions of China) is a continuing source of inspiration; and (b) most Western economists specializing in the study of centrally planned economies.[21] But the intellectual agreement, now partially translated into policy in China, may be misleading. In conversations with the Chinese, I have yet to find anyone who will openly argue for a return to the concepts and practices of the radical plan. On the contrary, one detects in the careful opinions expressed on the matter a hint of trepidation at the prospect of Maoism's resurgence. It was a "mistake" that will not be repeated now that Mao is confined to his mausoleum in Tienanmen Square. But, one learns, the mistake was not absolute: Mao, as he himself admitted after the Leap, was not an economist. More significantly, as a leader, he was 70 percent right (before 1958) and 30 percent wrong (after 1958). It would be more encouraging for the future course of China's current adjustments and hesitant reforms if the ratios were reversed.

Maoism as a model and strategy of social change is not confined to Mao the man or encased in a crystal casket. It is a state of mind that draws on an impatient but, by and large, accurate interpretation of Marxist dialectical teachings on class antagonisms. Nor is the Maoist frame of mind temporally limited. It is present in the Stalinplan and in the conservative and liberal neoclassical derivatives of the Stalinplan. In China, it was inherent in the earliest rectification campaigns of the now-glorified Yenan period and in the many terrorisms that preceded and accompanied the classical plan (1953–1957).[22]

The Maoplan had many beneficiaries as well as victims. The beneficiaries, currently cowed but unrepentant, number in the millions. Their wish to live to see a settling of accounts when the adjustment efforts

FIGURE 4.1

Chinese Economy Yearly Growth Path: Selected Aggregative Indicators, 1949–1980

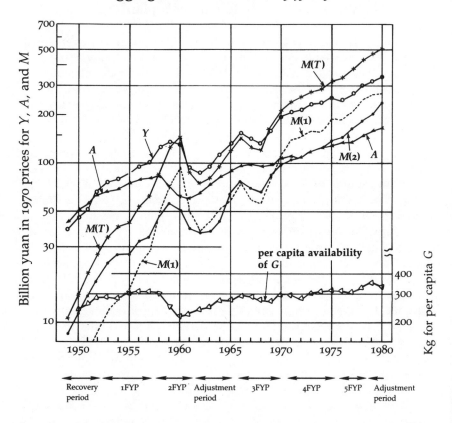

SOURCE: Shigeru Ishikawa, "China's Economic Growth Since 1949: An Assessment," *The China Quarterly*, no. 94 (June 1983): 247.

NOTATIONS: Y = "national income" (a Chinese concept, crudely similar to net domestic material product); A = total value of agricultural production; $M(T)$ = total value of industrial production; $M(1)$ = total value of heavy industrial production; $M(2)$ = total value of light industrial production; G = quantity of national food grain production; FYP = five-year plan.

fail (as they believe will happen) must be considered a not-negligible factor in China's future. The possibility of such a settling of old scores makes many middle-level cadres nervous, passive, or obstructionist, which in itself raises the odds against the success of the new course. A party rectification campaign ("reregistration") launched in 1983 and scheduled to last three years reportedly targeted 3 million party members (more than 10 percent of party membership) for expulsion by reason of their ultraleftist sociopolitical and ideological backgrounds. Maoplan adherents object to the growing income differentials resulting from the partial operation of market forces in the countryside and point to widespread corruption that (they claim) was either nonexistent or forcefully suppressed before. These moral reservations about giving the bird too much room in which to fly are not simply idle talk on the part of a few malcontents. The Chinese government has responded to the corruption accusations by a mass campaign of police repression, with daily executions widely advertised.[23]

Then there are also the chameleons of totalitarian dialectical reality. Some of the new rich peasants of China's post-Mao neoclassical conservative plan (1979–present) who are exhibited to foreign newspaper correspondents are former brigade and other local party secretaries, now chiefs of villages (such as Liu Liquan of Gaojia village, Sichuan province [where the neoclassical plan's "household responsibility" system began; see Chapter 9]). At the same time as they prosper under the new system, these people justify their past zigzag actions (including enforcement of the Maoplan) as, quite simply, carrying out the party's orders of the moment. "And, if the policy changes, the loyal Mr. Liu says that, however reluctantly, he will do what is asked of him," reports one correspondent.[24]

Although compared with the Maoplan's peak phases, the neoclassical conservatism of the post-Mao era is rational, that in itself is no guarantee of the neoclassical plan's survival, much less of its extension into liberalism and neomarkets. Another attempt to smash the cage and kill the bird cannot be dismissed as an altogether unlikely happening.

CHAPTER FIVE

Neomarket Yugoplan

Significance of the Model and the Experiment

Both the idea behind the Yugoslav experiment (with its fusion of market and worker control) and the experiment itself have excited widespread interest, enthusiasm, and wrath among economists and politicians of the West and East alike. Most of the praise has been lavished by Western economists of social democratic inclinations (for example, Vanek); some enthusiasm, as well as skepticism, has been expressed by Yugoslav economists (one of whom describes the system as "a mixture of totalitarianism and anarchy");[1] and scorn has been poured on the concept and its embodiment at various times by the Soviets, their allies, and the Maoists. The Yugoslav neomarket (or Yugoplan) is indeed a curious blend of many compatible and contrary elements, "a strange mixture of distorted market and state intervention."[2] The reason for the interest and emotion generated by the Yugoslav experiment is understandable. Its rejection of Soviet-type administrative central planning and resort (at least during some periods) to market-type bargaining and "planning from below" appeal to free marketers; its vesting of the management of firms and their assets directly in the working people strikes a responsive chord in socialists of various persuasions, particularly those who have always been uncomfortable with both capitalist and Soviet-type *edinochalie*. Equally, of course, it irritates state socialists who criticize the system's necessary linkage between workers' management and market-type behavior (lateral bargaining, horizontal relations, and so on). After 1978, the Chinese joined the crowd of interested onlookers. In sum, the Yugoplan neomarket appears to be a happy combination of the quest for allocative efficiency and distributional equity, or, alternatively, as the *haute trahison* of Marxism-Leninism. Its interest is enhanced by the rich variety of forms it has assumed since the early 1950s and by the changing proportions in which plan and market have been combined.

I think, however, that the interest in the Yugomarket will wane for two reasons. First, although the idea may be of universal appeal, the experiment is parochial, many of its elements being closely bound up with the specifics of an ethnically balkanized, multinational, culturally heterogeneous, regionally very unequally developed country. Second, the track record of the Yugoplan is mixed. Though the growth rate has been very respectable, personal incomes have risen faster than labor productivity, inflation and unemployment are high, industrial productivity has been sluggish, the investment rate has been inflated, and the effectiveness of investment poor (40 percent of gross social product in 1982, with a dismal capital-output ratio of 5:1). There have been strikes—the spectacle of workers striking against themselves—and management inefficiencies have been glaring. There is a balance of payments disequilibrium and a monumental foreign debt (more than 19 billion dollars at the end of 1982 in hard currencies [much more in total hard and soft debt], with a per capita indebtedness of 1000 dollars, that is, 300 dollars more than in bankrupt Poland).[3] In addition, there are signs of creeping centralization and instances of slapdash administrative interventionism. Even the kingpin of the whole system—the workers' management of firms—is beset by theoretical and practical problems that contribute in important ways to the system's troubles.[4]

Because the organization of the firm and its associated property rights is the foundation of the entire system, we will discuss it first under the heading "Property."

Property

The characteristic feature of Yugoslavia's system is the internal organization of the firm. The firm in Yugoslavia can be established or expanded by any unit of the government (from the local commune to the federal government), by five or more individuals who pool their assets, and by the splitting-up or merging of an existing firm. The firm, or working organization, is comprised of so-called Basic Organizations of Associated Labor (BOALs).[5] The BOAL is a technical unit that produces a marketable product or service.[6] All workers (from six to several hundred) within that unit belong to the BOAL. The BOAL makes decisions regarding the distribution of its (separately calculated) net income within the parameters of various "self-management agreements" and "social compacts" to which it is a party. These agreements and compacts are concluded, in conformity with general principles laid down by law, among economic organizations (BOALs, firms, banks) and sociopolitical "communities," trade unions, and associations or chambers of firms (*komori*), and they define the rights and responsibilities of the economic units toward one another and toward national policies. A firm is an association of BOALs. Each BOAL or firm of more than thirty workers has two organs: (a) a workers' council, elected by the workers by secret ballot from within the BOAL and from a list of people selected by labor unions liberally sprinkled with communist party members; and (b) a manager assisted by a managerial board. The latter is appointed by a special commission composed of workers' council representatives, trade unions, and a people's committee selected by the local political organ, the commune. A firm's operational plans must be approved by all constituent BOALs. The profit to be distributed is calculated for each BOAL in accounting prices internal to the firm, which are subject to inter-BOAL self-management agreements and are related both to the overall performance of the firm and the contribution of each BOAL to that performance. Within the boundaries of the agreements and compacts, the workers' councils have wide powers concerning decisions about the volume and assortment of production, prices, wage rates ("payment by results"), and about the distribution of profits as supplementary compensation to workers, payments into social funds, and investments. Managers (members of Milovan Djilas's "new class") have the dual function of carrying out the directives of the workers' councils and obeying the law that embodies the government and the party's macroeconomic social or regional objectives. Managerial positions are advertised and appointment is by competitive examination (plus pull?). The manager and his board cannot hire, discipline, or fire workers without the consent of the workers' council, nor do they have the right to determine the distribution of income within the BOAL-firm independently of the council. Managers and managerial boards can be dismissed either by the workers' councils or by the local communes.

In sum, the Yugoslav system rests on "social" property (not BOAL-firm property) and workers' management of assets (broad rights of use and disposal of fixed assets and profits) achieved through a multi-layered organization of representative workers' councils and professional managers responsible to both the councils and local political authorities (communes [local governments] and economic chambers [compulsory semigovernmental associations of firms], and, through these, republican and federal powers). Members of the League of Communists of Yugoslavia (LCY, or communist party) play an active and influential role within this complex setup. The sharing of the right of appointment between the BOAL-firm and political authority (commune) and the manager's dual responsibility limit the BOAL-firm's effective property rights in the "social" assets.

The socialized sector employs about 50 percent of the civilian labor force and accounts for more than 80 percent of the gross social product. Outside agriculture, the private sector is limited to firms employing not more than five salaried people. About 85 percent of the farmland consists of small (less than ten hectares) private farms employing 30 percent of the labor force and producing almost 60 percent of the marketed output. Another 5 percent of the labor force works on state farms and agricultural cooperatives modeled on the Soviet *kolkhoz*. Private farmers can come together in a BOAL and form a voluntary cooperative (not of the Soviet type) to take advantage of economies of input purchasing, output marketing, cheap credit from the State Agricultural Bank, and research. There are some five thousand such agricultural self-help cooperatives. They are managed by their members (private farmers) and do quite a bit of farming as well.[7]

Information

Prices are the primary carriers of information in the system. Most prices, however, are not determined by market competition but are, in various degrees, controlled. The main agency of control is the Federal Bureau of Prices. As in the neoclassical plan, but with important differences, the Yugoplan uses multicategory prices. There are four major categories: (1) *Free prices.* These prices, primarily of consumer goods, are determined by relatively free competition of buyers and sellers in the market. (2) *State-set prices.* These prices—of, for example, of oil products and some consumer goods of mass consumption—are fixed and can be changed only by the Federal Bureau of Prices. (3) *Approved self-management agreement prices.* These prices—of, for example, equipment, chemicals, and intermediate products—are negotiated among producers and between producers and users in self-management agreements that must be approved by the Federal Bureau of Prices. (4) *Self-management prices.* These prices—of metals and raw materials, for example—are negotiated among producers in self-management agreements relating to imported inputs and export goods and often set by reference to world market prices.[8] Prices of agricultural products purchased by the state from private farmers are negotiated between the two parties and approximate market prices.

The description of price formation understates the importance of price control in the Yugoslav system. Thus, the self-management price agreements are made within a broader framework of social compacts among sociopolitical entities that define the permissible limits of price formation (especially of price rises). The Federal Bureau of Prices has the power to change the goods that comprise the four price categories. It can also order price freezes or ban certain investments, and it has availed itself erratically of these prerogatives.

Most investment is now self-financed by firms and carried out within investment guidelines laid down in social compacts. Investments are also made by borrowing from banks, and there is some interfirm investment based on specific agreements. Interest is payable on borrowed capital, but is determined administratively and does not emerge from the competitive bidding of a capital market (that is, it is not an equilibrium rate). The rate of interest has been kept low for long periods of time: in recent years, it has stood at roughly one-quarter the rate of inflation.[9] There is no economic rent. When differential rent is recognized, it is fixed in special self-management agreements and compacts, and has little to do with demand and supply equilibrium. Wages are paid out of BOAL enterprise income, wage rates being decided on by workers' councils (but only within guidelines and limits spelled out in social compacts and self-management agreements). Foreign exchange rates are controlled by the state (primarily at the republican level), and foreign exchange transactions are monitored by the banking system.

Given this rather restricted freedom of prices, profit is unlikely to be a good indicator of social cost. In any case, it has been noted that the Yugoslav worker-managed firm has a propensity to maximize not total profit but net product per employee, that is, that part of profit intended for the workers' personal consumption. The tendency is to distribute the greater part of gross profit, then to borrow from the bank and pursue laborsaving, capital-intensive investments; this is all the more so when the interest rate is kept at artificially low levels. Such profit-distribution–bank-borrowing–capital-intensive investment action is conducive to investment inflation and unemployment. Where the laborsaving capital variant must be imported from hard-currency areas, there will be negative repercusssions on the payments balance. All this, in turn, will build pressures for deflecting the councils' decisions away from such a course and for some form of investment planning. The commune committee of the communist party seems always to be ready to help with economic policy whenever the model shows any weakness.

Coordination

The coordinating role of the market in the neomarket Yugoplan is not very great. Entry is restricted by the need for administrative approval to establish a new firm and by the threat of loss of control over the new firm to workers' councils. Firms do not go under. The competitive market operates as a coordinating device for many consumer goods and services. It does not function (or its operation is modified) in other spheres: labor, capital, raw materials, semimanufactures, public goods, and social services. The modification takes the form of a network of social compacts and self-management agreements among BOALs-firms and sociopolitical units of all kinds in which market considerations are tempered and tampered with by guidelines (sometimes orders) originating in nonmarket sources. This complex of lateral and vertical negotiations, compromises, multilateral bargaining, consensus, state guidance, party influence, and workers' management gives rise to a "rolling" (continuous), primarily indicative plan. In contrast with the neoclassical plan (both conservative and liberal), there is more give-and-take to the Yugoplan, more genuine consultation and participation, much more inclination toward horizontal transactions, better accommodation of competing interests, and less savaging of people. The plan is humanized; the market is tamed and socialized. One is reminded of the ravens who have the run of the Tower of London: they hop around the spacious grounds, but do not fly away. Their wings have been clipped.

If official statements are to be believed, the Yugoslav method of coordinating microeconomic decisions with the macro interest through social consensus (the intricate network of compacts and agreements) is superior to coordination by the competitive market. But not everyone agrees. Some see it as just another modification of market signals for the sake of equity, interregional solidarity, nation-building, or simply for the particularistic interest of localities or firms. They are mistrustful of the phraseology of "solidarity," detecting behind it a drift away from market-determined results to politically determined bailouts, subsidies, safety nets, and protection. Consensual accords, such people fear, represent an erosion of market socialism's principles and the abandonment of arbitration by market price. There is danger, they argue, that if the workers' self-managed firms do not respond to market demand, sooner or later they will have to respond to the need as defined and dictated by some administrative, noneconomic process.

The Yugoplan would then become just another variant of the neoclassical Soviet-type plan, and workers' self-management would be reduced to an empty shell.

Motivation

The model's central idea is that people will work better if they are meaningfully associated in the management of their workplaces. Alienation is minimized and the human personality expresses itself more fully when people participate directly in decisions regarding production and income distribution. Labor management of the firm, combined with a decentralized market economy, promotes individual freedom and eliminates class distinctions by banishing the tyranny of capitalists, corporation managers, and state bureaucrats—the "bad guys" of the market and plan. Labor management in the setting of markets is the quintessence of the socialist ideal: it makes the state largely irrelevant as the mover and coordinator of economic activity.

Yugoslav practice has fallen short of the ideal. Workers' self-management does not appeal to all workers; among workers, it has the greatest attraction for aspirants to managerial posts. Many crucial technical and financial decisions must be left by the workers to professional managers because of lack of time, worker expertise, or both. The tendency to maximize net income per employee restricts employment opportunities, gives rise to undermanning of equipment in the better-off firms, creates sizable differences in per capita income among firms (that is, violates the principle of equal work for equal pay), and helps fuel inflation through high distributions of net profits combined with high borrowing for investment.[10] The combination of workers' management of firms with markets that peaked during the period from 1965 to 1975 entailed some far-reaching neglect of external economies and diseconomies and the "fragmentation of systemic links."[11] This, together with a deteriorating balance of payments and foreign debt situation, led to the present relative taming of the market by social compacts and spasmodic ad hoc state interventions. It remains to be seen whether the practice of workers' management can prosper in the company of the Yugoplan's many social contracts and agreements, or whether it will be smothered by them.

CHAPTER SIX

Additional Issues

There are some additional issues that have a bearing on what has been said thus far, but require more explicit discussion.

Level of Development

An uncomfortable feeling persists among economists who deal with comparisons of economic systems that they are not handling well the problem of the level of economic development as measured by the level of per capita income. In Figure 1.1, the less developed socialist countries—China and Albania excepted—are notable by their absence. In recent decades, there has been a spectacular growth in the number of Third World countries adopting the command plan as the main instrument of goal selection and resource allocation. The literature on the less-developed centrally planned economies (apart from that of Cuba) is sparse, and this not exclusively due to the paucity of data. There is a good deal of ambivalence about how these economies fit into the conceptual framework of comparative economic systems, about whether perhaps they would best be left to the scrutiny of development economists and economic anthropologists.

Opinion on this question is split. At one end are level-of-development determinists, who argue that economic systems are a function of the level of per capita income. These people are often (though not invariably) adherents of what is known in German as *Stufenlehre*, or "stage" theory, which posits unilineal economic development accompanied by systemic transformations at every stage. Marx belongs to that school. The trouble with stage theory is that the level of economic development can fall as well as rise; economic institutions do not always correlate well with the level of development; and some economies skip a stage here and there. Even within the confines of Marxian historical materialism, it can be asked in what sense Marx's conception of history is linear—a continuous upward march from darkness to light, punctuated by dialectical revolutionary "jumps" (*skatchoki*)—and in what sense it is circular, beginning and ending with a property-less society. The circular view of history is suggested by Marx's *Critique of Political Economy* (in which he implies a movement from public ownership to private ownership, then back to public ownership; or primitive communal society, class society, communist society).

Another group of economists denies the systemic effects of an economy's developmental level, pointing to sharp differences in per capita income among countries belonging to the same systemic family.

Between the two extremes are those who think that the level of development exercises some influence on the institutional structure of an economy, but that this influence is not decisive. (American economist Morris Bornstein proposes to include less developed economies in a consideration of economic systems, but to exclude primitive nonmonetized tribal economies where economic relations are guided primarily by custom and tradition rather than market exchange or administrative command.)[1]

The history of the plan suggests that the less-developed countries—czarist Russia heading the list—provide a more receptive ground for implanting the plan than do developed market economies. There are various reasons for the apparent correlation of plan and low per capita income: many of the countries choosing the plan were former colonies of the Western powers; colonialism became associated in the minds of local elites and in the popular psyche with capitalism. When independence day came, the baby was thrown out with the bath water. There is also a widespread belief (not fully borne out by empirical evidence) that the plan reduces the market's often glaring personal income inequalities (in the advanced market democracies, these are lessened by fiscal redistribution). Marxist philosophy is strongly preoccupied with distributive justice (understood as rough equality of results), a preoccupation absent in the ethos of the marketplace. In many less-developed market economies, personal income inequalities tend to be very marked, and political capital can be made out of the promise to change this by changing the system. At times it has been argued that the plan, being a powerful engine for bringing about fundamental change, will engender a temptation to use it in low-income peasant societies gripped by institutional immobility. The plan, especially in its classical version, ruthlessly uproots seemingly insuperable institutional obstacles to economic growth.

Economist Kenneth Boulding raises the question of the relationship between the level of development and the economic system in a somewhat different context: the length of time the system has been in existence. Countries that opted for the plan through an indigenous revolutionary or (more rarely) electoral act (rather than having the plan thrust on them by Soviet arms) did so at an early stage in the development of their market economies. The opposite can also be hypothesized: transition from plan to market is possible and most likely to occur only during the plan's early stages.[2] If this reasoning is correct, the prospects for marketization and privatization reforms in the USSR and other more-developed socialist economies are not good. The reasoning appears to conflict with the hypothesis of socio-technical convergence of market and plan systems presumed to occur at an advanced level of each system's development. The convergence idea has received more attention than its analytical substance deserves.[3] Empirical evidence of convergent trends is at best ambiguous.

Level of development may influence attitudes toward the pace of capital replacement. In less-developed economies in which capital is scarce, there will tend to be a bias in favor of long capital life spans, which adversely affects the rate of technological diffusion where new technology is embodied in capital equipment. In the classical and neoclassical plans, this level of development-related impediment strengthens the existing systemic obstacles to technological innovation and the embodiment of that innovation in production.

Yet another linkage between plan and level of development is to be found in the increasing interdependence of the developed economy's constituent parts and in the growing complexity of that interdependence with its ever-larger numbers of intermediaries and shifting input-output coefficients.[4] In a developed economy, supply scarcities (plan tautness), allocative errors, and all manner of misjudgments by the planners cannot be easily localized and confined to this or that sector. They spread through the system, their secondary and tertiary effects causing widespread losses and making remedial action difficult.

Low levels of foreign trade, characteristic of the Stalinplan (as in the USSR and China), may be explained not only as the result of a conscious policy of self-reliance, but also as a function of low per capita income. The same can be said of the relative neglect of services.

Self-sufficiency of basic economic units, characteristic of the radical Maoplan, can also be explained in part by the low developmental level of a nonmarket economy. Low development means modest skills, simple planning machinery severely constrained in its capacity for co-ordination, and rudimentary communications. In such a setting, "all-roundness" at the level of the local primary producing unit makes more sense than advanced division of labor. The same argument may be used to help explain the Maoplan's propensity toward administrative decentralization, although (as noted earlier) other, probably more powerful, forces were actually at work (one of such forces being the weakening of the formal organs of central authority, resulting in decentralization by default).

Environmental Ecosystems

Economic systems function within an environment of cognitive and normative human behavior or culture. Culture covers a wide variety of phenomena: intellectual, methodological, ethical, aesthetic, social, political, and national traditions and legacies, which influence, and are in turn influenced by, the system of economic organization. The fact that the classical plan turned out to be what it was (see Chapter 2) surely had something to do with the cultural environment of the Russia in which it was nurtured. The evolution of Marxist scientism into Marxist-Leninist-Stalinist dogma is similarly linked to traditional patterns of Russian cognition. Adopted by China, the plan's institutional structure and explanatory ideology assumed distinctively Chinese cultural forms. Among these, mention should be made of bureaucratism and its propensity toward patriarchy, nepotism, autocracy, factionalism, and *guanxi* ("protective interpersonal connections," or "pull"). Although not absent in other national manifestations of the plan, they assume a particularly pervasive and virulent form in China.[5]

Nationalism

Among the components of the environmental ecosystem is nationalism. Marx never understood it; his theoretical scheme of property-defined classes cutting across national boundaries and nationalist feelings reflects that deficiency of understanding. The practitioners of Marxism, however, once in power, learned to use nationalism in the cause of socialist construction (as in the cases of Stalin in World War II and János Kádár after 1956, to mention only two examples). Nevertheless, nationalism has not been satisfactorily absorbed into the Marxist theoretical frame. It provides in some countries (for example, Poland) a competing perspective, and presents a policy threat to the existing order.

The Hero in History

Marxism appealed to Lenin, Stalin, Mao, and other dictators in no small measure because of the authoritarian license inherent in the doctrine. In the classical and neoclassical plans, Lenin, Stalin, and Mao gave the theory a practical totalitarian content. The pathology of the classical plan cannot be understood without Stalin, nor can the radical neoclassical plan be comprehended without Mao. Lesser builders of socialism (for example, Khrushchev and Brezhnev) have left their personal imprint on the conservative neoclassical plan. The question can be posed as to whether the neomarket Yugoplan would have been possible without Tito, and whether the Hungarian liberal variant of the plan can survive into the 1980s without Kádár or a Kádár-like successor acceptable to both the Hungarian people and the Kremlin. The post-1978 Chinese adjustments and their increasingly liberal drift (evident in 1984) are correctly associated with Teng Hsiao-p'ing, the great revisionist. So, in addition to the level of development and cultural environment, we must consider the influence of the individual birdman on the configuration and resilience of the cage. In other words, a good deal of what happens in a dictatorial society can be explained by the personal characteristics of the dictator, which are not captured by statistical averages.

Entrepreneurship

The critical problem of entrepreneurship under the plan has been touched on in earlier chapters. Entrepreneurship is understood here in its definition by Austrian economist Joseph A. Schumpeter as the establishment of "new formations": the introduction of new goods or goods of different quality and of new methods of production, the opening-up of new markets, the conquest of new sources of supply, and the carrying-out of new forms of organization.[6] In a centrally planned administrative command economy, the entrepreneurial function devolves on the central planners and is thus governmentalized and routinized. In addition, the entrepreneurs should be where the action is—at the grass roots of the economy, not at its pinnacle. Informally (and most of the time, illegally), the entrepreneurial function is appropriated by managers of firms, specialized contact men (*tolkachi*),

workers, collective farm peasants, and consumers; it becomes synonymous with the manipulation of official policies and officials, with the
rechanneling of inputs and outputs, and with other "nonrational" processes, rather than with innovation and the production of new goods.
The qualities it calls for in such circumstances are of the outwitting and
old "street-smart" variety, more suitable to thievery and the curb market than to economic creativity. Risk-taking, though sizable, is by and
large a redistributive phenomenon.

The suppression of entrepreneurship is not limited to the plan. It
exists in premarket and preplan oligarchic *dirigiste* societies, of which
parts of Latin America are excellent examples. In Peru, for instance,
"entrepreneurs cannot operate legally because of an oppressive bureaucracy built to protect those on top from competition from people below.
But they operate anyway, because that's the only way they have to
survive."[7] Entrepreneurship is also crippled in some welfare state societies, of which England before Margaret Thatcher is a suitable example.

Normative and Positive Economics and the Question of Systemic Collapse

One of the discreet themes of the preceding chapters is that adjustment
and (better still) reform of the plan are needed if the plan is to overcome the paralyzing institutional problems that beset it, and if it is to
do better than just muddle along. Indeed, unless something more than
cosmetic change is implemented, chances are good that the plan will
eventually collapse. But how and when does an economic system collapse? Poland's economy, for example, has gone under repeatedly; the
people have been alienated from their sociopolitical environment, and
the economic system has been thoroughly discredited in practice as
well as theory. Yet the economy keeps sputtering along.

The answer to this question is to be found in the relationship of
economic problems to political revolt, and in the further relationship of
positive to normative economics within the plan.

Whatever the economic system, whether market or plan, there is a
threshold beyond which economic problems turn into political dislocations. At some level of unemployment, inflation, goods shortages, consumption costs, per capita consumption, or distributional inequity, the
failure of economic institutions manifested in static, dynamic, and X-
inefficiencies, or more simply in the neglect of people as individual
participants in the system, is transformed into political unrest: the system is either voted out or booted out by revolutionary action.[8]

The precise threshold of tolerance at which this transformation occurs, as well as its timing, are difficult to determine. They depend, among other things, on cultural heritage (for example, the Russians seem to have a higher level of tolerance for nonsense and nuisance than do the Poles or the Hungarians); on the level of development (for example, in a low-income economy with a history of stagnation, a 1 percent annual increase in per capita consumption might be enough to stave off political turmoil); and on the personality of the leading decision maker (the Stalinplan, for example, was done away with only after Stalin's death, and could probably not have been disposed of before that event). Of course, in a self-respecting police state, political opposition and dissent that would alter the economic system in a peaceful way can be neutralized, and revolt can be suppressed by force of arms. In the absence of change initiated from on high, the system can continue to function for a considerable time with the help of brute force and intimidation. However, the underlying economic disequilibrium will continue to produce recurrent tremors of the political landscape. Change need not be unilineal, inexorably headed toward marketization and privatization; it need not inevitably be reform. It is likely to be continued intrasystemic adjustment in the direction of greater decentralization of the liberal neoclassical or Yugoplan varieties. But adjustment could also move the other way, toward the Stalinplan or, as in China, toward the Maoplan. The chances of structural intersystemic reform materializing are, on present evidence, not very great. Too many formidable political and ideological forces and vested interests are arrayed against systemic reform. But without such reform, the disabilities of the existing plan variants will not be resolved, though they may be lessened. This raises the possibility that the threshold of tolerance will indeed be crossed at some not very distant future time.

A plausible attempt at identifying the economic threshold has been made by Berliner.[9] He first distinguishes a level of per capita consumption threshold defined in political terms as "the level below which dissatisfaction would result in outbursts of disorder that would strain the authorities' instruments of political control" (the "bang" threshold). The bang can be avoided if the growth rate of income per capita ceases to decline and stabilizes at some positive, even if chronically low, rate. The exact annual rate of income increase that would result in per capita consumption above this political threshold is not easily defined—perhaps 2–3 percent for some countries, or as little as 1 percent for others. It should be added that the components of consumption are also important, not just the level. The growth of income should be in a direction more consonant with consumer preferences than has been usual under the plan. If the system keeps supplying generous quantities of rotten cabbage when what the consumers want is fresh meat, the "safe" level of consumption loses much of its crisis-dampening significance.

Berliner identifies a second threshold, lower than the political bang. This is the "incentives threshold," at which the economy begins to suffer from an erosion of motivation. When that threshold is crossed, it becomes difficult to sustain even a low level of stable growth, and a reciprocal downward push of output and consumption ensues until the bang. Problems with "labor discipline" in most countries of the neoclassical plan, particularly with the appropriation of social time for private moonlighting activities, suggest that the incentives threshold is being approached.

Economic issues are translated into political terms in both market and plan systems. Under the plan, however, the politicization of economics is much greater and more direct than it is in the market. The market has a way of depoliticizing, or at least obscuring, the political origin and content of economic decisions. This is much less so in the plan, where every achievement as well as misallocation and qualitative deficiency can be (and is) identified with the political leadership in charge of the economy—the "they" (as opposed to "us") of everyday parlance. In its defense, the leadership further politicizes the economic problem by saddling counterrevolutionaries, enemies of the state, wreckers, capitalist roaders, and lackeys of imperialism with everything from the shortage of sheet steel to blackened cabbage, while taking credit itself for skylabs. Marxist economics is normative, political, and cast in sociological terms (for example, capital = the retrograde exploiting class; labor = the progressive proletariat; value = surplus value extracted from the progressive proletarians by the retrograde capitalists). In short, every Marxist fact is a value. The same is true of the institutional structure of the plan. As noted earlier, even the sale of substandard goods becomes a constitutional issue to be solved by criminal law rather than by business loss and firm failure. This assimilation of economics with politics in the plan ensures that the consumption and incentives thresholds rapidly become contentious political issues.

The Three Economies of State Socialism

Our discussion has focused on the plan's civilian economy. Passing reference was made to two other economies that exist within the plan: the military–secret police economy and the underground market economy. The results of the former are visible in the awesome weaponry of the Soviet Union and its allies. The latter is symptomatic of the calcification of state socialism's societal substance. The coexistence of the three economies helps explain the paradox of the plan's apparent failure side by side with the manifest power of state socialism.

The least-known of the three is the military–secret police economy. Yet it is the one that needs to be understood most thoroughly because of its enormous influence on the "official" planned civilian economy. Many of the problems besetting the civilian economy, including some institutional malfunctions, are due in some measure to the diversion of scarce resources to the military–public security apparatus. The drain is quantitatively and qualitatively significant: the best materials and talents go to make weapons and refine methods of citizen surveillance. A study made by the U.S. Defense Intelligence Agency in 1983 concluded that the Soviet military industrial base "is by far the world's largest in number of facilities and physical size and it produces more individual military systems in greater quantities than any other nation." The study put the number of people employed in Soviet military industry in 1981 at 9 million, up 64 percent from 1965. Defense spending since 1970 grew at an estimated rate of 6–7 percent per year. In 1981, it absorbed between 14 and 16 percent of the USSR's gross national product.[10] Although market economies (but not in Japan) make sizable commitments to defense, the impact on the civilian sector in the market economies is different from what it is in the plan. Market economies suffer recurrently from aggregate demand deficiencies. In the setting of resource underutilization, military expenditures will have demand-stimulating spillover effects on the civilian sector. This is not so in a resource-constrained economy (the plan), where military and secret police expenditures aggravate supply scarcities and increase plan tautness in the civilian economy, with adverse repercussions on the consumer (and on the consumer as citizen). There is also another reason why positive spillovers to the civilian economy from the military and the police are small under the plan, namely, state socialism's already-noted fixation on secrecy. The larger part of information in the civilian system is treated as if it were a military secret (for to give out information is to give power to the recipients).[11] Under such conditions, military-related information with possible civilian applications is locked into the military–secret police economy. When some of it does seep out, its spread effect is hampered by the vertical ministerial and other divisions of the civilian economy.

This still leaves unanswered the question of why the military–secret police economy apparently performs so well. Elements of an answer may be found in our earlier analysis, and they essentially boil down to (a) quantitative and qualitative resource largess (there is no thought here of funding and input shortages), and (b) the application of lateral links and competition within the closed vertical military–secret police economy. The principles and operational rules of central command planning are bent to promote the interests of the state's armed power abroad and the maintenance of public order at home.

There is, however, an important qualifier to all this. The fact that military establishments get the best of everything (and very liberally so) does not necessarily mean they are invariably more efficient. Quasi-free supplies of skill, equipment, technology (some of it purloined abroad), and funds often encourage slack procedures and waste. A study carried out by the Yunnan Economics Research Institute between 1982 and 1983 showed that the province's military industries had two to three times as many trained technicians as did civilian industries—a ratio that probably applied to China as a whole. The productivity of cutting machines in the military factories, however, was only half that in civilian factories, and labor productivity was almost two-fifths lower.[12]

Scarce material (as well as human and technological) resources are diverted from the civilian to the military–public security economy with some small feedbacks. But the civilian economy is, on balance, a loser in this transaction: it is impoverished by the transfer. Similarly, resources are diverted by employees of the planned civilian economy into the underground market system, where they are redistributed in accordance with the dictates of supply and demand, not according to plan. Some of the resources return to the planned civilian economy, but the recipients are not those designated by material balances, allocation certificates, the state budget, and the credit and cash plans. In terms of physical resources, there is probably a net gain in consumer and producer welfare as a result of the underground activities of the market economy. The supply of consumer goods and services is more nearly consistent with actual consumer preferences (the leaking faucet gets fixed, even though the fixing is not in the plan), and producers are enabled to fulfill their output targets by using market-procured inputs. So in this sense, the official civilian economy gains from the operation of illegal markets. At another level of analysis, however, the planned civilian economy is a loser. A good example of this is in relation to the planned distribution of the labor force. By virtue of income derived from underground market activities, those who cannot find officially sanctioned employment in areas of the country they prefer are resistant to wage differentials, bonus schemes, housing amenities, and other enticements proffered by the planners and designed to move labor from labor-surplus to labor-deficiency areas, or, more generally, in directions dictated by planners' preferences with regard to the civilian economy. Since the profits reaped in underground activities cannot be legally invested in plants and equipment or research and development, they are used to buy officials and consumer goods.[13] The large-scale diversion of resources through stealing from the planned civilian to the shadow market economy testifies to the failure of planning. Everybody knows that without such transfer, the planned economy would function worse than it does. In other words, what we have here is not just a movement of resources from one economy to another, but the loss of legitimacy of the official plan—an erosion of economic ethos and ideological belief, which affects the motivational system by fostering attitudes of indifference, cynicism, and resentment. The major psychological spillover from the underground market economy to the planned civilian economy is the mentality and ethics of *blat* (an amalgam of corruption and influence peddling). On balance, the planned civilian economy is a loser again. The incentives threshold is crossed at numerous points every day. This gives work to the magnificently equipped public security economy, which, by resorting to its peculiar instruments of social control, keeps the planned civilian economy functioning (if not quite on course).

In all communist countries there exist two other civilian economies that are formally (if secretly) legal, but morally repugnant. The first consists of special unmarked stores for the *nachal'stvo* (leaders) in which the communist nobility is able to purchase, at cut-rate prices, goods and services unavailable elsewhere in the system and unimaginable for the ordinary citizen. These stores are of various grades of quality, and are accessible to the privileged in ascending order of *nomenklatura* rank. The second phenomenon, also legal but more conspicuous, consists of hard-currency stores (*Beriozki* in the USSR, Friendship Stores in China) in which imported capitalist goods and the best domestic products unavailable in ordinary stores are sold to foreigners and some domestic purchasers for capitalist currency. Normally citizens of the country in which the stores are located are not permitted inside. A major exception is made for a segment of party and state officials and for the official literary and technical elite, who are paid part of their salary in special rubles, yuan, or other "hardened" socialist currencies. Soviet diplomats, artists who perform abroad, and others who have earned convertible currency for the state are issued these certificate rubles at favorable exchange rates. Domestic currency is not accepted in this market.

Plans and Outcomes

One way to judge the probity of a man is to measure the degree of correspondence between what he says he will do and what he actually does. Often there is a marked difference between the two—sometimes a huge one. Similarly, any economy will, in its final outcomes, diverge from its original intent as revealed in the economy's idealized model of private and social preferences. Certainly in terms of the civilian sector, centrally planned economies have typically arrived at outcomes far removed from the plans' announced intents. While peasant living standards were collapsing and urban ones were subject to the "law" of rational low wages, Stalin kept repeating that the goal of socialist production was to assure the maximum satisfaction of the continual growing material and cultural needs of society, and that men produce not for production's sake, but in order to satisfy their needs. Every Stalin-plan, from first to last, announced its intent to raise civilian consumption at impressive rates. In the Soviet Second Five-Year Plan, for example, consumption was to rise by no less than 133 percent. This was clearly not to be. Two aspects of the problem of divergence between planned goals and actual plan outcomes should, I think, be considered.

First, consistency of goals and outcomes is determined by three things: the plan, the behavior of the system's units, and the environment (social, political, cultural, international).[14] The plan must be sufficiently powerful to enforce its will. In practice, though powerful and important, the plan is not all-powerful and all-important; it is full of gaps and contradictions. Without total power, there at least should be total cooperation with the plan by the plan's executors, and no serious disturbances from the side of the environment. This cooperation is particularly important in the area of information: executors, especially those at the economy's base, must supply the planners with accurate and complete information on what is occurring at the base (something only they really know) regarding resource availabilities and costs, past performance, and present compliance with the plan's directives. Indeed, perfect compliance with perfectly formulated and flawlessly transmitted plan directives is a sine qua non of plan intent = plan outcomes. This, of course, never happens. The quality of plan formulation, transmission, and compliance is often barely tolerable.[15] In fact, those who view the command economy as a species of centralized pluralism or decentralized monolith, see the plan as a ritual exercise designed to convey the impression of rational order where there is disorder and to lend legitimacy to the ruling group. The theoretical orderliness of the plan also serves to impress the more impressionable observers abroad, whose understanding of the plan stops at the document with its elegant iterative adjustments, input-output coefficients, and inverted Leontief matrices.

Second, the correspondence of the plan's secret intent with actual outcomes has generally been greater than the correspondence of officially announced intent with outcomes. The frenetic buildup of Soviet military power after World War II, for example, did not figure as the first and overriding objective of the Soviet neoclassical conservative plan, but has turned out to be that. This is a question of what one says not being what one means. In military matters, the plan's power is more comprehensive and stringent, and there is less tolerance for game playing by the executors (there is also less reason, for inputs are abundant).

II
CASES

CHAPTER SEVEN

USSR: The Role of Collective Farm Property in the Stalinplan and the Neoclassical Conservative Plan

I. THE ATTEMPTED USE OF COLLECTIVE PROPERTY FOR INDUSTRIALIZATION: THE *KOLKHOZ* AS A CONTROL DEVICE AND A SOURCE OF FORCED SAVINGS IN THE STALINPLAN

In Chapter 2, we noted the following points: (1) the classical plan requires that, together with urban consumers and workers (but even more so), collectivized peasants be used for the benefit of heavy industrialization, and an important function of the collective farm is to act as a forced savings device rather than as an efficient unit of agricultural production; (2) investment (the funds for which come from forced savings raised by taxation) is favored over consumption and in fact, consumption postponement becomes a permanent feature of the plan; (3) the classical plan is inward-oriented—self-reliance and a closed economy are preferred over foreign involvement. These three sets of classical plan characteristics go in tandem and reinforce each other. Isolation from outside sources of developmental funding, together with a preference for high rates of investment in industries with long payoff periods in terms of income generation (producer goods industries), naturally point to the underdeveloped country's largest sector, agriculture, as a potential (in fact, under the circumstances, major) available source of savings. The preferred rate of industrial investment will dictate the rate of squeeze that will be put on the peasants and others.

There is a problem, however. People will not willingly submit to confiscatory taxation, no matter what the long-term social benefits of the tax are alleged to be. This is especially true of people who, like the more prosperous and entrepreneurial peasants of Russia's New Economic Policy (NEP) period, had little use for the Bolshevik regime. Preobrazhenskii and those who, during what has come to be known as the Great Industrialization Debate on the strategy options for Soviet economic development in the 1920s, cast the peasants in the role of tribute payers to industry, did not have (or pretended not to have) a clear conception of how the tribute was to be exacted from the peasants without causing massive peasant disaffection and disruption of farm production and marketing.[1] The answer, of course, was inherent in the concept of forced savings. Moreover, it fit in nicely with the violent (not to mention terroristic) interpretation given (correctly, I think) to Marxist theory by Lenin and the Leninist concentration on control.[2] The solution was to herd the peasants into an organizational corral in which they had no choice but to do what was required of them by the planners. Having gone through the heady experience of private property and free marketings during the NEP period, they were to be regimented, caged, and made peons of anew within a thorough control organization strictly responsive to the party's will. This organization was the collective farm. Because the purpose of the *kolkhoz* (tight political control and confiscatory taxation) was intuitively understood and vehemently resisted by the peasants—especially by the more successful ones, now branded as *kulaks*—collectivization had to be imposed by force. Indeed, it was carried out with unspeakable brutality by the secret police, armed party activists, and workers' militias aided by artificially fanned "class warfare" in the villages (setting the poor against the rich), at the cost of millions of lives and untold human suffering (an estimated 4.5–7 million victims of starvation in the Ukraine). The *kolkhoz* helped expand the Stalinplan's public security economy (see Chapter 6)—the vast network of labor camps—which has since been trimmed and modernized by the inclusion of psychiatric hospitals for opponents of the regime, but has never been eliminated. The collectivization process, begun in 1929, was completed by the mid-1930s.[3] In other countries of the Stalinplan, collectivization was also accompanied by force, although the degree of peasant resistance and the human and economic costs of the operation differed from place to place.[4]

Attention is given here to the collective farm because the farm is the classical Stalinplan's central mechanism of political control over the peasantry (that is, over the majority of the population), and is an important contributor to unbalanced industrial development from indigenous sources. There is no Stalinplan without the *kolkhoz*. Thus, for example, in China, classical administrative command planning began not in 1953, when the First Five-Year Stalinplan was officially inaugurated (though not published), but in 1956, when agricultural collectivization on the model of the *kolkhoz* had been completed. Agricultural collectivization of this type is a necessary condition of the classical plan, no matter where it is implemented. It represents a systemic change of enormous political, economic, and social significance.

The following account of the *kolkhoz* mechanism of control and rural savings extraction is cast in a generalized form. It is a composite picture, a "consolidated" rendition of the Stalinist Soviet-type collective farm, based on the operational Soviet example of the 1930s through the mid-1950s, but not necessarily adhering to that example in every detail. The aim is to present the concept of control and rural forced savings, based on the Soviet organizational experience of the Stalinist years.

Over the years, the number of collective farms has decreased through mergers and conversions into state farms. Today, more than half the arable land is in state farms. Farm size has grown. At present, an average collective farm in the USSR has about 6,000 hectares of land (roughly 60 percent of it sown) and a labor force of about five hundred. State farms average 17,200 hectares of farmland, 30 percent sown.

The Stalinist *Kolkhoz:*
Property, Information, and Coordination

The Economics and Politics of Control

In dialectical logic, things are never what they seem to be. Most often, they are the opposite. Thus, officially and for public knowledge (embodied in the *kolkhoz* model charter of 1935 and its 1969 revision), the collective farm of Stalin's creation is an independent association of rural producers who voluntarily band together to cultivate their jointly owned land, using means of production that each producer had originally contributed as his share in the *kolkhoz*, but that is now unified property. *Kolkhoz* members not only freely join the association, but can leave it at will, presumably taking with them (if they so desire) the equity share they brought in. The *kolkhoz*, according to theory, is a democratic organization. The general meeting of members elects a management board, which includes a chairman, his deputy, and other administrators (usually from a half-dozen to a dozen people). These elected officials are answerable to the membership, as elected officials ought to be in democratic societies. The management decides on the collective's course of action, subject to approval by the membership. Income is distributed to members in accordance with the share of work each member has individually contributed to the collective ("to each according to his work"). For operational purposes, the collective farm is divided into brigades, each in charge of a brigadier and his helpers, who are also democratically elected.

This highly un-Leninist organizational blueprint was not used in practice. In practice, collectivization was forced. There was no voluntary quality to it whatsoever. Once in, members experienced great difficulty in leaving the *kolkhoz* without official consent: under the Stalinplan (in fact, until 1975) collective farmers, together with prisoners in jails and labor camps, did not possess the internal passport that was (and remains) the first prerequisite for locational and job mobility. In effect, the peasant was tied to the *kolkhoz* like a serf. Work for the collective replaced the old feudal labor service obligation, the *barshchina*.[5] Those leaving the *kolkhoz* could not claim any part of the equity share that they originally contributed to the farm's now solidly indivisible fund.

Collectivization was, in effect, synonymous with expropriation. The general meeting of members was a purely nominal and frivolous exercise in democratic centralism. The chairman and other farm officials were (and continue to be) nominated by the party from the *nomenklatura* (see Chapter 2). They could be disciplined only by party-government superiors and, as party members, were answerable only to their superiors, a situation unchanged to this day. The farm's production configuration and schedules were not matters of local, democratic, and independent decision; they were mandated by the plan, handed down to the farm by superior supervisory party-government–ministerial authorities. The most important component of the collective farm's plan was procurement of grain and other produce by the state, that is, the farm's delivery obligation. The state's interest under the Stalinplan was in that portion of total output that the state acquired—the "marketed" portion, not the total output. Nevertheless, in line with the unidimensional nature of the state's commands, the farm's plan included, in addition to the compulsory delivery quota, specifications regarding gross output, sown acreage, cropping patterns, and other production configurations and schedules (including, in some cases, the dates of sowing). The plan also determined the volume and structure of key inputs, including the minimum labor participation in collective work, the share of retained earnings to be devoted to the farm's capital fund (the collective's principal source of capital under the Stalinplan), the availability and prices of current inputs, and the deductions from gross revenue for the farm's social-cultural fund (under the Stalinplan, collective farmers were not included in national social security insurance, and there was not much culture). The emphasis throughout was short-term: fulfilling and over-fulfilling the annual procurement plan. Such concentration on the short run, typical of the classical plan (but also present in the neoclassical plan), was bound to have negative consequences for agriculture in the long run that were more serious than the consequences of short-term planning on industry. Superimposed on these short-term goals were longer-range mass political campaigns, of which Stalin's drive for the "transformation of nature" was among the more notorious. The theories of quack scientists (for example, Trofim Denisovich Lysenko) were forcibly popularized and imposed on farm managements by political *ukaz* ("executive order").

In sum, Stalinist collectivization of agriculture uprooted what voluntariness and horizontal information and coordination there had been during the NEP period. Market price signals were replaced by mandatory physical quotas, nonscarcity state-set prices, and administratively determined income distribution. With one exception, property was socialized and centralized. Because the peasants could not make a living under the new arrangement, private property rights of use were granted to collective farm families in small plots of socially owned land (the household "private" plot). Produce from these plots went to feed the family, and any surplus remaining after compulsory deliveries to the state could be sold for cash on the relatively free "collective farm markets" (*kolkhoznye rynoki*). These *rynoki* were (and remain) a thorn in the side of local party *apparatchiki* ("bureaucrats," members of the "machine"), who harassed them as best they could. All manifestations of institutional spontaneity (*samotyok*) were suppressed. Administrative orders were administratively carried out without regard to local conditions in accordance with what Nove calls " 'planning' by set pattern" (*shablon*), a type of bureaucratic rigidity.[6]

Under the Stalinplan, the presence of the Communist Party and the secret police in planning and management was pervasive and their influence on economic policy decisive. Both were direct emanations of Stalin, which distinguished them from their continued presence, pervasiveness, and influence today. The economic literacy of party and police members was modest at best. In the collective farm sector, machine tractor stations were used to provide the party-state with extra control over the peasants and *kolkhoz* managements. These stations—outposts of the proletariat in the countryside—were staffed with state employees, tractor drivers and "mechanizers" of all sorts, agricultural specialists, and political activists. Their control over the crucially important input planning within the collective farm sector was far-reaching. Until 1958 (when they were finally liquidated), the machine tractor stations, not the farms, owned the mechanized means of agricultural production (tractors, threshers, combines) and monopolized the pool of agronomic expertise.

The Mechanism of Savings Extraction

Economically, the function of the *kolkhoz* (however arrived at, whether deliberately or by chance) was to force savings out of the controlled peasantry through a reduction of the peasants' living standards. The savings were transferred to the state, which then used them in accordance with its developmental goal priorities (that is, in support of heavy industrialization at rapid rates, a process referred to by Stalin as *perekachka*, or "pumping over"). It should be noted that the burden of industrialization was also borne by urban consumers and workers whose living standards (during the 1930s) declined as a result of the combined application of the "law" of rational low wages (see Chapter 2), consumer goods famine, and high and rising state-set prices of consumer goods. The question of the real burden of industrialization borne by the peasantry during the first Five-Year Plan (1928–1933) has been the subject of controversy among Western economists. Millar, as we saw in Chapter 2, argues that collectivization was such an unmitigated disaster (contributing importantly to the famine of 1932–1934, when the per capita income of the peasants had fallen to about half the 1928 level), that before the First Five-Year Plan was over, the state had to turn around and help agriculture through investments designed to replace some of the assets lost through peasant resistance during the collectivization drive.[7] The compression of rural living standards and the gross transfer of income from peasants to the state as a result of collectivization are, nevertheless, beyond doubt.

If collectivized agriculture in Russia did not, in fact, generate the massive net transfer of resources from agriculture to industry that had been assumed in Western discussions of this question, what was primarily affected was the postmortem judgement on the Stalinist *kolkhoz:* the collectivization mechanism was not, as had been supposed, cruel but effective—it was cruel and ineffective.[8] The state did extract a much larger share of produce from a roughly constant output of grain in the early 1930s. What was taken out of agriculture was food and feed; what was put in was tractors for the (state sector) machine tractor stations, not industrial consumer goods for the peasants. The burden on the peasants was, therefore, real in terms of lowered living standards. It was, in addition, developmentally pointless. A tributary conclusion of the Millar argument is that collectivization was not a carefully thought-out, consciously planned exercise designed to transfer resources from agriculture to industry, but was instead the result of compounded stumbling along. In this interpretation, the principal factors contributing to the decision to collectivize were: ideological preference for social ownership of production means (that is, desire to put an end to peasant private enterprise, which the Bolsheviks abhorred), doctrinal bias in favor of preferential treatment for industrial workers, the wish to eliminate market and pecuniary relations from the economy (the collective farm sector was, in essence, demarketized and demonetized), and Stalin's sham grain delivery crisis of 1926–27. If indeed the peasants were holding back on grain deliveries to the state, they did so not because of adverse (for them) overall terms of trade between agricultural and industrial products—a holding-back expected of them by Bolshevik left-wing theoreticians—but because they were feeding grain to their livestock. They fed grain to their livestock because the relative prices of grain (including bread) and meat were such as to make feeding grain to livestock profitable, while supplying grain to the state at low state-set grain prices was unprofitable. The grain marketing crisis could have been solved by a simple change in the relative prices of grain and meat rather than by the institutional trauma of collectivization.

The Stalinplan's collective farm taxed the peasants many times in hidden but (for the payers) highly tangible and intelligible ways. The peasants could not evade this taxation because they had been imprisoned in the organizational framework of the *kolkhoz*. This can be seen from a consideration of *kolkhoz* revenues and expenditures (see Table 7.1).[9] Revenues and expenditures consisted partly of money and mostly of goods.

Revenues

1. Under the classical plan, the state became quasi-monopsonist vis-à-vis the collective farms. It purchased by far the greater part of the collective farms' marketed output at prices set by itself. The physical amount of state purchases (procurements) was specified in a compulsory quota, which under the Stalinplan was very high relative to the farms' capacity to produce and to the farms' internal needs. In fact, the quota for food grains, cash crops, and many other items was fixed on the basis of the farms' sown (later arable) area, not on the basis of output performance. This meant that any shortfall in production caused by, for example, weather vagaries would be absorbed by the farms, not by the state. After delivering the compulsory quota, the farms were encouraged (*pressured,* through input blackmail, would be a more appropriate word) to sell additional amounts of produce to the state at the state's discretion. The quotas were unpredictable and often changed at short notice (or with no notice). Compulsory quota deliveries were paid for at very low prices—"low" compared with (a) the farms' production costs (insofar as these could be calculated—see below); (b) the prices of industrial inputs used by the farms; and (c) the prices for comparable products on the free ("collective farm") markets. Above-quota deliveries were bought at higher prices, but these were still "low" in the three senses just mentioned. The combination of high

TABLE 7.1
USSR: REVENUES AND EXPENDITURES OF THE COLLECTIVE FARM—
THE MECHANISM OF EXTRACTION
(Stalinplan)

Revenues	*Expenditures*

(1) Sales of produce to the state
    a) quota
    b) above quota (*zakupka*)
    at state-set procurement prices
 (2) Sales of produce on the free
    ("collective farm") urban market
    (*rynok*) at market prices
 (3) Miscellaneous revenues
    a) *kontraktatsiia* sales
    b) sale of "industrial" prod-
    ucts and handicrafts
    c) provision of services
	(1) Taxes
	 (2) Machine tractor stations
	 (3) Insurance
	 (4) Capital fund
	 (5) Social-cultural fund
	 (6) Current production inputs
	 (7) Reserves
	 (8) Administration
	 (9) Residual payment to members
	    (workdays, *trudodni*)

quotas and low (often nominal) procurement prices amounted to a confiscatory tax on the farms (let us call this "tax #1"). The state obtained farm produce at prices well below those it would have had to pay, at that point in time, had it been obliged to buy this produce directly from independent peasants equipped with private property and responding to market price information (see Table 7.2).

In 1948, the state bought a ton of rye from the collective farms for 8 rubles—the same price as in 1928. The rye was sold to state millers for 338 rubles a ton. Most of the difference between 8 and 338 rubles was accounted for by the turnover tax, which (as Nove points out) should be seen as "both a tax on the peasants and on urban consumers in conceptually uncertain proportions."[10] In 1948, the price of bread was thirty times what it had been in 1928; prices of goods bought by the collective farms and farmers were also much higher than they had been in 1928.

2. What was left after point 1 (state purchases) could be sold by the *kolkhoz* on free markets maintained by local authorities in the towns, kept on the farm for reserve purposes, or reinvested. Under the Stalinplan, sales on the free market were the most important source of cash revenue for the farms. Although sales transactions with the state resulted in a net loss for the farms, this was not the case with sales on the free market, where urban purchasers did much of their food shop-

ping. Some analysts of the Stalinplan (for example, Millar, and British economist Michael Ellman) conclude from this that in practice, the market (*rynok*) tail came to wag the *kolkhoz* dog. While the state exploited the peasants through low procurement prices, the peasants struck back by charging equilibrium prices on the free market, thereby switching around the overall terms of trade in their favor and shifting much of the pressure on their own living standards to those of the urban workers.

When, in the mid-1950s, after many adjustments, collective farm costs of production were calculated, it was found that state procurement prices for most products did not cover the average production costs of those products, and that in many cases even the higher above-quota prices failed to meet average production costs.

Individual collective farm families could also sell the untaxed portion of the produce from their private plots on the free market. Zealous local officials, ever on the lookout for capitalist exploitation (that is,

TABLE 7.2

USSR: Indexes of Average Prices on Collective Farm Sales to the State by Product, Selected Years

Product	1952	1958	1962	1965[a]	1966	1969	1972	1973
Grain	8	65	88	100	107	110	112	108
Potatoes	7	59	71	100	100	98	115	108
Vegetables	24	na	na	100	113	122	151	152
Sunflowers	9	69	61	100	105	85	88	100
Sugar beets	37	80	86	100	103	92	110	125
Cotton	69	73	74	100	95	103	117	118
Milk	17	72	78	100	100	101	126	132
Cattle[b]	4	53	69	100	104	118	141	141
Pigs[b]	5	58	69	100	102	109	113	114
Sheep and goats[b]	5	76	76	100	107	123	140	140
Wool	26	75	93	100	98	110	124	132
Eggs	28	91	94	100	100	107	118	112

NOTE: na = not available.

SOURCE: Morris Bornstein, "Soviet Price Policy in the 1970s," in U.S. Congress Joint Economic Committee, *Soviet Economy in a New Perspective* (Washington, D.C.: U.S. Government Printing Office, 1976), p. 35.

[a]1965 = 100.

[b]Live weight.

market clearing prices in conditions of food scarcity), frequently intervened (and still do) in the operation of the markets with administratively determined price ceilings and other restrictive controls.

In 1950, 63 percent of collective farm revenues came from sales of
produce to the state, and 27 percent from sales on the market. In 1957,
the respective shares were 78 and 14 percent.[11]

3. Miscellaneous revenues were derived from a variety of nonfarm
activities. These included (a) sales of some crops (for example, sugar
beets) directly to state firms at prices negotiated in advance (*kontraktat-
siia*); (b) sales of products turned out by the collective farms' small-scale
industries (for example, farm implements, construction materials, food
processing) and handicrafts; and (c) provision of local transportation
services to other units (the renting out of horses and carts), and the
like. Such revenues were important for collective farms located in the
vicinity of large cities.

Expenditures

1. Having been taxed once through nominal procurement prices,
the collective farms were taxed again on their gross revenue ("tax #2").
Until 1965, the tax rate was 12.5 percent.

2. Fees for services rendered by the machine tractor stations were
paid in produce, and in effect constituted an addition to the procurement quota. The fees were, as a rule, excessive, and were, in fact, a tax
("tax #3"). It should be noted that the tax on gross revenue and fees
for machine tractor station services were priority charges on the farms'
gross revenue.

3. Insurance against loss of assets through fire or other causes had
to be taken out, because such loss was not replaceable free of charge
from the state budget as it was in state enterprises (including the state
farms [*sovkhozy*—see below]).

4. Government regulations specified the annual rate at which deductions from the farms' gross revenues were to be made for the ("indivisible") capital fund. This was practically the only source of capital
for the collective farms.

5. The model collective farm statute specified the maximum rate of
deduction from gross revenues for the farms' social-cultural fund (2
percent per year).

6. Current production expenses had to be covered out of gross
revenue. The inputs purchased by the farms were paid for at state
retail prices, which, carrying the turnover tax, were higher than the
state wholesale prices at which the same goods were sold to state
enterprises ("tax #4"). Since the farms were not considered to be parts

of a priority sector, the needed inputs were often unavailable to the farms, no matter what the price. This was especially true of electricity.

7. At the discretion of farm management, a portion of gross revenue in kind was put in reserve.

8. Administrative expenses consisted mainly of salaries for chairman and board members (who were also paid in work points for farm work). The model statute limited these expenses to 2 percent of gross revenues, but this limit was regularly exceeded in practice.

9. After covering these eight expenditures, anything left over was available for distribution to members for their labor contribution to the collective. In other words, the collective farmer was a residual legatee, the last claimant on the collective farm's revenue. Unlike state sector workers, whose wages were the first claim on enterprise revenue (after taxes), the *kolkhoznik* got what was left over. In 1952, 29 percent of total collective farm expenditures were paid to peasants as workdays. In 1956, the share was 45 percent.[12]

Motivation

Payment to collective farm members was made according to a system of workdays (*trudodni*). Peasants were allotted jobs that they were expected to perform in the course of a working day. Where a piece-rate variant of the system prevailed, each job had a certain number of work points attached to it. This constituted the day norm for that job. Completing a particular job (described in physical terms) earned that job's norm work points; another job earned a different number of work points. Usually, the more skilled the job, the greater the number of work points it earned.[13] Overfulfilling the norm earned bonus points; underfilling it resulted in points being deducted. At the end of the farming year (the main harvest), the total number of points earned by all working members was divided into the revenue remaining after the first eight expenditures had been met. This gave the value of one work point for that particular year, that is,

$$
\frac{\text{Revenues left after meeting expenditures one through eight}}{\text{Total number of work points earned by members during the year}} = \frac{\text{Value of a work}}{\text{point in rubles}}
$$

Payment in cash and kind (mostly in kind) was then made to each member according to the number of work points he (or, usually, she) accumulated during the year.

Notice the following characteristics of this particular motivational system:

a. There was bound to be conflict over work-point attribution. The arithmetical literacy of most work-point recorders was not high—certainly not as high as their class prejudice.

b. There was no definite scale of payment for work done—that is, those working did not know what their work would actually earn. The value of a work point depended on a variety of exogenous forces (not just weather, but state policy on quotas, procurement prices, prices of inputs, machine tractor station fees, taxes, and so on). These changed from year to year, often capriciously during the year.

c. The job, not the person, was graded. Unlike the practice in industry, where a person's wage depended on his skill classification, in the *kolkhoz* it was the nature of the job that determined how many work points the worker earned.[14]

d. The number of work points attached to a particular job was, by and large, arbitrary. "Average" work of "average" quality was graded 1 work point per day norm, unskilled work was graded 0.5 points per day norm, and skilled work was put at 2.5 work points per day norm (why not 3 or 3.5?).

e. The payment was a residual—made when there was something left over—not a fixed charge on gross revenue.

f. Until the 1950s, payments were made only once a year. The banking system was not allowed to extend credit to the farms for this purpose. In other words, the peasant was expected to work for an unknown and uncertain compensation payable in a distant future.[15]

g. Most of the time, the payment was tiny. In fact (as in China at the time of Mao's death), most peasants could not live on earnings from collective work. A portion of the payment was in forage used by peasants for private plot livestock, and the bulk of the payment was in produce, not cash.

h. Payment for labor being a residual of unknown value, it was not possible to calculate labor costs or identify the profit element. Under the circumstances, it was not possible to apply cost accounting to the collective farms. Production was carried out in an accounting vacuum.

The *trudoden'* system of compensation, together with the quota and procurement price policies, had an unfortunate impact on incentives, labor productivity, farm efficiency, and peasant living standards. It produced an agricultural slum. The planners did, however, obtain the grain, potatoes, cabbage, and other farm produce (wage goods) that they used partly to feed urban workers and partly for export, in return for which industrial machinery and equipment were imported in line with the state's industrial goal priorities. Taking the 1927–28 year to equal 100, the index of grain output from 1954 to 1958 (when the Stalin-plan began to be changed) was 152, while the index of gross marketings was 270. Throughout the Stalinplan, the rate of increase in grain market-ing exceeded the rate of increase of grain output. The difference was even more marked when net, rather than gross, marketings are con-sidered (net marketings are gross marketings minus repurchases by the peasant sector itself). In the 1932–33 year (the last year for which net marketing data are available, and also a famine year), the index of gross marketing was 120, and that of net grain marketing was 165.[16] A more rapid increase in grain marketing than in grain output was precisely what was intended. What was not intended, but in fact happened, was that the process of squeezing blood out of the turnip caused such rural devastation that the Soviet planners apparently ended up transferring more resources into agriculture than they got out of it.

Oppressed by the plan on the collective farm, the peasant sought relief by work on his private plot. But the hand of the state reached there, too. A portion of private plot output had to be surrendered to the state at the low procurement prices applicable to compulsory collec-tive farm deliveries ("tax #5"). Until 1953, the deliveries were specified by individual commodities and had to be made whether or not the plot produced such commodities. Often, the farmer had to buy these tax goods on the free market at high prices and surrender them to the state at the low state procurement prices.

By comparison with collective land, the private plots were (and continue to be) very productive. The plots represent about 3 percent of the sown area but produce more than 25 percent of the produce. The key ingredient to this success is the direct link that has always existed between individualized input of effort and personal reward. In 1966, according to a sample survey in the Ukraine, collective farmers ob-tained from their private plots practically all their potatoes, vegetables, milk, meat, and lard.[17]

When the farmer bought (inferior) consumer goods in the village cooperative store (when these were available), he had to pay a surtax on them (*sel'skaia nadbavka*) on top of the usual turnover tax ("tax #6"). The surtax could add as much as 70 percent to the retail price.

A final note on the combination of unidimensional, mandatory information expressed in physical terms with large-scale operations and the incentive system. Soviet tractor drivers are paid primarily on a piece-rate basis, the "piece" being the area they plow. The more they plow, the more they earn. As maximizing individuals, they plow shal-low, even though this is not in the social interest (that is, in the interest of a good harvest). So inspectors are needed to see to it that plowing is done to the proper depth. Information costs rise. Nove puts it well:

> The problem is to link reward with final outcome. On the huge multipurpose farms this link is at best tenuous. One does not have to tell a Western peasant to plough to an adequate depth, because he is directly interested in the final outcome, in the size of the harvest. If he employs a few labourers, the link between effort, pay, and result is still much easier to define than in Soviet large-scale agriculture. Yet: 'Who does not watch the work of the ploughman: the accountant, the supervisor, the brigadier, the representative of the People's Control, the rural Soviet, the agronomist, the agitator-political-organizer, and even a volunteer-quality-controller. Yet what sort of peasant is it, if it is necessary to follow him about to ensure that he ploughs and harrows properly.'[18]

The proper question is, What sort of system is it that produces such a peasant? It is no wonder that the job of a collective farm chairman has never been prestigious and that the turnover of chairmen remains high.

A Note on State Farms (*Sovkhozy*)

The Stalinplan and its successor recognize three property forms in agriculture. Ranging from the ideologically-socially "highest" to "lowest," they are: state property (the state farm, or *sovkhoz*), collective property (*kolkhoz*), and private property (the "private," or household, plot). Under the Stalinplan, the differences between state farms and collective farms are technical, economic, and ideological.

Technically, the *sovkhozy*, compared with *kolkhozy*, are (a) larger, (b) more specialized, and (c) more mechanized.

Economically, the *sovkhoz* (a) is a state sector enterprise—structurally similar to other state firms, financed from the state budget, subject to detailed state input and output planning, and operating on *khozraschet* ("economic accounting"); (b) has state farm workers, who are paid regular wages (like industrial workers), the level of tariff (basic) wages being determined by the worker's skill (the wage rates are set at a high level in the planning hierarchy), and who are included in the state system of social security; (c) has managers who are appointed in the same way as managers of other state enterprises (as compared with the "elected" *kolkhoz* chairmen).

Ideologically, (a) the *sovkhoz* is considered to be superior to the *kolkhoz* as a property form since it is owned "by the whole people"; and (b) although the prices paid for *sovkhoz* produce are not much higher than those paid by the state for *kolkhoz* deliveries, the *sovkhoz* is not seen as a forced savings device—its losses are made good by subsidies from the state budget, it purchases its current production inputs at state industrial wholesale prices rather than higher state retail prices, and (as already noted) its capital needs are supplied from the state budget rather than from its own revenue.

> ## II. THE SEARCH FOR ECONOMIC INTENSIFICATION: CHANGES IN THE *KOLKHOZ* UNDER THE NEOCLASSICAL CONSERVATIVE PLAN

The neoclassical plan—whether conservative, liberal, or radical—was introduced in state socialist countries in reaction to the Stalinplan's serious limitations in promoting quality economic performance. The classical plan was a violent, war-type agent of one-sided industrialization: heavy industry came first; within heavy industry, machine tools, steel, and power had priority. As we have seen, the plan relied on administrative force and command to accomplish a narrow range of high-priority goals—primarily growth of output, irrespective of cost. In fact, in agriculture (the largest and most populous sector of the Stalinplan) there was no cost accounting at all. Although growth of output in the priority sectors was impressive in gross terms, it was accomplished primarily by large additions of factor inputs (especially labor and, in industry, capital)—by "extensive" means, rather than by significant improvements in factor productivity, that is, rather than by "intensive" means. Over the long period from 1928 to 1966, capital productivity in the Soviet Union declined at an annual rate of 1.9 percent, and at 3.9 percent per year over the shorter period from 1950 to 1962.[19] Over the long period from 1928 to 1966, less than two-fifths of Soviet output growth was attributable to factor productivity improvements (better use of inputs). Extensive growth is expensive growth: additions of capital are made at the cost of current consumption, and labor is added at the expense of leisure.[20] But these measures do not capture the full human cost of the operation as it unfolded in Stalin's time and beyond.

One of the principal reasons (perhaps the main one) for the post-Stalin changes in the classical plan was the concern on the part of Stalin's successors in Russia (and on the part of successors to would-be Stalins in Eastern Europe) with the drag on growth exerted by poor quality performance in the low-priority sectors—agriculture heading the list. The purpose of the changes was (and still is) to "modernize" the Stalinplan through intraplan administrative adjustments of information, coordination, property, and motivation. This effort involves both a reshuffling of planners' goal priorities and selective repairs and renovations of the institutional apparatus—in short, working through the system to improve it, fine-tuning the status quo. Nowhere has this been clearer than in the adjustments made to the control and savings extraction mechanisms of the *kolkhoz*.

Changes in *Kolkhoz* Organization

After Stalin's death, many adjustments were made in the formal organization of the collective farm. The changes revealed contradictory trends: some were intended to enlarge the narrow scope of collective farm decisions; others worked in the direction of greater decision-making centralization. The first trend is illustrated by the abolition of the machine tractor stations in 1958; the emergence of the brigade as the basic production unit; the extension of the "election" principle to the brigade level; the (occasional) emergence of the "autonomous" mechanized link (*zveno*)—a subdivision of the brigade working on contract with the brigade on given tasks from start to finish;[21] the off-and-on attempts to strengthen the prerogatives of *kolkhoz* management boards vis-à-vis local party authorities; the improvement in the educational level of the managerial boards' personnel; the relative relaxation of central input controls; the vesting in *kolkhoz* management of decisions regarding capital fund contributions; and the greater latitude granted farm managements regarding the manner of plan fulfillment.

All these adjustments add up to modest administrative decentralization—nothing system-shattering; this is all the more so since the adjustments went hand in hand with administrative centralizations best represented by collective farm amalgamations and with the conversion of many collective farms into state farms. Collective farms today are much larger than they were in the Stalinplan years, and they are more mechanized. In this technical sense, they have come to resemble state farms, even though most of them are still all-purpose units (whereas the *sovkhozy* tend to be more specialized).

The early years of the Soviet neoclassical conservative plan (the Khrushchev years, 1954–1964) were marked by several mass political campaigns in agriculture. These included the virgin lands, corn-growing, and "catch up with the United States" campaigns that produced short-term positive and long-term negative results. It should be pointed out that mass political campaigning, though it thrives well under the radical plan, is a characteristic inherited from the Stalinplan. Indeed, the Stalinist strategy of economic growth is a leap strategy that relies heavily on political (police-type) mass mobilization.

Revenues and Expenditures

More interesting changes than reorganization of the *kolkhoz* occurred in the collective farms' revenues and expenditures. Here, too, the changes were intrasystemic, of the institutional adjustment kind. There has been no thought of marketization of information, coordination, and motivation, and no discernible move toward the privatization of property rights (as there was in China after 1978 [see Chapter 9]). The objective of the Soviet adjustments has been to elevate the collective farms' standing on the rank order of planners' priorities, to desist from treating the collective farmers as serfs and the collective farms as sources of forced savings, and to raise the status of collective farmers from second- to (almost) first-class citizens.

Revenues

The most important decision made by the post-Stalin leadership was to improve incentives to collective farms and collective farmers, and to monetize those incentives. The decision implied a shift (ever so small) from specific physical commands enforced by bureaucratic and police methods to more indirect guidance through "economic levers." The shift was discreet, not unlike the slight thaw in political and cultural life at that time. The "economics" of the levers was not revolutionized by marketization and privatization. In practice, the decision amounted to a series of pragmatic improvisations within a slightly reorganized Leninist-Stalinist framework.

Procurement prices were raised several times, and the hikes were substantial: between 1952 and 1956, average procurement prices of potatoes were raised 815 percent, of wheat 647 percent, of beef 508 percent, and of milk 336 percent.[22] By the mid-1960s, "normally functioning" collective farms were said to have been making a profit on their transactions with the state; Nove cites a profitability (as compared with costs) of 20 percent in 1964, although the profitability rate varied considerably between individual products and product groups (profitability on livestock was −17 percent, for example).[23] Above-quota deliveries and prices were abolished in 1958, but were partially restored in 1965 (for grain and some other products), these prices being on the average 50 percent higher than quota prices. At the same time, above-quota sales became compulsory.

Price differentials among commodities were calibrated more carefully to encourage the production of goods the state wanted to acquire. This was not always successful. Thus, milk and meat prices were set at levels where any expansion in their production would have increased the collective farms' losses. This occurred at the very time that the "catch up with the United States in milk and meat" campaign was being vigorously pursued. In the USSR, as elsewhere, the neoclassical plan is not very good at dealing with relative prices to stimulate or discourage the production of particular items. Ultimately, this is done by administrative pressure, whatever the price relationships. Although neoclassical plan prices play a marginally more important guiding role than they did in the Stalinplan, it is not a leading one. Bureaucratic habits are still much in evidence, and the economy is run largely by memoranda.

While procurement prices were raised sharply, the decision was made to hold the line on food retail prices. The result has been a rapid rise in agricultural subsidies, especially for livestock products.[24] Notice that these are state subsidies to protect the urban consumer from inefficient, high-cost collective and state agriculture, without hurting the peasants.

There was improvement with regard to the fixing of delivery quotas. By and large, the quotas were made more stable (less unpredictable) and rational. Whereas formerly the quota was fixed in accordance with the planners' industrial development objectives, after the change it was set with at least some regard to the farms' productive capacity, costs, and needs.

In 1956, cost accounting was introduced in the collective farm sector. It was at first a slapdash affair, quite unscientific. Since at that time the *trudoden'* system was still in force (that is, labor costs were a residual, and profit could not be identified), collective farm labor costs were calculated on the assumption that they were the same as those of neighboring state farms—which most of the time they were not. In 1966, the collective farms were ordered to abandon the old *trudoden'* system of remuneration and to guarantee minimum wages at state farm rates. Resort could be made to loans from the state banks in situations where the collective farms' financial position made it impossible to meet the payroll out of current revenue.

Expenditures

The most important change on the expenditures side has already been mentioned: the abandonment of the workday system and the introduction of a minimum tariff wage. Collective farm members are now guaranteed a minimum payment for work done, which reduces their burden of risk. Their compensation is determined by:

$$\frac{\text{Total net product}}{\text{Total number of hours worked by members}} = \frac{\text{Hourly compensation}}{\text{rate in rubles}}$$

A member can increase his share by working more. Notice that the peasant still does not know in advance what the hourly rate will be, since he can neither foresee the size of the net product nor the number of hours worked by all members. Nor can he predict the quality of the work put in by a large number of his coworkers. In contrast to state farm workers, who are paid fixed tariff wages known to them in advance, the collective farmer is paid only for work actually done. Collective farmers are now covered by the national social security system, and the farms are supposed to operate on *khozraschet*. The introduction of the hourly dividend system in 1966 was preceded by more frequent cash advances to members in the course of the farming year. These were financed by bank loans.

Other changes favoring collective farms (under the heading of expenditures) included the already-mentioned vesting in farm managements of decisions on capital fund deductions. Tax rates were lowered and calculated on the basis of net, rather than gross, revenue (see below). The machine tractor stations were dissolved in 1958; their machinery was sold to the collective farms on credit, the debt being eventually written off. All this meant that after 1958, the state had to purchase (at by then higher procurement prices) that portion of the farms' produce formerly delivered (at exorbitant rates) as payment for machine tractor stations' services. (Incidentally, the former employees of the machine tractor stations—state sector employees on regular wages—were collectivized; that is, they went on the *trudoden'* system of residual payments, although attempts were made to help them maintain a semblance of their former higher status and pay. Still, many of these employees left the farms and migrated into the urban state sector.) The collective farms under the neoclassical plan benefit from state budgetary expenditures on land improvement, which have risen significantly. Investment in agriculture, which in 1950 was 16 percent of total investment, rose to roughly 30 percent of a much larger investment outlay in the 1970s, and to 38 percent by 1980. Capital inputs into agriculture rose 2½ times between 1950 and 1960, 2⅓ times between 1960 and 1970, and 2 times between 1970 and 1980. Out of its budget the state also helps collective farms with capital and operational grants. Current production inputs are sold to the collective farms at industrial wholesale prices rather than higher retail prices. An effort has been made to supply the countryside with better-quality consumer goods and to provide it with cultural facilities. (A key reason cited by young people for leaving the countryside has been the absence of such amenities in rural areas.) The *sel'skaia nadbavka* has been abolished, as have compulsory deliveries from private plots. Collective farmers now have an internal passport, like everybody else, which at least theoretically makes it possible for them to move around. (There are, however, still many administrative hindrances to personal mobility.)

As a result of measures taken on the sides of both revenues and expenditures, the financial situation of the collective farms and the income position of collective farm members at first improved considerably from low levels. (Farm finances deteriorated again, though, in the 1970s.) Between 1953 and 1967, total peasant income from collective and private plot work doubled, then doubled again between 1967 and 1979. As a result of the improvement in the income flow from the collective and that income's higher cash component, the share of total peasant income derived from private plot activity declined from 36 percent in 1965 to about 25 percent in 1985. Collective farmers' earnings have become comparable to those of state farm workers, and the difference between rural and urban living standards has been considerably narrowed (though it is still significant).

That a heroic effort of bureaucratic imagination has been made— not only to put an end to the Stalinplan's squeeze on the collective farm sector, but also to assist that sector through state largess—is beyond question. The Soviet neoclassical conservative plan's objective is to raise the low quality of collective farm operations, reduce costs, and make the collective farm into an efficient unit of production. Throughout, the assumption has been that this can be done by administrative reorganization and intrasystemic adjustments in the plan's institutions of information, coordination, property, and (especially) motivation. However, until 1984, there was no perceptible movement in the USSR toward subdividing labor to the level of the family unit; toward delegating broad property rights in land and the means of production to that private unit; or toward establishing a market information, coordination, and incentive nexus at the private unit level. In this regard, the Soviet neoclassical plan has been, until very recently, much more conservative than the Chinese adjustments carried out after 1978, which (by 1985) were skirting systemic reform (see Chapter 9). In 1983, however, things began to change in the USSR too with the Politburo's formal approval of the *zveno*-based system of contractual responsibility.

In 1983, movement toward what might conceivably turn out to be almost a reform of the collective farm system was prompted, among other contributory causes, by the growing dependence of the *kolkhozy* on state aid. In the 1970s, farm indebtedness rose more than ten times, while short-term debts rose three times. At the same time, attempts to put the farms on economic self-accounting (*khozraschet*) for all practical purposes collapsed. In 1980, only 8 percent of collective farm teams and brigades were on *khozraschet*.[25] This neoreformist movement, which had been stalled many times before, will be discussed briefly in Section III.

Effects of Neoclassical Conservative Adjustments

How has Soviet *kolkhoz* and *sovkhoz* agriculture responded to the generous ministrations of the neoclassical plan?[26] It has responded in a number of ways, including the following:

1. In the 1950s, the annual growth rate of output was 4.9 percent, reflecting the positive initial impact of the virgin lands campaign, the dismantling of the machine tractor stations, and the significant increases in procurement prices. In the 1960s, the effect of these adjustments began to dissipate: the annual growth rate declined to 3 percent. In the 1970s, it fell to 2 percent.

2. In the late 1950s, output per unit of inputs increased at an average annual rate of 2.1 percent. During the 1960s, the increase was 0.9 percent, and 0.4 percent in the 1970s.

3. The cost of agricultural production (in constant prices) rose by more than 50 percent between 1965 and 1980. Between 1966 and 1976, material costs per unit of output increased by 77 percent; payments for inputs from outside agriculture increased 110 percent. One consequence of this has been that in 1980, half of the *kolkhozy* and *sovkhozy* were operating at a financial loss and had to be subsidized from the state budget.

4. Because retail prices of most foods with a low-income demand elasticity have been kept unchanged since 1962 while costs have risen sharply, state subsidies for purchasing and processing one kilogram of meat rose from 2.2 (1980) to 2.8 (1983) times the retail price. The corresponding figures for butter were 1.8 (1980) to 2.3 (1983) times the retail price. In 1980, the total agricultural subsidy came to about 35 billion rubles (50 billion dollars), 23 billion rubles (35 billion dollars) of which went for wheat and dairy products. The relative prices of bread and meat have induced distortions in the demand for both products. (Peasants, for example, buy bread at low prices and feed it to their livestock

[reminiscent of the "grain crisis" of 1928]. They purchase meat at retail and feed it to foxes, selling the fur at a handsome profit.)

5. Soviet agriculture's sensitivity to changes in weather conditions (due in part to deficient storage and infrastructural facilities, especially roads) has not been significantly reduced. This translates into production cycles and frequent shortages of particular food items. The weather problem, which is real, exaggerates built-in system defects, or, when the year is exceptionally good, overcomes them (as in 1978).[27]

6. Complaints about loss of produce through spoilage continue. In a typical year, 20 percent of the grain, vegetables, and fruit produced is lost, as is half the potato crop (equivalent to the total annual U.S. production). This is due in part to inadequate storage and transportation, but also (perhaps more importantly) to poor work organization, in large part a result of overcentralized information, coordination, and property, and still an inadequate motivational system.[28] The improvement in the material condition of collective farm workers has apparently failed to elicit the expected productivity response. There has been no movement at all toward decentralization of farm management and planning.

7. Articles in the Soviet press suggest that three major problems continue to afflict Soviet agriculture: shortage of fertilizers, overcropping, and neglect of fallow land. The resultant ecological damage has been serious. Between 1960 and 1980, 7.5 million hectares of agricultural land were lost.

8. Imports of grain have risen from 200,000 metric tons in 1960 to about 35 million metric tons in 1982 (43 million in 1981). Grain exports declined from 7 million tons in 1960 to 2 million tons in 1982 (3 million tons in 1981). Grain imports are used to supplement shortfalls in domestic production of food grains. They are also used to feed livestock, the intent being to expand domestic meat supplies and improve the citizens' diet. Since 1950, the per capita consumption of food has, in fact, improved—both quantitatively and qualitatively. Per capita consumption of protein foods (for example, meat) has risen both absolutely and relative to starches, but actual meat consumption (fifty-four pounds per head per year in 1981) falls short of official norms.[29]

In a review of an important work on communist agriculture, American political scientist Roy D. Laird summarizes the systemic sources of the persistent farm problem:

> Why are the inefficiencies and shortcomings tolerated? In spite of the many 'reforms' announced (and some adopted) from Stalin's day to the present, first priority has been to retain, and indeed maximize, central political control over the farms and the peasants. Economic control is, of course, the prime tool for achieving political control, and agricultural policy in the So-

viet Union and Eastern Europe is, first of all, political. However, emphasis on ideology and power has extracted a most 'costly tribute.'[30]

Specifically, the crucial linkage between input of effort and reward has not been established. The adjustments carried out in the post-Stalin-plan period have failed to link effort to result or incentive to both effort and result. There have been several reasons for this. First, there is the peasant's continued uncertainty regarding the size of his (now) hourly pay. Second, the success indicator for kolkhoz managements (plan fulfillment) differs from the peasants' preoccupation with hourly compensation. If the farm's output or deliveries to the state fall below the plan, then management, unconstrained by labor costs, will try to remedy the situation by adding labor hours, even where the marginal product of labor is small (that is, as long as average product is larger than zero). In such a situation, more hours worked will mean less pay per hour.[31] Third, except for experiments with the contractual zveno ("link," discussed below), organizational diseconomies of scale (especially the cost of supervision) persist. Fourth, despite injunctions against meddling with the quota, procurement quotas are, in fact, arbitrarily changed. At the level of the kolkhoz, there has been no systemic change so far in the distribution of allocative power—no marketization, no privatization. Managerial boards are still appointed and remain responsible upward to their nomenklatura patrons, not downward to collective farm members. But real change of the reform species may perhaps be on its way. To be sure, it has been on its way for a long time now—but one never can tell.

III. BEYOND ADJUSTMENT?

Reference was made earlier to the zveno, or "link" (actually, to the narod-noe zveno, or "unregulated link"). The zveno has a long and checkered history going back to the years immediately following World War II. The idea behind the link was to find an organizational form smaller than the collective or brigade, relatively independent of the parent stem, that would be vested (by contract) with responsibility for production and that would be rewarded according to results. This idea has been revived lately in the form of the so-called collective contract (kollektivnyi podriad), which bears a striking resemblance to the Chinese post-1978 system of contractual production responsibility to small groups (including households; see Chapter 9). The collective contract idea was formally approved by the Soviet Politburo in February 1983 and is currently (1986) in the process of apparently widespread implementation.

This is how the collective contract works (or is supposed to work).

A small group of collective (or state farm) workers—a half-dozen to dozen people—is recognized as a legal person within the farm. The farm signs a contract with the group (which may be a household) for production on a given area of the farm's land or for livestock raising (the livestock, like the land, remains the legal propertʸ of the collective farm). The contract specifies the mutual obligations of the parties, including terms of payment for work done, supply of inputs, and so on. The group is entirely responsible for organizing its work under the contract, and distributes its revenue among the members. Establishment of groups is to be voluntary and autonomous. The assignment of land and other means of production under the contract is to be made on a long-term basis, to encourage proper care of the land and other assets. Payment is to be linked directly to results.

If implemented in conformity with the theoretical blueprint, the system of collective contracts, like its Chinese counterpart, would signal a movement toward privatization and marketization, that is, toward a reform of the system, not just a simple adjustment. The idea has strong support within the top leadership from, among others, Mikhail Gorbachev. The implications of the move are understood both by the movers and their opponents. There is talk of a sense of "proprietorship" within the small groups that will improve the production climate. Proponents stress economic advantages in the form of increased labor productivity (apparently 15–20 percent higher in the groups than in the *kolkhozy* and their brigades), higher yields (20–30 percent higher), and more output per unit of assets (5–8 percent better).[32] Opponents (rather quiet of late) are worried about loss of control and possible throwbacks to the so-called private property mentality of petty producers. This is a familiar scenario.

The result of the battle, presently joined, will depend to no small extent on the attitude of the bureaucracy at all echelons, but especially at the local level. In China, these local-level bureaucrats, threatened not only with loss of power but of jobs, have put formidable obstacles in the way of the production responsibility system. In addition, the idea of doing something voluntarily and autonomously does not sit well with the Soviets; in fact, it is quite incomprehensible to the Soviet mind. The prospects for rural systemic reform in Russia, therefore, are uncertain at best.[33] What is certain is that over the next decade, the demand for food in the USSR will continue to grow at a rapid rate (as it has over the past fifteen years), and hence, the problem of adjustment versus reform will continue to be posed acutely.

CHAPTER EIGHT

USSR: Information, Coordination, and Motivation in the Neoclassical Conservative Plan

In this chapter we will look at some adjustments made in the Stalin-plan's institutions of information, coordination, and motivation by the Soviet neoclassical conservative plan since the mid-1950s. It would be, I think, fair to say that (a) the theoretical debate on the needed changes, as that need was perceived by the discussants (many of whom were party-affiliated academics), was at all times bolder than the actual implementation of changes; and (b) that after an initial, almost reformist zeal for decentralization (which, however, never went beyond administrative decentralization), there was disappointment, recrimination (an "I told you so" attitude on the part of the centralizers), counterreform, and a return to sclerotic bureaucratic habits. The neoreformist zeal peaked toward the end of the 1960s. The 1970s and early 1980s witnessed a partial return to Stalinist origins—with the new addition of mathematics and computers.

In terms of the philosophical controversy of the 1920s, the neoclassical conservative plan, as it has existed in the USSR from the mid-late 1950s to the present time, represents a movement from the teleological to the geneticist conception of the plan (see Chapter 2). It pays more attention than did the Stalinplan (at least at the verbal and conceptual levels) to "objective" economic conditions or regularities that put feasibility limits on goal formulation in all economic systems. The Soviet neoclassical conservative plan is also willing (at the conceptual and verbal levels, and sometimes even in controlled experimental practice) to acknowledge the money nexus and importance of financial relations in the plan. In this sense, it is less "leftist" in its interpretation of the Marxist theoretical legacy, which visualizes demonetized (high technology, resource unconstrained) economy as the ideal to be attained.

Information

Physical-Technical Indicators (Normativy)

The original intent of the neoclassical conservative adjustment was to eliminate, or at least drastically trim, the "petty tutelage" exercised by the center over enterprises through numerous physical-technical indicators (*normativy*). Although in former times the central planners handed down to enterprises several dozens of such norms, the gross value of output indicator took precedence over all others. At first the neoclassical plan reduced the number of centrally formulated indicators to eight, and replaced the gross value of output index with a combined index of profitability and profit (or sales).

The eight indicators were physical output of key products, sales revenue, quality indices, total wages bill, profit, profitability, payments into the state budget, and allocations from the budget. In the 1970s, indicators of labor productivity, average wages, employment, product assortment, utilization of capacity, fulfillment of delivery contracts, and cost savings were added. By the mid-1980s, the principal indicator was sales revenue corrected for the proportion of delivery targets successfully met. This was accompanied by other indicators, notably profit, cost reductions, improvements in utilization of capacity, and improvement of product quality.

The *normativy* reduction was not designed to replace central control with managerial autonomy. On the contrary, it was intended to make central control stronger by making it more efficient. If it is true that there are now somewhat fewer central norms than there were before the mid-1950s, it is equally true that those in place are very broad and pervasive. The distortions generated by the managers' preoccupation with profits, sales, and profitability—expressed in prices that do not adequately, nor even remotely, reflect relative scarcities, opportunity costs, and demand, and that, moreover, are not fully coordinated with physical-technical indices—has led to renewed additions to the lists specifying the volume and assortment of output of principal products and to the lists fixing the supply of key materials and equipment in physical terms. In addition, numerous ad hoc administrative corrections are made all the time. As early as 1969, for example, the Ministry of Meat and Dairy Industries sent forty thousand administrative instructions to its enterprises to supplement the eight central indicators.

It was originally hoped that the eight indicators, combined with the right price constellation, would by themselves do the job. By 1980, not much was left of the original modest bureaucratic decentralization.

Whether expressed in physical or financial (cost-plus value) terms, the readjusted indicators remained unidimensional information. Thus, when sales revenue became a leading indicator, enterprises purchased expensive inputs as the easiest and (from the standpoint of the indicator) most rational way of fulfilling the indicator—and getting bonuses for it. When net value of output was tried as the indicator, enterprises began to select products with high processing costs. When profit was the leading indicator, enterprises emphasized those products within their total product mix that, though perhaps having a lower profit rate, had a higher ratio of profit to processing cost. The high cost of materials in this context was a matter of indifference to the enterprise. The overall result was an increase in costs, so a cost reduction indicator had to be brought in. There is another way of looking at the reduction in centrally formulated enterprise indicators: whenever an indicator is dropped, managers will ignore or neglect that dimension of production expressed by the dropped indicator; this means that soon the indicator must be put back in again.

A former Soviet planning worker puts it this way:

> In instances when Soviet planners have stipulated a revised set of leading indicators and tied incentive funds to them, other indicators have moved in undesirable directions. Specifically, delivery contracts were not met, labor productivity declined, and costs grew. Planners found that, once again, only direct regulation could bring an improvement for any individual economic indicator.[1]

Industrial Wholesale Price Revision

In addition to both the already-discussed changes in the collective farm system (including the farms' system of compensation) and the revision of industrial wages (see below, "Motivation"), the Soviet neoclassical conservative plan made adjustments in long-neglected industrial wholesale prices. A general revision of industrial wholesale prices in the USSR was carried out in the 1966–67 year.

Adjustment of industrial wholesale prices as the planners' and managers' secondary conveyor of information means changes in the prices of Grossman's Quadrant IV (see Figure 2.1), that is, in prices set by the state on the basis of cost, with little attention to equating supply and demand, since supply and demand are primarily determined by the planners' physical rationing of inputs (S) and mandatory targeting of outputs (*D*). The adjustment concentrated on the costing formula: the calculation of "prime cost" (*sebestoimost'*) and the profit markup. The results are shown in Table 8.1 and its accompanying explanatory notes, which draw on the pioneering work in this field done by Bornstein (see Chapter 3, note 9).

Specifically, the mid-1960s revision of Soviet industrial wholesale prices (the "Kosygin 'reform' ") set out to accomplish four things. The new prices were to be set in such a way that they would (1) reflect current costs ("socially necessary expenditures of labor") more accurately than did the old prices, most of which had not been changed for many years; (2) ensure a "normal" level of profitability in most branches of industry and in every "normally working" enterprise, and thus "help convert profit into a real index of the effectiveness with which the productive funds allocated to the enterprise by the state are used";[2] (3) serve as major stimulants to innovation, quality improvement, and technical progress; and (4) be flexible in the short run (that is, more sensitive to changing cost and demand conditions) than had been the old prices.

These four aims of the price adjustment were carried out as follows:

1. To make wholesale prices correspond more accurately to current production costs, the components of existing prices were changed in several respects. These changes represent a revision of cost and profit accounting methodology based on Marxist principles as read by the revisionists of the time: (a) regular bonuses to managerial, office, and engineering-technical personnel were to be included in enterprise profit rather than prime cost (as had been done previously); (b) interest on short-term bank loans, instead of being counted as part of cost, was now to be counted as a charge against profit; (c) expenses for geological prospecting and forest maintenance, formerly covered by the state out of budgetary grants, were to be included in enterprise costs of production; (d) a capital charge ("interest") on the average annual value of enterprises' undepreciated fixed and circulating capital as shown on the balance sheets was to be included in profit calculation; (e) in some extractive enterprises, a fixed differential rent charge was to be introduced; and (f) the enterprises' average, branch, planned profit markup (or loss deduction) was to be calculated primarily as a percentage of branch total (fixed and circulating) capital instead of as a percentage of cost. This latter adjustment did not significantly change depreciation rates, which had been too low to begin with, and did not depart from the concept of average, branch, planned adjusted, weighted cost (*sebestoimost'*) and average, branch, planned profit markup or loss deduction.[3] In essence, therefore, the new wholesale prices remained centrally fixed, average-planned, cost-plus prices; there was no real reform here.

Perhaps the most interesting innovation was the introduction of a capital charge levied on gross enterprise profits, the profits compared to sales rather than to gross output as before. For industry as a whole, the charge (in the 1966–67 year) was set at 6 percent per year; in some exceptional cases (for example, coal), it was set at 3 percent, and in two subbranches of the food industry, at 10 percent. There was to be no charge for planned loss enterprises. Within these guidelines, the precise rate of the charge was to be set by ministries for each enterprise under a given ministry's control. The charge was to be paid to the state treasury out of gross enterprise profits, which were planned for industry as a whole at 15 percent of total capital. It should be pointed out that the capital charge was (and remains) rather arbitrary, its main function being redistribution of profits. It is price-determining, rather than price-determined. It does not emerge as a residual of optimal allocation prices (that is, opportunity cost of capital), and does not, therefore, reflect the social marginal productivity of capital. Thus there is, again, no reform.

Nor has the neoclassical adjustment given any consideration to the opportunity cost of land (social marginal productivity of land, expressed in rent). Although for a short while changes in costing methodology succeeded in making the new prices better indicators of current production costs, they did not introduce opportunity cost prices. Such prices could have arisen had enterprises been allowed to negotiate contracts directly and competitively, the contract prices emerging from these lateral negotiations (marketization). However, the closer approximation of prices to better-calculated current production costs did make it easier for enterprises to conduct their affairs on the basis of self-accounting (*khozraschet*) for a time, and made it possible for the center to better enforce its preferences by greater resort to "value" tools ("economic levers"). Ministries and other administrative authorities, however, were unwilling to lay down their physical control weapons. Moreover, some of the new prices remained under the nefarious influence of the gross value of output (*val*).

2. The second aim of the industrial wholesale price revision was to make most branches of industry profitable on the average, and to reduce the number of enterprises operating at planned losses (subsidized enterprises). Since profitability (*rentabel'nost'*) was to become the key index of the effectiveness of enterprise performance, it was essential for price levels to be such as to ensure a "normal" level of profitability (decreed to be about 15 percent for industry as a whole) in most branches.[4] This was to be achieved by substantial increases in the wholesale prices of most commodities and of freight rates. The price of

TABLE 8.1
USSR: Neoclassical Conservative Plan—Composition of State-Set Industrial Wholesale and Retail Prices
(average cost-plus method)

Ex-Factory (or Enterprise, Firm) Wholesale Prices

(1) Average planned cost of production of enterprises in the branch[a]
    a) cost of material inputs, including energy
    b) depreciation of plant and equipment[b]
    c) direct and indirect labor[c]

+

(2) Average planned profit (or loss, or none) of enterprises in the branch[d]

+

(3) Turnover tax (if any) previously paid by the enterprise on any inputs used in making the product (but no turnover tax on the product itself)[e]

+

(4) Average transportation charges (usually to station of destination) where the enterprise is responsible for delivery of the product

---

Industrial Branch Wholesale Prices

(1) Ex-factory (or enterprise, firm) wholesale price

+

(2) Turnover tax (if any) on the product[e]

+

(3) Planned profit of central wholesale organization

+

(4) Average transportation charges, if borne by the wholesale organization rather than buyer (usually to station of destination)

State Retail Prices[f]

(1) Industrial wholesale price

+

(2) Planned profit at retail

+

(3) Transportation charges, if borne by the buyer

[a]The cost (*sebestoimost'*, or "prime cost" of production) is average for the branch; *planned* to take account of proposed or expected cost reductions or increases; *weighted* by the output levels of the various enterprises in the branch; and *adjusted* to exclude the highest cost (marginal) producers (not considered to be "socially necessary").

[b]Depreciation (amortization) funds are, in part, remitted to the state treasury. Rates of depreciation on plant and equipment are based on the expected life of assets. They are considered by many socialist economists to be too low (that is, they inhibit the timely replacement of assets). In China (1981), the usual depreciation period for machinery was thirty years. No depreciation was charged on urban residential buildings. Depreciation does not include charges for obsolescence.

[c]Includes basic (tariff) wages and salaries and social insurance payments (social insurance tax calculated as a fixed percentage of each enterprise's wages bill). Also included are overhead expenses and expenses for geological prospecting and maintenance of forests.

[d]The planned profit markup is set to provide a "normal" level of profitability for most "normally operating" firms. In arriving at the markup, the following charges against profit are taken into account: (a) bonuses of managers, technicians, and clerks; (b) short-term and long-term interest on bank loans; (c) capital charge (tax) on the average annual value of the firm's undepreciated fixed and working capital; (d) differential rent payments in some extractive industry firms (see Bornstein, "Soviet Price Policy," p. 21). Under the classical plan, managerial-technical-clerical bonuses were treated as cost of production items, as was interest on short-term bank loans. Since the ex-factory price is the same for all firms in the branch producing a given product, differences in production costs are reflected in (sometimes considerable) variations among firms in actual profitability. That portion of the difference attributable to "objective" reasons (location, geological formations) can be adjusted by a differential rent charge. In the Soviet neoclassical plan, profits are calculated primarily, but not exclusively, as a percentage of branch total (fixed and circulating) capital (but see Bornstein, "Soviet Price Policy," p. 22). In the Chinese neoclassical plan (post-1978), profit was calculated on the basis of cost as it had been in the Soviet Stalinplan. The size of the profit markup is also determined by considerations of the quality of the product, but not always very effectively. The greater part of planned enterprise profits is remitted to the state budget. A part of above-plan profits is also remitted. The size of the profit remittances is dictated largely by government policies with respect to taxing or subsidizing specific funds: production development (self-investment by the firm outside the plan); bonus (primarily for management, in some countries also for workers); and social-cultural uses (especially worker and employee housing). The rules for payments into and out of the funds are laid down by the state.

[e]The turnover tax is levied at each stage of production and delivery. It is usually calculated as a percentage of the value of gross receipts, varying according to the type of commodity or service. In the USSR, the tax typically has been levied primarily on consumer goods and collected at the industrial wholesale level. In other countries (for example, China) the tax is imposed at the factory level and enters the ex-factory price. (See also Kornai, "The Prospects of the Hungarian Economic Reform," p. 232.)

[f]The general level of consumer goods prices is set so that (it is to be hoped) the total value of consumer goods and services (V) plus savings (S) absorbs the total consumer disposable income (Y):

$$V + S = Y$$

The price levels set for individual commodities depend on a variety of planners' goals. Among these are (a) the planners' appreciation of a good's social utility or disutility (for example, children's clothing—subsidized, relatively low prices); and (b) the need to bring consumer demand into equality with planner-determined supply (for example, automobiles), or supply into equality with planner-determined demand (for example, above-quota farm produce, wages in Siberia). (See Grossman's Quadrants II and III, fig. 2.1.)

For an updated version see Morris Bornstein, "The Soviet Industrial Price Revision," in G. Fink, ed., *Socialist Economy and Economic Policy: Essays in Honour of Friedrich Levcik* (Vienna and New York: Springer Verlag, 1985), pp. 157–170.

coal, for example, was raised by 78 percent; that of crude oil, by 130 percent. The result was that all branches of industry were made nominally profitable, the spread of interbranch profitability was reduced, and the number of planned loss enterprises was drastically cut down. However, there remained wide spreads in the profitability of the various items produced by each industry branch, by individual plants, and between enterprises within a branch. This has meant that, not infrequently, a plant has concentrated on producing the most profitable items while neglecting others perhaps socially more necessary. To check this trend, the center added more "unprofitable" items to the enterprises' *nomenklatura* lists (lists defining for the enterprise in physical-technical terms the items—and their assortment—it was obliged to produce). This renewed resort to "economic physics" weakened and distorted the intent of the reform, which was to enhance the use of prices to guide enterprise behavior.

The rise in the level of wholesale prices was not allowed to be fully reflected in state retail prices, nor was it permitted to affect the terms of trade with agriculture. Basic wages and salaries were not to be changed except for earlier commitments made with respect to raising the minimum wages of workers and employees, minimum collective farmers' earnings, basic rates for service workers, and supplements for workers and employees in climatically hostile or geographically remote areas (see below, "Wages"). These constraints meant that the reform of industrial wholesale prices amounted to not much more than a redistribution of costs and dues within the producer and consumer goods supplying sectors. The insulation of reformed wholesale prices from retail prices and of retail prices from wages narrowed the intended effectiveness of prices as instruments of coordination, incentive, limited allocation, and control.

Actually, the level of industrial wholesale prices after the reform rose significantly—more than had been programmed—due to the exaggeration by enterprises of information about "socially necessary" costs and to the swelling of "temporary," "new," "one-time," and "single-item" prices set by ministries and enterprises. Most often, the new products, on which inflated temporary prices were set, were really old products that had been repackaged or only slightly altered. The center's reaction to the cost-push inflation of wholesale prices was to fall back increasingly on old administrative decree-type controls.

By the early 1980s, when yet another general revision of industrial wholesale prices was scheduled, the price adjustment of the 1960s had been readjusted almost back to where it had been before. Complaints were being voiced again (as they had been in the 1950s, 1960s, and 1970s) about wholesale prices being totally unrelated to the level and structure of costs, especially labor costs (that is, the prices were generally below costs, many enterprises were operating at a financial loss, economic accounting [*khozraschet*] was difficult, and so on). For the most part, these complaints were dealt with by administrative decrees, which produced new distortions on top of old.

3. In order to make wholesale prices act as stimulants to innovation, technical progress, and quality upgrading, an effort was made to set the prices of substitute products in such a way as to encourage the use of more advanced products without, by the same token, creating financial difficulties for enterprises. Price markups for products of above-average quality were also inaugurated. New quality standards were promulgated for a number of key commodities (for example, metals, cement, timber), and the new prices took these standards into account. However, the effectiveness of theoretical price inducements was greatly lessened by a persistent sellers' market and by the fact that innovation requires retooling. Expenditures for retooling, which take a long time to recoup, are an immediate subtraction from current income. They reduce profits and (under the revised system) managerial bonuses in the short run.

4. The objective of making the new wholesale prices more flexible in the short run, that is, more responsive to shifts in cost and demand conditions, has not been achieved at all. The new prices could only be changed by central decision, and central decision makers were busy with other things. After the 1966–67 year, several rather modest upward adjustments were made in industrial wholesale prices, primarily in the manufacturing industry. They failed to capture the rapidity and complexity of the underlying changes in the level and structure of costs. The demand side remained, as always, neglected. Key inputs were physically rationed out as of old, and demand was commanded by mandatory physical output norms. Like their predecessors, the revised prices failed to establish the vital link between the preferences of consumers, enterprises, and government—between the private and the social interest, even the social interest as perceived by single-party planners. In sum, under the neoclassical conservative plan today, Soviet industrial wholesale prices are somewhat better-computed (from the standpoint of Marxist cost-accounting theory) supplementary instruments of central control and of enterprise performance evaluation. Their contribution to the attainment of allocative and motivational optimality, however, is either negative or zero.

Coordination

Formal Organization

In the post-Stalinplan era, numerous reorganizations of the plan have been (and continue to be) made. These are intrasystemic changes carried out on the administrative centralization-decentralization axis. The natural response of an administrative centrally planned command system to economic problems is to reorganize the administration.

Regionalization. As noted in Chapter 3, the dissolution of branch ministries and the creation of regional councils of the national economy (*sovnarkhozy*) by Khrushchev in 1957 were attempts to decentralize the bureaucratic system on the regional ("territorial") principle. The replacement of branch ministries with *sovnarkhozy* meant that individual enterprises were subordinated to new supervisory authorities (regional councils rather than branch ministries). Enterprise decision-making power was not enlarged. The economic problems of information, coordination, property, and motivation that had troubled the industrial branches earlier now troubled the regions. The *sovnarkhozy* organizational adjustment was put away in 1964, together with its author, by the ascendant technocrats and party regulators.

Material-Technical Supplies. There was some talk in the mid-1960s about abolishing (or partly dismantling) the State Committee on Material and Technical Supply (*Gossnab*, the agency in charge of physically rationing key inputs) and the ministerial supply departments. The talk was that these supplies would be progressively distributed through "commercial" wholesale channels, presumably in response to reformed (not merely adjusted) industrial wholesale prices. But this was only talk—nothing came of it. Today (1985), 98 percent of producer goods are allocated physically by *Gossnab* and ministerial material-technical supply departments. Had something been done in this crucial area along the lines envisaged by the talk, such a change could almost have amounted to systemic reform. As long as *Gossnab* and the ministries physically allocate key resources (and not so key ones, for example, ski poles), marketization is out of the question.[5]

Associations. The creation of "associations" (*ob'edineniia*) in the 1970s was mentioned in Chapter 3. This is an administrative adjustment designed to give industrial organization greater flexibility while reducing administrative costs and strengthening central control. Two basic types of associations should be distinguished: the production association, which is a very large production enterprise (although it assumes several varied subforms); and the industrial association, which is a unit of administration roughly equivalent to (on occasion even replacing) a ministerial department (*glavk*), although it may also be an administrative unit subordinate to the *glavk*.

Nove lists six reasons for the creation of the associations: (1) administrative economy (that is, easier and more effective central control through reduction in the number of units that must be planned and supervised from the center); (2) economies of scale (but there may also be scale diseconomies; in terms of employment, Soviet firms are, on the average, much larger than firms in developed market economies); (3) the facilitation of technical progress through closer linking of production and research in the larger association, or through the establishment of "scientific and production associations"; (4) the increasing of management's powers and status; (5) the consolidation within one firm of the output of products formerly produced by many smaller enterprises; (6) the redistribution of economic power among ministerial departments, managers, and party officials.[6]

The net effect of the association phenomenon appears to have been greater centralization of decision making. Former contributor to Soviet planning Fyodor I. Kushnirsky sums up the trend this way:

> There was a tremendous growth in [the *Gosplan*] powers in the 1970s. During this period, it strengthened its influence in annual planning, where most inputs are allocated and appropriations are made—this despite the initial intent of the 1965 reform to concentrate *Gosplan*'s efforts on long-term planning and to devolve to the ministries the task of annual planning. Far from dispersing control of resources among ministries, *Gosplan* actually increased its supervisory role, especially in the distribution of metals and energy . . . Moreover, *Gosplan*'s functions were broadened from planning to direct monitoring of the performance of ministries, industrial associations, and enterprises in meeting plan targets . . . Of even more significance have been the shifts in decision-making from the *Gosplan* and the USSR Council of Ministers, on the one hand, to the apparatus of the party Central Committee, on the other. The party apparatus has always exercised considerable control over economic activity in the Soviet Union, but in the Brezhnev era it began to monitor even day-to-day operational decisions.[7]

Physical Coordination[8]

The Soviet neoclassical conservative plan (the "Khrushchev-Brezhnev model") is the Stalinplan modernized, but not structurally reformed: it is equipped with computers, mathematical techniques, automated supply, production scheduling, inventory control, and information retrieval systems; with more nearly scientific (in an engineering sense) norms of input and output; and with peripherally more sophisticated planning (input-output) and optimization (linear programming) methodologies. *Peripherally* is meant to indicate that these methods remain, by and large, in the experimental domain of research institutes and mathematics-economics bureaus within planning departments, but that they are not used as generalized policy instruments. A rising portion of the annual plans is calculated by *Gosplan* and ministerial computers; the Central Statistical Administration is highly computerized, as is the allocation of physical-technical inputs by *Gossnab;* and so on. These are important changes.[9] By accelerating data processing, greatly increasing information storage capacity, and resorting to increasingly sophisticated models for translating information into decisions, the very substance of planning may in time be affected. So far, however, these changes have been changes in planning techniques, not in the economic genetics of the plan. Technocratic substitution can only go so far in alleviating systemic ills.

Computerization and the design of information systems has proceeded from the bottom up—from the level of enterprises-associations (record-keeping, inventory control, production scheduling) toward the integration of these enterprise-association systems in ministerial branch systems, and subsequently toward their integration in a *Gosplan*-controlled, economy-wide system. A "confidential" paper on the existing planning system, prepared by researchers at the Novosibirsk Institute of Economics of the USSR Academy of Sciences and allegedly leaked to Western correspondents in Moscow in the summer of 1983 (extracts from which are given in Appendix B of this book), criticized what it described as the gain in the decision-making power of ministries at the expense of the *Gosplan* on the one hand and enterprises-associations on the other.[10] This could conceivably have happened if ministries had secured control over the design and development of the computer and information systems within their branches and had geared those systems to the particular needs of the branches as perceived by ministerial-level authorities. It would have provided the ministries with a greatly enlarged volume of rapidly processed information about conditions within the branches, and thus enabled them to increase their control over their constituent enterprises-associations and to enlarge their power vis-à-vis the *Gosplan*. This, in turn, would have strengthened the Soviet economy's already-marked propensity toward "compartmentalism." The trend suggested by the Novosibirsk critique has been disputed by some emigré former planners.

Kushnirsky (above) maintains that during discussions on the automated system of planning calculations in the 1970s, ministry specialists argued that information transmitted by enterprises should be processed by the ministries and submitted by them as inputs into the *Gosplan* system. The designers of the system, however, maintained that the *Gosplan* should obtain data directly from the enterprises. In this way, the reliability of data obtained by *Gosplan* would be greater, as would be *Gosplan's* control over the ministries. Apparently the *Gosplan* argument prevailed.[11]

The computerization of the centralized economy can also mean the more rapid spread of erroneous information through the system. This is a real danger in a central planning system, compartmentalized into competing (sometimes antagonistic) bureaucratic interests. Under such circumstances, the supply of accurate information may not be in the interest of any one compartment, although being in the interest of the social whole as perceived by the top planners.

The Marxist distrust of the monetization of economic relations and the importance attached to physical (as opposed to financial-value) planning, continues to dominate Soviet thinking. The significance and usefulness of financial-value levers, especially as plan control mechanisms, is better understood, but without significantly affecting the dominant position of administrative instructions couched in physical-technical terms.

Within this more up-to-date framework of planning techniques, physical planning is still carried on primarily by the method of material balances. The material balance as a planning tool has been discussed in Chapter 2 (see Table 2.1) and in Chapter 3. Here we will add a few details.

Material balances in the USSR are constructed for four major categories of goods: (1) funded commodities, (2) centrally planned commodities, (3) decentrally planned commodities, and (4) nonplanned commodities. Balances for funded commodities are prepared by *Gosplan*. There are about two thousand such balances for more or less aggregated commodity groups (for example, steel, machinery), but these represent approximately 80 percent of the value of all allocated commodities.[12] Balances for centrally planned commodities are prepared by *Gossnab*, the material-technical supply committee under the Council of Ministers, and its supply and sales administrations (*Gossnab's snabsbyty*). About twenty thousand commodities are so balanced. Decentrally planned commodities are balanced and distributed by *Gossnab's* territorial (republican, and so on) administrations without specific permission from higher organs. Roughly fifty thousand balances are involved. Nonplanned commodity balances are prepared by ministries. These concern

(a) goods produced by enterprises within the ministerial branch and distributed to other enterprises in the branch, and (b) some commodities not included in the *Gosplan* or *Gossnab* balances, which are produced by the ministerial branch but distributed to other ministries. About twenty-five thousand balances are involved.

The following points should be noticed: (a) not all commodities produced and used by the system are covered by individual material balances—some goods are not covered at all; others are included in a very aggregated way; (b) not all the production of a commodity for which a balance is constructed is included in the balance (suppose commodity X is produced as the principal output of industry A and also as a side product of industry B; in such a case it is likely that the output of X in industry B will not be included in the material balance of X, because such subsidiary output is probably not known to the central planners or to ministry officials in industry A); (c) the material balances are predicated on fairly unrealistic technological assumptions that exclude non-constant returns to scale, nonproportional inputs, and input substitutability; (d) the fixed input coefficients (norms) are, as a rule, weighted averages (weighted in favor of the more efficient producers)—this creates efficiency and consistency problems. (First, the better producers have insufficient incentives to efficiency ["soft norms"], while the less efficient producers may find the norms out of reach; second, "when during the process of plan calculations the relative outputs of plants with different input-output relationships is altered, this alters the actual mean input-output relationship. If the planners continue to use a given norm, then inconsistencies will result");[13] (e) finally, the system of material balances is not well-integrated with other balances of the national economy—if only because of the magnitude and complexity of the task, the integration tends to be tenuous and haphazard; the formal relationship between the material balances and other balances of the economy may be seen from Figure 8.1.

In sum, because of the major gaps (gaps in commodities covered by material balances, gaps between the material balances system and other balances of the economy, gaps between technological assumptions and technological reality), it is not possible to establish intercommodity and intersectoral consistency and efficiency of resource supply and distribution.

Soviet planners are concerned first and foremost with balancing the input needs and output of a single commodity, rather than with lesser-order adjustments needed in all balances directly or indirectly linked to the production of that commodity (see Figure 8.2).

Any change in the output of commodity 1 (as in the upper, rather than lower, part of Figure 8.2) would require adjustments in the output of commodity 2 and others serving as inputs into 1. This, in turn, would require adjustments in the output of all commodities entering as inputs into 2, and so on. In Soviet planning practice, the tendency has been to make adjustments in first-order relationships. In Figure 8.2, this means that if the planned output (uses) of 1 is raised, the inputs into 1 must be raised by amounts needed to produce the additional amount of 1. However, no adjustments are made for the additional resources needed to produce the extra inputs that go into 1, except where the secondary effects are obvious. This makes inconsistencies of inputs and outputs inevitable.[14]

Instead of engaging in laborious iterations arising from the secondary effects on interindustry outputs of a decision to increase the deficit commodity's output, spending precious foreign exchange to import the deficit commodity, or drawing down strategic stocks of the commodity, the planners typically make up the deficit at the expense of the consumer. Specifically, they reduce the allocation of the deficit commodity to lower priority industries (consumer goods), and treat final household demand for consumer goods and housing as a residual that can be trimmed at will. When steel is in short supply, the production of tanks and trucks will not suffer. The input of steel into the refrigerator industry will be reduced and fewer refrigerators will be available for private consumption. The buyer of refrigerators cannot directly and immediately take out his frustrations on the planners' priority industries although, over the longer run, pawning off shortages on the consumer will have adverse effects on labor productivity and socialist enthusiasm for production. In addition, shifting input shortages to the low-priority "buffer" industries will increase plan tautness in these industries, which sooner or later shows up in substandard quality and in the wrong assortment of consumer goods. Some of the input shortage burden may even be distributed among higher-priority industries to force them to economize on inputs. But too many supply problems cannot be shifted to those industries for fear that they, too, will cut corners on quality.

Thus, the first round adjustment (usually the only one) is an adjustment carried out at the consumer's expense. This has been so in the past, and is true today, though marginally less so because consumer goods industries do not rank as low on the planners' scale of what is important as they used to in the days of the Stalinplan.

These are adjustments at the level of plan formulation. In line with what has been said earlier (see Chapter 6) about divergence of planning intent from actual plan outcomes, adjustments (that is, responses to

FIGURE 8.1

Soviet Economic Balances

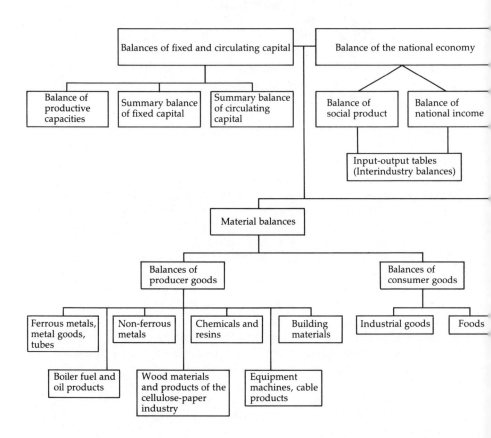

SOURCE: Ellman, *Soviet Planning Today,* p. 71.

material imbalances) will be made in the course of plan implementation as enterprises, associations, *glavki,* ministries, and others reshuffle inputs and outputs and manipulate performance indicators to make actual plan outcomes formally conform to the plan's intent. More even than the bargaining stage of plan preparation ("democratic centralism"), the mutual bureaucratic accommodation, exchange of favors, and useful contacts stage of plan implementation influences what finally comes out

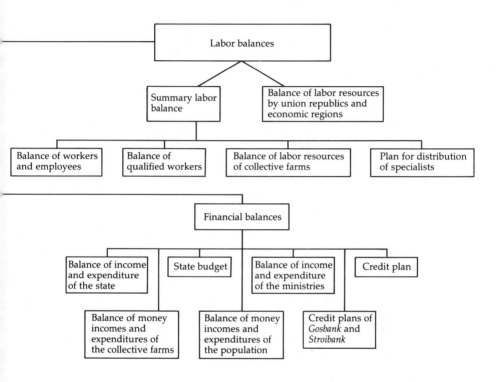

of the morass of material balances. The underground economy plays an important part in this reshuffling of inputs and outputs.[15] Despite inter-agency accommodations and compromises, conflict among agencies and their ability to block each others' decisions is a serious problem that causes distress to enterprise managers. Bureaucratic crisis management of this kind results in real plan outcomes often being quite different from what they formally appear to be. Even when the plan is said to be 100

FIGURE 8.2

Material Balances in the Classical and Neoclassical Conservative Plans

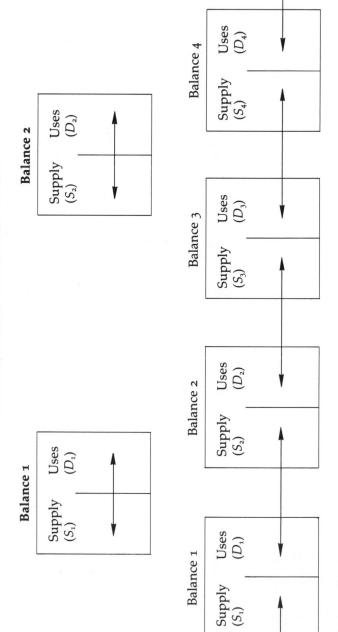

SOURCE: Ellman, *Soviet Planning Today*, p. 73.

percent fulfilled in every respect, the actual result will almost certainly be quite different from the announced result. If the plan targets the production of 50 million tons of steel and 50 million tons are produced, the actual outcome may be somewhat different from what was intended if half the steel cannot be used because it is of inferior quality, of an incorrect assortment, in the wrong location, or has been stolen. "It is," as one Soviet economist put it, "easier to plan than to fulfill plans."[16]

Within the material-technical supply system as practiced in the USSR, suppliers of the balanced materials are specified for customer enterprises by *Gossnab;* that is, buyer and seller are tied to each other by administrative order. The suppliers of the various inputs needed by the customer firms are specified for those firms by the plan. The supply allocation certificates that the customer firms receive from the planners (via their ministries) are valid only for the supplying enterprises identified in the certificates. A supply contract is then worked out specifying the transaction details, but the contract can be concluded only between the firms named by the planners and only within the parameters of the allocation certificate. User enterprises do not have the right to choose their own suppliers, nor can supplying enterprises competitively offer their wares to potential buyers. Information and coordination are administrative and vertical on the theory that the center knows (and knows best) which suppliers should serve which customers in the best interests of society as a whole—a theory that is, in fact, incorrect. Motivation also remains vertical, since each supplier will strive to satisfy not his customer, but instead his order-giving, reward- and punishment-dispensing administrative superiors:

> The whole experience of the centrally planned economies indicates . . .
> that without a price and market mechanism the centre is deprived of vital
> information about what is most urgently needed, *and* that the micro de-
> tail would in most cases have to be decided at lower levels, closer to the
> suppliers and their customers.[17]

The material balances method of physical plan formulation suffers from a number of drawbacks, some of which have been mentioned earlier (see Chapter 2). One important handicap is that the calculation and reconciliation of balances (even just one round) takes a great deal of time, so that finalized plans are invariably late in arriving at the enterprise level. This suggests that during perhaps as much as one quarter of the planning year the Soviet economy operates on an ad hoc basis. This inconvenience could be overcome by the adoption of the input-output table method of formulating an internally consistent plan. Input-output tables for the Soviet economy have, in fact, been constructed for a number of years (beginning with 1959), but the method has not been adopted in operational planning. The reasons for the apparent reluctance of Soviet authorities to resort to a very useful and promising planning tool range from ideological to practical. The ideological obstacle is that the input-output table shows that land and capital are scarce factors, and, as such, must carry scarcity (opportunity cost) prices, which runs counter to the Marxist labor theory of value. But this sort of ideological rigidity can be overcome (as with Kantorovich's "objectively determined valuations"). The main practical problem seems to be threefold in nature. First, the Soviet information system, rooted as it is in multiproduct branch ministerial data reporting (not to mention data withholding and falsification), is not well suited to the product data requirements of an input-output matrix. Second, even the more advanced experiments with a national input-output table have so far arrived at a matrix of less than 1000 by 1000, which is less than the degree of disaggregation obtained by the currently used material balances. Third, where (because of their heterogeneity) products entering the input-output table have to be expressed in value terms, problems arise; this is because the industrial wholesale prices in which the product values are expressed are not indicators of relative scarcities. Nevertheless, input-output methodology (see Appendix A) has the potential to make Soviet planning more expeditious and to improve the internal consistency of the plan's parts.[18]

Optimization

Optimization of the plan means that, among the various possible and feasible internally consistent plan variants, one is chosen that is "best." The best variant is the one that maximizes some objective function within certain well-defined scarcity (resource availability) parameters.

The problem of the conscious optimization of the whole plan (as distinct from optimization of small parts of the plan) is difficult in theory, and even more so in practice. This is understood by Soviet mathematical economists and those Western economists who have studied the subject at close range (for example, Alfred Zauberman, Holland Hunter, and Michael Ellman—see Bibliography). There is a large and growing Soviet literature on the subject, but so far not much action in planning practice. In the Soviet neoclassical conservative plan, optimization still takes the back seat to the quest for tolerable plan consistency. Although less than in the Stalinplan, optimizing is still by and large a question of doing better this year what was done last year (the "ratchet principle"), "better" often being synonymous with "more."

The difficulties are inherent in what is to be maximized (the objective function) and what the resource constraints are. Whatever the suggested objective function for the economy as a whole, it is too aggregated, too vague, too broad, and too diffuse. Some Soviet economists have proposed maximizing total social utility (as did Stalin—recall his goal of assuring "the maximum satisfaction of the continual growing material and cultural needs of society" [Chapter 6]). A question that arises immediately is, How does one measure total social utility, especially when there are rather passive, cost-plus prices? An alternative (but not more helpful) formulation is that the objective function to be maximized is "planners' preferences," or the level of output that maximizes the satisfactions of the plan's top decision-making authorities. This begs the essential question of what these preferences are—in workable detail. In practice, they appear to be an unsteady amalgam of the views of powerful special interest lobbies, habitués of the Politburo, committee chairmen, party secretaries, ministers, and other upper *nomenklatura* types. In the USSR, as elsewhere in the world of the plan, the objective function has not been identified with the operational detail needed, nor has it been agreed on beyond the general proposition that it should reflect "party policy." (Some cynics have suggested that the objective function to be maximized consists of the personal interests of the members of the top party bureaucracy, but this formulation, too, is more amusing than enlightening. The elite interest explanation is, however, more suggestive than the maximization of total social utility.)

The problem with determining precisely the resource availability constraints is no less elusive. The main difficulty is faulty information transmitted from below regarding the resource situation at the lower levels. This faulty information is then aggregated (coordinated) to produce a bigger informational flaw. Thus, as in the case of the objective function, one settles for a compromise. The ratchet is hauled out and put to use on the constraints side: top priority sectors, industries, and projects are accorded all the resources they claim to need, while everyone else goes without. Notice that the deficient and distorted information flowing through the system is in part due to motivational incompatibility. There is little (if any) motivation for enterprises to reveal their correct capacity and other resource-related information to the planners, for what the planners (in their macro wisdom) wish to maximize may not be (and most often is not) in the maximizing micro interest of the enterprises.

In practice, therefore, despite the enormous advances of mathematical planning techniques and the increase in computational facilities, the Soviet economy continues to operate at conspicuously suboptimal levels. Indeed, because of the increasing complexity of economic relationships, the waste may conceivably be greater than in the rough and simple days of the Stalinplan.

Financial Coordination

Financial coordination of the physical plan has several dimensions. We will briefly examine two of them: monetary control over the plan carried out by the state banking system, and fiscal control exercised through the state budget (*gosbiudzhet*). Prices as subsidiary coordinating devices have been discussed earlier under the section on information.

Banking. Formal control over money flows in the plan is exercised by the state banking system. Basically, the system consists of the State Bank (*Gosbank*), the Construction Bank (*Stroibank*), and the Foreign Trade Bank (*Vneshtorgbank*).

The State Bank (equipped with thirty-five hundred branches) has six major functions: (1) the fulfillment of those of a central bank (the issuing of legal tender, maintaining of gold reserves, and making of international payments [the latter through a special branch]); (2) the administration of tax receipts and current state expenditures (that is, payments of turnover, profit, and other taxes and payments out of the state budget account with the bank); (3) the execution of monetary control over plan fulfillment; (4) the issuance of short-term (thirty- to ninety-day) credit to enterprises; (5) the extension of certain long-term investment credits to enterprises; (6) the acceptance of savings deposits from individuals through a network of some seventy-five thousand savings banks (*sberkassy*).

The State Bank's monetary control functions over the plan are made possible by the fact that all state enterprises and organizations are required to keep accounts with the bank and to transact all business (including wage and salary payments) through those accounts, that is, by book transfers in the bank ("control by the ruble"). These bank balances cannot be converted into freely spendable cash.

The State Bank provides short-term credit to state enterprises over and above the working capital they receive from the state ("charter fund") and charges a flat rate of interest (about 2 percent) on it. All such loan requests must be approved by the *Gosplan* as part of quarterly plans. They are usually extended for inventory purposes, seasonal variations, and to smooth out cash flow problems. Resort to short-term bank credit is necessary because the free charter funds are, as a rule, not sufficient to take care of the enterprises' maximum needs. The State Bank also extends building credits to both construction co-operatives formed by groups and some few private contractors; it also extends some long-term credit to state enterprises and collective farms (for which a slightly higher interest rate is charged).

The State Bank's monetary policy functions are minor compared with those of a central bank in a market economy. Monetary policy, conceived primarily as the establishment of a financial macrobalance for the economy and all its subunits (to correspond with physical output and input decisions), is decided elsewhere: within the central planning network, including prominently the Ministry of Finance. Since there are no financial markets in the USSR and no government bond market, it is not the State Bank's function to manipulate the flow of credit through an interest-rate policy (credit flows are determined by the plan). As noted, the interest charged by the bank on its short- and long-term loans is, in effect, a flat-rate tax. The bank's function is not to make monetary policy, but to manage and monitor that policy as made by the plan.

The State Bank's resources come from state budgetary surpluses, budgetary grants, and enterprise deposits. Its savings offices are the only banking facilities directly available to citizens. The interest rate paid on individual savings accounts is typically around 3 percent. The interest earned can be converted into a lottery that pays winners up to double the amount of their converted savings. Special deposit accounts for the purchase of apartments by individual families are also available. The State Bank's savings offices collect personal income and other direct taxes on the population, housing rents, and payments for utilities.

The Construction Bank is charged with channeling investment funds from the state budget to state enterprises, and with supervising all investment expenditures in accordance with the state investment plan.

The Soviet neoclassical adjustments of 1965 (also known as the "Kosygin reforms") envisioned a much-enlarged credit disbursement, and more generally, plan coordination function for the state banking system. Although bank credit became available, it could not be used by firms for decentralized investment because the needed inputs for such investment could not be bought by the firms from the material-technical supply network (*Gossnab*); that is, the inputs were all committed to the plan beforehand, by physical decisions. (Hence the enterprise managers' complaint: "We have the money, but there is nothing to buy with it.") Additionally, in the spirit of the 1965 adjustments, the banking system was to take over a rising portion of state centralized investment that was formerly carried out almost exclusively through nonreturnable, interest-free state budgetary grants to state sector enterprises. This, too, did not come to pass. At the present time (1985), the share of bank credits in total Soviet centralized state investment is not much more than 3 percent. The collapse of the intent to increase the role of credit and the banking system in the Soviet neoclassical conservative plan thus seems to be directly related to the failure to marketize investments, or at least, the failure to partially "commercialize" the apparatus of central material-technical input supply allocations.

The outline of formally planned bank activities should not distract attention from the fact that in actual practice, both the State Bank and the Construction Bank do pay out more money every year than planned. Together with inflated ministry- and enterprise-set (one-time, temporary, new-product) prices, the banking system has been and remains a contributor to the Soviet system's suppressed inflation.

The Foreign Trade Bank receives and disburses foreign exchange, monitors foreign transactions, keeps the Soviet gold stock, and manages the USSR's foreign currency reserves. The ruble is nonconvertible, which means that (a) it is not used for purchases abroad (the dollar, other convertible currencies, and gold are used for this purpose), and (b) ruble bank deposits and cash balances of state enterprises, cooperatives, and individuals have no external purchasing power (that is, Soviet firms and individuals are insulated from foreign markets).[19]

State Budget. Almost half the gross national product of the USSR is allocated to consumption, investment, defense, and administration through the consolidated state budget of the central government, republican governments, and local governments. (This compares with about 20 percent in the United States.) State sector enterprises and agencies receive the greater part of their capital from the state budget. Nonbudgetary sources of finance include enterprise retained profits, leftover amortization funds, and bank credits. About half the consolidated state budget is administered by republican and local governments in broad conformity with the all-union government's instructions. These governments have their own revenues derived from *kolkhoz* and cooperative taxes, from about half the income tax, and from most of the state's share of enterprise profits. The budget is usually published in December of each year.

The two sources of state budgetary revenues are the social sector (state and collective) and the private sector. Revenues from the social sector include the turnover tax, deductions from enterprise profits, social security receipts, income taxes on organizations (primarily on collective farms), customs duties, and miscellaneous taxes. Revenues from the private sector are derived from income tax on population, state bonds bought by the population, money-goods lotteries, and a few other relatively minor sources.

Since the 1930s, revenues from the social sector have regularly accounted for some 90 percent of total state budgetary income. About 60–70 percent of total income was attributable to receipts from the turnover and enterprise profits taxes.

Budgetary expenditures may be grouped under six headings: (1) the financing of the national economy (capital investment, planned increases in working capital, subsidies for planned losses of enterprises and organizations); (2) social-cultural projects; (3) defense; (4) central, provincial (republican), and local administration; (5) loan service to the population (payment of interest and repayment of principal on the national debt); and (6) other expenditures, which include some parts of a special vote for the KGB, allocations to investment banks to increase their resources, emergency reserve funds, rebates to retail trade connected with changes in prices (accounts for price regulation), price subsidies to agriculture, geological prospecting (since the 1965 reform, much of this is charged to enterprises), and state gold purchases. Financing the national economy typically accounts for more than 40 percent of total annual budgetary expenditures. Social-cultural outlays usually represent 40–50 percent of all budgetary outlays. About 90 percent of the cost of education, health, physical culture, social insurance, and social security is financed out of the state budget, the remainder from a portion of enterprise-retained profits, collective farms' cultural funds, and trade union funds. About half the total amount spent on industry and construction comes from the state budget; the other half comes from a portion of enterprise-retained profits, amortization funds of enterprises, and bank credits. The state budget also finances roughly half the total amount spent on state farms and agricultural produce procurement organizations. A simplified consolidated state budget for selected years is given in Table 8.2.

Taxes in the Soviet system perform two main functions: they furnish revenue to the state (this revenue being eventually expended in accordance with the state's preferences), and they are instrumental in achieving a financial macro and micro balance.[20]

The main taxes on the social sector are the turnover tax, enterprise profits tax, income taxes on organizations (especially on collective farms), social security tax, and miscellaneous taxes. The main taxes on the population (private sector in budgetary terms) have been the personal income tax, state bonds (nominally voluntary, but in past practice,

TABLE 8.2
USSR: CONSOLIDATED STATE BUDGET, SELECTED YEARS
(percent of total)

Revenue						
	1937	*1940*	*1950*	*1960*	*1970*	*1978*
Social sector						
Turnover tax	69	59	56	41	32	32
Deductions from enterprise profits and income tax on organizations (collectives)	9	12	10	24	35	30
Social insurance receipts	6	5	5	5	5	5
Miscellaneous[a]	12	19	20	23	20	25
Private sector						
Taxes on population, state loans, and miscellaneous	4	5	9	7	8	8
Total revenue	100	100	100	100	100	100

Expenditure						
	1937	*1940*	*1950*	*1960*	*1970*	*1978*
Financing the national economy[b]	41	33	38	47	48	54
Social-cultural expenditure	24	24	28	34	36	34
Defense	17	33	20	13	12	7
Administration and justice	4	4	3	2	1	1
Loan service and miscellaneous[a]	14	6	11	4	3	4
Total expenditure	100	100	100	100	100	100
Budgetary surplus/deficit						

SOURCES: Calculated from Soviet statistical manuals for various years and Bergson, *Economics of Soviet Planning*, p. 362.
[a]Miscellaneous total (both sectors).
[b]Main components: industry and construction; agriculture; procurement and forestry; domestic and foreign trade; transport and communications; municipal economy and housing.

compulsory), inheritance tax, agricultural tax paid by collective farmers on income derived from private plots, and miscellaneous taxes.

The *turnover tax*, introduced in 1930, has played an important role throughout the Soviet plan experience, both as a supplier of revenue for the state and as a means of financial macro and micro balancing. At its peak in 1937, the turnover tax contributed just under 70 percent of the state's budgetary revenues. By 1980, its share was one-third. The decline in the relative contribution of the tax to state budgetary revenues in the 1950s, 1960s, and 1970s may be attributed to the fact that bigger payments to farmers for larger supplies of food were not compensated for by proportionate increases in the retail food prices.

With some exceptions, the tax is applied to consumer goods and to materials used in making consumer goods. The tax has two aspects: regarding some commodities (matches, tobacco, salt, alcoholic beverages), it is principally an excise tax imposed as a lump sum per commodity unit; regarding other goods (for example, textiles, clothing, bread, sugar, consumer durables), it is primarily a "gap tax."[21] In the latter case, prices of individual goods are set so as to clear the shelves (see Grossman's Quadrant III, Figure 2.1).

For accounting purposes, the tax paid by consumers to the sellers is not part of the sellers' revenue. Sellers must periodically (every few days) remit to the Ministry of Finance ruble amounts equal to their planned turnover tax receipts.

The turnover tax was at all times a major constituent of consumer retail prices, because the quantity of consumer goods the state decided to produce lagged behind consumer disposable money incomes.

In the late 1960s and 1970s, about 60 percent of centrally planned enterprise profits were paid into the state budget through the *enterprise profits tax*. The remainder was retained by enterprises and used for "decentralized" capital investment (under ministerial guidance), for increases in working capital and to cover planned losses, and for improvement of enterprise housing and payment of cash bonuses and premia to managerial and technical staffs. Enterprise managements are required to transmit an amount equal to the nonretainable share of their planned profits to the Ministry of Finance every month. When, as sometimes happens, profits actually earned run below planned profits during any part of the planning period, the enterprise will find itself short of cash. Before the 1965 adjustments, about 20 percent of enterprise overplan profits had to be surrendered to the state. The balance could be used for bonuses and premia, enterprise housing, and other specified purposes. After the adjustment, practically all overplan profits went to the state treasury, but a larger share than previously of planned profits actually earned could be used by the enterprises for decentralized investment, bonuses, and social-cultural projects.

Income taxes on organizations include, as their most important component, the tax on collective farm income (discussed earlier). In 1965, the *kolkhoz* income tax base was changed from gross to net income, and the incidence of the tax on the poorer farms was reduced.

The *social security tax* is calculated as a fixed percentage of enterprise wages fund.

Miscellaneous taxes on the social sector included, at various times, local taxes on construction, local transport, livestock, and *kolkhoz* markets; a ground rent tax (abolished in 1959) applied to land occupied by state enterprises; stamp duties; automobile registration fees; and a tax on timber cutting. Until 1958, miscellaneous revenue from the social sector also included machine tractor stations revenue.

The most important tax on the population—but still of relatively small importance for the state budget (of which it has comprised 5–8 percent over the years)—is the mildly progressive *personal income tax,* applied to all money incomes of individuals with the exception of those of collective farmers derived from work in the collective. The tax depends partly on the level of money earnings, partly on the origin of the earnings. Thus, lower rates are applied to income from work in the social sector than to the same level of income derived from similar private activities. In 1970, the maximum rate was 13 percent (more than three times as high for the same income derived from private activity).

State bonds, or nominally voluntary mass subscription loans, were common in the 1930s and 1940s. Because citizens really had no choice in the matter and refusal to buy bonds was interpreted as a symptom of treasonable propensities, the bonds were, in fact, a form of direct tax. Their economic function was to help absorb excess money purchasing power in the hands of the population, this excess having arisen from the unwillingness of the state to produce enough consumer goods. In the period from 1952 to 1954, the volume of these forced loans was cut in half. In 1958, the practice of bonding the people without their consent was stopped. Bonds that had formerly been sold to individual citizens on a genuinely voluntary basis were not to be defaulted on. Such sales were continued in subsequent years.

Bequests and inheritance of private assets are legal in the Soviet Union, subject to a relatively small *inheritance tax.* Exempt from the tax are funds deposited in state savings banks, state bonds, personal insurance benefits, copyright earnings, and authors' fees.

Collective farmers and (with some exceptions) state employees are required to pay an *agricultural tax* on income earned from activity on their household allotments. Before 1958, they were also assessed for compulsory deliveries to the state of produce from the plots. The agricultural tax is based on the state's assessment of the livestock owned and area sown. The state's policy toward private allotments varied considerably over time. In the last years of Khrushchev's tenure of power, the policy became unusually harsh and restrictive. Extra taxes were imposed on the plots, rights to collective pastures and supplies of hay were narrowed down, stringent limits were imposed on the size of plots and number of privately owned livestock, and numerous restrictions were placed on trade in *kolkhoz* markets (including the fixing of prices by administrative order). Most of these measures were removed after 1964.

Miscellaneous taxes on the private sector included, at various times, a "bachelor tax" on single persons and on couples with no children or up to two children. The tax was removed in 1958 except on single men and couples with no children. Even in these cases, however, low incomes were exempt. In the 1930s and 1940s, a number of fines were levied on private enterprises and other allegedly antisocial elements—for example, on workers who were late for work or came to work drunk. In the 1930s, a cultural and housing tax (in addition to the income tax) was levied on personal incomes. Miscellaneous taxes also included passport fees, an entertainment tax, private passenger automobile registration fees, and (from 1941 to 1945) a war tax based on income.

Motivation

Industrial Wage Structure and Determination

In Chapter 7, we had occasion to examine both the motivational system as it operated in the Stalinplan's collective farm sector and the changes made in that system after Stalin's death. Here we will concern ourselves with the wage structure and wage determination process in Soviet industry under the Stalinplan and in the neoclassical conservative plan. The subject is of more than parochial interest because all state socialist countries have adopted the Soviet practice (albeit with local adaptations). They have followed the Soviet example during the Stalinplan and imitated the post-Stalin adjustments of the Soviet industrial wage system. As noted in Chapter 3, in all state socialist economies, both during the Stalinplan and under the neoclassical plan (conservative and liberal), the wage-fixing function is monopolized by the state at a high level of the planning hierarchy—at the level of a Council of Ministers' commission, with the party's highest organs (for example, the Politburo) taking an active interest and having a decisive say in formulating the basic principles of wage determination.[22]

Plan and Market. Under the Stalinplan and its successor, the Soviet industrial wage has had to take into account market forces. In the absence of complete administrative allocation of labor, the wage belongs to Grossman's Quadrant II (see Figure 2.1). It is a price of labor services set by the state to equate individualized (private) labor supply (S) with plan-determined demand (D). Because of administrative-police restrictions (through internal passports, labor books, residence permits) on the mobility of people as citizens and workers, the "market" for labor is quite imperfect, but it is present (both in the Stalinplan and neoclassical plan), and must be taken into account by the planners when determining wage levels and differentials.[23] The individualized (private) labor supply is especially important in the short run. Over the longer run, the state can influence it through educational policies. One difference between the Stalinplan and its neoclassical successor is that under the former, the labor market is more imperfect than under the latter. For one thing, in the Stalinplan, a significantly larger proportion of labor is allocated by administrative means—through the forced labor camp system (*gulag*). Between 1940 and 1956, in addition to restrictions in the forms of passports, labor books, and residence permits, individual workers were prohibited by law from leaving their jobs. (In a setting of severe labor shortages, supply and demand soon reasserted themselves: labor books were "lost" during the war, and authorities looked the other way when workers changed their jobs as state firms, anxious to fulfill their plans, manipulated the wage system in a number of informal ways [which we will be examining].) Still, the Stalinplan was more willing than its successor to accept the distortions and anomalies that developed over time as a consequence of ignoring the underlying changes in the real cost of and demand for labor. An important aspect of the "economic" nature of the post-Stalin changes (using "economic levers") was that the existence of market forces (no matter how poorly competitive or hampered in their operation by layers of bureaucracy) was conceptually recognized and taken account of in the formulation of the state's wage policy.

Although wage determination in the USSR was (and remains) an exercise in Quadrant II price-setting (adapting private S to state-determined D)—that is, fixing wage levels and relativities in such a way that labor will move in the right quantity and skill composition into the right employments and locations ("right" being synonymous with planners' preferences)—the fact that the state is not a monolithic lump also plays a part on the side of state-determined demand. State firms working within a very taut plan will bid for labor among themselves. Since they cannot compete through price (determining wage rates is not within their competence), they do it in other, mcre round-about ways. The point is that state firms will manipulate the wage structure at their level and, therefore, that the labor "market" exerts an influence on state wage policy not only on the supply side (through individualized labor supply) but also on the side of state demand (through the "individualization" of the state at the firm level—each firm, in its concern with plan fulfillment, being a micro state in its right). The firms will be able to carry on in this way because they have information at their level the planners do not; because they can find ways of keeping that information to themselves; and because the rules set by the planners governing wage determination are broad enough (and enough crevices exist) for local adaptation of the plan to the labor market realities to take place (though at the cost of distortions elsewhere in the system).

Under the Stalinplan (from 1933 through the mid-1950s), no general restructuring of work grades, wage rates, and wage relativities took place. Adjustments of relative wages were made here and there, and some general increases were decreed in order to keep up with rising prices of derationed basic necessities. Since the mid-1950s, much more attention has been paid to the wage system. There has been concern with eliminating the drift between basic wage rates as set by the state and actual earnings (take-home pay) through "spontaneous" enterprise level adjustments of the wage rate to labor market realities as perceived by enterprise managers. In other words, while keeping a grip on the labor market through administrative regulations of labor mobility and central wage controls, the new regulations and controls at least try not to ignore the market to the extent that the Stalinplan did.

The Stalinplan used sharp money wage differentials to encourage mobility of "free" (non-*gulag*) labor in consonance with the sectoral and other priorities of the planners. The best wages were in the top-priority sectors and subsectors of the economy—heavy industry. Wages in light industry were lower. In consumer services, they were lower still. They were lowest of all in state agriculture (not to mention the residual earnings of the collective peasants). In wage terms, high skill was prized; low skill despised. Nove shows that in the 1930s wage differentials between workers ranged up to 1:4.4, while if "auxiliary" workers (janitors, cleaners, and so on) were included, the differential would have been 1:12.[24]

The general principle of unequal money compensation—the inequality being in (rough) accordance with the planners' intersectoral and intrasectoral priorities—has been accepted by the neoclassical conservative plan. In fact, the current wage structure in industry and trade suggests that planners' preferences between heavy industry, light industry, trade, and agriculture have not undergone any dramatic change. Heavy industry still comes first, and this is reflected in wage levels for that subsector being higher than elsewhere. However, subsectoral and sectoral wage differentials have been narrowed. The same has been true of wage spreads between lower- and higher-skilled workers, and between workers and engineering-technical personnel earnings. Thus, though the general principle of using money wages to direct labor into occupations, skills, and locations desired by the party planners (and supported by the educational system over the long run) remains the same, a considerable narrowing (as compared with the Stalinplan) of basic wage differentials has occurred. This primarily appears to have benefited the lower-paid workers. A minimum wage was introduced in 1956 and has risen steadily since.

The Stalinist "law" of rational low wages has been done away with. It articulated the planners' strong preference for investment over consumption and, under the circumstances of the time, was enforced by means of the turnover tax applied to most consumer goods (food included). Although the post-Stalin planners still prefer investment to consumption, these days they are of the opinion (a) that this preference can be taken care of by taxing the profits of state firms rather than taxing basic foods (in fact, some basic consumer items now carry a negative turnover tax); and (b) that a continuation of consumer goods neglect à la Stalinplan is motivationally self-defeating. Soviet consumers complain that now they have the money, but there is not much they can buy with it—at least not much they want. In other words, (b) has meant a shift toward consumer free choice, but not toward consumer sovereignty (that is, a situation in which consumer demand determines the volume and pattern of production). The planners still dictate the volume and assortment of consumer goods, although (as we have seen) they listen somewhat more attentively to the chirps coming from the cage.

The Soviet neoclassical plan's consumer goods pricing policy suggests that the planners are interested in having real income inequality be smaller than the inequality of money incomes. Goods considered by the planners to be necessities (for example, basic foods such as bread and, these days, meat) or to be socially desirable (for example, children's apparel) are priced low at retail—often below production cost; planner-designated luxuries (for example, automobiles) and socially undesirable goods (vodka), on the other hand, carry high turnover taxes. At the highest levels of the hierarchy (the top 1–2 percent of the population), all this has little effect, since the most desirable goods are available only at special party stores not open to the general public, and are sold to the topmost elite at, reportedly, very reasonable prices.[25] In the special shops, consumer sovereignty comes alive.

The Mechanism of Wage Control and Evasion. The planned wage has three main components: basic (or tariff) wage, bonus wage, and social wage.

The basic wage takes into account the principle of unequal money compensation (differential material incentives) described in doctrinal terms as the socialist principle of "from each according to his ability, to each according to his work."[26] Both ability and work contribution are defined by the state in line with its preferences, modified these days by what the planners make of consumer rumblings. The bonus wage is also determined by reference to the principle of unequal money compensation and is linked to state-determined indicators. For example, under the neoclassical conservative plan, for managers the bonus is linked to enterprise profits, profitability, sales, labor productivity indices, and the like, rather than (only) to the gross value of output (*val*) used in the Stalinplan.

Central planners' control over basic wage rates is greater than over the bonus wage. This is so because it is impossible for the planners to know what the fulfillment, overfulfillment, or underfulfillment of each and every norm is at the enterprise-production association level, and hence what exactly goes on with actual bonus payments (especially where piece-rate norms are involved). Planners can (and do) try to increase compliance by decreeing maximum bonus payments defined as a percentage of the basic wage and by controlling the total (basic and bonus) wages fund; despite this, however, bonus schemes give managements greater opportunity for independent maneuver than does the schedule of basic wages. As we will see, managements tend to "correct" the planners' bonus scheme according to their own interpretation of the labor supply and demand pressures within their own particular cages.

The payment of the social wage (social benefits of all kinds) is made in accordance with need, as perceived by the planners, rather than in accordance with work.

Basic wages in the Soviet Union are determined at the level of the Council of Ministers, specifically, by the State Committee for Labor and Wages, assisted by the *Gosplan* and the All-Union Central Council of Trade Unions.

Each ministry is informed of the size of the wages fund allocated to it for a given planning year. This size will depend on both the previous year's situation and on the planners' estimates for the following year for such items as increases in labor productivity, changes in the size of the labor force and in its age and skill composition, the availability of consumer goods, the absolute level of consumer goods prices, the savings ratio of the population, tax receipts, and the structure of relative consumer goods prices. This is no easy job. Each ministry then divides up its share of the wages fund among its various subordinate enterprises and deposits the appropriate shares in the enterprises' (production associations') accounts at the State Bank (*Gosbank*).

For any given enterprise, there is a system of job grades for production workers (see Table 8.3). Separate schedules exist for managerial and engineering-technical personnel. The production workers' grades normally (but not invariably) range from grade one (lowest-skilled worker) to grade six (highest-skilled worker, roughly equivalent to foreman). The number of job grades and their spread in wage terms has decreased since the Stalinplan. The requirements for each occupational classification are defined by the planners in tariff and qualifications manuals. There is a general manual that applies to interbranch (interministerial) occupations (such as bricklaying and truck driving), and there are tariff manuals concerned with jobs specific to given industrial branches. The general manual covers 60–70 percent of all industrial jobs.

The tariff and qualifications manuals include: (a) description of the type of work involved under the job grade; (b) examples of the work; and (c) skill and knowledge qualifications, including formal educational requirements. Job grades have work coefficients (*setki*) attached to them. The coefficient attaching to labor grade one is always 1 (the base coefficient). Under the Stalinplan there were about 1,900 different coefficient schedules. After 1975, this number was reduced to 3. Coefficients attaching to higher job grades are multiples of the base coefficient. Job grade one has a ruble wage (base wage rate, or *stavka*) attached to it. Under the Stalinplan there were 1,000 different base wages. After 1975 this number was reduced to 17. In the USSR since 1965, the *stavka* has been predominantly a time-based wage. The wage rates for higher labor grades are the wage for labor grade one multiplied by the appropriate coefficient (that is, the coefficient attaching to each successive labor grade [see Table 8.3]). Fulfillment of 100 percent of the norm for a given job grade would earn the wage rate attaching to that grade. Where piecework is used (in approximately one-quarter of the labor force under the neoclassical conservative plan in the USSR), the hourly wage in rubles is tied to a physical output norm. The rate is then payable if, for example, in one hour the worker produces y units of the product conforming to specified quality standards. Shifts in the

TABLE 8.3

USSR: REPRESENTATIVE MODEL WAGE SCALE APPLICABLE TO
PIECEWORKERS IN AN INDUSTRIAL ENTERPRISE UNDER NORMAL
WORKING CONDITIONS

Labor Grade	1	2	3	4	5	6
Coefficient (setka)	1.00	1.2	1.3	1.5	1.7	2.0
Wage rate (stavka) (hourly rate in rubles)	0.30	0.36	0.39	0.45	0.51	0.60

labor force desired by the planners can be achieved by altering the basic wage in this or that branch. The acquisition and distribution of skills desired by the planners can be achieved by altering the job coefficients (setki).

Basic wages corresponding to the job grades are adjusted, by means of a regional system of coefficients and supplements, to take account of adverse climatic or locational conditions. Their comparative levels also reflect, as we have seen, planners' inter- and intraindustry priorities. Adjustments are also made for dangerous or unpleasant work.

Managerial and technical personnel basic salary schedules are published in separate manuals, and are usually expressed in ranges at monthly rates of pay.

A copy of the enterprises' planned wages and salary fund is deposited with the State Bank. The bank will release payments from the fund only in accordance with the plan. Such approval will normally be given only if it conforms to centrally defined procedures for payment of basic wages-salaries and bonuses for plan overfulfillment, or if it can be proved to be justified by extraordinary circumstances. This is an important component of "control by the ruble."

Bonus wages and premia of all kinds are interlaced with the system of basic wages and salaries. Bonuses and premia may be awarded to individual workers for overfulfillment of the production plan, cost reductions, economical use of raw materials, high-quality performance, and so on. They may also be given to teams of workers, shops, enterprises, or other collectives.

These days central regulations stipulate that bonuses must not exceed 20–30 percent of basic wages and salaries. This proportion is about half of what it was under the Stalinplan when piece-rate payments to workers were more important. In principle, bonuses to production workers (paid out of the wages fund) are not counted as part of the "prime cost of production" (*sebestoimost'*; see above section, "Prices"). The reasoning behind this is that the extra cost involved is offset by economies on overheads, which may not always be the case.

Evasion of wage control by enterprise managements (or whatever the basic production unit) has typically taken two forms. The enterprise has manipulated norms of output and time, and it has reclassified its workers among job categories. To recapitulate, both manipulation of norms and reclassification of workers were done in line with the enterprise management's reading of signals emanating in the labor market, with its interpretation of supply responses by workers to wage levels and differentials, and with its understanding of the competing demand for labor of other enterprises.

Manipulation of output norms usually took the form of filtering only such information to the planners as would induce the planning center to set norms that could easily be overfulfilled by most workers in the firm (the "soft plan"). Once such overfulfillment took place, the enterprise could switch to bonus payments, over which central control was (and remains) less stringent than control over basic pay. The successful pursuit of this strategy has resulted in wide differences between what a job was supposed to pay (tariff rate) and what it actually paid (tariff plus bonus). With increased resort to time-based wages (where bonus-tampering is more difficult than with piece rates), this wage drift has been slowed down, but not halted.

Manipulation of job grades usually took the form of inflated enterprise estimates of the number of workers needed in the higher, better-paid grades. Workers whose skills were applicable to lower grades were classified in higher grades by enterprise managements. (In fact, low-paid clerks were sometimes reclassified in higher-paid production workers' grades.) Without such deception, the enterprise might well have found itself unable to recruit scarce manpower—and therefore unable to overfulfill the plan and obtain the bonuses. When the authorities finally began revising the wage structure after 1955, they found that there were no workers in the unskilled and low-skill categories in the USSR.

In spite of the strict regulations governing payments out of the wages fund, enterprises found it possible to persuade their supervisory ministries to intervene on their behalf with higher authorities in order to authorize supplementary wage payments (not originally planned) in the course of plan execution. This was (and still is) happening because the ministry has a stake in its enterprises' fulfilling and overfulfilling the plan, and understands that without friendly assistance, some enterprises might find it difficult to finish their plan. This situation added to the upward pressure on wage costs.

After 1965, the enterprise manager (or production association head) theoretically no longer needed to obtain approval of his ministry to redistribute his work force and total wages fund among job categories. In practice, however, ministries have continued to exercise their former rights in this regard.

In general, the Soviet neoclassical conservative plan does not extend managerial decision-making rights to the enterprise labor force. Ministerial and other higher-level supervisory and planning authorities continue to keep a tight grip over the wages fund and its distribution, as well as somewhat looser controls over bonuses and premia. The right to hire and fire does not belong to the enterprise manager.

The *social wage* is the third component of the workers' and managers' total income packet. It consists of cash benefits and free or subsidized services in the areas of health, education, housing, vacations, and general welfare; it represents roughly one-quarter of the total wage-salary. Under the neoclassical conservative plan in the USSR, the state social wage covers more workers (for example, collective farmers) and benefits are better than in the past. State-controlled trade unions marginally increase their role in managing these benefits on behalf of the state. The unions' "transmission belt" function (that is, transmitting planners' commands from the planners to the workers) becomes more positive: social benefit inducements are resorted to in preference to criminal or civil law punishments. There is, however, no evolution of trade unions toward more autonomy vis-à-vis the state.

Three other wage-like elements should be mentioned. The first consists of fringe benefits accruing to higher-grade officials of the party and state—the "privilegentsia." These include chauffeured limousines, choicer vacation spots, and, above all, access to goods unavailable to others. Such benefits are not easily quantified. Even less quantifiable is the political power-income (clout) that goes with one's location on the *nomenklatura* list. Political power-income differentials in all socialist single-party economies are very wide. In the words of the London *Economist,* in the USSR and other communist countries "there are two measures of real power—high party office and personal patronage, or a tail in the party: the string of cronies [an official] can promote to key jobs."[27] Finally, there is income derived from the underground economy. Moonlighting and exchange of goods and services in the second economy represent a sizable appropriation by individuals, both of time paid for by the state and of state property.

The preceding review of Soviet wage structure and determination reveals a great deal about disposable money income. It does not, however, indicate much about the incentive effects of that money income on labor productivity and on the quality of workmanship. Unfortunately, under the neoclassical conservative plan in the USSR, consumer goods shortages persist, as does the divergence of available goods assortments from (presumed) consumer preferences ("presumed" because consumer preferences still have no institutional way of declaring themselves or affecting the volume and pattern of production). Not much improvement has been made in the quality of consumer goods; shoddiness remains the rule. The imbalance between disposable money income and the supply of quality goods desired by consumers is a major structural flaw of the neoclassical plan, as it was of the Stalinplan. Between 1976 and 1980, wages and salaries in the USSR increased by 28 percent, consumer goods production by 21 percent, and retail trade turnover by 22 percent. Over this period, personal savings ("deferred demand," or *otlozhennyi spros*) rose from 91 to 156 billion rubles. In the meantime, extractive and primary industries absorbed 50 percent of the gross social product, 40 percent of all fixed capital and labor, and almost 30 percent of all capital investment.[28]

Administrative Controls over Labor

Although manipulation of wage levels and differentials is the principal means used today to equate the supply of labor with planner demand for labor, other nonmarket means are also employed. The long-run structure of labor supply is importantly influenced by the government's educational policy. Communist Party members are obliged to serve where the party decides, although there is considerable concealed traffic and influence-peddling in this regard. Members of the Communist Youth Organization (*Komsomol*) are supposed to respond to the organization's employment instructions, especially when it comes to going north or helping with the harvest. Under the Stalinplan, massive transfers of collective farm labor to industry were carried out (frequently on a compulsory quota basis) by the Administration of Organized Labor Recruitment (*Orgnabor*). Graduates of secondary and vocational schools are often placed in local enterprises by local authorities. College and university graduates are obliged to work for three years in jobs assigned to them by the authorities; this measure is justified as repayment of the scholarships granted to the students throughout their college careers. There are also many administrative controls over labor mobility, some of which were mentioned earlier (the internal passport, residence permits, de facto rationing of housing, and so on).

Nomenklatura controls over choice appointments have also been discussed. The appointments are not only choice—they are key. Hence, a strategically important segment of the total employment picture escapes even the modest marketization of Grossman's Quadrant II (see Figure 2.1). Last but not least, there is concentration camp labor—down from its peak of 7–15 million prisoners during and immediately after World War II, but still significant.

Managerial Motivation:
Economic Stimulation Funds at the Enterprise Level

The Soviet neoclassical plan adjustment of the 1960s, which in its broad operational principles applies to this day (with only rather minor technical revisions), brought into being three types of enterprise "economic stimulation funds": material incentives funds, production development funds, and funds for social-cultural measures and housing construction. The revenue for these funds was to come from retained planned profits, amortization deductions, proceeds from the sale of surplus equipment (the latter two applicable only to the production development funds), and a few other minor sources.

The norms for forming enterprise stimulation funds were centrally determined and ministry-administered, while the norms for payments out of the funds were usually set by ministries on the basis of centrally determined guidelines. The system of norms (or coefficients) was very complex: in 1968, for example, there were more than thirty distinct systems for forming the material incentive funds alone.

The objective of an enterprise's material incentives fund was to rationalize incentives to managers, technicians, and office personnel by tying bonuses to the enterprise's profit and sales performance, and later (as we have seen), to other indicators as well. Retained planned profits were to be by far the most important source from which material incentives fund monies were to be drawn. Bonuses paid to managers, technical personnel, and office workers were paid from the material incentives fund. The bulk of production workers' bonuses was still paid (as in the past) out of the enterprise wages fund. The basic condition for payments of bonuses out of the material incentives fund was fulfillment of the volume (and, later, assortment) of output indicators. Since these indicators were still formulated centrally on the basis of administrative rather than economic criteria, this provision tended to restrict the intended economic effectiveness of material incentives fund payments.

Payments into the material incentives fund were made according to rather complex formulae that brought together an enterprise's profit (or sales) and profitability performance. Profitability was calculated as a percentage of fixed and working capital. Thus, assuming the fulfillment of volume and assortment of output targets, the manager would try to maximize his profits or sales as compared with the previous period; he would then use a formula to translate the percentage increases in profits (or sales) and profitability norms into money amounts to be paid into the material incentives fund.

The idea of tying managerial bonuses to profits, sales, and profitability was rational and clever in the abstract. If properly used, it could have promoted the neoclassical plan's intent to make greater reference to market-related multidimensional information on enterprise performance (to the "law of value") instead of using unidimensional physical indicators. In practice, the problem was that profits and sales were (and are) expressed in planned average, cost-plus, centrally determined prices, not in market-generated, opportunity cost prices, and that in addition to attempting to maximize his material incentives fund by fulfilling his profit (or sales) and profitability plan, the manager had to strive to carry out the volume and assortment plan using many administratively rationed (funded) commodities. The "economic" solution was, in fact, dependent on prior administrative decisions, and the two did not always (or even usually) mesh. Even more significant is that payments out of the material incentives fund were (in practice) not made in accordance with the monies available in the fund, but in response to ad hoc administrative suggestions, instructions, persuasions, and pressures of other sorts from above. These administrative inducements always ultimately prevailed. They were an amalgam of what the planners wanted done and the interpretation put on that desire by ministries, chief administrations, and other bodies in pursuit of their own interests.

The objective of the production development funds was to give enterprises the right to make certain investment decisions outside the central plan—to reduce investment tutelage. The revenues for the funds were drawn from amortization deductions (the depreciation fund), from some retained profits, and from sales of surplus plants and equipment. Amortization deductions in the Stalinplan were paid into a central fund. Under the neoclassical conservative plan, enterprises were allowed to transfer to their production development funds from 30 to 50 percent of such deductions.[29] Norms for forming production development funds were set centrally and supervised by ministries. With regard to money transfers from retained planned profits, the rules were broadly similar to those governing the material incentives funds. Had the production development funds been used in the way outlined, they would indeed have represented a move toward the decentralization of decision making. Evidence suggests, however, that, at least in the USSR, (a) production development fund investment tended to be a small part of total industrial investment; (b) disbursements from the production development funds did not use all the monies available in the funds; (c) most payments out of the funds were made for capital repairs. The obstacles to enterprise-sponsored investment seemed to be the shortage of raw materials and other investment inputs outside the state plan, and the unwillingness of local construction organizations to tie themselves up in decentralized investment work while their hands were already full meeting the state investment plan's assignments. It is not surprising, therefore, that Soviet enterprise managers were easily persuaded by their ministries to switch production development fund monies to centralized investment projects. In addition, the *Gosplan* and the state committee in charge of distributing funded commodities apparently raised all sorts of objections in the course of confirming projects to be financed from the production development funds. Under the neoclassical conservative plan, despite talk of decentralization and trust, there is still great reluctance to give enterprise managements real decision-making power over the future of the economy (over investment), and in the context of strained central plans (and consequently input shortages), decentralized investment is regarded as an annoying whim that must be restrained.

The criteria for deductions from retained planned enterprise profits into the funds for social-cultural measures and housing construction were broadly similar to those governing deductions from the material incentive funds. As with the other funds, actual deductions from the former lagged behind the monies available for disbursement, and for very much the same reasons.

Adjustment in the Traditional Wages Fund

In 1983, during the brief regency of Iurii Andropov, a new method of allocating wages funds to enterprises was tried. Its aim was to strengthen managerial motivation to seek labor productivity improvements and encourage workers to do the same. The traditional method of allocating a wages fund to an enterprise was to calculate the fund each year by multiplying the average wage by the planned employment. Thus, if the planned employment is 1,000 workers for the year 1985 (first year of the five-year plan) and the average wage is 1,100 rubles a year, the wages fund "confirmed" by the ministry for the enterprise will be 1.1 million rubles.[30] Suppose the enterprise in 1986 exceeds the output plan by 10 percent through increasing labor productivity, that is, raising output 10 percent with an unchanged labor force. The result under the traditional system will be as follows: (a) managers will receive bonuses from the enterprise material incentive fund; (b) workers' wages will be increased through extra payments for meeting production norms; (c) the enterprise's wages fund will remain the same (1,000 × 1,100 rubles = 1.1 million rubles)—that is, it will not reflect the improvement in labor productivity.

Under the new system, the following takes place. In 1985 (first year of the five-year plan), indicators for the enterprise and actual results are as follows:

Output target: 6 million rubles

Actual output: 9 million rubles

Negotiated wage coefficients (to remain unchanged
for five years): 0.10

Planned and actual number of workers: 1,000

Wages fund: 1.1 million rubles

In 1986, the wages fund will be calculated as follows: add to the average wage (1,100 rubles) an amount equal to 0.10 times the increase in labor productivity (9,000 rubles − 6,000 rubles), times the labor force (1,000), or:

1,100 rubles + 0.10 (9,000 − 6,000 rubles) = 1,400 rubles × 1,000 =
1.4 million rubles (1986 wages fund).

The 1986 wages fund available for distribution is greater than the 1980 fund by 300,000 rubles, reflecting increases in labor productivity. The labor force remains unchanged as do basic (tariff) wage rates. The 300,000 rubles may be used by the manager to pay bonuses to those workers responsible for the productivity increase. Management and workers presumably now have an interest in increasing labor productivity. If the coefficient (0.10) really remains the same over the five-year period (and past experience is not reassuring on this score), the incentive to raise labor productivity will be reinforced because the "ratchet" threat of having production targets raised in 1986 due to plan overfulfillment in 1985 will have been removed. The 300,000-ruble wage increase will not be inflationary because the coefficient is presumably set at a level such that the increase in wages cannot exceed the increase in productivity. Pressure for increasing labor productivity may, however, induce managers to increase their use of other nonlabor inputs (for example, fuels and capital) to raise output per unit of labor, or to resort to other simulations and formalisms.[31] There is, in other words, the distinct possibility that this particular measure will go the way of other incremental remedies applied to individual parts of a complex system in the past—that is, it will not achieve its intended purpose (see Chapter 3). In any case, what goods are the workers to purchase with the extra money? At best it might come in useful to buy officials and thereby purchase better goods from the economy's nether regions.

As with other aspects of Stalinplan adjustment, the changes in the managerial system of motivation must be implemented by the very agencies most opposed to them. These bureaucracies are quick both to point out every failure of market-type techniques to elicit the efficiency and innovation responses intended by the adjustments, and to blame most shortcomings on what they believe to be the wrong course. Their instinctive reaction is to resurrect administrative methods of conducting the business of society. However, they are not alone in this. Many enterprise managers have become used to administrative ways of running their enterprises. They know the ins and outs of bureaucracy, the safe ways to maneuver around troublesome regulations, and they draw comfort, financial benefit, and status from the old routine. It would be wrong to contend that most of these managers chafe at the bit and wish to assume risks and responsibilities to which they are not accustomed and for which they do not have the temperament. They would certainly prefer lower output targets, higher input allocations, and bigger bonuses. But it is not at all clear that they would be prepared to go broke in the cause of managerial independence. Real marketization of the economy would spell more trouble for the manager from below, for it might sooner or later extend itself to the workers. There is a "why rock the boat?" attitude in the Soviet neoclassical plan that is not limited to the conservatives in the ministries on up, but is shared by many routinized enterprise and production association managers as well.

Real marketization and privatization of the Soviet industrial economy would, therefore, necessitate a profound transformation in the psychology and intellectual makeup of the bureaucratized and party-affiliated fraternity of managers—a revolutionary process of relearning. After more than half a century in the cage, the bird's wings have become atrophied. Still, they could conceivably be revitalized if managements were made truly and fully responsible for the resources they use—with all the economic risks, benefits, and punishments this entails. In the Soviet industrial economy, decentralized decision making "will be of no avail unless production units are made responsible for the national resources they utilize. Such a decentralization of economic responsibility is inseparable from the fundamental problem of property ownership."[32] The cage must be taken apart.

CHAPTER NINE

China: Stalinplan, Maoplan, Neoclassical Conservative Plan, and Beyond

When communism triumphed over the Nationalists in China after decades of ruinous warfare, its remaining enemy was China's poverty. In 1952, three years after the takeover, after the worst physical damage had been repaired, per capita gross national product came to fifty 1952 dollars, and per capita output of grain—the main ingredient of the people's diet—came to 288 kilograms. There were two persons per acre of cultivated land and a population of 568 million, four-fifths of whom were engaged in farming pursuits. The rate of natural increase, which hovered around 1 percent per year in the years of the republic, was just beginning to undergo a dramatic increase, primarily due to a reduction in the mortality rate as the economy stabilized. Population increased by 2 percent a year from 1952 to 1966, and by 2.3 percent a year from 1966 through 1976.[1] Contributing to the demographic upsurge was the absence of a comprehensive family planning policy, caused by ideologically related disagreements on the subject. The new court doctrine of Marxism-Leninism was interpreted much of the time as teaching that an expanding population was not a major impediment to economic development and the improvement of the people's living standard. According to this understanding of the doctrine, the threat came from the wrong kind of economic organization ("social relations of production" in Marxist terms). A radical change in the economic system, it was believed, would release the hitherto unused forces of production in industry and agriculture. Following the Soviet Stalinist model, the economy had to be demarketized and deprivatized. Decision making regarding the determination of social objectives and the allocation of resources to chosen objectives was to be transferred from private interests and the Old Regime to administrators of the new proletarian party-state. In the process, the old "exploiting" classes (landlords, "rich" peasants, and capitalists) were to be destroyed together with the bourgeois state machine, class relations being delineated in accordance with Marxist analysis altered by China's own revolutionary insights. The favored beneficiary of this societal transformation was to be industry, especially heavy industry; this was along the lines of historical progression traced by the experience of Stalin's Russia. In 1952, crude steel output in China was 2 kilograms per head (273 kilograms in the USSR on the eve of Soviet socialist industrialization—1926–1928); the output of pig iron was 3 kilograms (22 kilograms in the USSR); and the output of electric power generation next to nothing—a mere 0.005 kilowatts per capita (0.01 kilowatts in pre-Stalin Russia).

Although Chinese reliance on the Soviet model in these early years was heavy, it was neither total nor slavish. It was promoted by communist China's isolation from the nonsocialist world after the Korean War and by the absence of a noncapitalist blueprint for economic construction. (The Yugoslav market socialist "deviation" was in its early untried and perilous stages.) At the same time, the blueprint was qualified by several considerations that were to grow in importance as the years went by. The first consisted of the peasant origins of China's Marxist revolutionary experience, which had several consequences that gradually surfaced. Not least of these was a deep suspicion of urban life, seen as the carrier of bourgeois "spiritual pollution." This suspicion was reinforced by the peasant-soldier origins of many of China's new leaders (Mao prominently included). Combined with parochialism, easily fanned xenophobia, and peasant anti-intellectualism, it encouraged isolationist tendencies and a (partially justifiable) distrust of things foreign—socialist foreign things included. What might be called the "Yenan syndrome"—the guerrilla-cum-pioneer experience of living on the margin of subsistence, where equal sharing was not so much a matter of choice as of necessity—gave Chinese communism an inclination toward egalitarian modes of income distribution while making it fear and reject what was perceived to be the shallowness and spiritually destructive potentialities of material wealth. In later years, this leaning translated itself into a paradoxical glorification of the revolutionary virtues of poverty (which the revolution was designed to abolish). The monastic simplicity and Mao's idealist insistence on the irresistible creative power of the correctly inspired, ideologically inflamed masses, were, I believe, genuine (although not always practiced by the preachers) and were not simply opportunistic rationalizations of China's impoverished material circumstances. They found sympathetic response in much of the Western literature on China at the time, and are still fondly remembered by leftist segments of China's current leadership, especially at the middle echelons. Finally (but not unimportantly), Mao's personal exposure to Soviet style and substance in Moscow in 1950 must have left him with some unanswered questions about Soviet designs and about the political cost-benefit calculus of accepting fraternal aid. These doubts were surely confirmed by firsthand Chinese exposure to Soviet experts during China's First Five-Year Plan (1953–1957) and by the spectacle of the Soviets' treatment of their East European dependents in the wake of World War II.

Remaking the Economic System

During the period from 1949 to 1956, China's new rulers engaged in a vast operation that may be best described as "destructive construction." The aim was to uproot the then-existing economic organization (destruction) and to replace it with a system of central administrative command planning (construction). The operation was concluded in June of 1956 with the completion of rural collectivization on the model of the "advanced" Soviet collective (*kolkhoz*). On the ashes of the old arose another system of economic, social, and political relationships and a totalitarian cultural order whose basic postulates have survived the many spectacular changes introduced since then.

It is interesting and instructive to note at this point that the process of sovietization (with the caveats just mentioned) has never been repudiated in its essence. Indeed, the people who were in charge of the apocalyptic event (minus those who are now gone due to natural and unnatural deaths) are largely the ones in charge today—Teng Hsiaop'ing, former Propaganda Chief Chou Yang, and Chen Yün among them. What happened in the intervening period was a series of events—including the Great Leap Forward, the Reconstruction of 1961–1965, the Cultural Revolution (1966–1976), and the post-Mao Great Self-Criticism and Renewed Reconstruction (1977–today)—constituting a succession of palace revolutions of enormous significance to private lives and to the future of China. There has still, however, been no fundamental change in the philosophical assumptions and institutional makeup of the system. With one important exception (the post-1978 discreet family tenancy system in the countryside, which will be described presently), the economic organization of China today remains in its quintessence soviet (not *Soviet*, or *Russian*, but centralized, administrative, state-planned, dictatorial, and collective). Of equal importance is the fact that allowing for accumulated experience, personal misfortune, and the passage of time, the thinking of those in charge of China's affairs remains by and large unchanged. This does not hold true of the intellectual community (both old and young), but does apply to policy makers—and in China (as elsewhere, only more so), it is not the intellectuals who make policy. They do not, in fact, even influence it much. The older people bend with the wind and the young become co-opted, while the unbridled ones end up in places of re-education through labor.

All of which is to say, again, that a careful distinction should be drawn between intrasystemic adjustment—the renovation of the system—and intersystemic reform. There has been only one reform so far—that of 1949–1956—but there have been many adjustments, of which the post-Mao course of the Four Modernizations and the Open Door are the latest variation on a classical theme. However, by the mid-1980s what had begun as minor repair of China's planned economic system, which was savaged by the radicalism of the Cultural Revolution (1966–1976), through the internal logic of the process had developed into a serious attempt to restructure China's Soviet-type command economy. Marketization and privatization had advanced most in agriculture, albeit against determined opposition from sections of the party and bureaucracy. As of 1985, in this sector one could speak of the beginnings of systemic reform: a centrally approved drift beyond not only neoclassical conservatism, but also the borders of neoclassical liberalism.

Destruction of the Market and of Private Property

Destruction meant the forcible removal, at large cost in human life (upward of 2 million landlords dead, not counting other class undesirables), of the dominant groups and of the institutionalized societal interrelationships inherited from the past. The body count tells only part of the story, because the operation was primarily designed to "re-educate" (or, in Marxist terms, to fundamentally reshape) the "superstructure" of ideas—both of individual psychologies and social ideologies (such as religion, culture, and philosophy) and of institutions (laws, government, the educational system, the media, and the family). This drive to alter the individual and collective psyche was particularly important in the scheme of Chinese communism. It was intended to eradicate "feudal" and capitalist ideological contaminations and to prepare the way for the emergence of the new socialist man. At least superficially, it was successful.

The principal means used to achieve the objective was the mass campaign of terror and intimidation, controlled by the center and meticulously orchestrated by local cadres. It resulted in a veritable rout of old habits and ways of thinking and in the disappearance of established institutions. As it turns out, these habits and beliefs were merely driven underground, where they led a precarious and fearful existence and provided those in power with an excuse for organizing bigger and more intensive hunts. The most important drives aimed at the economy during this time of systemic trauma were those of land reform and the subsequent (1955–56) collectivization, and the Five-Anti terrorism directed at the native ("national") capitalist sector in industry and commerce. "Our party . . . wiped out the national bourgeois class while in alliance with it."[2]

The key economic institutions banished during this time were market information, coordination, and motivation, and private property in the means of production and distribution (see Table 9.1).

The comparatively small private industrial sector in 1952 is explained by the communist government's early confiscation of about half of industry belonging to the nationalist government ("bureaucrat capital"), foreign corporations, and big domestic capitalists. In 1952, almost all the peasant families counted in the socialized sector (the 40 percent, or 50 million households) were banded together in loosely organized, mostly seasonal, mutual aid teams. The peasants' socialization was, therefore, at this stage quite nominal. After collectivization (1956), farm families were allowed to cultivate small household plots on the Soviet model and to dispose of the produce of those plots (approximately 5 percent of arable area) as best they could, including through sales on fairly free village markets.

The destruction of private enterprise in commerce, the handicrafts, and agriculture, described by China's official statistical manual *Ten Great Years* (1960) as "a great victory of the socialist revolution," imposed unnecessary hardships on the country's urban and rural population.[3] The number of retail outlets and service establishments dwindled (the planners preferring a few big centers so as to better control them), and rural household sideline production (for example, pig raising) was drastically reduced, with deleterious effects on peasant family incomes and quality of service. It was not until 1977 and the years following, under pressure of urban unemployment and with Mao safely dead, that private enterprise in the cities (primarily one-man and one-family business) was resurrected. In 1984, the urban private sector employed about 2 percent of urban workers and employees (not a system-shattering figure). In the countryside, a more extensive (if disguised and circumscribed) privatization occurred.

TABLE 9.1
THE CHINESE PRIVATE SECTOR, 1952 AND 1956
(percent)

	1952	1956
Industry	17	0
Commerce (retail)	57	4
Handicrafts	97	8
Agriculture	60	4
National income generated in private sector	79	7

SOURCE: State Statistical Bureau, *Ten Great Years* (Peking: Foreign Language Publishing House, 1960), pp. 35–40.
NOTE: Industry = percent of gross output value (handicrafts excluded); commerce = percent of retail sales; handicrafts = percent of number of handicraftsmen; agriculture = percent of peasant households.

Construction of the Classical Stalinplan

Construction meant the further building, with Soviet assistance, of an administrative apparatus of central planning and control that by 1956 had taken over the functions formerly performed by tradition and the market (with the exception of trade on village fairs). It also meant the socialization (nationalization and collectivization) of property in the means of production and distribution.

The quantitative picture of the socialization of property inferred from Table 9.1 needs little comment. In theory, the destruction of private property was not to be instantaneous any more than was the passage from market to administrative resource allocation. An elaborate gradation of transitional property forms between private and state property was worked out for industry, commerce, handicrafts, and agriculture.[4] Private property and markets were to be eased out, not thrown out. There is reason to believe that certain relatively moderate sections of the leadership (by and large those in power today) took seriously the idea of gradual socialization. This was primarily for technical reasons; these leaders believed that the "material forces of production," the crucial variable in the pseudoscience of historical materialism, were not ready for the ideologically "higher" socialist property relations implied in nationalization and artel-type collectivization. Even if this were true, these people were ignored and socialization was accomplished by a quantum jump. The turning point for industry and commerce was the Five-Anti campaign of 1952; for agriculture, it was the "little big leap" of 1955–56. In December of 1955, half the peasant households were in the private sector; by June of 1956, there were none. These and later leaps in property relations have contributed to the erratic, cyclical course of the economy over the past thirty-five years.[5]

As markets crumbled, there arose an imposing edifice of central planning (a Chinese Stalinplan) built on Soviet foundations with the help of Soviet social architects.[6] In addition to the takeover of the banking system (accomplished by 1952), an important landmark in the replacement of market by plan was the introduction in 1953–54 of the "planned purchase and planned supply system" through which the government all but monopolized the trade in food grains, oil seeds, edible oils, raw cotton, cotton yarn, and cotton cloth (so-called first-category goods), and in hemp, jute, tobacco, sugarcane, sugar, silkworm cocoons, tea, live hogs, and other commodities ("second-category" goods). First-category goods were purchased exclusively by the government at government-set prices and were distributed by the newly formed State Planning Commission. Second-category goods were acquired by the government from collective farms under a contractual (compulsory) delivery quota system at state-determined prices, the collectives being able to sell any surplus above the quota at less-controlled prices at peasant fairs.[7] Only "minor native products" could be produced and traded freely outside the state network. State procurement under the system rose sharply in the first few years; this had disincentive effects on the producers, since state purchase prices were well below market levels and were perceived by the peasants as being confiscatory—a form of tax. Eventually, state procurement of grain stabilized at 15 percent of total output, and cotton procurement at 80 percent.

Also in the early to mid-1950s, key industrial inputs began to be distributed among state firms by physical rationing determined by the planners and supervised by the State Bureau of Material Supplies; that is, all vestiges of the market in raw materials and producer goods were erased. Material balances for a growing number of materials and capital goods began to be prepared at the central planning echelon and at the level of provinces, municipalities, and counties (for less important products). In 1952, there were 28 balances. By 1956, their number had risen to 235. The practical implementation of these physical rationing decisions was made by general contracts concluded between the supplying and user ministries (each in charge of a particular commodity group or service) and, within these general contracts, by particular contracts entered into by producing and user enterprises under the ministries.

After a checkered history, which included the vandalization of the planning network during Mao's Great Leap Forward (1958–1960) and the Cultural Revolution (1966–1976), the number of material balances constructed at the central and provincial levels in the early 1980s was in the neighborhood of 600, but this figure has been challenged as too high. Nationwide rationing of food grains and basic consumer goods was introduced in 1955 (local grain and edible oil rationing had been in effect since 1953). Cotton cloth rationing was discontinued in January of 1984 due to increased supply of synthetic fibers sold at higher prices.

The state also began to set industrial wholesale and retail prices on the basis of Soviet-inspired prime cost-plus formulae, and to determine wages for state sector workers (also done on the Soviet model). Labor placement and mobility were subject to state control. Collectivized farmers were paid according to the Soviet-type work-point system; that is, they became residual claimants on the collective farms' net income. Cooperative sector industrial and service workers were recompensed out of their enterprises' earnings remaining after payment of taxes, centrally prescribed accumulation and social fund contributions, and deductions for current operating expenses. Prices in the system (especially industrial wholesale and state agricultural quota procurement prices) were intended to be allocatively neutral. They were to be subsidiary instruments, supportive of administratively determined physical allocation. All transactions among state and collective enterprises and governmental (including army) units were made through book entries at the People's Bank ("control through the yuan," the equivalent of the Soviet "control by the ruble"). Foreign trade transactions were the monopoly of state trading corporations under the Ministry of Foreign Trade and were subject to financial control by the Bank of China.

Adjustments to the Left:
The Neoclassical Radical Maoplan

The early results of the operation of the classical Stalinplan were not all negative by any means. In terms of the quantity of output, especially heavy industrial output, the results were impressive (see Table 9.2). Moreover, inflation was brought under control, government revenues were increased, the budget was balanced, open unemployment was avoided (it began to show up again in the cities in 1957–58), a fairly equitable system of distributing basic commodities was in place, and income polarization of the peasantry was reduced. From the standpoint

TABLE 9.2
QUANTITATIVE RESULTS OF THE CLASSICAL STALINPLAN
IN CHINA, 1957[a]

Gross value of agricultural output	124.8
Gross value of industrial output	228.6
Gross value of heavy industrial output	310.7
Gross value of light industrial output	183.2
National income (gross domestic material product)	153.0
Government revenues	168.9
Government expenditures	172.8
Total capital construction investment	317.2
Volume of railv·ay freight	223.6
Total volume of retail sales	171.3
Total volume of imports and exports	161.8
Total volume of imports	133.3
Total volume of exports	201.1
Total population	112.5
Labor force	114.7
Workers and staff members	193.5
Grain output[b]	118.6

SOURCE: State Statistical Bureau, "National Economy: Major Targets," *Beijing Review*, November 29, 1982, p. 19; for grain output; National Foreign Assessment Center, *China: Economic Indicators* (Washington, D.C., 1978), p. 11.
[a] 1952 = 100. For output, based on current prices for gross value of agriculture and gross value of industrial output.
[b] Grain output per capita in 1952 = 288 kg; 1957 = 306 kg.

of the new regime, the most significant achievement was the elimination of traditional class alignments, and thereby of the power base from which forces opposed to socialist construction could stage a comeback.

But there were also problems associated with the classical Stalinist system of economic organization. The quantitative troubles were most tangible in agriculture. Collectivization had not improved the land-population ratio through any significant expansion of the cultivated area (although the sown acreage increased through double cropping), and the expected upsurge of grain production did not materialize. The reasons for this were to be found in the qualitative shortcomings of the organizational transformation. Reduction of income differentials in the countryside and income distribution problems inherent in the Soviet-type collective method of farm management had disincentive effects on the newly collectivized peasantry, especially on the former rich and upper-middle peasants, who were unenthusiastic about the whole enterprise to begin with. Shortages of capable farm managers and accountants added to the difficulty. State investments in agriculture during the period from 1953 to 1957 were less than 8 percent of state capital construction outlays. Even if collective and private investment is added (4 billion yuan a year), the total (15 percent of all investment) was just enough to take care of depreciation of existing fixed capital, but not enough to have any marked positive impact on output and labor productivity through capital deepening and technological advance. In industry, the capital-intensive method of industrialization was unable to absorb the annual cohorts of job seekers, and urban unemployment became troublesome by 1957. The labor force between 1952 and 1957 rose by 4 million a year, while industrial employment annually absorbed only 400,000 people. Light industry experienced shortages of current inputs due to the slow advance of agriculture, which supplied 70 percent of light industry's raw materials. In other words, lopsided development was beginning to give rise to the same sort of difficulties in China it had earlier caused in the USSR and other centrally planned state socialist economies.

Shortages of raw materials and consumer goods, sluggish performance of agriculture, bottlenecks and surpluses, open and disguised unemployment, inflationary pressures, long construction cycles, low productivity of labor and capital (especially in agriculture), difficulties with technological innovation and diffusion (due in large measure to the suppression of individual entrepreneurship), and a growing problem of perverse incentives to managers (originating in defective information and coordination instruments, that is, the absence of a price system that would indicate the relative social costs and utilities in the economy), produced disillusion with the newly created system and prompted attempts at modifying it. Although these reasons were important in encouraging the leadership to take a fresh look at the usefulness and effectiveness of the classical Soviet model for China, other considerations were involved. These centered on ideological interpretations of the purpose and means of economic development. Another factor contributing to the re-examination was the deteriorating state of China's political relations with the Soviet Union.

In what followed, ideological considerations took precedence. In 1956–57, at the very time that the process of systemic destruction-construction was completed, an acerbic debate on the future shape and direction of the system began within the leadership—a "two-line struggle," as it was later to be called. The debate, sheltered from public view, took place between September 1956 and the summer of 1957. It started with the "right" wing dominating the September 1956 Eighth Party Congress, which approved a draft Second Five-Year Plan (1958–1962) modeled on the first Stalinist one (1953–1957). Already at that time, however, it was clear that something had to be done about the inadequacies of the system. What was done was partial retrenchment and liberalization of the economy, which lasted from October of 1956 through early June of 1957. This short-lived "adjustment to the right," or movement toward neoclassical conservatism (including a 7 percent cutback in state investment), was accompanied by an overtly liberal cultural interlude known as the "Hundred Flowers." Launched at the end of April 1957, it was terminated in early June when a chilling "anti-rightist" campaign was unleashed with near-unprecedented fury. By the end of 1957, the debate had been settled in favor of radical "leftist" (Maoist) theses on the shape and direction of the system.

The radical theses underlay the Great Leap Forward (1958–1960) and were resurrected in modified form during the Cultural Revolution (1966–1976), especially during that event's peak phase from 1966 to 1969. The Leap and the Cultural Revolution represent the two major leftward adjustments of the classical system of central administrative command planning. Though extreme and spectacular, they were not fundamental reforms of the system. The leftward adjustments revolved around six theses concerning speed, level of socialization, mass mobilization, motivation, distribution, and innovation.

Speed

The left spurned what it considered to be the too-leisurely pace of the classical plan under almost every one of the above headings. (Notice that the orthodox draft Second Five-Year Plan in fact foresaw development at breakneck speed.) In this respect, the leftward adjustment (the Maoist solution) was simply Stalinism at a faster speed. For example, under the First (Stalinist) Five-Year Plan, domestic investment represented 24 percent of national income (net domestic material product). From 1958 to 1962 (covering the Leap, as well as the Leap-generated depression), domestic investment jumped to 31 percent of national income, followed by a figure of 30 percent during the Cultural Revolution (1966–1976).[8] The ratio of state investment in heavy industry (light industry = 1) was 8.5 during the orthodox First Five-Year Plan, 11 during the Leap and post-Leap depression (1958–1962), 14 at the height of the Cultural Revolution (1966–1970), and 10 during the less exalted stages of the Cultural Revolution (1971–1975).[9] Remnants of the market and quasi-private property rights in household plots were to have been phased out over an indeterminate number of years (they still exist in the USSR, more than half a century after collectivization, and their importance in supplying the citizens with high-quality foods has not diminished). The plots and village markets were abolished overnight at the outset of the Leap and the Cultural Revolution. (They were resuscitated in the intervening period). It took six months to collectivize 120 million peasant households; it took just four months to put them all into communes (September–December, 1958). In 1957, the irrigated area increased by 3 million hectares; in 1958, the claim was 32 million hectares. During the whole First Five-Year Plan, 770 large projects drawing water from rivers were built; in 1958 alone, the claim was 1,800 projects. Two reservations must be entered here. First, the 1958 statistics took a leap into unreality. One factor to be considered is that the State Statistical Bureau was dismantled (after being rebuilt from 1961 to 1965, it was again razed to the ground in 1966, leaving thirteen practicing statisticians for the whole of China). Second, the quality of output was not only poor, it was often counterproductive. Large-scale ecological damage was inflicted by ill-informed digging of ditches and reservoirs. Between one-third and one-half of the steel made during the Leap (especially that coming from backyard furnaces) was unusable: good pots and pans went into the furnaces and junk came out. In other words, the leftward adjustments markedly accentuated the Stalinplan's qualitative problems on both the input and output sides. The speed was not sustainable materially, organizationally, or psychologically. This "leap to nowhere" engendered a catastrophic downturn that lasted from 1960 through 1962. The gross value of industrial and agricultural production fell by 31 percent in 1961 and 10 percent in 1962; then again by 10 percent in 1967 and 4 percent in 1968 (representing the effects of the Cultural Revolution's peak phase). During more restrained leftist adjustments, the damage was smaller: in 1974 (the "little" Cultural Revolution), the gross value of industrial and agricultural output rose by 1.4 percent, and then by 1.7 percent during the left resurgence of early 1976.[10] Thus, putting the economy in high gear meant, in effect, putting it into reverse—and breaking the gears in the process (see Table 9.3). Not captured by the statistics is the incalculable damage done to China's small pool of expertise by both adjustments, especially by the anti-cultural exercise of 1966–1976.

Level of Socialization

Among other things, speed meant rapid transition from "lower" to "higher" relations of production, especially property relations; that is,

TABLE 9.3
SOME ECONOMIC CONSEQUENCES OF LEFTWARD ADJUSTMENTS IN CHINA: THE GREAT LEAP FORWARD AND THE CULTURAL REVOLUTION
(percent compared with previous year)

	Great Leap Forward			Cultural Revolution			
	1958–59	1959–60	1960–61	1966–67	1967–68	1975–76	1976–77
Grain output	−17	−9	8	5	−7 (−4)	0.3 (0.4)	−0.7 (−1)
Cotton output	−29[a]	−25[b]	−10[c]	5[d]	−5[e]	−4[f]	−13[g]
Agricultural output	−22 (−13.6)	−11	5 (−2.4)	5 (1.6)	−7 (−2.5)	0	−3
Industrial output	22	5	−42	−13	9 (−5)	0	14
Steel output	25 (67)	35 (35)	−57	−33 (−33)	−10 (−10)	−14	16
Gross national product	−5 (8.2)	−3	−21	−4	0.4 (−?)	−0.2 (−?)	−8
Foreign trade value	16	−7	−25	−5	−5	8 (8)	14
Population		−1.5[b]	−0.5[c]		−5		
Labor productivity in state enterprises	−5.4[h]				2.5[i]	−0.3[j]	−8.6

SOURCE: Cheng, *China's Economic Development*, pp. 310–11. Based on U.S. government estimates and Chinese official sources, from *Beijing Review*, March 23, 1981, p. 25; population from Ishikawa, "China's Economic Growth Since 1949," p. 248; Robert C. Hsu, *Food For One Billion: China's Agriculture Since 1949* (Boulder, Colo.: Westview Press, 1982), p. 40.

NOTE: "Again in the ten years of the Cultural Revolution (June 1966–October 1976), there were fairly large fluctuations in the national economy, sometimes up, sometimes down, sometimes at a standstill, and then going down, till it finally was at the brink of collapse" *Beijing Review*, May 11, 1979, p. 15.

[a]1959. [b]1960. [c]1961. [d]1967. [e]1968. [f]1976.
[g]1977. [h]1958–1962. [i]1968–1970. [j]1971–1975.

it meant more advanced socialization. The left had no patience with the right's insistence on the need for deliberateness and gradualness in passing from one Marx-defined property grade to the next without skipping any of the grades. As already mentioned, an array of transitional property forms had been worked out for agriculture, industry, commerce, and the handicrafts, only to be bypassed by recurrent left adjustments, of which the rural "little big leap" of 1955–56 is a good example.[11] Such transitional forms of property as did survive the Great Leap Forward (or as were nursed back to life in the first few years after the Leap) were liquidated by the onrush of the Cultural Revolution (between 1966 and 1968).

The most eye-catching jump in socialization was the creation of the rural people's communes in 1958—the transformation in a brief time span of 740,000 collective farms into 24,000 communes and the elimination of household plots. According to the original intent of the Leap, the commune was to be the production and income distribution unit. It owned all property, including peasant houses, domestic animals, poultry, and private bank deposits. The commune was also given governmental, paramilitary, security, educational, and public health functions formerly exercised by the townships. It became apparent very soon (as early as May 1959) that the arrangement was unworkable. Beginning in 1961, a rightward adjustment was made. The production team (equivalent to the former large village) became the production and accounting unit, most productive property was now owned by the team, and "private" family plots were restored.

There were two related reasons for the retreat from the mania for social gigantism. First, the size of the commune made effective control over production activities extremely difficult ("conducting production in a blind way"). From the standpoint of the span of control, the production unit was quite simply too large. One of the results of the communes' vast new responsibilities was the diversion of peasant labor to manual farmland capital construction (the digging of ditches, and terracing and leveling of hills) and to labor-intensive commune mini-industries. Much of this effort produced negative results. Among these was the fall in crop output, caused by an acute labor shortage that was a direct consequence of the diversion of manpower to nonagricultural tasks. (Additionally, large numbers of peasants fled to the cities to avoid communization, adding to an already-serious problem of urban unemployment.) Second, the distribution of income could not be carried out at the commune level without grievous disincentive effects on the labor force. To facilitate its work, the commune distributed incomes equally to individual workers, half in the form of "free supplies," half in haphazardly estimated wages with tenuous regard to individual work contribution. (The "free supply" system meant, for example, that instead of ration grain being distributed to households, it was allocated to the communes' dining halls and received by the peasants in the form of free meals.)

That leaps into higher states of socialization do not promote material welfare was later documented. One example among many is given in Table 9.4. If 1960–61 (when the full effect of the communes was felt) had been included in Table 9.4, the story would have been even more revealing.[12]

Defense Minister P'eng Teh-huai censured the left adjustment of 1958 in a ten thousand-character memorial addressed to Mao and distributed among those attending the party's central committee gathering at Lushan in August of 1959. He was promptly dismissed. Years later (in 1979), *Kuang-ming jih-pao* eulogized a poem entitled "On Visiting My Native Village" composed by P'eng at the apogee of the leap into communism (December 1958):

> Grain was scattered all over the place,
> And sweet potatoes had withered.
> The young and the able-bodied were away making steel;
> And only the children and the women were left behind to bring in
>   the crops.
> I applaud and cheer for the people.

In 1958, said *Kuang-ming jih-pao*, the poem had been "like a beacon in a foggy sea, a luminous pearl in a dark night."[13]

Mass Mobilization

The left's prescription for problem solving consists of political mobilization of the masses based on the concept of class warfare and mass frontal assault. The two main ideas are (a) putting to full use China's most abundant resource, muscle power ("full use" implies extending the number of hours worked each day and the number of working days per year); and (b) assuring the effectiveness of mass work by collective political stimulation (which implies restricting personal economic incentives). Mass political mobilization encompasses the recruitment of planners, statisticians, administrators, managers, and other "nonproductive" workers of the planning apparatus for work in the fields and factories. Without a market information and coordination

TABLE 9.4
LEVEL OF SOCIALIZATION AND GRAIN DEFICIENCY,
XIGUAN PRODUCTION BRIGADE
(Mouping County, Shandong Province)

Stage of Socialization Progress	Year	Average Per Capita Income (yuan)	Households Deficient in Food-grains (number)
Beginning of agricultural cooperation (mutual aid teams)	1953	53	37
Cooperation completed (advanced collectives)[a]	1957	51	41
Communization (rural people's communes founded)[b]	1958	31	86

SOURCE: Wei Min, "Back to the Right Track," Beijing Review, January 19, 1981, p.27.
[a]"Due to lack of experience, things were hurried up a little bit in setting up cooperatives."
[b]The workday value in 1958 was 0.8 yuan.

mechanism, the absence of these people (the plan's information conveyors, processors, and coordinators) from their desks ensures that physical work in the fields and factories will be anarchic and unproductive. The most disastrous ecological damage during the Great Leap Forward occurred in places where the greatest effort at digging, terracing, leveling, and changing the course of rivers had been expended. The worst steel was that produced by the most people. When there is no market there must be a plan, and this requires bureaucrats to do the planning.

The antibureaucratic aspect of mass mobilization (letting the bureaucrats know how it feels to plant paddy rice) has never been far distant from leftist thinking in China and has distinct class overtones: the establishment bureaucrats are accused of "capitalist-roading." This aspect of leftist thinking became particularly prominent during the second adjustment of the Cultural Revolution.[14] Although mass campaigns have been the common property of both left and right, the difference lies in the right's insistence on strict bureaucratic control over each campaign and on the insulation of the higher party and governmental apparats from the effects of these storms.

Motivation

Any leftward radical adjustment of classical central administrative command planning involves substantial changes in the system's incentive structure. In fact, differing intraparty views on how to motivate economic agents to perform their tasks productively and efficiently, how the motivational system should be constructed, and what combination of prods it should contain in order to reconcile the micro interests of the agents with the macro interest of society (as defined by the planners) are central to what has come to be known as China's "two-line struggle."[15] Despite assurances to the contrary, the struggle is not over with by any means. Indeed, the linkage between planners' preferences and the interests of enterprise managements (the problem of "success indicators" to firms) is among the more crucial weak links of the system. Rarely are the two amicably reconciled; more often they are at odds, with harmful repercussions on consumer want satisfaction.[16] Economic activity becomes a game of wits between planners and enterprise managers.

The left radical (Maoplan) solution to the problem of the malfunctioning Visible Hand is to remold the individual (and hence his interest) in the image of the single-party state through political education. This education includes the use of nonmaterial, collective, cooperative, positive and negative incentives and the simultaneous downgrading of material, individual, competitive incentives. The desire for private material wealth (the meaning of "private" being extended to the family) in competition with others is relegated to the category of negative acts skirting the counterrevolutionary. Any manifestation of affluence, however modest, is viewed as bourgeois conspicuous consumption, a flaunting of the proletarian ethos. The end purpose of this educational effort is to extinguish individual material wants for anything not contained in the planners' preference schedule, and to proscribe the maximization of individual want satisfactions. This is the essence of the rationed "free supply" of planner-determined "everyday necessities" and of the attempts to eliminate money relations (money being seen correctly as coined freedom).

When the alleged omnipotence of political consciousness fails to produce the expected results, as it has on at least two occasions (1958–1960, 1966–1976), the damage inflicted on the individual psyche is not easily undone. The leftist adjustments induce a wealth phobia even in those (and they are many) who are sorely tempted to improve their material lot and perceive opportunities to do so. The cadres in charge of the reversal are equally fearful: "There are some comrades who still feel insecure [with the post-Mao rightward adjustment] and are always whispering: 'Does this conform to socialist orientation? Is it still a collective economy?' Some others even sigh with anxiety: 'The results are gratifying, but the direction is worrisome.' "[17]

Distribution

In the matter of distribution, the left presses for rough egalitarianism guaranteed at a low level of income. Egalitarianism, rough or not, means that people are paid according to need determined by "society," that is, by the Standing Committee of the Politburo or some other similarly restricted (usually senescent) body, rather than in accordance with their marginal contribution to production (marginal productivity or, in Marxist terms, "to each according to his work"). This will work if the recipients of equalized income have been transformed by political campaigns of mass mobilization and other methods of re-education into selfless, nonmaximizing, collective beings—or socialist people. In that state of other-mindedness, they do not care whether, or by how much, their material rewards deviate from their work contributions, and their productivity is, therefore, not affected in the least. If, on the other hand, they have not been so transubstantiated, labor productivity will suffer—especially the productivity of the more skilled workers. Moreover, recruitment into the skilled categories will suffer, too, because it will not be worth people's while to make the extra effort and bear the costs of working one's way up the nonexistent income ladder. Rough equalization of personal incomes in agriculture was tried during the Great Leap Forward (in an equal shares and free supply system) and at various points during the Cultural Revolution (in experiments with egalitarian systems of work-point distribution). According to right-wing criticism, this contributed to the collapse of work incentives in the countryside and to the decline of agricultural labor productivity, estimated at between one-quarter and one-third from 1957 to 1975.[18] Wage differentials in industry were narrowed during the two Maoplans by phasing out the top wage brackets and promoting workers in the lower brackets in a wholesale way. With few exceptions (for example, textiles), industrial labor productivity in 1958 dropped by at least 50 percent, after rising 8.7 percent a year during the First Five-Year Plan (1953–1957). Between 1957 and 1978 (a period that included the two major leftward adjustments), labor productivity increased at only 0.7 percent per year.[19]

By itself, low income is not regarded by the Maoplan as a damp-
ener of worker and peasant "enthusiasm for production," provided the
income is equitably (meaning reasonably equally) shared and is secure,
that is, guaranteed by physical rationing of basic commodities at subsidized prices, or, better still, without prices. The basic income guarantee is reinforced by job security (not a specifically leftist characteristic).
In China, as in other state socialist countries, it is very difficult for the
enterprise director or (formerly) collective farm manager to fire the
loafers and the inept, who, in times of the dominance of left radical
views on incentives, comprise a large portion of the work force.

Guaranteed, equally shared low income is known as the phenomenon of the "iron pot"—the "unbreakable rice bowl." According to post-
Mao analysis, "unbreakable rice bowls exist because there is a common
pot. This practice is very harmful . . . We must break the unbreakable
rice bowls. The first thing we must do is get rid of the iron pot."[20]

However, at a low level of income, it is difficult to break the unbreakable rice bowl (dismiss people from their jobs) and get rid of the
iron pot (guaranteed equalized income) without causing unemployment and human destitution.

It should be noted that not only was the reasonably equally shared,
guaranteed income low during the more virulent phases of the leftward
adjustments, it was also stagnant. Industrial money wages barely rose
between 1957 and 1976 (industrial labor productivity went up 15 percent
during the period), and the cost of living index for urban worker households increased 30 percent.[21] Moreover, the quality and assortment of
rationed produce deteriorated during this time and consumer costs
mounted (in the form of lines outside of stores, and frequent goods and
services shortages). During the post-Leap depression, there was starvation in some parts of the country.

Data on peasant incomes are less reliable for the Maoplan periods
than those for industrial workers' wages. They are, however, not absent, and point to long-term stagnation. Japanese economist Shigeru
Ishikawa's calculations show that in 1957, annual labor remuneration
per employed person from the collective sector in agriculture was 98
yuan (35 yuan per capita of member household) in real terms, that is,
deflated by the cost of living index (1952 = 100). In 1976, it was 111 yuan
(42 yuan per capita) in real (1952) terms. In 1976, however, the opportunities for earning private sector supplements to the meager collective
sector income were more restricted than they had been in 1957. The
decisive fact is that in 1976, to "subsist" in the countryside (as Chinese
economist Du Runsheng put it), an annual total per capita income of 95
(current) yuan was needed. But in 1976, collective work paid only 63

(current) yuan per head, or two-thirds of what was needed for subsistence, while possibilities for supplementing this income from private sources were restricted and regarded as reprehensible.[22]

Innovation

The systemic hindrance to technical innovation and its translation into usable products are accentuated, according to current Chinese thought, by left radical theses on who is to do the innovating and how it is to be done. The question of who is answered in a class way: the poor and lower-middle peasants not only should, but, given the correct social environment, actually will do the innovating. Their inventions must be instantly emulated and popularized, as with the Leap's foot-pedaled earth pounders and double-share plows. Although advanced technology not devised by the masses is not to be spurned (in line with the principle of "walking on two legs"—a modern leg and a traditional one), peasant, worker, and soldier innovations are preferred. As to how to do the innovating, the injunction is to learn through doing and keep away from books (except those team-written on a narrow range of political subjects). This is not a caricature of the leftist position on innovation. It is fair to say that the results of its implementation during the two leftward adjustments of the classical Stalinplan have been detrimental to China's economy and will have retarding effects for years to come. The systemic propensity to multiply smokestack industries based on currently available technology, and the difficulty the classical centrally planned system experiences in sensing the direction of technological progress, are compounded by the left's preference for ox cart- and bicycle-type technology—its obsession with self-reliance, anti-intellectualism, and utopianism. Largely because of the Cultural Revolution, technologically China fell needlessly further behind the advanced countries of the world, particularly in revolutionary growth areas such as microelectronics, optics, and biotechnology.

Adjustments to the Right:
Neoclassical Conservative Plan

There have been two major rightward adjustments since the classical centrally planned administrative command structure (Stalinplan) was completed in 1956. Both have been reactions to the damage done to the economy (and especially to the steering mechanism) by the swings to the left. The first rightward adjustment took place from 1961 to 1965.[23]

It was undone by the Cultural Revolution, and the people in charge of it were disgraced. The second adjustment, still in progress and showing signs of moving in a liberal direction (as of 1985), began after the death of Mao and the liquidation of the leftist chiefs (the Gang of Four) in September and October of 1976, but got in stride only after 1978.

Because rightward adjustments toward a neoclassical conservative plan have been primarily reactive, they have typically devoted considerable initial attention to rebuilding the institutional structure of central planning cannibalized by the left's chiliastic upheavals. In that important sense, movements to the right in China have been restorations of orthodoxy with appropriate modifications to allow for the lapse of time. Nevertheless, residues of the earlier left-wrought changes in institutions and ways of thinking always remained in the reconstructed edifice of central planning. When the radical vision of the people's commune failed in 1959, the commune was refashioned to allow for three levels of ownership (commune, brigade, team), and most farming and income distribution functions were delegated to the production team. But the skeletal structure of the commune and its underlying modes of thought remained. Commune authorities, for example, constantly interfered in team affairs, conscripted team labor without pay, and so on. The Leap's proliferation of native mini-industries was subsequently curbed and the most obviously inefficient backyard furnaces were scrapped, but the expansion of village industries was not brought to an end and the idea behind their creation was not repudiated. The idea, it was said, was fine—it simply got out of hand and "went too far." To this day, after ten years of pushing the pendulum away from the extreme left position of 1976, portions of the rebuilt economic mechanism have their origins in the leftward swing, and leftist notions on economic organization and policy are still in circulation (though diminishing in force). With each swing of the pendulum, however, leftist ideas and policies have been reinterpreted to conform to new perceptions of truth, a process manifest in the current leadership's translations and annotations of Mao Tse-tung's Thought.[24]

Paradoxically, rebuilding the institutions of classical central command planning, that is, rebureaucratization and recentralization of the economy, goes hand in hand with cautious marketization and limited privatization of property rights—both essentially decentralizing measures. In the past, these have not been carried very far, certainly not far enough to amount to systemic reform. The paradox is easily explained. Rightward adjustments, certainly in their early stages, are emergency operations in times of severe crisis. In 1960–61 and in 1976, the economy was chaotic. Maoism had tried the impossible: to run an economy with no markets and without a plan. When chaos strikes and ruin threatens (as in Russia after the civil war), the instinctive reaction of communist regimes is to let people take care of themselves, within limits, through markets and the exercise of private property rights. When conditions improve and/or new dislocations appear, markets are curbed and property rights are resocialized.

The key issue faced by the communist establishment during periods of rightward change is how to combine market and plan and broad usufructuary rights with public property without fundamentally altering the system of central command. Under attack from unnamed critics, the post-Mao leaders have endlessly dwelt on this theme without satisfactorily resolving the problem it poses. A few establishment economists show acute awareness of the fact that to remedy the qualitative ills, the economy has to be not merely adjusted, but reformed: what is needed is a conversion, not simply ritualistic prayers to the Invisible Hand.

In the remaining pages, we will concentrate on the latest rightward changes made in the economy since the death of Mao, particularly since 1979. These changes have many similarities to those of 1961–1965, but go well beyond them.

Central Planning Apparatus

The ministerial system of central administrative command planning vandalized during the Cultural Revolution has been rebuilt. At least 20 million officials are involved in about forty central ministries and commissions and five hundred departments and bureaus at the provincial and municipal levels. Most important among these are the State Planning Commission under the State Council; the State Bureau of Supplies, which physically rations most key commodities (including the bulk of producer goods); the State Statistical Bureau; the State Bureau of Prices (the government's price-setting agency); the People's Bank and the banks under it (the Agricultural Bank; and the Bank of China, which deals with foreign exchange transactions); and the People's Construction Bank under the Ministry of Finance.

Lines of authority have been reestablished and formalized. Various neopopulist revolutionary committees and other management organs left over from the Cultural Revolution have been dissolved and replaced by the old directorial principle (personal responsibility of the manager of the firm, the old Soviet *edinochalie*). Laws and regulations have been enacted to govern economic relations and give them stability and a degree of predictability. Accounting is again in good graces.

In brief, the economy has been institutionally restored in accordance with an updated version of the classical central administrative command planning principle of 1956. The updating primarily has to do with attempts to make the administrative structure more flexible through some administrative decentralization (mainly to the provincial level; to an extent, this is a leftist legacy); with an increase in the still-restricted autonomy of firms; with limited price flexibility; and with a relatively liberal attitude toward market transactions and private initative (especially in agriculture). These marketization and privatization initiatives have proved useful in some areas, particularly in agriculture. However, they have also worked at cross-purposes with the restored plan; their existence hangs in the balance, all the more so since the whole idea of markets and privatized social property rights is distasteful not only to the left, but to many establishment pragmatists as well, who resort to it out of necessity but do not like its psychological, political, and philosophical implications.[25] They need not worry much: the rebuilt apparatus of central planning overshadows the market. This does not mean that central control is complete: runaway investments by local authorities are proof to the contrary (the central budget controls only about half the country's expenditures). But it does mean that the realm of markets—that is, of voluntary, lateral, competitive buyer-seller relations—is limited.

Price System

The price system reflects this situation. It is (except, increasingly, in agriculture) a regime of state-fixed prices that bear little relation to relative costs and utilities in the economy. Rigid state-fixed prices (industrial wholesale prices, retail prices, agricultural procurement prices) in the early 1980s accounted for 70 percent of the value of all commodities. They dominated the economic landscape, but played a minor and subsidiary allocative role. Allocation of the bulk of producer goods was done by physical orders, and many consumer goods (including most basics) were physically rationed with the help of subsidized prices. The food price subsidy alone ran to 30 billion yuan a year and represented a big drain on the state budget (see Chapter 3). The neoclassical conservative plan also uses so-called negotiated prices that cover primarily agricultural commodities not subject to state-set quotas or procurement targets. These prices are arrived at through bargaining between state and cooperative and/or private sector buyers and sellers, and are a species of market price. There are also free market prices frequently interfered with by local party authorities who dislike them. These prices prevail on rural and urban fairs. Together with negotiated prices, in the early 1980s they accounted for 20 percent of the value of all commodities. Then there are floating prices set by the state at the central and local levels. These are permitted to move about the state-set base within a range determined by the state, no limits being put on price reductions below the base. In the early 1980s, floating prices accounted for 10 percent of the value of all commodities.

The regime of state-fixed, cost-plus prices and wages has been adjusted many times since 1976. Money wages have been raised and bonuses reintroduced. Relative prices have been changed to reflect more accurately relative cost structures, and cost accounting has been improved. Agricultural procurement prices have been raised to improve farm incentives. All of this has had some positive results, primarily (indeed, spectacularly so) in agriculture, but has also caused new distortions. Until 1985, the intervention in the price system has been partial and ad hoc—a tinkering with individual prices and groups of prices, but not a reform of the price system. The price system (especially its industrial component) remains unsatisfactory as a means of information, coordination, and motivation. It does not indicate opportunity costs. Together with the system of physical-technical-administrative commands issued by the planners, it is largely responsible for most of the economy's qualitative deficiencies, especially for static resource misallocation and for the poor quality of outputs and inputs (low factor productivity, extravagant materials utilization rates). Although somewhat less so, it is true today as it was in 1979 that "there is little variety in the goods produced . . . They are of inferior quality, . . . efficiency is low, and the amount of raw materials and other things consumed in the process of production is very large."[26]

Under these conditions, profits do not necessarily indicate the efficiency of operations—in fact, the contrary can (and does) happen in a quite random way. Imported up-to-date technology under such circumstances runs a good chance of being wasted, because the economy's information conveyors do not reliably indicate where the technology is needed and where it will do the most good.

A reform of prices designed to overcome the serious shortcomings of the neoclassical conservative plan would have profound philosophical, political, and economic implications.[27] Philosophically, a reform would mean a change from dictatorial ways of doing business to voluntariness of contracts, and a revolutionary increase in the number of decision-making units: it would mean pluralism, if not democracy. Utility and profit-maximizing thinking would have to replace the paternalistic state mentality. Politically, a reform would require putting herds of bureaucrats out to pasture as state price fixers and memo writers were replaced by the market. Featherbedded jobs would be discarded and subsidized prices for basic goods would rise dramatically in the short run. Economically, marketization of the price system would alter the cost and profit structure of the economy and the budgetary situation of the government; it would change the present distribution of income (in a less egalitarian direction) and would thus necessitate the introduction of a new complex of direct taxes levied on firms and individuals; and it would almost certainly strengthen inflationary pressures and cause open unemployment during the structural adjustment period. These are formidable deterrents to reform. Only Yugoslavia and Hungary took to this road in the 1960s and 1970s, but they have backtracked since.

A partial, gradual freeing of industrial prices (together with an extension of state enterprise property rights) was decreed by the State Council on May 10, 1984. It was followed on October 20 by a decision by the party's Central Committee to make significant liberalizing changes in the industrial price system (marketization) and to bring about an equally far-reaching expansion in the decision-making rights of state-owned enterprises (privatization). I have analyzed and evaluated this reform intent elsewhere.[28]

In agriculture, further liberalization of an already quite liberalized price system has been undertaken. State purchase quotas for all but a small number of basic ("first-category") commodities (such as grain and cotton) were to be abolished beginning in 1985. Prices of most agricultural commodities (grain and cotton excepted) were to be allowed to float in accordance with market supply and demand. Included were prices of pigs, aquatic products, and vegetables produced for sale in large- and medium-sized cities and mining areas. The state was to continue purchasing grain and cotton, but would also permit these to be sold at free market prices once the contracted quotas had been met. The contracted amounts of grain and cotton procured by the state from peasant family tenant farmers (see below) would continue to be paid for at the listed state procurement prices. However, if the market prices fell below the listed price level, the state obligated itself to purchase all available grain at the listed state price (a form of parity pricing). Free market sales of medicinal herbs have also been permitted with a few exceptions. Bans on free market sales of timber produced by collectives have been lifted, and state forestry farms have been allowed to sign labor or joint management contracts with their workers and local peasants. These agricultural price system reforms go beyond neoclassical liberalism. They herald—indeed, initiate—systemic reform.

Reordering Goal Priorities

The latest (post-Mao) rightward adjustment, like its 1961–1965 predecessor, has rearranged the policy priorities from heavy industry, light industry, and agriculture (in that order) to agriculture, light industry, and heavy industry. It is now conceded that in the earlier adjustment, the change remained unfulfilled and heavy industry forged ahead. There has been trouble with that, this time too. The heavy industry lobby has been active, especially since 1982. In addition, the very structure of the system favors continued expansion of producer goods industries.

There appear to be two motivations behind the switch of priorities. The first is to restore a measure of intersectoral balance to the economy. The imbalance created over the thirty years is seen as being in large part responsible for recurrent supply bottlenecks, materials shortages, and erratic growth patterns. The idea for the change is officially attributed to Mao:

> We must take the amount of grain and raw materials and the market
> scale provided by agriculture as the starting point for developing our national economy as a whole. In 1959 Mao Zedong stated that we must
> arrange the development of our national economy in the order of priority
> of agriculture, light industry, and heavy industry.[29]

The second motivation behind the change in the ranking of policy objectives is the need to back money wage increases in industry and cash income increases in agriculture with consumer goods, preferably those actually desired by consumers. Otherwise, the incentive effect of more money in people's pockets will not materialize; inflationary pressures will simply worsen. This has, in fact, happened in the years following the wage hikes, inflation manifesting itself on the free and "negotiated" markets, and prompting state sellers to raise officially fixed prices in unauthorized, "disguised" ways. The same motivation (plus a desire to see juvenile unemployment in the cities drop) has been behind both the post-Mao government's relatively generous attitude toward self-employment and the encouragement of small cooperative ventures in the urban services sector.

The improvement in urban workers' and employees' money earnings in the past few years can be seen from Table 9.5.

TABLE 9.5
THE MATERIAL CONDITION OF CHINESE WORKERS AND EMPLOYEES

Average Annual Money Wages of Workers and Staff Members in China
(yuan)

	1978	1979	1980	1981	1982	1983
All workers and staff	614	668	762	772	798	826
State sector	644	705	803	812	836	
Collective sector in cities and towns	505	542	624	642	671	

Rise in Urban Cost of Living Index
(percent)

1979	1980	1981	1982	1983	1984
1.9	7.5	2.5	5.8	2.1	3.0

Annual Per Capita Total and Disposable Income of Families of Workers and Staff[a]
(yuan)

	1978	1981	1982	1983	1984
Total income			500	535		
Income that can be spent on living expenses (disposable income)	316	464	495	526	608

Annual Per Capita Expenditures of Families of Workers and Staff[a]

	1981		1982	
	Yuan	% of total	Yuan	% of total
Living expenses	457	100	471	100
Food	259	56.7	276	58.6
Clothing	68	14.9	68	14.4
Rent	6	1.3	7	1.5
Utilities (water, gas, electricity)	5	1.1	6	1.3
Transportation	6	1.3	7	1.5
Medical expenses	3	0.7	3	0.6

TABLE 9.5 (continued)

	Average Annual Per Capita Consumption				
	1952	1957	1965	1978	1983
	Yuan in current prices				
	76	102	125	175	288
	Index (Based on comparable prices) (1952 = 100)				
National average	100	122.9	132.4	177.0	250.1
Rural average	100	117.1	124.8	157.5	249.4
Urban average	100	126.3	136.8	219.9	238.2

Sources: Data furnished by State Statistical Bureau, in Beijing Review, July 6, 1979, p. 40; May 19, 1980, p. 24; May 18, 1981, p. 20; May 17, 1982, p. 23; May 9, 1983, p. xi; October 24, 1983, pp. 24–25; August 27, 1984, special tables; March 25, 1985, p. viii. State Statistical Bureau, Statistical Yearbook of China 1983 (Hong Kong: Economic Information Agency, 1983), pp. 483–87. Current prices.

[a]Based on sample survey of 8,715 households (1981) and 9,020 households (1982) from 29 provinces, municipalities, and autonomous regions; 12,050 households (1984) in 82 cities. No comparable statistics are available for 1965–1980. Disposable income in 1957 (current prices) = 235 yuan.

Technological Policy: Opening the Door

The organic tendency of the Soviet-type economy to be inward-oriented was encouraged for many years by the Maoplan's anticosmopolitan, guerrilla-like, rural concentration on the advantages of self-reliance. This has now been changed (for the second time) to a policy of "leaning to all sides" in international trade and finance—especially to the advanced capitalist side. During his visit to Washington in January 1984, Premier Zhao Ziyang assured his hosts that China would continue to pursue its Open Door policy initiated after 1976. China, Zhao indicated, will allow the United States to give it economic aid, especially long-term, low-interest developmental loans that the United States advances to friendly developing countries. China is also interested in nuclear cooperation and transfers of advanced technology. The acquisition of state-of-the-art technology to replace the (by now) mostly obsolete high-cost technology used by China's industries and the poor-peasant–invented techniques in the countryside is the main reason for the Open Door and for the welcome mat spread outside it. The United States has responded favorably to this: more than a third of the value of Sino-foreign joint ventures in 1983 was with U.S. firms; the Trade and Development Assistance Act (PL-480), which provides for sales of food on highly concessionary terms, is now applicable to China; the U.S. State Department's International Development Agency is funding a feasibility study for ten major Chinese investment projects; and so on.

Two difficult questions are raised by the Open Door. The first, already encountered in the preceding pages, concerns the usefulness of technology purchases without a thorough reform of China's economic system. There are many examples of expensive blunders made by the post-Mao leadership because the economic system did not generate the allocative optimality signals needed to make rational purchasing decisions. Once imported, the capital and know-how could not be absorbed. The second question is more political. Is it in the interest of the United States to help China blaze a new trail and build socialism, with or without Chinese characteristics? There are those who argue that, apart from agriculture, the main thrust of the post-Mao adjustment has been to rebuild the system of central administrative command planning and to make it work better by resort to mathematical modeling and computers. The costs and benefits of this development to the United States and other market democracies have not been fully determined.[30]

Changing the Rural Commune System

A very important change has taken place in agriculture—an adjustment bordering on systemic reform. Indeed, some argue that what has happened to China's farm economy since 1979 (but especially after 1981) does constitute a reform of the system.[31] The change has two major elements: the so-called production responsibility system, and the administrative reorganization of the people's commune.

The production responsibility system is an arrangement under which the production team (in the commune system, the basic unit of production and accounting) enters into contracts either with small groups (four to six families) or with individual families for the delivery to the team of specified produce at state-set prices. Three types of contracts have emerged since 1979. The first two represent a fairly conservative adjustment; the last skirts systemic reform.[32] The first type of contract, dominant in 1979, is known as production responsibility to groups (*pao-ch'an tao tsu*). Here the production team assigns land to small groups of four to six households under a contract that specifies the delivery by the groups of agreed-upon output, which is paid for in work points. All or a part of any surplus is kept by the groups. Typically, the groups do the field work, from planting to harvesting, while the team supplies chemical fertilizers, draft animals, and other means of production and does the plowing. The second type of contract (*pao-ch'an tao hu*), dominant in 1980, does very much the same, except that the contract is entered into with individual families; land and draft animals are allotted to these families, and all the surplus production is typically retained by the family. Under both these types of contracts, the production team is still the production planning and income distribution agency. Both types of contracts (but especially the contracts to groups) have a long history in China: they were employed in two crisis periods, following collectivization (1956) and during the first rightward adjustment after the collapse of the Great Leap Forward (1961–1965).

The third type of contract goes beyond these rather timid administrative decentralizations. Known as *pao-kan tao hu* (or farming contract with households), it is described by a Chinese source in the following way:

> The state decides what crops and other products are to be undertaken in a region. Based on the state plan, the collective (production team) contracts out tracts of land to peasant households who guarantee to grow certain quantities of certain crops. Peasant households pay agricultural taxes and sell a required quota of their produce to the state. The production team retains a share of earnings from product sales to cover irrigation, power, and public welfare, and the households get the rest.[33]

In other words, individual families deliver a given quantity of contracted-for produce to the team at state-set prices and pay the agricultural tax (in produce) and flat levies for the team's accumulation, social, and welfare funds. (Some of this goes to pay cadres, teachers, and health workers, and to provide relief for families in need.) The delivery obligation at state-determined prices constitutes a quasi-rent, and the whole arrangement amounts to a system of family tenancy, the landlord being the state. Within the constraint imposed by the "rent," tax, and collective funds obligation, the household makes its own production decisions and distributes its income. Work points are abolished. The team, village, and sometimes township provide certain services (for example, mechanized plowing, veterinary care, crop protection, water supply) for which payment is made by the households. Anything produced over the quota, tax, levies, and other expenses can be disposed of by the households as they please; the households can sell such produce on the free market, or sell it to the state at prices negotiated with the state on the basis of prevailing free market prices. The legal ownership of the land allocated to families under the contract remains collective. Land allotment to each family is based on the number of family members and number of able-bodied workers in the family. The land cannot be sold by the family; originally, it could not be rented out, either. This caused problems as the number of family members and workers changed, and prevented the efficient use of land where efficiency is related to farm size. Beginning in 1984, subletting of land was authorized provided permission was obtained from the team. Such interfamily exchanges of the right to use land include provisions for compensating the transferor family for investments made in the land transferred. Originally, land leases ran from one to three years. This inhibited long-term investment in the land by families (why invest in land that in a few years might go to one's neighbor?) and led in many instances to abusive use of the land. The same document that authorized land sublets extended the term of land leases to fifteen years (and longer, in some places).[34] Such is the logic of privatization: it does not like half measures. Originally, draft animals were rotated among households (in 1982, there were 58 million draft animals for 183 million peasant households). This led to overworking of the animals. Now draft animals are either purchased outright by the households or rented from those who own them. Households are allowed to hire a limited number of workers. Originally, families were not allowed to own tractors and other mechanized means of production. Now this is encouraged. In the past few years, in addition to individuals buying machinery, the collective farm machine stations have contracted half of their tractors to individuals. The contractors are paid a portion of the peasant's final income. In some cases, the collective's tractors were sold to individuals. Today, more than 90 percent of China's tractors are owned by, or are under contract to, individual peasants. In other words, most farm machines are managed by individual families. The number of families who derive their income primarily from operating farm machines is increasing rapidly. Some of them use the machines chiefly to cultivate large tracts of land that they have contracted, but most provide cultivation services for other peasants. Many of the collectively owned farm machine stations have become service organizations. They offer cultivation services, repair machines, train drivers for those families who also offer mechanized service, and supply replacement parts and fuel oil. At present, 9.98 million Chinese people are operating farm machines.[35]

A late development has been the creation of households specialized in grain production. These have emerged as a resullt of the consolidation of land holdings under the now-permitted system of transfer of land use rights among families. The farms are sizable, they benefit from economies of scale, and (as of 1984) they were being actively encouraged by the authorities. The result has been that in some places a small minority of (rich) farmers delivers most or all the contractual delivery quota. Other households specialize in the provision of a variety of agricultural and nonfarm services (for example, raising pigs, caring for orchards, farming fish, raising silkworms, making handicrafts). In the past, peasants were not allowed to engage in nonagricultural pursuits except when hired by commune or brigade mini-industries. Now they are free to trade—not only on the free market, but as professional traders. These Chinese NEP-men can buy goods not subject to quota deliveries, transport them over short or long distances, and own or rent means of transportation (for example, rent railroad cars, trucks, or boats) in pursuit of their trade.[36] Specialized village workshops have made their appearance in some localities. Owned and operated by peasant families, they provide a variety of services (such as sewing and knitting) and occasionally do subcontract work for urban firms.[37] In fact, where the system has been most successful in raising peasant incomes, most of the increased income has come from nonfarm employment of family members.

In addition to privatization of property rights, new forms of voluntary cooperation among peasant families have come into being. These voluntary associations are not really so new. They represent a revival of mutual aid associations of all kinds that long existed in China's presocialist countryside. The cooperatives are of different sizes, are formed for different purposes, and combine in different ways labor, capital, and know-how contributions of their members. Of the 2 million tractors privately owned in 1983, 600,000 were owned by such private cooperatives of peasant families. The co-ops were responsible for their own profits and losses, which they shared out on the basis of the individual families' respective contributions to the venture.

Small industries formerly run by communes or production brigades have been, on occasion, rented out to family cooperatives or individuals. The new lessees are granted broad managerial rights, including the right to hire and fire personnel.

As already noted, the marketization and privatization of the rural economy is to be expanded through the gradual abolition of the quota and through the extension of market pricing to the bulk of agricultural commodities. If implemented, the change would amount to the quasi-total removal of the rural responsibility contract (the quota), a significant further marketization of buyer-seller transactions, and to an important extension of de facto private property rights in the countryside. Such an arrangement would go beyond neoclassical liberalism and amount to a crossing of systemic borders in agriculture. A serious deterioration in the weather, in the political climate, or in both could rather quickly put an end to what is sometimes referred to as China's "second" revolution (the first having consisted of the installation of the Stalinplan).

A second aspect of the post-1978 change in the configuration of China's rural economy has been the organizational decommunization of the commune. The commune's administrative functions have been vested in the revived townships (*hsiang*). Production brigades have been reconstituted as villages. Although in theory this change is designed to re-emphasize the administrative autonomy of local governmental authorities and to separate economic from governmental tasks, the political power structure within the townships and villages has not been reformed. Former rural power holders are still very much in charge. In fact, many commune, brigade, and team cadres have been quick to accommodate themselves to the new system stressing rich peasant elites.[38] Through their position in the power structure, these grassroots cadres have either become an integral part of the new rich peasant elite by awarding themselves the best contracts and the better lands, or they have joined the rich peasants in informal "I scratch your back, you scratch mine" arrangements. From being the spokesmen for the poor peasants under the Maoplan, they have become ardent advocates of the new order based on the rich peasants. And if the line changes, they will make a self-criticism and then do what is asked of them by the party. They will put the bird right back in the cage, if ordered to do so, or they will chop it up.

Commune and brigade technical offices have been transformed into companies that provide specialized services of all kinds (for example, veterinary services, agricultural extension, crop protection) to individual families under contract.

Changes have also been made in supply and marketing cooperatives and credit cooperatives. The general intent of these changes was to revitalize these organizations by making them more truly cooperative (that is, owned by their members) rather than agencies of the state and of the People's Bank (which they had been for many years), and to gear them to the needs of the new tenant family farms.

In income, output, and labor-land productivity terms, the new system has been a great success over the short term (see Tables 9.6, 9.7,

TABLE 9.6
PER CAPITA NET INCOME AND EXPENDITURES OF
PEASANT HOUSEHOLDS IN CHINA[a]
(yuan)

	Income					
	1978	1979	1980	1981	1982	1983
Average per capita net income	134	160	191	223	270	310
From collective work	89	102	108	116	140	273
From domestic sideline production (private sector)	36	44	63	85	103	
From other nonborrowing sources	9	14	20	23	27	37

	Expenditure					
	1978	1979	1980	1981	1982	1983
Average per capita living expenditures	116	355	162	191	220	248
Consumer goods	113	131	158	186	215	
Food	79	86	100	114	133	147
Clothing	15	18	20	24	25	28
Fuel	8	8	10	11	12	
Housing	4	8	13	19	23	28
Articles of daily use	8	11	15	20	22	27
Recreation and services	3	4	4	5	5	

SOURCE: Data furnished by the State Statistical Bureau, in *Beijing Review*, October 24, 1983, pp. 22–23; ibid., May 14, 1984, p. x. Figures rounded to nearest yuan; current prices.

NOTE: In 1978, 33.3 percent of the rural population had a net average per capita income of less than 100 yuan, and 2.4 percent an income in excess of 300 yuan. In 1983, the proportion of rural population with less than 100 yuan per capita was 1.4 percent, and that with over 300 yuan was 46.4 percent—a dramatic transformation (*Beijing Review*, August 27, 1984, special tables).

[a]Number of households survyed: 1978: 6,095; 1979: 10,282; 1980: 15,914; 1981: 18,529; 1982: 22,775 in 29 provinces, municipalities, and autonomous regions; 1983: 30,427 in 28 provinces, municipalities, and autonomous regions. 1952 net income (at current prices) = 73 yuan.

TABLE 9.7
PER CAPITA GRAIN OUTPUT IN CHINA
(kilograms)

	Kilograms	1957 = 100
1957	294	100
1977	284	97
1978	318	108
1979	342	116
1980	324	110
1981	326	111
1982	348	118
1983	387	126

SOURCE: Derived from State Statistical Bureau, *Statistical Yearbook of China 1983*, pp. 103 and 158; and from *Beijing Review*, March 25, 1985, pp. ii and viii.

and 9.8). Grain output per capita has risen, but the battle is uphill (see Table 9.7). Because of the diversification of agricultural production, the content of the diet in both city and country has improved over the past several years. Increases in grain output were obtained through higher yields: between 1978 and 1983, the harvested area fell by 6 percent, while grain output rose by 23 percent. Important yield increases were also registered for industrial crops (for example, 91 percent for rapeseed, 78 percent for sugar beets). Efficiency of pork production increased in terms of the ratio of annual pig slaughter to herd numbers and in terms of slaughter weights.[39]

Labor productivity has risen dramatically, releasing large numbers of formerly underemployed workers who are seeking employment in local (county, township, village) industries. The intent of the authorities is that the peasants, no longer needed on the land, should leave the land but not the countryside, and that they should go into (rural) factories without going into the cities. Despite prohibitions, underemployed rural workers are beginning to move massively to the larger cities. In the Party Central Document Number 1 (1984), it was noted that

> with the increase in labor productivity not so many people are needed to till the fields; in quite a number of economically developed areas where diversified operations are well managed, the portion of labor used to till the land has, over the years, dropped from 70 or 80 percent in the past to just 20 or 30 percent today. . . . At present [1984] surplus labor in rural areas is generally estimated to be 30 to 40 percent of the total labor force [90–120 million people] and in some areas it exceeds 60 percent.[40]

If things go on as they have since 1979, by the end of the century, surplus labor in agriculture may well exceed 200 million people.

There is no doubt that the improvement in the agricultural situation is due, for the most part, to the partial but quite extensive marketization and privatization of production relations in the countryside. The contract system has worked because it has given a private production unit (the family) the right to arrange its production schedule as it sees fit (subject to the quota constraint); has permitted this private unit to sell its after-quota, after-tax, after-levy produce at market prices; and has allowed this private unit to distribute its income as it wishes. There has been a great increase in peasant interest in farm technology of all kinds and in the acquisition of mechanical aids to production, as well as a considerable movement toward household specialization in farm-related trade, service, and transportation tasks. In industry, where production responsibility has been tried, it has not worked very well because the basic production unit with which contracts are concluded is not private (it is the state or cooperative firm); because surplus produce is sold at negotiated, floating, or other neomarket (but not competitive) prices; and because the use of retained profits is subject to many restrictions imposed by the state.

It is indisputable that institutional flexibility has been the rule in agriculture since 1979 and that it has succeeded in raising peasant living standards from the low levels of the Cultural Revolution. In some respects, the current system of information, coordination, property, and motivation in the countryside resembles the Soviet NEP of 1921–1928, but seems to go beyond it.

Several qualifications must be made about the degree of marketization and privatization and the possible future development of rural

TABLE 9.8
OUTPUT INCREASES IN CHINA, 1978–1983
(percent)

Food grains	23
Cotton	114
Oilseeds	102
Sugarcane and beets	69
Tea	50
Meat (except poultry)	64

SOURCE: Derived from State Statistical Bureau, *Statistical Yearbook of China 1983*, p. 158; and from *Beijing Review*, March 25, 1985, p. ii.

production responsibility in China. The system of markets and broad rights of use by families to collective property is still restricted by numerous state limitations and collective obligations. These include the obligatory payment of the quasi "rent," determined both by quantity of produce and by state price (this quasi "rent" is to be gradually abolished, however); the payment of the agricultural tax; the payments into the collective capital and social funds; the collective's continued legal ownership of land, irrigation and drainage facilities, some draft power, and machinery; the fact that the state is the provider to the households of all producer goods, many current inputs (for example, chemical fertilizers, electricity), most industrial consumer goods, and all credit; the inability of individual peasants to move away from their production team without state permission; the fact that a growing part of household income is derived from part-time or full-time work for collectively owned small industries; the recent proliferation of collective (commune, brigade, or team) arrangements to undertake pest control, seed selection, and chemical fertilization; the frequent harassment of the more entrepreneurial and prosperous peasants by middle-echelon (commune-level) cadres who see themselves losing their jobs in the face of peasant self-initiative; and the ideological enmity of important sections of the party who consider the system to be equivalent to capitalist restoration. Progress has been from very low output levels. Use has been made of previously unused or scandalously underutilized potential. To sustain the momentum (especially of peasant investment) in future years will require expanding the realm of individual peasant freedom and institutionalizing it in truly participatory local government bodies (village councils). This is not likely to happen. Powerful voices are already raised against too much democracy ("anarchy"), against the widening income differentials in the countryside and resultant class polarization, against the "exploitation" of industrial workers by the peasantry (which never fails to rally Marxist purists), against the negative attitude of peasant families toward army recruitment of boys who can now be better used on the family tract of land, against the reluctance of parents to send children to school when they could be more profitably used in the fields, against the reluctance of households to pay their share of contributions into the collective social and capital funds and against the consequent deterioration of rural infrastructures. The party worries about control slipping through its fingers as incomes and output grow. Historical experience shows that whenever a conflict between control and welfare develops in communist societies, the control argument prevails. As Lenin put it, "trust is good, control is better."[41]

The production responsibility system, foremost in its specialized household form, is a system that relies on, benefits, and encourages the rich peasant—not a favorite figure in the Marxist-Leninist ideological pantheon. The justification for the system is that the growing prosperity of a (relatively) few households will trickle down to the poorer strata of rural society. The rich will pull up the poor. In the meantime, the de facto decollectivization of the collective has made the lot of many poor peasant families harder, if only through the abandonment of the common iron pot principle of egalitarian income distribution.

All of this poses a potentially formidable social threat to the production responsibility system. The possibility of mass rural exodus is an economic danger, as is the neglect of infrastructural facilities and other public goods formerly taken care of by the collectivity. There are those within the leadership who, no doubt, urge a strengthening of administrative controls over rural labor mobility. There are also those in the leadership who are unhappy with the turn in the terms of rural-urban trade in favor of rural areas brought about by the procurement price increases of 1979 and subsequent purchases by the government of a growing volume of produce at the higher above-quota prices.[42] To protect urban living standards, food grains and other basics are sold at retail prices lower than the state procurement prices for those goods. The resulting agricultural subsidy has been rising rapidly since 1978 and is now a staggering 20 to 25 billion yuan a year. This is roughly a measure of the resources that, before 1979, under the regime of low procurement prices, agriculture annually transferred to urban areas. The partly marketized and privatized rural economy continues to operate within a broader environment of an industrially planned system.

China's hesitation to initiate a marketization reform of the state industrial wholesale and retail price system, finally broken (but how resolutely?) in October of 1984, is indicative of broader sociopolitical and ideological restraints on reform. In the absence of systemic reform outside agriculture, the successful rural household production responsibility system will operate in a hostile, or at least incompatible, environment and run the risk of being economically suffocated—if it is not politically decapitated.

CHAPTER TEN

Hungary: Neoclassical Liberal Plan

Chronology

The history of the plan in Hungary falls into four periods: (1) the Stalinplan, 1948–49 to 1967; (2) the New Economic Mechanism (NEM) First Try, 1968–1972; (3) the Partial Recentralization, 1973–1978; and (4) the NEM Second Try, 1979 to the present time. The Stalinplan built by Stalin's Hungarian stand-in, Mátyás Rákosi, was a faithful copy of the Soviet prototype:

> Decisions were made at the top by planners working under the politbureau's direction. What and how much was to be produced was planned in detail. The planners' decisions were enforced through rationing. Materials were rationed by administrative orders; labor by controls over wages; and capital investment by direct allocation not only of funds but also of construction materials, plant and machinery. In the early 1950s Hungary was, according to the predetermined 'statistics' of any planned economy, ploughing back some 35–37% of its national income.
>
> Prices were fixed by Rákosi's planners and changed rarely. Industrial wholesale prices—the prices that firms charge each other—were fixed on a cost-plus basis in which the firms concerned were able to earn sufficient revenue to cover current (but not capital) expenditure and show a small profit. Retail prices for the goods people wanted were deliberately kept too low, as shown by the persistent shortage of this, that or the other. Agricultural prices were held down while the prices of fertilizers, fuel, machines and everything else farmers needed from industry were kept relatively high, thus simultaneously encouraging demand and discouraging supply.
>
> In foreign trade, totally unrealistic exchange rates and a complicated structure of taxes and subsidies isolated domestic prices from foreign

ones. With foreign trade conducted by special import-export firms, the factories had no direct contact with foreign customers and suppliers and no real interest in foreign trade.[1]

The blunders, waste, and inefficiency of the Stalinplan; its unsuitability for a small, natural resource–deficient, foreign trade–dependent, narrow domestic-market country; and a politically repressive regime subservient to the Soviet Union were directly responsible for the Hungarian revolution of 1956. More quietly and a little earlier, a few Hungarian economists had advocated changes in the Stalinist system in the direction of decentralization of decisions. These arguments began to surface in 1954, a year or so after Stalin's death.[2] Interrupted by the 1956 revolution, they gained momentum in the mid-1960s, involving at that time not only academic economists, but party and government policymakers as well. The elaboration of a relatively liberal blueprint for the revision of the Stalinist economy thus became a joint national effort (*nemzeti konzenszus*) unique in the annals of Eastern Europe's socialist vassal states.

The theoretical consensus-cum-compromise was embodied on January 1, 1968, in documents that put the NEM (or, as we would call it, the neoclassical liberal plan) into practice. The transition from the Stalinplan (or slightly modified version of it) to the liberal plan was made in one comprehensive move.[3] It was a blanket revision rather than a staggered patchwork of adjustments. This was the time when the Soviet Union itself was engaged on a course of piecemeal adjustments of a much more conservative bent. Soviet attention was thus temporarily diverted, and Soviet temper was "reformist." However, as an additional precaution, the Hungarians built several institutional brakes into their NEM. These were applied from time to time, with increasing pressure as time went on, not only to allay Soviet fears of capitalist restoration, but to humor those opponents of the NEM among the Hungarian party elite whose cooperation in implementing the changes had to be secured. The brakes were also built in to lessen the disruptions that an orchestrated and relatively bold adjustment of the Stalinplan was bound to cause. The brakes included price and average wage controls, many ad hoc administrative interventions, and the central setting of limits on the use of enterprise funds formed from retained profits.

Three events—one internal, two external—made the adjusters slam on the brakes and reverse gear in 1972, 1973, and 1974. The first event was domestic in origin but applauded by the Soviets. It revolved around the contradiction between the necessary conditions for efficiency and what Hungarian economist János Kornai calls "the ethical principles of a socialist economy."[4] This contradiction found its quintessential expression in large income inequalities, which adversely affected workers in the larger, cumbersome, inefficient, overstaffed, noncompetitive, complacent, and coddled state-owned industries. Managers of these industries joined their employees in clamoring for the NEM changes to be stopped—or better still, reversed. The problem was quickly politicized as "the social situation of certain groups and subclasses . . . [especially] the most important subclass—workers in the large industrial plants—developed the least favorably."[5] The proletariat and the holders of sinecures were fighting for their jobs, which were threatened by productivity-promoting adjustments. In 1973, fifty large "political" factories built during the Stalinplan were exempted from the efficiency-promoting rules of the NEM and given large subsidies.

Domestic reasons for backtracking on the early NEM were joined in 1973 by the external shock administered to the Hungarian economy by the oil crisis and its accompanying inflation.[6] This was followed by worldwide stagflation, which continued on its recessionary course until the early 1980s, and by the Soviet decision to deny its East European dependencies oil at preferential prices. The Hungarian planners' response was to plan more during such troublesome times, even though the record of the NEM until 1972–73 had been encouraging. Between 1967 and 1973, net material product (which had stagnated before) increased at an average annual rate of more than 6 percent, and consumption at 5.7 percent. Between 1962–1967 and 1967–1972, factor productivity more than doubled. Inventory ratios were significantly reduced. Overall, there was a notable reduction in firm costs and an increase in the alacrity of enterprise response to domestic and foreign demands. Between 1967 and 1973, the rate of increase of gross agricultural output almost doubled to 3 percent per year. During the same period, exports rose at an average annual rate of 12 percent. The increase was especially marked for exports to developed market economies (annual rate of 24 percent).[7]

In the face of deteriorating external conditions, Hungary decided to maintain past (NEM) rates of domestic growth. This involved an increased rate of imports (to sustain the growth of domestic consumption, investment, and stocks of raw materials), a decline of the export rate in a recessionary world and in the context of strong domestic demand, and a deterioration in hard-currency terms of trade. A large convertible-currency trade deficit quickly developed, necessitating recourse to foreign borrowing. Net foreign indebtedness in convertible currencies, which was 900 million dollars in 1970–1973, rose to 5.2 billion dollars in

1978–1980.[8] To deal with the 1972 domestic income inequality phenomenon, central controls over profit sharing by enterprise managements were introduced, controls over labor mobility were tightened, and enterprise investments were aligned more closely with state preferences. To deal with the external (1973–74) threats, export taxes, import subsidies, and foreign exchange restrictions were reintroduced (once again effectively insulating domestic producer prices from world market prices); detailed planning by ministries of enterprise activities was again taken up; and physical indicators began to multiply and again take precedence over value indices. The withdrawal from greater reliance on (limited) market forces and (partial) privatization of allocative decisions that characterized the NEM was not a retreat all the way back to the Stalinplan. It was, however, a shift away from the liberal toward a conservative variant of the neoclassical plan.

On January 1, 1980, the NEM was reintroduced in a form nominally more liberal than its 1968–1972 aborted predecessor but, in the opinion of reform-minded Hungarian economists, one that was inconsistent and haphazard. The resurrected national consensus was that to translate Hungary's potential comparative advantage in hard-currency international trade into domestic growth and efficiency, the institutional arrangements and goals of the neoclassical liberal plan had to be reinstated. (A few years later, in 1984, a parallel intellectual and policy development occurred in Tengist China.)

Basic Concepts of the Neoclassical Liberal Plan

From the broad picture of the neoclassical plan in Chapter 3, what specific ideas emerge as defining the liberal variant of the plan under the four institutions and societal goals?

Information

1. Primary reliance is placed on value-type (financial-price) information, the values themselves being increasingly synthetic expressions of competitive, contractual, buyer-seller (market) relationships, that is, indicators of cost to producers and utility to users. This involves: (a) progressive alignment of domestic producer prices with world market prices (which implies import and exchange rate liberalization); (b) alignment of consumer prices with producer prices, that is, reduction of disparities between the two sets of prices resulting from subsidies and socially or politically motivated tax differentials; (c) broader (but

not broad) right granted to enterprises to set uncontrolled prices, especially the prices of new products (here, too, the right remains restricted); (d) a movement toward the use of profit expressed in "competitive prices" as the only indicator of enterprise performance.

All of this means a transition from reliance on obligatory physical-technical norms set by the planners to price signals, and within price signals, movement from Grossman's Quadrant IV (see Figure 2.1) toward Quadrant I. It means progress toward the marketization of information. The trend is in the direction of economic (as opposed to administrative) decentralization of allocative decisions.

2. Implied in (1) is an important change in the character of the information generated in and transmitted through the system. Under the liberal plan, information is made increasingly general and voluntary. Information that used to be addressee-specific (for example, addressed by the planners to particular enterprise managers) and obligatory or quasi-obligatory for the recipient, now tends toward generalized "pure" information about scarcity conditions in the system, to which the recipients adapt as best they see fit, that is, in accordance with their maximizing calculus. This voluntary adaptation is, in turn, transmitted through prices to the other party or parties to the transaction. Rather than being handed down as an obligation, information is exchanged.

Rarely (and then only cautiously) articulated is the idea of pluralizing the political process—of introducing a democratic modernization, once talked about in China (1978–79), but neither implemented there nor anywhere else in the world of the plan (except very briefly and imperfectly during the Czech spring of 1968, and in Poland before the December 13, 1981, imposition of martial law).

Coordination

1. Plan directives, as a system, are progressively replaced by direct linkages of increasingly autonomous firms through an expanding market-type price system. Increased autonomy means expansion of the firm's decision-making powers, including the right to make investment decisions, to make use of new opportunities for production, and to obtain inputs through multiple "commercial" channels. The role of the banking system in enterprise investment decisions is enlarged (though the banking system remains centralized), and state budgetary support is restricted.

2. The system of mandatory output targets and the physical rationing (funding) of key inputs to firms by obligatory quotas are, by and

large, done away with. The trend is toward the elimination of the material-technical supply network and the commercialization of wholesale trade.[9] However, a considerable amount of indirect, informal control from above remains "for the time being"—a fateful escape clause. This control is enforced by discreet command ("suggestions"), and by the use of selective financial instruments (differentiated taxes, centralized credits, subsidies).

3. Administrative reorganization aims at a reduction in the number and, it is to be hoped, policy influence of the planning and supervisory bureaucracies.

4. The semilicit and illicit "unregistered" market economy is tolerated, and parts of it are legalized or otherwise absorbed by the official economy as auxiliary means of coordination.

Property

1. As noted in Chapter 3, the neoclassical plan in both variants accommodates itself to wide extensions of private property rights in the means of production, retail distribution, and the service trades. This is particularly so regarding expanded rights of use granted to the actual operators of legally designated public assets, known under the code name of "rational separation of capital ownership functions from government control of the economy."[10] The difference between a conservative and a liberal approach to this delicate issue (delicate for Marxists) is to be found in the pragmatic graciousness with which the reality of privatization is accepted by the communist establishment. In the conservative Polish plan, peasant families legally own their farms (restricted in size), but they are persuasively hampered in the free exercise of their legal rights by the state's hostility toward the institution of private property. In Hungary (and, increasingly, in China), the state's attitude toward de facto private property in household plots and in some other assets has fluctuated over time (for example, as with the crackdown of the mid-1970s), but on the whole has been relatively benign (and even supportive, within limits), at least since the introduction of the first NEM in 1968. The benignity and support are not uniformly approved of by all members of the Hungarian party and government bureaucracies ("one should not believe that everybody is 'pragmatic' in Hungary"), but they are at least more marked and less self-conscious than in other parts of the planned world.[11]

2. This support for de facto extension of private property rights finds expression in a broad range of organizational forms in which the borderline between public and private property is blurred. There are

many such flexible arrangements, including lower-level cooperatives, cooperative-private partnerships, state-private and cooperative-private subcontracting and leasing deals, and joint ventures with foreign capitalists. Post-Mao China, like Hungary, is experimenting with a growing number of small- and medium-sized, loosely organized units of this kind in which the range of property rights vested in the unit is judged primarily by efficiency criteria. In some respects, this is a throwback to the organizational mixed property forms used before the massive wave of Stalinplan socialization.[12]

3. Points (1) and (2) apply to legalized mixed and private property. A similar, though officially less accommodating, attitude exists toward private property in the legally unrecognized underground economy. Although private appropriation of state property and state-paid time are common in both the conservative and liberal variants of the plan, in the liberal variant there are more shades of illegality and more "color blindness" on the part of law enforcers. (This does not mean that official corruption in the liberal plan is any more widespread than in the conservative plan. It is simply tacitly co-opted, accepted as the inevitable condition of state socialism.) The following is the color scheme of the liberal plan:

> Work carried out with one's own tools and during one's free time—grey; with state-owned tools but not during working hours—light brown; with state-owned tools *and* during working hours—dark brown. The illegal renting of land, premises, or a dwelling—brown; above a certain constantly changing limit—black. Illicit property deals—black. Loans to individuals or groups for the (partial or total) financing of their projects—black. All these activities contribute toward increasing the GNP.[13]

Motivation

1. Primary reliance is on positive material incentives to workers and managers. This includes turning a myopic eye to private income generated in the semilicit or illicit economy from grey to dark brown, sometimes black. Marginal opportunities are provided for the investment of private savings in the official economy.

2. In accordance with a post-Stalinplan implicit social compact between the authorities and the citizenry, the "law" of rational low wages is laid to rest, official wages (including earnings from overtime work) rising more or less in concert with, or slightly faster than, the rise in official consumer goods prices—with occasional exceptions. These exceptions are not trivial, and erosion of real living standards tends to occur (temporarily, it is hoped) as prices are freed. Income

disparities grow. In a Hungarian (also, lately, Chinese) version of the trickle-down theory,

> if the income of some people is rising more rapidly than that of others, but everybody's income is rising anyway, this is usually tolerated by society. But if the income of people with low resources does not rise or even declines, while that of others conspicuously rises, the limit of tolerance of society may suddenly sink lower.[14]

When this happens, the liberal plan becomes subject to what Hungarian economist Rezsö Nyers calls "the pitfall of leveling of incomes," which applies to both the disposable income of efficient enterprises and to wages.[15] Consumption costs (see Chapter 3) are lowered through a reorientation of official goal priorities in favor of consumer goods supply (or at least in disfavor of those whom Khrushchev once described as the "metal eaters"), and through the consumption opportunities provided by the unofficial economy—the expansion of the "nonstate sphere."

3. Enterprise managements are involved in wage determination to a greater extent than in the neoclassical conservative plan. However, central controls over wages are considerable. They are exercised through taxes and subsidies, which affect enterprise profits, and, more directly, through wage legislation.

4. Managerial and worker bonuses are tied to profit performance.

5. The firms' budget constraint is hardened; that is, unprofitable firms are shut down.

6. Enterprise managers have the right to hire and dismiss workers. State sector guaranteed lifelong employment is abolished. Some form of intrafirm "democratic" control over the firm's leadership may (but need not) be introduced. Enterprise directors are still members of the *nomenklatura*.

The goals of the neoclassical liberal plan are comparatively consumer- and outward-oriented.

It should be noted that changes toward partial marketization and privatization of the neoclassical liberal plan's institutional structure have qualifiers attached to them at every step. The liberal adjustments "tend" in a marketizing and privatizing direction; the material-technical supply network is dismantled "by and large"; plan directives are "progressively" replaced by direct linkages of "increasingly" independent firms through an "expanding," "market-type" price system; administrative reorganization "aims at" a reduction in the planning and supervisory bureaucracies; and so on. There is an inclination to marketize and privatize an increasingly complex economic structure that eludes centralization by presently available means, but the goods are never quite delivered—least of all in the state sector. In 1983, after sixteen years of the NEM, Kornai concluded that in Hungary

> there does not exist a built-in mechanism that could assert itself in the behavioral rules of the state enterprise, that could hold it back from the investment drive, and that could force it to adjust to demand. The factors that guarantee moderation of growth policy and a favorable internal supply of goods to the population are not sufficiently 'institutionalized.' This could only be secured by a really comprehensive reform of the economic mechanism that also deeply permeates the state sector.[16]

The Hungarian liberal plan experiment remains tentative, inconsistent, subject to contradictory domestic pulls, threatened by powerful vested interests and offended ideological sensibilities, and dependent upon the goodwill of a reactionary Soviet Union. The liberal plan is unfinished business—perhaps unfinishable within the institutional framework of the plan; it is an amalgam of radical half-measures only halfway implemented. It tries to find the economically rational and politically feasible dimensions of the cage without simultaneously trying to determine where exactly socialism ends and capitalism begins (a provocative problem). As the Czechs found in 1968 to their grief, the less said about such things the better. The "leading political role" (that is, the monopoly) of the party is reaffirmed at every step. But the monopoly role of the party in politics is in itself an enormous obstacle to pluralizing the economy.

"We do not lull ourselves into the belief of complete freedom of action," writes one Hungarian economist (a coauthor of the liberal plan), "yet we make efforts to grasp as much as possible of the possibilities for action as they arise . . . We are between the past and the future."[17] In this "twilight zone," much that goes by the name of marketization and privatization, lateral buyer-seller bargaining, and competitive pricing is really simulated and orchestrated by underemployed planners "with extremely complicated legal rules, on a desk."[18]

What Has Happened

In light of the basic concepts of the neoclassical liberal plan, let us now see what actually has been done in the Hungarian economy since the inauguration of the NEM in 1968 and its reinauguration in 1980 after the slippage of 1973–1978.

Information

1. Two things are beyond doubt: compared with the economies of the neoclassical conservative plan, as a matter of principle greater reliance is placed on value-type (financial-price) information, and an attempt is made to make the values reflect scarcity relationships within the economy and between domestic and world market prices for internationally traded goods (nonruble trade). In other words, the degree of marketization of information is greater in the Hungarian liberal plan than in its conservative Soviet and East European counterparts.

a. On January 1, 1980, the government introduced new producer prices based on world market prices for roughly two-thirds of its firms. The share of these "competitive" prices was 80 percent in machine building, 50 percent in the chemical industry, and 20 percent in food processing. Two kinds of firms were affected: those exporting more than 5 percent of their output in convertible-currency trade, and those using a high proportion of materials imported in such trade. In the first case, the domestic prices of industrial products were set on the basis of profit margins that reflected the domestic cost of earning convertible currencies in exports.[19] The firms could raise the domestic price if the export price rose, and had to lower the domestic price when the export price fell. When there was no domestic competition for a good, the export-based domestic price gave rise to excess demand. However, the firm was not allowed to establish market equilibrium by raising the domestic price. In the second case (firms using a high proportion of materials imported in hard-currency trade), the domestic prices of raw materials, fuels, and basic intermediate products were equated to import prices in convertible-currency trade, with the differences between these and prices of imports from planned economies (ruble trade) being made up by taxes and subsidies. This alignment necessitated increases in the domestic prices of energy (57 percent), and raw materials and basic intermediate products (30 percent). From then on, the domestic prices of raw materials and basic intermediate products were to fluctuate in accordance with changes in prices paid in convertible-currency trade and with changes in the exchange rate. Energy prices were fixed centrally and were to be adjusted from time to time in line with changes in world market prices.[20]

Because of incomes and living standards policies, domestic prices of agricultural products (wheat included) are not generally aligned with world market prices, even though some domestically produced commodities are competitive at world prices (for example, wheat). However, the influence of wheat market prices on the calculation of domestic prices has been increasing over time, particularly for (i) those products where the proportion of (convertible-currency) imports is large (for example, protein feeds), and (ii) those products that act as substitutes for (convertible-currency) imports (some seeds). Products not entering hard-currency trade and primarily consumed at home continued to be priced according to domestic input costs, and remained unrelated to world prices (for example, early vegetables, four-fifths of which are produced privately).[21]

In the "noncompetitive" sphere of the economy (20 percent of machine building, 50 percent of chemicals, 80 percent of food processing), firms were allowed to set their domestic prices with a 6 percent profit margin, and subsequently to adjust those prices in line with increases or decreases in costs. Noncompetitive–pricing sphere enterprises must report to the government Materials and Price Office whenever their profitability exceeds 6 percent (9 percent in the service trades). The Materials and Price Office can then forbid further price increases, unless the portion of profit above 6 (or 9) percent is expected to be absorbed by increased costs. However, there are many exemptions from the obligation to report. The liberality of the exemption depends to a considerable extent on the quality of the enterprise's bureaucratic connections with superior authorities. In the past, many enterprises received favored treatment under the pricing regulations because they argued that they were the only suppliers of a particular product. Monopolistic pricing behavior was thus encouraged and rewarded.[22]

Hungarian economists point out that the "competitive" prices are not really competitive—they are simulated by the ex-planners:

> Our price mechanism presupposes the market mechanism, and many of
> our problems are due to this fact or to the situation that in practice we
> have a simulated rather than a real market. We can expect an appropriate
> solution only if steps are taken to establish a real market mechanism and
> competition.[23]
>
> How can prices be based on world market prices without organic links
> with the world market? How can they be 'competitive prices' without
> competition? If the new price system would function according to its
> principle, that would really mean a step forward as compared with
> former practice, which was characterized by simple cost-plus pricing. The
> new pricing principle means, however, a retreat in comparison with the

1968 principle because it excludes the influence of domestic demand and supply on prices from the price formation. Moreover, it is replaced not by the direct influence of foreign markets but by taking foreign trade prices into consideration in a rather peculiar pricing procedure. Therefore, the pricing principle of 1980 is not only a step forward but at the same time a retreat, reflecting the fact that the 'reformers' have lost their belief in the real functioning of a *real* market.[24]

Kornai shows that the spirit of the original competitive pricing idea has been frequently and grossly violated. Thus, when the profitability of exports declined, the firms were theoretically obliged to reduce their domestic prices accordingly, which in most cases meant a reduction in their profitabilities (which in turn was bad news for worker and management profit-sharing wage and salary supplements). A study of 167 firms subject to the competitive price system showed that the profitability of domestic sales was greater than that of hard-currency export sales. In several cases, the two profitabilities moved in opposite directions compared with the pre-1980 period: domestic profitabilities increased, while export profitabilities declined.[25] This was due to the generous use of taxes and subsidies to compensate or overcompensate firms for the effect of the price revision.

Although firms have a reasonable amount of latitude with respect to convertible-currency area exports, imports continue to be strictly controlled by the center. There is no import competition to speak of. In the absence of such competition, there is no full alignment of domestic manufacturing producer prices with world market prices.

Until recent years, there were two exchange rates for the forint: a commercial rate, and a lower tourist rate. In mid-1981, the two rates were unified—a step, some say, toward the convertibility of the forint. The exchange rate is based on the average cost of exports and necessitates the subsidization of a significant part of exports. Under the General Agreement on Tariffs and Trade, Hungary has obligated itself to carry out a progressive tariff reduction (tariffs now average 24 percent, plus additional import charges of 4 percent). Import licensing is pervasive. This has led to the creation of domestic industries that are noncompetitive on world markets as to cost, quality, or both.

b. An attempt has been made to reduce the disparities between the structure of producer and consumer prices through the reduction or partial removal of differential taxes and subsidies. This reduction and removal are, however, far from complete. The most important disparity is between the producer prices of agricultural staples and the domestic retail prices of those staples. The calculation of correct farm costs of production is vitiated by what one writer calls the "inability" to determine appropriate scarcity charges for land use (rent).[26] Although there are land taxes that depend on quality differentials, the differentiation appears to be too small. Processed agricultural exports receive higher tax rebates than exports of manufactured products. High taxes are levied on certain goods deemed to be socially undesirable (for example, alcoholic beverages), while tax exemptions or subsidies are applied to other goods deemed socially desirable (children's clothing; housing; heating materials; and public utilities consumed by the citizens, not tourists). The price system, therefore, continues to be fairly distorted (see Kornai, above). Free market prices in 1980 constituted 50 percent of retail trade (37 percent in 1978), 80 pecent of industrial producer prices, and 30 percent of agricultural prices. Important agricultural products (for example, grain, animals, animal products, and sugar beets) are purchased by the state at long-term contractual, fixed or regulated prices. Above-quota sales are made at daily determined market prices.

These ratios of free prices (which include maxima or floating prices) to controlled prices raise three problems. The first concerns the relative weight of each price in the economy. Let us assume that an economy has only two goods, one widely consumed (for example, bread), the other not (yo-yos, for instance). If the price of bread is controlled and the price of yo-yos is fixed, one could conclude that in this economy half the prices are fixed and half are free, which would not get us very far in our understanding of reality. But this is precisely the problem with listing the proportions of controlled and free prices in Hungary. Many prices of staples, fuels, raw materials, basic intermediate products, and processed foods are controlled; the prices of "luxuries" are not.

This raises the second problem. Nominal control over prices should be distinguished from effective control. Not unlike tariff theory (where the effective rate of tariff protection of a good is calculated as the tariff rate of the good plus the tariff rate on inputs used to produce the good), calculation of the effective control over output prices should include the degree of control over the prices of inputs.[27] The price of yo-yos may be free, but the price of the wood from which the yo-yo is made is controlled.

The third problem is that the "free" trade and free pricing of producer goods (the 80 percent) takes place in monopolistic markets where buyers' free choice remains strictly formal and where the crucial ingredient of competition is missing.

There is also a wide sphere of free prices on the grey to black market. Practically everyone in Hungary engages in some form of moonlighting activity, which involves all sorts of competitive transactions and represents in its totality a significant addition to the income earned in the official economy. (This subject is discussed more fully under "Coordination and Motivation," below.)

Economists both in and out of Hungary agree that the differences between producer and consumer prices need to be further narrowed, and consumer prices need to be made more flexible so they can transmit information about changes in demand to the producers.[28]

c. The right of Hungarian firms to set the prices of their products—even where these prices are in the free sphere—is quite limited, being restricted by many specific legal rules.[29] The firms spend quite a bit of time and expend much ingenuity (which could be more productively used elsewhere) trying to circumvent the rules. In this regard, the basic relationship remains, by and large, vertical (between the seller and the government Materials and Price Office), but the verticality is less formal than before. As Kornai puts it, the relationship resembles "repeated matches in a game," a "regulator game"—more popularly known as finagling.[30] Every firm must submit detailed price documentation to the Materials and Price Office every six months. The intent behind this requirement is to keep an eye on the profit levels of individual firms and confiscate "unfair" profits. The ability of a firm to evade the regulations and have the upper hand in the regulator game depends on the product group. Where a firm produces a narrow range of standardized products, the Materials and Price Office can keep a close tab on the relationship of the firm's costs and prices. Where differentiated products are involved and the output is sold in several markets, enforcement of the legal price rules becomes extremely elusive. Given the difficulty experienced by Hungarian firms to change even free-sphere prices, there has been a tendency to come up with new products—some innovative, others sham. In such cases, latitude for enterprise price setting is comparatively greater (as it is in the other countries of the plan). There is thus quite a bit of innovation going on in Hungarian industry, but the larger part of it—as in other state socialist countries—consists of changing labels and pouring old Tokay into new bottles.

In agriculture, the 30 percent of freely set prices are less burdened with explicit and informal regulations. Included in the 30 percent are prices charged by collective farms to the state for above-contract purchases and prices ruling on the urban and rural free markets.

d. Given all the above, there is, of course, little chance of or point in profit and profitability rates becoming the only indicator of enterprise performance as required by the basic concepts of the neoclassical liberal plan. The Hungarian experience shows two things. First, when firm profits and profitabilities emerged from the changed system of "competitive" prices, they were quickly annulled by differentiated taxes and subsidies, the result of which was to restore the status quo ante. Of a total of 1,135 industrial units, 971 (or 85.5 percent) reverted to the old allocatively useless profitabilities within less than two years of the "competitive" price system's introduction. Between 1968 and 1980, more than one hundred orders and legal rules were introduced to regulate the profits and profit-sharing decisions of the firms. About two-thirds of enterprise gross profits were taxed away and redistributed by the ex-planners. Thus, one cannot help but wonder what has happened to the NEM. Second, other criteria of enterprise success were and are being used in addition to profit: production of cheap consumer goods, exports to hard-currency areas, fulfillment of CMEA export contracts, "sales responsibility" (sale of output, very stringently supervised), and so on. This is perhaps just as well, because in the absence of truly competitive market prices, the profit criterion is (as it always has been) not a rational indicator of the efficiency of resource allocation—it means nothing.

In socialized agriculture, profit maximization, though more important, is not the only criterion of success, either. Between one-quarter and two-fifths of the cooperative farms are subsidized (because of land quality differentials). These farms are unlikely to maximize profits.

The consensus of expert opinion on the Hungarian price system in the early to mid 1980s was that there were still many formal and informal controls exercised over the so-called free pricing sphere, and that a significant portion of prices (including the prices of strategic inputs) remained in the sphere of direct government regulation. The changed Hungarian price system, therefore, only marginally played an allocative role—one somewhat greater than in countries of the conservative neoclassical plan, but still very restricted.

A powerful external constraint on the freeing of prices and their alignment with world market prices is Hungary's commitment to export and import under bilateral and multilateral CMEA contracts. This is not very popular with the Hungarians (perhaps illogically, since most of the goods sold in that trade would find no takers on the more sophisticated convertible-currency markets). Popular or not (but certainly nationalistically offensive), this commitment (under CMEA contracts) absorbs a great deal of capital and labor. Roughly one-third of Hungary's exports and one-quarter of imports involved in this intraplan trade consist of binding obligations under the bloc's "socialist division of labor." This means that a significant part of Hungary's industry working toward fulfilling such fraternal obligations of necessity must remain outside the reach of price liberation and other market-oriented adjustments.

2. Since the inauguration of the NEM in 1968, what has happened in Hungary is not the actual implementation of generalized, voluntary, pure information about scarcity conditions in the system, but rather the establishment of both general principles endorsing progress in that direction and of simulated "competitive" price exercises designed to activate that progress. At least under the liberal plan there are general principles, endorsed by the party and government, that are favorably inclined toward the idea of competitive, lateral, contractual information directly and spontaneously generated by buyer-seller transactions. Departures from these principles may be (and are) made—so many, in fact, that in the course of implementation the new information system falls far short of its ideals. The information system remains mixed, with vertical information remaining predominant (although the verticality is less formal than in the neoclassical conservative plan and the realm of horizontal information is larger). The once highly visible hand of the planners becomes invisible. Firms are advised, rather than ordered, to do certain centrally desired things, and they are counseled to behave in specified ways. The advice and counsel are in practice as binding as the formal ministerial orders, norms, balances, and allocation certificates were in the plan's earlier incarnation—the firms subject themselves, "almost voluntarily, to patronage."[31] There is also greater tolerance of the lateral, competitive underground information network. It is accepted by the liberal plan, with cynical bemusement on the part of officials and citizenry alike.

In terms of political marketization (democratization), there has been what American political scientist Ivan Volgyes calls "an alliance policy": repression but not terror; remarkable instances of free expression, but no free association or free political action. The three basic characteristics of this alliance dating back to 1968 appear to be the total depoliticization of Hungarian life; the "Greyhound effect" (in which one can discuss anything one pleases, preferably in private, but must "leave the driving to us"—the Party); and *ez van-ezt kell szeretni,* or "this is what there is; this is what you must love" (that is, only Kádár rule exists; there is no possible alternative).[32] As in other East European communist countries, the social compact exchanges relative prosperity for absolute docility. In the other countries, however, delivery by the state of relative prosperity is becoming increasingly difficult. The amount of democracy in Hungary is consistent with the amount of marketization and privatization of the Hungarian economy. Both are greater than elsewhere—but not enough to love.

Coordination

1. Plan directives mandatory on the state firms and rural cooperatives have been abolished as a system (exceptions exist). In the nonagricultural sector,

> enterprises consult the ministry while drafting their plans and even sub-
> mit the plan to the ministry; in turn the ministry often directs the enter-
> prise to do or not to do something. But neither the ministry nor the
> planning office total up the plan figures supplied by enterprises [there is
> no aggregation of material and other balances].[33]

The abolition of balance aggregation and disaggregation is one of the
characteristics distinguishing the liberal plan from its conservative
counterparts in other state socialist countries. Enterprises spend less
time bargaining about the plan with superior (ministerial and other)
authorities, and more time dealing with "more essential problems."
They do, however, still spend more time "consulting" and "cooperat-
ing" with their overseers (the Ministry of Industry and the National
Materials and Price Office).

In agriculture, the system of vertical coordination is even more relaxed (though not horizontal and voluntary either). Contractual deliveries to the state of grain, animals, animal products, sugar beets, sunflowers, and some other important products at state-set, long-term
prices are centrally determined "according to plan." The prices are not
exploitative. However, more than in industry, the coordinating mechanism in Hungarian agriculture relies on the agricultural cooperatives'
perception of their individual material interest and on their relatively
autonomous pursuit of that interest. The state helps shape that perception through extensive use of indirect financial indicators: prices, wages,
credits, taxes, and subsidies. Socialized farming units' pursuit of their
own financial interest takes place, therefore, within only a partially marketized price system (see above, "Information"). The rural cooperatives'
investment decisions are regulated primarily by the National Bank's
control over credit allocation. Long-, medium-, and short-term credit is
examined by the National Bank in accordance with plan priorities. Some
investment decisions are out of the farms' hands altogether; they are
made instead by county-level authorities.

2. The system of mandatory output targets and the physical rationing (funding) of key inputs to firms by obligatory quotas has been

eliminated. As noted earlier, there is no aggregation and disaggregation of balances. Material-technical supply as it exists in the USSR has been replaced by multiple channel wholesale trade in the means of production. There remain several "brakes" on this truly significant dismantling of a key institutional arrangement of the old Stalinplan: (a) rules exist limiting the scope of wholesaling in the means of production; these rules are supposed to be temporary exceptions to the general principle and confined to certain problem areas (they do, however, have a way of becoming permanent and transforming themselves into the guiding principle); (b) informal interventions by the authorities are very common; though they are not blanket interventions, they distort what was meant to be market-type allocation; (c) as noted earlier, wholesale trade in materials, semifabricates, and producer goods is dominated by monopolistic state firms, so that competitive bidding is not much in evidence; and (d) the wholesale "market" is a seller's market, so that free choice by buyers is not much in evidence either.

3. The number of industrial branch ministries has been reduced to one: the Ministry of Industry. However, it is not numbers that matter, but power. The one remaining "super" ministry has considerable influence, which it shares with the Materials and Price Office:

> The Hungarian system of 'neither planning targets nor market' has meant not only releasing enterprise decisions from control from above through plan instructions, but at the same time preserving bureaucratic control by the economic elite, at present including both party and state officials in charge of economic matters and top managers of big enterprises. There have been no significant moves towards restriction of this elite's decisionmaking power by the market or by parliamentary democracy and public opinion.[34]

Members of the privileged class have managed to hold onto the power levers, and are not, as in other countries of the plan, receptive to the expansion of market influences, that is, to power sharing. It is this organizationally reshuffled elite at the liberal plan's center that has succeeded in, among other things, restricting the mobility of labor (restriction of the labor market), imposing its preference on investment allocations and putting a brake on investment after 1978 (restriction of the capital market), confiscating the development funds of foreign trade enterprises in 1970–71 (restriction of foreign trade markets), and cracking down on the market-oriented private plot and auxiliary activities of rural cooperatives and on the unregistered (second) market economy in 1975.

4. Despite these outbursts against the legal and unregistered mar-

ket economy, one of the characteristic features of the neoclassical liberal plan is the symbiosis of the plan and the shadowy "nonplanned sphere," where legal private enterprise imperceptibly merges into illegal pursuits. Altogether, 1.2 million man-years are believed to be expended in the legal private economy by an economically active population of 5.2 million ingenious souls. Many more million man-years are spent in extralegal private activities. Much of the success of the liberal plan in regard to consumer welfare through an easing of consumer costs is due to the official tolerance (indeed, integration) of the shadow economy in the official one. "The extension of the nonstate sphere," writes Kornai, "should be regarded as an organic part of the reform process."[35] Although overall this merging has had many positive material consequences for the consumer, the picture is not without blemishes. Money-making activities in the second economy are largely responsible for the sharp income and wealth differentials that have emerged and that, in the view of some, severely strain the social fabric of Hungary. Correction of these disparities through progressive personal taxation is made difficult by the clandestine nature of most earnings. Since corruption and illegal markets of all colors are an integral part of state socialism, the friendly stance adopted by the liberal plan toward the underground market phenomenon may be seen as an attempt by the plan to reap some profits itself and at least tax some of the illicit earnings.

Property

1. The Hungarian firm—agricultural, commercial, and industrial— has broader decision-making powers than its counterpart in the neoclassical conservative plan. In fact, the major purpose of the NEM was to increase the autonomy of the basic producing units. That some progress has been made toward that goal is beyond question. As we have seen, the Hungarian firm has been significantly liberated on its input acquisition side through the commercialization of producer goods and materials supply. On the output side, too, the abolition of mandatory targets set by the planners has resulted in the expansion of firm autonomy. However, the central authorities still keep a tight grip on enterprise contractual delivery obligations ("sales" performance), so that on this side the room for maneuver by the firm is more limited. The firm has gained some rights to set prices (particularly of new products) and to make investments out of its own retained profits, but these rights remain residual. Still, compared with the past, the sphere of prices determined by direct agreements between buyer and seller has been

considerably enlarged. Although investment by firms remains comparatively small, investment decisions have been pluralized. Instead of being determined by a central planning board, they are now the joint responsibility of the central authorities, the state banking system, and the firms.

The extension of enterprise rights regarding the enterprises' fixed and circulating assets has been most evident in agriculture. Since the second collectivization in 1958 (completed in 1961), new members of the rural cooperatives have been permitted to own their livestock and were paid cash for the land they contributed to the collective. Members of cooperatives legally own their private plots. These plots are provided free to members and average 0.6 hectares. This area can be doubled by leasing from the collective or state farms land these farms find unsuitable for large-scale cultivation. Restrictions on the sale of tools, small machinery, fodder, fertilizer, pesticides, and other production inputs to households for use on these plots have been lifted (although, as noted earlier, from time to time there are second thoughts on this). Legal restrictions on the number of animals permitted on household plots have been abolished. Credit has been made available to households for livestock purchase, acquisition of equipment, and modernization of structures. The idea behind all of this is quite simple: small-scale private, medium-scale cooperative, and large-scale state properties are needed to take advantage of the economies and to avoid diseconomies of scale and organization. The wages bill of agricultural cooperatives is no longer centrally regulated. Members of agricultural cooperatives can work as many hours as they decide. Instead of paying a profits tax, cooperatives are subject to a differential income tax based on per capita personal incomes. An additional progressive income tax is levied on a cooperative whenever its average monthly per–man-hour income exceeds a centrally set norm. The proceeds of this tax are used to subsidize the incomes of workers in cooperatives with unfavorable natural conditions. Ancillary activities of the rural cooperatives are encouraged. In 1980, these activities accounted for 35 percent of the cooperatives' total output, more than double the proportion of a decade earlier. Ancillary activities include the production of simple farm implements, construction materials, and wood products; local construction; food processing; and the manufacture of parts for large industrial firms.[36]

In sum, property rights have been made slightly more collective in the state sector and have been decollectivized in the cooperative sector. Private property is feared less and is, in fact, used in the operation of the socialized economy in various formal ways.

2. The NEM accommodates a variety of flexible organizational

forms in which the borderline between social and private property is blurred. This is true of both industry and agriculture (more so of the latter than the former).

In agriculture, there are four basic organizational forms: state farms, cooperatives, small cooperatives, and private plots. The relatively highly mechanized state farms use 15 percent of cultivated land and concentrate primarily on grain. State farm workers are state sector employees; they are paid tariff wages plus bonuses. The basic work week is set officially at forty-eight hours, but workers are encouraged to work longer hours through monetary incentives. Cooperative farms take care of 70 percent of the cultivated land. Like the state farms (although less mechanized), they concentrate on crops in which the benefits derived from economies of scale are significant (grain, sugar beets, sunflowers). As already noted, cooperative members legally own their private plots, which can be (in whole or in part) rented to the cooperative. The private plot can be inherited by the member's survivors. However, if the family survivors are not members of the cooperative, they must sell the inherited land to the cooperative. Small cooperatives may be set up by state farms or cooperatives. They farm land that for one reason or another has been left out of cultivation by the larger state and cooperative units. Although originally the land of these small cooperatives was owned by the parent unit (state farm or cooperative), today members of the small co-op have broad property rights over certain assets of the co-op. There exist about three thousand such units, employing 250,000 people. As American economist James Mulick puts it,

> the most important point is that, in most cases, the small cooperatives are not subsidized in any way. Most of the products produced are more labor-intensive than those produced on a large scale. They tend to be products which are not viewed as basic commodities and, therefore, the price is not strictly controlled. Further, the authorities seem firm in their promise not to come to the aid of failing units. Because each of these units employs relatively small numbers of workers, large displacements will not result from bankruptcies.[37]

The small agricultural co-op illustrates the flexibility with which the NEM—certainly compared with broader similar experiments in the plan's conservative variant—tackles the problem of economies of scale and specialization. The small co-op is granted quasi-private property rights to the assets it uses, as well as facilities for acquiring the necessary inputs and access to relatively free markets. Private plots (in effect, 1.5 million mini-farms) of cooperative farm members and others (state farm workers, state sector industrial workers and employees) account for 15 percent of the cultivated land (as with state farms) but produce 44 percent of the gross value of agricultural output (and probably more).[38] (One would expect private-plot holders to underestimate output value for tax reasons.) Produce originating in the private plots and sold on the free market often exceeds by very substantial margins the wage earned in official state employment.

In industry, the picture is different. Although many organizational forms exist (some are discussed below), the problem is primarily one of the size distribution of state sector industrial enterprises. Hungary has one of the highest industrial concentration ratios in the world: a very small number of very large firms.[39] This concentration is the result of policy measures pursued through the 1960s and 1970s for reasons of ease of control, economies of scale, and technological diffusion. In fact, the Hungarian enterprise or firm is more like a trust or a Soviet "association." One of the consequences of this high concentration is the absence of competition over wide areas of the industrial economy, which in turn reduces the possible efficiency-producing effects of marketization of information and privatization of property rights. Since 1980, attempts have been made to break up these industrial dinosaurs, but progress has been sluggish. In 1982–83, there were 700 state-owned industrial enterprises (more than half of them with an annual output value of over 50 million forint, or 31 million rubles). Of these 700 firms, 275 produced 73 percent of the total industrial output value. In the following two years, some 80–90 smaller firms were created by breaking up the large enterprises. Hungarian industry thus continues to suffer from the rigidities of large size, especially in light industry, where flexibility is highly desirable. Less than 19 percent of all industrial workers are employed in enterprises with a total work force of under 100 each; in Sweden the equivalent ratio is 45 percent.

Small- and medium-sized firms can be created in Hungary not only through the breakup of large firms, but also by the establishment of new firms from the top down (or, more interestingly, from the bottom up). In 1982, regulations were issued (there must always be regulations) allowing ministries, local councils, and state-owned enterprises to set up affiliate firms. These are of two kinds: "enterprise business work partnerships"; and "business work partnerships," or simply "small cooperatives." The enterprise business work partnerships come in several variants. One of the more imaginative of these involves the new affiliate unit's subcontracting a part of the parent enterprise's operations—including use of the enterprise's fixed assets, paying a fee for this subcontracting, but keeping its own profits. These profits may be distributed as bonuses among the affiliate's workers. However, the affiliate workers' basic (tariff) wages are paid by the parent enterprise.[40]

The business work partnerships, or small cooperatives, can be set up by ministries, local councils, large enterprises, or individuals. There are fewer administrative and other restrictions on them than on the larger firms (as is the case with cooperatives generally), but they cannot ask for help from the founding authority in the event of financial difficulty. In 1980, with 3 percent of the industrial capital stock, they employed 14 percent of the industrial labor force, and accounted for 6 percent of gross industrial output (and a much larger share of net output). Small co-ops formed by individuals are common. They range in employment size from two to thirty people and are primarily concentrated in the service trades, including professional services (for example, management consulting, and the writing of computer software). The partners who supply the bulk of the capital (earned, no doubt, in the underground economy) are legally liable for all debts incurred by the co-op. Despite very progressive taxes imposed on the co-ops' profits, the lack of infrastructural facilities for small business in a land of giant enterprises, and bureaucratic foot-dragging, the productivity of these private co-ops is high: the per capita income of small private cooperatives is four times that of the orthodox operatives.[41] Unlike the typical traditional service cooperatives, the business work partnerships provide badly needed services (for example, plumbing, auto repairs) when they are needed—not two or three years later.

Another novel organizational and property form (from the bottom up) consists of "new operational systems." The new operational systems involve awarding to individuals, through auction, the right to lease small businesses of all kinds (restaurants, food stores, barbershops, tourist lodgings). The lease typically runs for five years, but can be renewed. With rare exceptions, each entrepreneur is limited to operating only one business unit; there are no chain stores here. The new operational systems are given considerable latitude in obtaining inputs and setting prices, and are fully responsible for their profits and losses. They do very well, their services being responsive to demand through the market. In early 1984, the new operational systems arrangement included twenty-two thousand people.

The public-private property enterprise combinations are shown in Table 10.1.

3. As has already been suggested, the liberal plan's attitude toward private property in the legally unrecognized (or simply overlooked) underground economy is tolerant, on condition that the size and scope of private possessions are not too blatant. Much of the

TABLE 10.1

Combinations of Public Ownership and Private Entrepreneurial Activities in Hungary

Owner of the means of production	User of the means of production	Arrangement for use of capital equipment	Typical branches
State enterprise or cooperative	Private person or group of private persons (in some cases, the lessee is chosen through auction [new operational systems])	Leasing fixed capital for a definite rent[a]	Catering, trade
State enterprise or public institution	"Economic team" formed from the employees (enterprise-business work partnerships; some business work partnerships)	The team works under the protection of the employer, and uses part of the fixed assets for which it pays rent	Maintenance, repair, fitting (as yet preliminarily planned)
Partly state enterprise or public institution, partly the user	Workers of the enterprise or institution in question	Illegal informal work done during regular working hours, perhaps with the use of employer's equipment	Construction, maintenance work, repairs, trucking

SOURCE: Kornai, "The Prospects of the Hungarian Economic Reform," p. 239.

[a]A related form is the so-called contractual operation; in this form, the owner enterprise or cooperative also procures a portion of the materials.

housing in the countryside (including secondary residences of urban dwellers) is of that kind. Some of these structures are quite elaborate, even by Western standards. They could not possibly have been built on the owners' earnings from official employment. Although the construction itself may be private and legal, the source of funds for such construction usually is not. (Legal private construction, incidentally, is believed to be responsible for the building of one-half of all dwellings, and absorbs the efforts of about 200,000 people.) These and many other possessions are evidence of the lively underground market and of the enormous amount of entrepreneurial ability expended on circumventing nonsensical rules. Still, though all of this ingenuity could have been more productively and creatively employed, it does contribute to Hungary's uncounted but real national product and does improve the consumer welfare of those smart enough to engage in it (the bulk of the population, though in differing degrees). The Hungarians say they earn four thousand forints a month, spend seven thousand, and bank the rest.

Motivation

1. There is no doubt whatsoever that the liberal plan relies on the proverbial carrot instead of the stick, and that the carrot includes the provision of marginal opportunities for investing private savings primarily accrued through single-minded involvement in the black or grey market.

2. One must be wary of official statistics on incomes and prices. The reported incomes capture only a small part of the real income flow: they deal primarily with wages and salaries in the official economy, or "sleeping money," as it is called (one sleeps on the official job so as to be fresh for the real job on the parallel market). Similarly, price indices are unreliable; in general, they understate real movements (especially upward) in the price level. In selling a private house, for example, one price is registered with the authorities (a low one, to avoid being accused of profiteering), while the real transaction takes place at a higher price. The balance between the statistical price and the actual is settled under the table by means of "key money." In addition, one wonders precisely what comprises the basket of goods from which the consumer price index is derived. The real annual inflation rate in Hungary over the past several years is estimated at between 15 and 20 percent.[42] The official figures are given in Table 10.2. For all its shortcomings, Table 10.2 shows an erosion of living standards between 1975 and 1980. This was one reason for the introduction of the small co-ops where extra

TABLE 10.2

PERSONAL INCOMES AND PRICES IN HUNGARY, 1960–1983

(percent)

Years	AVERAGE ANNUAL GROWTH		TOTAL GROWTH	
	Income	Prices	Income	Prices
1961–1965	3.3	0.4	18.1	1.9
1966–1970	6.2	0.8	35.0	4.0
1971–1975	4.5	2.8	25.0	14.6
1976–1980	1.6	6.3	8.1	35.5
1981	—	—	8.5	4.6
1982	—	—	7.6	6.9
1983	—	—	7.9	7.3

SOURCE: Official Hungarian sources in Tökés, "Hungarian Reform Imperatives," p. 7.

income could be made legally after hours by those with little access to the underground economy.

3. As noted in Chapter 3, in the neoclassical liberal plan the state retains control over wages in its own sector. This is done through differentiated enterprise profits taxes and subsidies, and through the direct intervention of laws and regulations governing wage increases in state-owned enterprises. Differential taxes and subsidies result in the redistribution of net income among enterprises, presumably in accordance with state preferences. This, in turn, affects enterprise wages. Laws and regulations governing wage increases fall into three categories.[43] (a) *Central determination of increases in the wage bills and wage levels of enterprises.* Roughly 30 percent of enterprises are so covered, including most of the larger ones; this sets the tone for the rest. (b) *Relative wage bill regulation.* Increases in enterprise wage bills are tied to changes in value added, but are limited by allowable increases in average wages. About 55 percent of enterprises are so covered. (c) *Relative wage level regulation.* This was intended to raise productivity through reduction in the firms' labor force, but did not happen. Instead, enterprises reduced average wages by hiring low-wage labor. To counter this trend, a variant of the relative wage regulation was introduced: allowable increases in wages are now tied to the growth of wages plus profits per worker. Some 14 percent of enterprises are governed by this regulation.

By and large, these regulations have not worked out the way they were supposed to; they did not markedly improve labor productivity. Under both (b) and (c), increases in average wages of more than 9 percent (originally 6 percent) a year are subject to a progressive tax, the starting rate of which is 150 percent and can go as high as 800 percent. This threat encourages game playing ("regulation game"). For example, firms that have room for improvements in efficiency use their opportunities slowly, so as to avoid going through the legal wage increase ceiling and getting slapped with the tax.

Not unreasonably, World Bank economist Bela A. Balassa counsels the NEM's architects to link wages to worker productivity. Since management, rather than workers, is responsible for the firm's profitability, a stronger link should be forged between managerial remuneration and profit performance. This necessitates the phaseout of bonuses that are presently based on the bureaucratic evaluation of managers by supervisory authorities. These "introduce subjective elements and reduce the manager's independence"; translated, this means that the manager is evaluated not on strictly economic efficiency criteria, but on political ones as well.[44]

4. As noted earlier, managerial and worker bonuses have been tied to profit performance, but not always only to profit performance; often they have been tied to profit after "corrective" subsidies and taxes. The profit motive is more important in the nonstate sphere, where profits reflect more accurately real marginal costs and utilities, and where the producers' budget constraint (in a "sink or swim" situation) is harder than in the coddled state sector.

5. For all the discussion of letting inefficient, money-losing firms go out of business, the state firms' budget constraint (especially the budget line of the large state firms) has not been significantly hardened. Few state firms go under in Hungary; they are usually saved through merger with financially healthy firms, or else are subsidized out of their plight. In 1980, only three state enterprises (relatively strong ones) were shut down. In the current still-defective state of the price information system, the question of whether a firm that is suffering persistent losses should be liquidated is one of multiple choice. The firm may be having losses (in terms of irrational prices) because it is (a) inefficient, (b) efficient, or (c) none of the above:

> The changes of 1979–1982 promised an epoch of 'hardness.' The combined result of the changes was that too many enterprises got into a situation that, in the absence of a state subsidy, would lead to a catastrophe. If only a small part of enterprises were menaced, the state might perhaps have let things take their course, and these enterprises would have gone bankrupt. But what can be expected if many economic units,

with quite a few very big ones among them, would stand at the brink of bankruptcy without support? The experience of the years 1979–1982 left a strong impression on enterprises: the promise of 'hardness' and the very different implementation, a combination of 'excessive hardness' and indulgence.[45]

In other words, if full marketization and privatization of the system were introduced today, Hungarian industry would czardas itself out of business.

6. Within the overall wage controls exercised by the state, Hungarian managers have the right, as directors of their enterprises, to hire workers; reassign workers to part-time jobs if no full-time work exists for them to do; fine workers for absenteeism, lateness, and other breaches of labor discipline; and dismiss them for cause. This last right is restricted by the socialist principle of employment security: lifelong job tenure in the state sector for all except political undesirables and the most incorrigible proletarian loafers. It is further restricted in some firms by "enterprise councils," which are to oversee the managers' longer-term (strategic) decisions (investment and expansion, but also employment policies). The enterprise councils are found primarily in large- and medium-scale state enterprises. In addition to the director and his deputies, they consist of managers of subdivisions, research workers, top technicians, as well as representatives of the party and government trade unions (the latter two having no vote, but much influence).[46] Boards of Supervision are being established for firms. They must be consulted on all strategic questions. The Boards of Supervision count among their members *nomenklatura* representatives from the government, the State Bank, the Chamber of Commerce, trade unions, the firms' management, and workers. They are to be responsible for the hiring and firing of managers, for general supervision of enterprise operations, for decisions on important changes in the scope of the firms' operations, and for liquidation of the firm. In smaller state enterprises, there are "elected managements." Yugoslav-type workers' councils and the control of enterprise property by the workers does not exist. Outside Yugoslavia, such arrangements are still seen as heretical.

The cautious and half-hearted experiments with participatory decision making at the enterprise management level have not been notably successful. Contrary to their overt decentralizing (power-sharing) intent, they have a centralizing influence on firm management. The central government is presented with yet another vehicle for inserting itself into the firm's affairs. Moreover, decisions by committees are slow and run counter to the theoretical intent of making enterprises more flexibly and quickly responsive to changing needs and entrepreneurial opportunities.

The second NEM has also addressed itself to the problem of the enterprise managers' managerial competence (as distinct from their political credentials). As in post-1978 China, Hungarian managers are to be chosen through open professional competition, which may involve some kind of examination. If the applicant successfully negotiates this hurdle, he is to be appointed for a period of five years, during which time he is to be reviewed annually by the enterprise council. In 1982, there were 103 newly appointed enterprise directors, 2 of whom were chosen through open competition. In the following year, 30–40 appointments were to have been made, some through competition.[47] The trouble with this scheme, in Hungary as in China, is that the changes are cosmetic. Underneath, the *nomenklatura* system acts as before. The managers and other top personnel of leading state enterprises (and most nonleading ones as well) are, as they have always been, party members—and not low-level party members at that. In inordinate numbers, they are members of

> the Party's Central Committee, deputies of the National Assembly, ex-officio members of county, city, and district councils, and executives of various Patriotic People's Front organizations. By virtue of their positions, these people have consultative or veto power over many things—including the implementation of economic reforms—while there are no meaningful external checks on their performance.[48]

For the most part, these people belong to the apparat, and lack adequate (or often, any) professional training for the managerial and technical jobs they hold. Their main interest is in their convivial survival as a class. This can be most successfully secured by encouraging the center's more reactionary instincts. The demands for more enterprise autonomy, the managers' freedom from peonage, and the bold entrepreneurship in a market environment come from reform-minded economists, not from the managers (or from state sector blue-collar workers, for that matter).

In the cooperative sector (particularly in agriculture), there is both more managerial autonomy and more nonorchestrated participation by co-op members in management. One should not be carried away by this freedom, since it is strictly relative to the authoritarianism of the neoclassical conservative plan's *kolkhoz*. Still, despite frequent governmental intervention in the affairs of the rural cooperatives (especially the bigger ones), there is a degree of independence and pluralism here not found elsewhere in the socialized economy and unthinkable in political life. In the winter of 1982–83, the members of one-fifth of the agricultural cooperatives rejected by vote the officially designated candidates for co-op chairmen, electing in their stead people of their own choosing.[49] Whether these elections actually held is not known.

Performance of the Hungarian Economy Under the Neoclassical Liberal Plan

When Hungarian reform-inclined economists (like Támás Bauer) speak of the NEM, they refer to the limited marketization and privatization measures as having been inconsistently and haphazardly carried out. They complain that the result of compromise and seesaw movement is an economy that is neither plan nor market. The characterization of the economy as "neither plan nor market" (no cage, no bird) is, I think, inaccurate.[50] The Hungarian economy after seventeen years of the NEM is both plan and market: plan first, market second; plan less formal but insistent, market more open but truncated. The cage has been enlarged, but the bird (much tamed) is still inside, though able to fly about more than before. The bird's continued imprisonment is not just due to Hungary's obligations under CMEA contracts (without the socialist world, where else would the Hungarians peddle their wares?) or to the fear of Soviet displeasure. It is due, first and last, to the Hungarian party's unchanged views on control. It is true that these views have been civilized and polished over the years—potentially competing nodes of power have been tamed and co-opted through united patriotic fronts (politics), joint ventures, overlapping preference zones, and "flexible' organizational forms (economics), rather than being forcibly suppressed.[51] But the party-state's exclusive rights of decision on major questions of goal setting and resource allocation are carefully preserved through indirect and direct intervention—indirect where possible, direct as a frequent last resort.

In terms of conventional statistical indicators, the Hungarian economy has done neither significantly better nor worse than other state socialist economies of Eastern Europe (those belonging to the confraternity of the neoclassical conservative plan).[52] Still, it has done better in some less easily measurable but important respects, and done somewhat worse in others. Its most notable success has been in reducing the consumer costs of competitive shopping: those innumerable frustrations and irritations arising from the conservative plan's quasi-permanent sellers' market in consumer goods and from the plan's apparent inability to overcome either the shoddiness of its products or the supply-demand mismatch. The great achievement of the liberal neoclassical plan, in other words, has been the betterment it has brought about in everyday consumer welfare. This is particularly true of food, which is plentiful and of good quality. Annual improvements in the Hungarian diet have been dramatic during the NEM period, greatly superior to those attained during the Stalinplan. Hungary today is self-sufficient in most agricultural goods (crops, animal products, live animals, processed foods) and, in addition, is an important exporter of such products. In the late 1970s, agricultural exports constituted just under one-quarter of Hungary's total exports, and about 30 percent of its hard-currency exports. Two-thirds of the agricultural exports consist of high value-added processed foods. Compared with other state socialist (CMEA) countries, during the 1970s Hungary had an average annual agricultural trade surplus of 600 million dollars, higher than that of any other CMEA country. Agriculture accounts for nearly 15 percent of net material product. Gross agricultural output rose between 1970 and 1980 at an average annual rate of 3.5 percent, more than in any other European country—East or West—with exportable production rising at a much faster pace. Domestic food consumption increased at an average yearly rate of 1.5 percent and was characterized by the already-noted shift toward higher-quality foods. Comrades from all over Eastern Europe and the USSR come to Hungary to fill their shopping nets with what the London *Economist* describes as "food, glorious food!"[53]

The success of Hungarian agriculture is traceable to the following causes: (a) the comparatively active (certainly compared with the USSR) process of making voluntary the membership in rural producers' cooperatives and de facto privatization of the collectives' property rights (that is, expanding the collectives' rights to the acquisition, use, and disposal of their assets); (b) the greater heed paid to market information; (c) the closer linking of effort to reward (increase in the relevance of the cooperatives' profit to individual members' earnings from collective work); (d) the contribution of marketized private farming and the symbiotic relationship between the socialized and private sectors of agriculture;[54] (e) the encouragement and expansion of the cooperatives' (as well as individual households') ancillary mini-industrial activities (which contribute significantly to the co-ops' employment and income):[55] (f) the relatively generous state investments in agriculture; and (g) the diffusion of technological innovation through the technically operated production systems.

In other areas, too, consumer costs have gone down and consumer welfare up, despite some erosion of officially computed living standards. The improvement is due to a more consumerist orientation of the state's goals, which manifests itself in the official acceptance of the second (market) economy in both its more broadly legalized and its still-illicit to -illegal manifestations. "The black market," reads the government paper *Magyar Hirlap*, "is a matter for the police, not a question of ideology."[56] Because of the dismantling of the formal network of plan controls and the partial collectivization (or process of making less statist) of the state sector, there is more flexibility and adaptability to changing consumer needs and cost conditions in Hungary's nonagricultural sectors compared with other socialist economies of the region. As with the expansion of the nonstate market-private sphere, the reduction in the planned component of the economy has been carried less than halfway. The system of partially disassembled plan and partially assembled market often produces results that reflect the worst of both worlds.

In addition to a large external (convertible-currency) debt and the normal inefficiencies of the neoclassical plan, the Hungarian system brings to the surface problems that in the conservative plan remain more or less suppressed. These include inflationary pressures (as subsidies are jettisoned and state retail prices are raised to cover costs), sharp income inequalities, and social tensions of all kinds. These translate themselves into the world's highest suicide rate, alcoholism rivaling the levels of Soviet intemperance, rising drug abuse, and a steep increase in violent crime. Naturally under such conditions there are calls for restoring socialist discipline (in China today, these calls revolve around the four basic principles of proletarian dictatorship under the party's leadership), if not quite à la Stalin, at least à la Andropov. And there are, from the other side, Aesopian calls for carrying the marketization and privatization process further—to its logical conclusion of systemic transformation.

CHAPTER ELEVEN

Yugoslavia: Workers' Self-Management and Market Syndicalism

A Model for Mankind or Manifestation of Parochialism?

The Yugoslavs' experience of more than thirty years of mixing market and plan demonstrates what has already been implied in the discussion of systemic models in Chapter 1: that in practice, there is no such thing as market socialism (if by socialism is meant state socialism, the administrative command plan).[1] The plan dominates the market, or the other way around. There may be degrees of domination and different styles of dominance, but there is no practical permanent mutation. The laws and procedures of the market may be modified by democratic social policy (as in Sweden and Britain, for example), and adjustments may be made in the plan through resort to market-like mechanics (as in Hungary [bold] and the USSR [timid]), but this is quite different from a genetic fusion of market and plan, which is what market socialism is about. Between approximately 1965 and 1976, Yugoslavia came close to crossing the systemic frontier—away from the plan and toward the market— a deceptively imminent transition accompanied by a peculiar privatization of property rights to worker collectives at the level of the firm. But the crossing of the border never occurred. Since 1975, the role of the market has been substantially reduced while property rights have been privatized still further, down to the component worker collective subunits of the firm. Yugoslavia has lost much of its former appeal to those who saw in it a market socialist utopia, if only because the market is hard to find in the welter of social agreements that more or less coordinate disparate economic activities. The Yugoslav case still speaks to those who see in worker management the economic liberation of mankind, even though there are troublesome questions about both the reality of management by workers and its effectiveness. The theoretically demonstrable superiority of labor management-cum-markets has been marred by the economy's actually demonstrated ills, among them double digit inflation, unemployment, balance of payments problems, huge foreign debt (the equivalent of approximately 20 billion dollars as of 1984), cyclical fluctuations, and regional inequalities. It used to be intellectually fashionable to associate these things with the market, but in Yugoslavia (certainly since 1975) they have flourished without what could honestly be called a market. Yugoslavia continues to attract the attention of Western students today more because it is important to the West politically and strategically than because its jumbled economic system contains a constructive lesson from which others may learn.[2] The Yugoslav "model" was never really transferable—a point made already in Chapter 5—and it is even less so today, beset as it is with current structural difficulties and uncertainties about its future course.

The neomarket Yugoplan is country-specific and culture-bound for a number of reasons. First, historically it was conceived of as a philosophical alternative to both Soviet Marxism-Leninism and Western bourgeois democracy—a "differentiated product," as one economist put it—required to theoretically legitimize the Yugoslav-Soviet rupture of the late 1940s.[3] (State socialist regimes and their leaders need "theoretical" formulations of this sort; every new leader must have his writings, no matter how unoriginal or unimaginative his thought.) Tito's theoretical product (borrowed from Yugoslav communist leader Edvard Kardelj) was workers' self-management, which has since become a national mystique not subject to fundamental criticism. This was later enriched by the mystique of the socialist market, and then (in 1975) transformed into the current myth of self-management and social compacts.[4] Self-management as a variant of socialist ideology was linked to Yugoslavia's partisan experience during World War II (the experience of the Tito-period and current party and government elite, or of the "Club of 1941") and emphasized self-governance minus elaborate federal-level bureaucracies.[5] The general economic theory of labor management and of how such management fits into market and plan came later, some of it from abroad.[6]

Second, the labor-managed, decentralized, neomarket economy represents a specific Yugoslav answer to the question of how to hold together a multinational country whose nationalities exhibit a lack of mutual affection. In Yugoslavia, the nationalities are more or less homologous with geographical regions. They can be kept together either by Stalinist terror or by granting to each wide rights of self-governance, which is what the Yugoslavs have done. In the economy, the nationalities question is compounded by a large north-south developmental problem. The lower down one goes in granting self-management rights (for example, to the level of the firm), the greater the chances that the self-managing unit will be coequal with a given nationality. Conversely, "a strong and activist government must, regardless of its policies, inevitably create discord among the eight major nationalities."[7] The very question of centralization of power in the federal government versus power dispersal takes on the overtones of a nationality struggle: the majority nation (the Serbs) is for it; the others oppose it.[8]

Third, Tito's personality came to dominate the model of self-managing socialism, thus (as one observer put it) "subtly subverting it."[9] Titoism was the glue that held together the self-managing units with help from the market during Tito's lifetime, and, now that Tito is gone, through the complex, cumbersome, and confusing network of agreements and compacts, as well as through prodding from the organizationally strengthened (as compared with pre-1975) but still regionalized party.

Chronology

Yugoslavia's experience with labor management, plan, and market falls into four periods: (1) 1945–1948—the classical Stalinplan; (2) 1949–1964—the development of workers' self-management (property-motivation) combined with indicative planning in a setting of (a) expanding markets, and (b) quite considerable state and party intervention in prices, capital allocation, and enterprise managerial appointments (information-coordination); (3) 1965–1975—the combination of by then consolidated workers' management and much-expanded market relations with less and lower-level government intervention (compared with the previous period); and (4) 1976 to the present—the highly decentralized workers' management combined with a system of social contracts and self-management agreements, which to a significant extent substitute themselves for the informational and coordinating roles of the market.

It is the change in property and motivation, represented by labor management of enterprises, that distinguishes Yugoslavia's experimentation with plan and market from the experiences of other countries that, like Yugoslavia, originally had been members of the Stalinplan family. In Yugoslavia, the principles and practice of self-management have been extended beyond the economy to "sociopolitical communities" comprised of the federation, republics, provinces, and basic non-economic decision-making units known as "communes." The term "worker" is used in Yugoslav parlance to denote all persons employed in the social sector and all wage earners in the private sector. Self-employed persons in the private sector are known as "working people."

We will be focusing on current institutional arrangements, that is, those in force since the mid-1970s—workers' self-management and compacts-agreements—with occasional reference to earlier arrangements, particularly those of the market-oriented interlude of 1965–1975. It was during that time that the Yugoslav economy gained (in some Western circles) the reputation of being market socialist.

Property and Motivation: Workers' Self-Management

The principle and practice of workers' self-management is comprised of two concepts: "social" ownership of enterprise assets, and worker control of enterprise policy. Social ownership means that the workers do not own outright the enterprise assets; they hold these assets in trust for society, that is, for all the people. Conceptually, property rights are not private (although they are privatized to the level of the enterprise workers' collectives), and they are not public in the public-state sense used in state socialist economies of the classical and neoclassical plan. Workers' self-management means that the workers directly or through democratically elected representatives (that is, elected by secret ballot with no shenanigans) have a determining say in the affairs of their workplace, whether that workplace is an enterprise or a subunit of the enterprise. This determining say is not absolute: it is exercised within the limits of state law and other external and internal constraints (to be discussed presently). Nevertheless, the principle of self-management requires that enterprise regulation by forces other than the workers be as small as possible, and that the greater part of the country's gross material product be subject to autonomous enterprise decision making rather than to government decisions. The workers' writ covers production, investment, and income distribution decisions.

The extent to which workers actually manage the units of which they are legally in charge is pivotal in a systemic sense. If they are in actuality masters of their enterprises (or other units), then decentralization of decision making constitutes an effective privatization of property rights to the level of the workers as a group—socialized privatization. If, on the other hand, internal and external forces limit the right of workers' self-management to the point where that right becomes purely nominal, then decentralization remains Leninist and administrative; the workers' collective becomes a mere cog in the state and party machinery, a device designed to take some of the burdens off the planners' backs. There are conflicting views on this in the Yugoslav case, so a clear-cut answer cannot be given. There is no doubt that workers' self-management in Yugoslavia is not a pretense and a fraud, as are labor unions in other state socialist countries. At the same time, however, it is something less than what its advocates would have one believe. The main internal constraint on workers' self-management comes from the business executive of the self-managed unit—the professional director and his staff. For a variety of reasons primarily having to do with practical things (such as the workers' lack of familiarity with—or even sustained interest in—either the day-to-day or the longer-term business and technical logistics), the influence of the professional executive on the self-managed unit's decision-making processes is substantial—perhaps, some would say, commanding. To prevent the directorial function from being perpetuated and directorial influence from overwhelming the decision-making process within the firm, executives are appointed by workers' representative bodies for fixed periods, although they can be (and are regularly) reappointed. The tenure of Yugoslav enterprise executives has not been exceptionally long as compared with the average tenure in CMEA countries or in American corporations. The system insists upon the rotation of executives, although frequently the rotation is horizontal; that is, the same person rotates among different decision-making organizations within the same enterprise. The nominating bodies (commissions) are comprised not only of elected workers' representatives but also of representatives from trade unions and professional associations selected by the local government organ—the commune and the commune's party committee.

A second source of limitation on the workers' decision-making power is the network of intra- and interenterprise agreements and compacts, including those concluded between the self-managing units and various political and social entities. These consensual agreements may dissimulate pressures put on the workers' perception of their particularistic interest by both professional management and external communal, republican, and federal agencies. Such pressures will tend to be important with regard to matters such as income distribution (wage restraint), investment, and pricing.[10] They have been exercised in the past by several agencies, the precise power of each changing with the times. Before the mid-1960s, the federal government intervened in micro decisions by enterprises through its general investment fund (derived from revenues yielded by taxes on enterprise profits). Between 1965 and 1975, the main interventionist agency was the banking system, which from 1969 to 1972 accounted for almost half the domestic fixed investment (the government comprising one-fifth, the enterprises the rest). The banks themselves were cooperative in nature; that is, they were controlled by the borrowing enterprises. Still, they enforced credit rationing rules that were viewed as being contrary to the notion of workers' self-management. After the mid-1970s, the interventionist role of the banks declined sharply, concurrently with a significant expansion of the investment role of the enterprises themselves. The party (League of Communists of Yugoslavia [LCY]) was slated by the 1970s revisions to become the main external force of intervention in enterprise and subenterprise affairs. How effective that intervention is in practice remains a matter of controversy. Party domination of practical self-management is believed by some to be far-reaching.[11] Others regard the party's role as relatively modest—relative, that is, to the role played by the party in other state socialist countries.[12] Although the party is organized along republican-nationalities lines (less so now than in the mid-1960s–mid-1970s), its operating procedures run to democratic centralism rather than consensual agreement, and its direct participation in state organs is guaranteed by the 1974 federal constitution.

Whereas before the mid-1970s workers' representative councils were enterprise-level bodies, they have since been decentralized to the level of the constituent functional units of the enterprise known as Basic Organizations of Associated Labor (BOALs). These have been defined and described earlier (see Chapter 5). Enterprise policy is formulated through a process of bargaining among enterprise BOALs and is incorporated in intraenterprise agreements (to be examined presently). The idea behind the decentralization of workers' self-management to the BOAL level was to ensure that workers exercise their managerial rights on the basis of equality. The move clearly pluralized decision-making power within each enterprise, weakening central administrative control. At the same time, this pluralization of economic power has been attended by microeconomic inefficiencies resulting from insufficient intraenterprise coordination and by a further blurring of responsibility for overall decisions affecting the firm's welfare as a whole. Consensual governance is time-consuming if consensus is more than an empty slogan.

Decentralization of self-management to the BOAL level went hand in hand with regionalization of government, with important powers being surrendered by the federal authorities to republics and their constituent administrative units. Mandatory consensus among the six republics and two provinces (Vojvodina and Kosovo) is required even on minor matters, giving regional governments de facto veto powers. This has led, among other things, to economic nationalism based on republics or provinces. The six constituent republics, for example, administer shares of the railroad network, with trains changing locomotives each time they pass republican borders: "Several of the republican train systems are arguing over which one will carry the coal, and in the meanwhile none of it is moving."[13] Instead of one stultifying bureaucracy, the adjustments of the 1970s have produced eight. Some people argue that the collegial leadership under which the federal presidency is rotated among the eight-member presidium makes it difficult for a leader to have an effect and invites mediocrity. On the other hand, the system— proposed by Tito and introduced in 1974—gives each region equal representation and contributes to social peace: "It's much more important to have national and social harmony," argues one senior Yugoslav official, "even at the expense of decision-making."[14]

As noted in Chapter 5, workers' self-management was introduced as a means of ending the alleged alienation of the worker from his product and from society. It was thought that by granting attenuated collective ownership rights to the workers, the motivational system would be vastly improved. In one fell swoop, both equity and efficiency would be achieved. This expectation has not been borne out. The arrangement does seem to have the support of the workers and of the population at large, even though it is criticized by some Yugoslav economists as a "sacred cow" and a fetish.

In self-managed firms and their constituent BOALs, workers are guaranteed a minimum annual wage. This must be paid irrespective of whether annual net earnings are sufficient to cover this minimum. If earnings are insufficient, the minimum wage must be paid out of internal reserves or by state subsidies. The rest of the workers' annual wage is paid from net income (income remaining after payment of taxes, business expenses, and other financial obligations) in accordance with decisions by the workers' councils of each BOAL, reconciled through inter-BOAL intraenterprise agreements and interenterprise compacts, and paid in conformity with the law. The workers' council also decides on the shares of net income that go to accumulation, reserves, and communal consumption. Payment for common services (such as education, health insurance, and social security) is made in line with "free exchange of labor" agreements concluded with so-called communities of interest.[15]

There is some evidence that in maximizing net income per worker, workers' councils have tended to opt for capital-intensive variants of any given production process, even though Yugoslavia is a labor surplus economy with approximately 20 percent of its labor force working abroad in the developed market economies of Western Europe. This compulsion has been one reason for investment inflation and capital misallocation (the latter being of grandiose proportions). It has also contributed to Yugoslavia's high unemployment rate, as entry into the more successful enterprises has been restricted by protectionist workers' council hiring practices aimed at ensuring that the net income available for distribution as wages is not distributed among too many workers (especially if the job-seekers are from other republics). Friends and relatives have been known to gain entry with less trouble than others. There has been the temptation (though not as much so as was predicted by theory) for workers' councils to go on wage-spending sprees. Strikes have been frequent. They have usually focused on wage demands rather than broad social issues. There has also been a tendency for wage hikes to outrun increases in labor productivity, and this has been one of the factors contributing to Yugoslav inflation (currently running at 50–60 percent per year). Failing units are regularly bailed out by government subsidies, and thus, enterprise-BOAL budget constraints are as soft as possible. In the large Feni nickel works, the four thousand worker-managers have decided to keep their firm in business and themselves on salary even though nobody is buying their nickel ore. Given the high unemployment rate in the country, external (governmental, LCY) pressures on the firm to shut down are not very strong. Wage differentials within BOALs-enterprises are determined by the workers' councils. Studies of the Yugoslav wage structure show that wage spreads both within and among BOALs-enterprises are narrower than in Western European market economies (despite Yugoslavia's lower developmental level) and that they are comparable to the formal wage differentials in East European neoclassical economies of the conservative bent.[16] The presumption is that workers' management operates in the direction of a relatively egalitarian income distribution, although the effect of informal pressures on workers' councils and managers by external government and party organs to keep wage inequalities within reasonable bounds must also be taken into account.

Workers' self-management of the Yugoslav style has probably not improved microefficiency by much (if at all). There is speculation that it might, in fact, have helped to lower it. The principal merit of workers' self-management is the opportunity it provides for the expression of divergent group economic interests at the grass roots–level of society. In this respect, self-management, even though probably more circumscribed in practice than it appears on paper, has helped buttress the legitimacy of the still-monopolistic (if regionally fractioned) political order. This is understood and much appreciated by the party.

Private Property in Agriculture

At its peak in 1950, socialization embraced a little more than one-third of agricultural land in Yugoslavia. After 1953, decollectivization proceeded rapidly as members were legally (and in fact) permitted to leave the collectives. Currently, roughly 15 percent of agricultural land is socialized, most of it under state farm workers' management. The state sector concentrates on large-scale cultivation and agro-industrial processes, while the relatively few cooperatives concentrate on technical services, marketing, and farm extension–type activities. Output performance has been satisfactory, but not spectacular. In the 1970s, the per capita annual rate of growth of agricultural output was 2.5 percent (3.5 percent overall). However, investment in agriculture has been comparatively feeble and the pace of modernization sluggish. Legal limits are imposed on the size of private farms and on hired private labor force.

Information and Coordination: Agreements and Compacts

It was during the late 1960s and early 1970s that market-type institutions of information and coordination played a relatively important role in the Yugoslav economy. Even then, however, the economy was nowhere close to crossing systemic borders. The difficulties and shortcomings attributed in the early 1970s to the market were due more to the restraints and exceptions applied to market information and coordination than to the market's "excessive" role:

> To a great extent the failure of the market in Yugoslavia was not the result of excessive reliance on the market mechanism per se, but rather of excessive reliance on a set of markets distorted by regional barriers to the flow of goods and factors of production, and by ad hoc interventions in market activity by government organizations, especially at the republican and communal levels . . . The resulting situation was aggravated by the absence of effective macroeconomic measures critical to the successful operation of a market system.[17]

As economist Ljubo Sirc has put it, "what Yugoslavia needs is a market economy—more market information and coordination, rather than less."[18] We have already referred to the labor market's imperfections, which are partly due to national parochialism and partly to the operation of workers' self-management. Additionally, a market for labor is rejected on ideological grounds: workers, it is argued, are not a commodity. The capital market (using the term loosely) is replete with rigidities and distortions. A large portion of investment is self-financed by firms. Interfirm investment is made in accordance with income and risk-sharing agreements. Regional authorities are reluctant to invest outside their jurisdictions. Investment credits are extended by the banks at interest that has little to do with market equilibrium rates. Nor are rents market-determined; they, too, are fixed by agreements among firms and organizations, with market criteria entering into the consensus by happenstance. All prices, including "free" ones, must conform to price policy guidelines expressed in agreements among sociopolitical communities (territorial units having political and administrative responsibilities, that is, the federation, republics, provinces, and communes). Set and changed by agreements concluded between producers and consumers of particular goods and services, the prices are not reliable carriers of information about relative scarcities in the system. Income distribution is decided by workers' councils according to considerations that include the notion of marginal product ("to each according to his labor") but also "solidarity"—"a cross," as one observer put it, "between equity and efficiency."[19] The precise ingredients of that cross are not clear.

Given the absence of central administrative planning and the peculiar nature of the Yugoslav market, coordination is achieved by means of interagency social compacts and self-management agreements. The social compacts are consensual "agreements concluded among government organizations (sociopolitical communities) or between government organizations and other agents in the economy, including enterprises, chambers of business, and trade unions."[20] They deal primarily with broad policy issues in areas such as prices, income distribution, employment, and foreign trade. Although they are not legally binding, they are in fact used in lieu of laws to govern conduct in the social interest. Self-management agreements deal with specific policies and are enforceable in the courts. Within enterprises, they are concluded among BOALs (and within the general framework of social compacts) regarding all major aspects of production, exchange, and income distribution.

Information and coordination by compacts and agreements has some serious drawbacks besides the problems connected with economic calculation. The process is time-consuming—to arrive at a voluntary consensus between Serbs and Croats is not an easy or speedy task. If the consensus is not reached voluntarily, chances are the agreements will not hold. The social compacts are very general and broadly gauged, giving republican and commune authorities wide discretion in interpreting them; this hampers coordination. Changes in policy requiring rapid action are slow to materialize as compacts and agreements are laboriously renegotiated.

Granick is probably right when he detects in the Yugoslav information and coordination system elements of syndicalism.[21] Neomarket syndicalism or not, the arrangement apparently works for the Yugoslavs. Or does it?

Economic Performance

On the surface, things appear to be good. "We do not look like a country where the average income is less than $3,000 a year," a senior Yugoslav Foreign Ministry official has been quoted as saying.[22] In the 1960s and 1970s, Yugoslav growth rates of gross national product and gross national product per capita were the highest in Europe (Eastern or Western) and were exceeded only by Japan. Structural transformation of the economy in a modernizing direction has been rapid: agriculture's share of total product and labor force has declined very fast compared with other developing countries. Labor income distribution has become comparatively equitable, less unequal than in the market economies of Western Europe. Yugoslav citizens have been free to travel and take up employment abroad, an opportunity of which they have availed themselves in large numbers.

On the other hand, serious problems have dogged the economy during each of its various incarnations. Unemployment rates have been high and persistent despite the massive employment of Yugoslav workers abroad. Inflation has eroded real incomes. Misallocation and duplication of investment have been rampant. Obviously inefficient, noncompetitive factories have been kept going by subsidies. Petty regional bureaucratism has flourished. The convertible-currency debt per capita is higher than that of bankrupt Poland. The debt is repeatedly being rescheduled by private Western bankers under prodding from their governments, which do not wish to see Yugoslavia slip into the Soviet orbit.[23] Income and wealth differentials among the country's various provinces have not been significantly reduced; indeed, they appear to be growing larger. Although consumer costs are lower than in the countries of the neoclassical conservative plan, shortages of particular consumer goods recur. Austere stabilization measures required by the

International Monetary Fund as a precondition for several million dollars' worth of loans were put into effect in 1983; they were expected to cut living standards by 10–15 percent. All this has given rise to acute social malaise and open talk of alienation of the working class. The Belgrade daily *Politika* has alluded to a deep corrosion of Yugoslav society, of "chaos, disorder, sluggishness, and lack of responsibility."[24]

CHAPTER TWELVE

Summary and Conclusions

In 1953, workers in Berlin took to the streets to bring to the attention of the authorities their dissatisfaction with the Stalinplan imposed on them by an idiosyncratic Soviet interpretation of wartime and postwar interallied agreements on the new world order. Three years later, workers in Poland and Hungary did the same, but on a more grandiose scale. Although the immediate official response was to activate state socialism's favorite and persuasive agency of social change, the tank, the notice given by the German, Polish, and Hungarian workers did not go intellectually unheeded in Moscow and in the capitals of Moscow's East European dependencies. Stalin was dead, internal power plays were in progress (the more rabid and agile Stalinists were abandoning ship posing as liberals), change was in the air, and there was talk of new beginnings—of a "new course." (Although when former premier Imre Nagy in Hungary tried to apply the new course in his country, he was shot). Gradually the thesis of "different roads to socialism" began to take hold—an East European rendition of China's blooming "Hundred Flowers." (However, as the Chinese who bloomed soon discovered, one must correctly distinguish between flowers and flowering weeds in the socialist garden, for the weeds must be uprooted.) The Berlin, Poznań, and Budapest events were merely reminders of the political need for economic changes and of the connection established in the minds of the citizenry between economic and political change (between bread and freedom). The deficiencies of the Stalinplan were there for all to see.

The fundamental flaw of the Stalinplan (and of its subsequent neoclassical incarnations) was the lack of correspondence between individual and social interest. The social interest was that of the state and was defined by a small, self-appointed, self-renewing elite. This interest was imposed upon the rest of society by command-type economic institutions of information, coordination, property, and motivation. These institutions left no room for the effective expression of private wants and aspirations. A similar disharmony existed between the interest of the state and the interests of the basic producing units—the state and collective enterprises. In short, the plan's motivational structure was defective, leading to rationally perverse behavior on the part of economic agents. The costly sparring between the regulators and the regulated was compounded by limitations inherent in the plan's informational, coordinating, and property arrangements: allocatively meaningless prices; unidimensional physical indicators for firms; an error- and distortion-prone process of aggregation and disaggregation of material and financial balances; arbitrariness of central materials rationing; lack of economically creative entrepreneurial initiative (as distinct from ingenuity in circumventing stifling rules) due to narrow property rights vested in enterprise managements and, more generally, in private individuals; the extreme politicization and bureaucratization of the economic process; and so on.

The end result of the Stalinplan was rapid allocatively inefficient growth of product on a very narrow front. Static misallocations (allocative waste) were monumental. The growth rate itself lost much of its appeal when corrected for useless or substandard output. Consumer costs and deprivation were high, and agriculture constituted a disaster area. Given the cat-and-mouse game between planners and plan executors in the course of plan formulation and fulfillment, plan outcomes represented neither the intent of the planners nor the wishes of the vast majority of the system's participants (consumers, workers, and firm managements). The plan was both harsh and ineffectual when it came to establishing a decent quality of life for the people (which is what economic systems are supposed to effect).

Freed from Stalin's presence, Stalin's surviving *nomenklatura* appointees addressed themselves to the question of what to do with the Stalinplan to make it less costly and more livable. The preferred solution, then as now, was to work within the institutional structure of the plan rather than reach outside it; to replace worn-out and obsolete parts with new ones; to repair, renovate, and rearrange rather than discard and start over again. In this process of adjustment, high hopes and great expectations were placed on economic techniques. Techniques were seen as the economic equivalent of political "style of work"—better kinetics to accomplish any given job, the job being given by largely unchanged philosophical and ethical assumptions and by unaltered political power alignments of the old totalitarian social order. At no time was there any question of sharing power with the people, either politically through competing parties, socially through organized interest groups, or economically through the market and through privatized property rights.[1] Capitalist institutions could be called upon to improve the plan's operation through Leninist decentralization, that is, by having lower administrations shoulder some of the responsibility for central decisions. But they were to be used only as techniques—as technical supplements to the institutional order of the plan, not as substitutes for that order. They were to be divorced from their natural political, social, and ethical context and applied the way one applies a tool to produce whatever one desires—using capitalism to build socialism, the market to invigorate the plan, and private property rights to solidify the state's hold over assets. It was quickly found that markets and private property rights are not, in fact, neutral techniques, separate from their environmental ecosystem—that they possess a logic deriving from that system, and are carriers of a broader pluralistic culture incompatible with the plan's monolithic assumptions and procedures and totalitarian political and social environment. Once introduced, markets and private property rights tend to take over. With ill-disguised dismay, the Chinese are finding this out today. In sum, adjustments to the "right," if carried far enough, may end up in systemic transformation—in what in party circles is called "capitalist restoration." The bird will not be imprisoned in the cage (if it is to be a bird and not a plaything of the planners): it must fly away. The realization of this and of the implications for their interest as members of the ruling class has led post-Stalin adjusters of the Stalinplan to mark time, proceed with caution, retreat, and act in general conformity with the laws of suspended animation. This has been particularly true in the Soviet Union, where the adjustments of the 1950s and 1960s had been readjusted almost out of existence by the early 1980s.

The original faith placed by the adjusters in the possibility of using capitalist techniques to make the plan work better without changing its institutional essence was extended to Western technology. By importing or (better still) stealing state-of-the-art technology, wonders would allegedly be done with the plan's institutional workings. Computers, for instance, would speed up the flow of information in the system and make coordination easy. This faith, too, has proved to be a distraction from reality. In the plan's bureaucratic morass, the computers have (among other interesting things) accelerated the transmission of erroneous information and have not reduced the foul-ups of plan coordination—the surpluses and shortages remain as big as ever. Viewing technology as a cure for paralytic economic institutions reached its apogeee in the 1970s (the years of détente with the West, and of massive infusions of Western credits and technology). It involved a trip up the blind alley of planometrics, the pursuit of the perfectly centralized electronic plan. At the end of the road was bankruptcy of the plan in Poland, centrally planned stagnation in the Soviet Union, and unimproved qualitative conditions elsewhere. The voices from Novosibirsk (see Appendix B) suggest that at least among the more intelligent members of the Soviet establishment, the complexities and impracticability of the planometric model are understood, and there is renewed interest in exploring more approachable avenues of marketizing and privatizing adjustments (and if the situation gets very bad, perhaps even of reform).

A similar understanding is apparent in some leading Chinese circles. Under Mao, China had tried to deal with the disabilities of the Stalinplan primarily through radical leftward adjustments. As a remedy for the ills of the Stalinplan, the Maoplan worked well only in the minds of Western armchair radicals. In China, it wreaked havoc with the economy. Despite its cogent lesson by negative example, a turning to Maoism in the future (in China and elsewhere) cannot be ruled out any more than can a return to a modernized version of Stalinist terror in the USSR. In the meantime, however, Tengist China has shown a growing inclination to move beyond the conservative to more advanced neoclassical liberal remedies for the economy's qualitative problems.

Our explorations show that changes of the adjustment type do not achieve the effency and quality objectives set for them. The liberal plan and the Yugoplan have been more successful than the neoclassical conservative plan in reducing consumer costs and marginally improving the quality of the plan's products, at least on an intrasystemic comparison (Hungarian and Yugoslav products are highly prized in Moscow). At the same time, the liberal adjustment has brought to the surface problems that had been suppressed before, and has created others—including open inflation, open unemployment (Yugoslavia), sharp income disparities (although the Stalinplan was not bereft of these), heavy foreign indebtedness, and social tensions. The liberal plan has not done away with, but instead has co-opted, the classical and neoclassical conservative plans' bribery and *blat*. The growth rate of the gross national product (both total and per capita) has not been significantly better in liberal-plan Hungary than in conservative-plan Romania, Bulgaria, or the USSR. Nor has the liberal plan arrested the secular decline in growth rates typical of all countries of the plan.[2]

Planometrics and the radical Maoplan not being serious contenders in the effort to reduce waste and increase quality, the results of the neoclassical liberal experiment (Hungary) being at best mixed, and the Yugoplan being out of bounds by reason of its participatory property prescriptions (and not particularly attractive in terms of actual performance), what are the adjusters to do? One answer, of course, is that they can do nothing, which means essentially that they continue doing what they have done in the past. Although easy, this is not a viable long-term answer. The threshold of tolerance in a number of countries of the plan has either been crossed (as in Poland) or such crossing is impending. Inaction and falling further behind in everything except military technology will simply not do. Using military technology to contain disequilibrium may work for a time. There will be a temptation, at least in the Soviet Union, to return to the Stalinplan. During his short tenure of power, Andropov showed an inclination to take this gutted road. There remains systemic reform, but it is rejected at present because of the enormous conceptual and practical problems inherent in a decision (to return to this book's epigraph) to dismantle the cage. To appreciate the immensity of the obstacles to plan reform and the cataclysmic event that reform would constitute, let us review the conditions necessary for reform.[3]

Conditions Required by Reform of the Plan

Information

Reform of plan information requires two things:

1. Vertical information reflecting planners' preferences must be transformed into horizontal information emerging from the maximizing decisions voluntarily arrived at through direct lateral contracts by competing buying and selling units (marketization of information). Such horizontal information must be the predominant form of information in the system. Voluntariness and competition are pivotal to the transformation.

2. Physical information expressed in nonsubstitutable quantities and unidimensional planner-set prices must be transformed into market price information that synthesizes for each commodity the multidimensional, relative scarcity (cost-utility) relationships involved in each and every transaction. Such market price information must be the predominant form of information to which buying and selling units adapt as they wish.

Under reform, (1) plus (2) means that mandatory, addressee-specific, unidimensional, primarily quantitative information reflecting planners' preferences is replaced by general, "pure," synthetic, price information reflecting the opportunity costs in the system as these emerge from competing, maximizing behavior of decision-autonomous buyers and sellers in the market.

Coordination

Reform of plan coordination requires the following:

1. The dismantling of the economic bureaucracy.

2. Abolition of vertical coordination through material-financial balances and physical rationing of key inputs, and its replacement by spontaneous market coordination.

Property

Reform of property requires two things:

1. Denationalization and decollectivization of large segments of the industrial, agricultural, commercial-financial, and other sectors of the economy. Denationalization and decollectivization should be embodied in law, but what really matters is de facto privatization of property rights, that is, the vesting of very broad rights to the acquisition, use, and disposal of assets in the actual users and custodians of those assets (whether these be individuals, private corporations, true [not nominal] cooperatives, or government-owned units). Broad rights to assets include the right of the firm to make capital investment and depreciation decisions; to allocate its after-tax profits as it chooses (the taxes not being confiscatory); to expand, diversify, innovate, relocate, contract, or liquidate its operations; and to be in charge of its wage policy through direct negotiations with its (independently unionized, where need be) labor force. The latter requires the freeing of the labor force; and the workers' ability to respond directly and laterally to wage offers by firms, and to move freely in and out of employments and locations. That is, the ownership of "labor power" alienated by the state must be returned to the worker.

An important but often unmentioned practical consideration in the privatization of plan property is the need to break up large state oligopolistic and monopolistic firms, trusts, associations, and other units. Privatization and the freeing of prices on which privatized decisions are based must be accompanied by interfirm competition, not by the transformation of public into private monopolies. Almost all centrally planned economies (China's somewhat less than others) exhibit very high industrial (and agricultural) concentration ratios, due in large part to the planners' preference for small numbers of large units, which are easier to control from the center than large numbers of small units. Consideration of economies and diseconomies of scale should enter into the breakup decision, but the state socialist dogma of "big is beautiful"—the automatic identification of large scale with large economies—must be qualified.

2. Privatized property in the above sense must become predominant in the system.

Motivation

Reform implies the following:

1. The marketization of positive and negative incentives to managers, workers, and farmers. This involves wage-setting at the level of the producing enterprise or group of enterprises through lateral negotiations, that is, removal of central determination of enterprise wages funds, wage rates, and so on. It also requires labor mobility—the workers' and managers' right to move both from job to job and geographically. Additionally, it requires that managers have the right to hire and fire workers, and that unprofitable firms go bankrupt (that is, it requires a hardening of the firms' budgetary constraint).

2. Firm performance is judged by the criterion of profit expressed in market prices. Worker performance is judged in relation to the worker's marginal revenue product.

These conditions for reform are in sharp contrast to everything for which the plan has stood. It is no wonder, therefore, that, however meager the efficiency results, adjustment is preferred to reform. But adjustment—even of the more liberal sort—will not suffice. By opting for half measures, by not letting markets be markets, and by treating private initiative as a nuisance to be tolerated (or even co-opted) during the "transition" from socialism to communism (a transition nobody believes in), adjustment compounds the known defects of the plan. It is, as the Chinese say, like "climbing the tree to catch the fish." The Hungarian NEM and the Yugoplan get better press outside Hungary and Yugoslavia than from Hungarian and Yugoslav economists on the inside. The plan is thus caught up in an apparently insoluble dilemma: intrasystemic changes do not work, while reforms of the system are excluded by (extraefficiency) economic, political, ideological, and psychological difficulties. The result over the years has been a situation described by the Chinese as one where "there's a lot of noise on the staircase but nobody's coming down." However, the plan's quality and efficiency problems are now such that someone had better "come down." Wrenching decisions on what to do with an increasingly unworkable plan will have to be made soon.

Input-Output Tables and Their Relevance to Planning

Input-Output Tables[1]

A hypothetical input-output table for an economy is shown in Table A.1, which is greatly simplified. The simplification consists of the following: (a) the economy represented in the table has only three output-producing industries (coal, electric power, and beer) and one factor input (labor); in even a simple real-life economy, there would be numerous very specific inputs and outputs; (b) it is assumed that only the transactions shown in the table took place over the period (calendar year 1985); (c) the outputs and inputs shown in the table (coal, electricity, beer, labor) are completely homogeneous; in even a simple real-life economy, these would, in fact, have many heterogeneous components; (d) it is assumed that there is only one technically feasible way of producing each output (the way implied by the table); that is, inputs cannot be substituted for each other, and an increase of output by, let us say, 10 percent, can be realized only through increasing all inputs by 10 percent (assuming constant returns to scale); (e) it is assumed that labor can be expanded at short notice according to need.

The three producing industries (coal, electric power, beer) are listed on the left-hand side of the table. These three industries are also consumers of coal, electric power, and perhaps even beer; as such they are listed horizontally across the top of the table. The left side of the table (the "interindustry uses" quadrant) indicates the producing sector of the economy in which all output of the three producing industries is fully used by those industries. In addition to the producing sector industries, there are the (primary) factor inputs of land, labor, and capital (the "value added" quadrant), with only labor shown in the

TABLE A.I
HYPOTHETICAL INPUT-OUTPUT TABLE

	CONSUMERS (USERS OF OUTPUT)							
	Interindustry Uses Quadrant			Final Uses Quadrant				
	Producing Sector Intermediate Demand			Autonomous Final Demand Sector				
Producers (suppliers of inputs)	(1) Coal per 1 million tons	(2) Electric power per 1 billion kwh	(3) Beer per 1 million gallons	(4) Households[a]	(5) Capital formation	(6) Government[b]	(7) Net export	(8) Total output
(1) Coal (million tons)	10 $(\frac{10}{50}=0.2)$	20 $(\frac{20}{100}=0.2)$	5 $(\frac{5}{50}=0.1)$	5	0	5	5	50
(2) Electric power (billion kwh)	20 $(\frac{20}{50}=0.4)$	10 $(\frac{10}{100}=0.1)$	5 $(\frac{5}{50}=0.1)$	20	15	20	10	100
(3) Beer (million gallons)	0 $(\frac{0}{50}=0)$	0 $(\frac{0}{100}=0)$	5 $(\frac{5}{50}=0.1)$	20	0	5	20	50
(4) Labor (million man-hours)	3 $(\frac{3}{50}=0.06)$	2 $(\frac{2}{100}=0.02)$	1 $(\frac{1}{50}=0.02)$	1	0	3	0	
	Value Added Quadrant			Direct Factor Purchase Quadrant				

NOTE: Direct technical and labor input coefficients in parentheses. The coefficients show the first round effects of a change in the total output of one industry on outputs of the industries from which the industry receives inputs, and on labor input.
[a]Private consumption column.
[b]Collective consumption column.

table (bottom row). How the labor input is used is shown by columns (1) through (7). Thus, in 1984, the coal industry used 3 million man-hours of labor, the electric power industry 2 million man-hours, and so on. Columns (4) through (7), all the way down the table, represent the final demand of households (private consumption), demand for capital formation (investment), government demand (collective consumption), and net exports. Thus, in 1985, households consumed 5 million tons of coal, 20 billion kwh of electricity, 20 million gallons of beer, and 1 million man-hours of services of store clerks, doctors, teachers, police-men, and so on (treated in the table as a homogeneous unit). Column (5), "capital formation," refers to the accumulation of plant, equip-ment, and inventories irrespective of who received them. All capital created during 1985 appears in this column, unless it has been com-pletely used up during the year. Column (6), "Government" demand, would (in a planned economy) exclude the receipt of capital goods by government enterprises (listed in the "producing sector" or subsumed under "capital formation"). Column (8) shows the total gross output of each producing industry and the total gross factor input (labor); thus, the total output of the coal industry (row [1]) in 1984 was (in million tons, read across the table): 10 + 20 + 5 + 5 + 0 + 5 + 5 = 50.

If, instead of expresssing the input magnitudes under each "pro-ducing sector" column (columns [1]–[3]) in physical terms, we were to express these magnitudes in money terms, we would obtain the cost involved for each producing industry. If we were to express the final demand magnitudes under each "final demand sector" column (col-umns [4]–[7]) in monetary terms, the sum of each column would be the total expenditure of, respectively, households (household consump-tion, C), new capital formation by enterprises (investment, I), govern-ment expenditures (collective consumption, G), and net exports (X)—or $C + I + G + X$ = gross national product. If, instead of expressing the rows of the table in physical terms, we were to express them in money terms, the last entry on the right side of each row would repre-sent both the total receipts of each industry that that industry derived from the sale of its product and the total incomes of the owners of factor inputs (landowners, workers, capitalists—in our table, workers only). The sum of the incomes of factor input owners would be the gross national income, which would be equal to the gross national product.

The table reveals the interdependence of the economy's industries and sectors. The output of one industry is the input or final demand of others. Thus, looking across row (1), we find (last entry on the right) that the coal industry in 1985 produced a total of 50 million tons of coal. Of this total coal output, coal industry itself used (in tons), 10, electric power industry 20, beer industry 5, households 5, capital formation 0, and government 5. Looking down column (1), we find that in order to produce this 50 million tons of coal, coal industry used as its inputs (in million tons) coal 10, electric power 20, beer 0, plus 3 million man-hours of labor.

Given the assumptions made earlier, the table implies certain technical relationships (direct technical coefficients) between inputs and outputs. These coefficients show the amount of inputs that each industry listed on the left of the table and labor must supply to produce one unit of the total output of the industry listed across the top of the table. The labor coefficient shows the same for the labor input needed. Thus, 10 million tons of coal were needed to produce 50 million tons of coal. Hence, 0.2 million tons of coal ($\frac{10}{50}$) were needed to produce 1 ton of coal. Also, 20 billion kwh of electricity were needed to produce 50 million tons of coal. Hence, 0.4 billion kwh of electricity ($\frac{20}{50}$) were needed to produce 1 ton of coal (and so on). The direct technical and labor input coefficients implicit in the table are shown in parentheses. To increase the total output of electric power by 1 billion kwh, the following first-round increases will be needed in both the output of the other industries that serve as inputs of the electric power industry and in labor input: 0.2 million tons of coal, 0.1 billion kwh of electric power, no increase in beer, and 0.02 million man-hours of labor. But this is only the first-round adjustment. In order to obtain, for example, an increase of 0.2 million tons in coal output, all other outputs (and labor) that are inputs of the coal industry must be increased (and so on, round after round).

Use of Input-Output in Planning

How can the input-output table be used for planning? This can be done by constructing a mathematical model of production interrelationships from the data contained in the table.[2] The following statement may be made with regard to each industry: the total output of coal must be large enough to supply all the coal needed by all intermediate users (electric power, beer). Each user need is expressed as the output of the using industry times the quantity of coal needed per unit of the using industry's output (input coefficient).

The above can be written as:

$$X_1 = a_{11}X_1 + a_{12}X_2 + a_{13}X_3 + \text{final demands } ([4],[5],[6],[7]),$$

where X is the (unknown) output level of an industry; 1, 2, and 3 are industries; and as are input coefficients.

Thus, a_{11} means the quantity of the product of industry 1 needed per unit of output of industry 1; a_{12} means the quantity of product of industry 1 needed per unit of output of industry 2; a_{13} means the quantity of product of industry 1 needed per unit of output of industry 3. In our input-output matrix there are three unknown levels of output (X), one for each of the three industries (1, 2, 3). Thus, there will be three equations, one for each industry for which the output level is to be found. When final demands are given, the set of three equations can be solved to find the output level for each industry.

Due to constraints such as the capacity of each industry or the inability to expand labor supply in the short run, the required output levels may not be achievable. In this event, it will be necessary to try alternative combinations of final demand and to find the one that is best and conforms to the constraints. This type of exercise can be carried out with the aid of computers with little trouble, even in the case of large and complex systems.[3]

APPENDIX B

The Novosibirsk Document, Summer 1983 (Extracts)

The following excerpt from the Novosibirsk document (referred to in the text) has been translated by *The New York Times*.[1] According to Western and Soviet samizdat sources mentioned by Kushnirsky,[2] the document was written by Tatiana Zaslavskaia, a member of the USSR Academy of Sciences working at the Novosibirsk Institute of Economics and Organization of Industrial Production.

Irrespective of the document's merits regarding precisely who has gained and who has lost decision-making powers in recent years (alleged weakening of the *Gosplan*, parallel weakening of enterprises and associations, strengthening of ministries and agencies), the document succinctly sums up the contemporary "main peculiarities of the system of state economic management" in the USSR as these have been inherited from the Stalinplan.

> The basic features of the existing state system of economic management were shaped roughly five decades ago [that is, in the 1930s]. This system has been repeatedly amended, renovated, and perfected, but it has never undergone a qualitative transformation that would reflect basic shifts in the forces of production.
>
> The main peculiarities of the system of state economic management include: a very high degree of centralization in economic decision-making; the highly regulated character of planning; the inhibition of market forces; a discrepancy between the prices of consumer goods and production costs; a centralized system of allocation of materials and supplies to all enterprises; the centralized regulation of all forms of material incen-

tives for workers; overlapping authority and resulting confusion among ministries and agencies; the limited economic authority and, as a result, the limited economic liability of enterprises for the results of their economic performance; and restrictions on all forms of unregulated economic activity in the sphere of production, service, and distribution.

All these elements reflect the dominance of administrative methods of management over economic methods, and of centralized methods over decentralized ones.

Within the framework of that system, people were regarded as "cogs" in the economic mechanism, and they behaved accordingly—obediently (passively), like machines and materials . . .

Even under the most rigid regimentation of economic behavior, the population always enjoys a certain amount of freedom to respond to the limitations imposed by the state. Hence, the possibility arises for overt and covert clashes of group and public interest.

When established rules and regulations, for instance, limitations on the size of private plots, fishing limits, etc., affect the vital interests of certain categories of people, they look for ways to circumvent the constraints and satisfy their requirements. Then the state introduces still harsher measures to block undesirable forms of activity, in response to which the population comes up with more refined methods that make it possible to meet their interests under the new conditions.

The type of worker that such a system cultivates not only falls short of the needs of developed socialism but also fails to match the requirements of modern production. His common traits are a low labor and production discipline, an indifferent attitude to work, a shoddy quality of work, social inactivity, a well-pronounced consumer mentality, and low code of ethics.

Also worthy of mention are such widespread activities as pilfering, all sorts of shady dealings at state expense, the proliferation of illicit business, and a taste for remuneration regardless of the results of work.

Thus we believe that the most important source of social tension in the economy is not just a lack of harmony, but an actual contradiction of interests among vertically dependent groups, workers and team leaders and managers, managers and ministers.

NOTES

Chapter 1

1. According to C. R. Prinsep (the translator of French economist Jean-Baptiste Say's *Traité d'économie politique* [1803]), the (market) entrepreneur (or "adventurer," as Prinsep calls him in English) is "the person who takes upon himself the immediate responsibility, risk, and conduct of a concern of industry, whether upon his own or a borrowed capital" (J.-B. Say, *A Treatise on Political Economy*, trans. C. R. Prinsep, 3rd ed. [Philadelphia: John Grigg, 1827], p. 18 n.). In a market system, the defining characteristics of a successful entrepreneur are said to be "vision, boundless energy, intellectual creativity, . . . a patience quota of zero, . . . ability to think like [his] customers, . . . [and] perseverance to the point of obsession; not reckless gambling, but no hesitation either to take substantial risks so as to remain competitive or protect a lead in technology; daring to fix things before they break; willingness to invest heavily in the future; focus on the long-term outlook; fierce independence and high economic motivation; putting top priority on developing and motivating employees; appetite for daring; experimentation; fanaticism for fundamentals regarding the firm's finances and external forces affecting the firm; personal involvement in every aspect of the business; and a propensity to stress informality rather than a highly structured environment" (Arthur Levitt, Jr., and Jack Albertine, "What It Takes to Become a Successful Entrepreneur," *The Asian Wall Street Journal*, September 1, 1983, p. 6). In a planned economy, the entrepreneurial function is nominally vested in the central planners, that is, in the state corporate establishment. This immediately raises problems of the bureaucratization and consequent routinization of entrepreneurship, which is the antithesis of "fierce independence," "appetite for daring," "personal involvement," "informality of structures," and so on. See Gregory Guroff and Fred V. Carstensen, eds., *Entrepreneurship in Imperial Russia and the Soviet Union* (Princeton, N.J.: Princeton University Press, 1983).

2. See Egon Neuberger, "Comparative Economic Systems" in Alan A. Brown, Egon Neuberger, and Malcolm Palmatier, eds., *Perspectives in Econom-*

ics: Economists Look at Their Fields of Study (New York: McGraw-Hill, 1971), pp. 252–66.

3. For more formal definitions of economic institutions, see Walter S. Buckingham, Jr., *Theoretical Economic Systems: A Comparative Analysis* (New York: The Ronald Press, 1958), p. 90: "norms, rules of conduct, or established ways of thinking"; Vaclav Holesovsky, *Economic Systems: Analysis and Comparison* (New York: McGraw-Hill, 1977), p. 25: "stabilized patterns of relationships which tie the participants together," or "particular forms and patterns of the process elements in action"; Morris Bornstein, "An Integration," in Alexander Eckstein, ed., *Comparison of Economic Systems: Theoretical and Methodological Approaches* (Berkeley: University of California Press, 1971), pp. 339–95: "relatively fundamental organizational arrangements for conducting production and distribution." Excellent discussions of information, coordination, property, and motivation are to be found in Friedrich A. Hayek, "The Use of Knowledge in Society," *American Economic Review* 35, no. 4 (September 1945): 519–30; Morris Bornstein, ed., *Comparative Economic Systems: Models and Cases*, 4th ed. (Homewood, Ill.: Irwin, 1979), pp. 49–60 (on information); Frederic L. Pryor, *A Guidebook to the Comparative Study of Economic Systems* (Englewood Cliffs, N.J.: Prentice-Hall, 1984), chaps. 8 (on motivation) and 4 (on property); and Neuberger, "Comparative Economic Systems" (also available in Bornstein, *Comparative Economic Systems*, pp. 23–24 [on motivation], pp. 24–25 [on information], pp. 25–26 [on coordination]).

4. "The producers of wood . . . do not have to know whether the demand for pencils has gone up because of a baby boom or because 14,000 more government forms have to be filled out in pencil. They don't even have to know that the demand for pencils has gone up. They need to know only that someone is willing to pay more for wood and that the higher price is likely to last long enough to make it worthwhile to satisfy the demand." From Milton and Rose Friedman, *Free To Choose: A Personal Statement* (New York: Harcourt Brace Jovanovich, 1980), p. 15.

5. These attributes interact. For whatever the reasons, resistance by participants to the use of economic institutions (unacceptability) raises the institutions' cost and lowers their accuracy, flexibility, and coherence. In turn, incoherent, uneconomical, inaccurate, and inflexible institutions adversely affect their acceptability, and so question the legitimacy of the organizational structure. Poland of the 1970s, and well into the 1980s, is an excellent example of unacceptability of the economic order to participants, and of the system's consequent loss of legitimacy. At such a point the system is maintained by the use of armed force and political intimidation.

6. Competition need not be textbook perfect or pure, but it must be workable or effective. *Horizontal* means that neither party to the transaction is deemed superior to the other. *Profit maximizing* includes the notion of profit "satisficing," or profitable growth. On the concept of profit "satisficing," see Herbert A. Simon, "A Behavioral Model of Economic Growth," *Quarterly Journal of Economics* 69 (1955): 99–118. Bela Balassa defines a market as a system of

mathematical equations that solves the demand functions of consumers, the transformation functions of producers, and the supply functions of production factors, through the reallocation of production and consumption (Bela A. Balassa, *The Hungarian Experience in Economic Planning: A Theoretical and Empirical Study* [New Haven, Conn.: Yale University Press, 1959], pp. 239–43). An excellent discussion of markets is to be found in Pryor, *Comparative Study of Economic Systems*, chap. 6.

7. On the "prisoners' dilemma," see Michael Ellman, *Socialist Planning* (New York: Cambridge University Press, 1979), pp. 5–6; Amartya Sen, "The Profit Motive," *Lloyd's Bank Review*, no. 147 (January 1983), pp. 1–20. Exceptions to the doctrine of the Invisible Hand (that is, market failures) were examined early on by, among others, Adam Smith (*The Wealth of Nations*, 1776), Alfred Marshall (*Principles of Economics*, 1891), and A. C. Pigou (*The Economics of Welfare*, 1920). For a more recent account, see Francis M. Bator, "An Anatomy of Market Failures," *Quarterly Journal of Economics* 52, no. 3 (August 1958): 351–79. The Invisible Hand does its job of harmony well, but only under stringent and not always practicable conditions.

8. "We believe that the most important source of social tension in the economy is not just a lack of harmony, but an actual contradiction of interest among vertically dependent groups, workers and team leaders, team leaders and managers, managers and ministers" ("Confidential Memorandum on Soviet Economic Organization" [prepared by economists associated with the Siberian Division of the Soviet Academy of Sciences, Novosibirsk], *The New York Times*, August 5, 1983, p. A4). A suggestion for a general theory of nonmarket (administered economy) static efficiency failures is contained in Charles Wolf, Jr., "A Theory of Nonmarket Failure: Framework for Implementation Analysis," *Journal of Law and Economics* 22, no. 1 (April 1979): 107–39.

9. Friedman and Friedman, *Free to Choose*, p. 11. This is so because of the essentially individualistic, voluntaristic, and competitive assumptions of the market, and the collectivist, authoritarian, and monistic assumptions of the plan.

10. A Russian reflecting on the police crackdown on absenteeism in 1983 put it this way: "You can compare our economy with a cart pulled by three tired horses. You have to change the horses and the cart if you want the economy to be effective. Andropov isn't going to do that, but he is using the whip" (*The Wall Street Journal*, July 21, 1983, pp. 1, 21). In this case, *adjustment* meant rounding up people in the streets (where they were hunting for scarce goods) and sending them back to the offices, factories, and shops where they were supposed to be. The assumption was that if the people were back at their jobs, they would work. The motivational structure of the system, however, precluded that, and this systemic deficiency was left quite untouched by the adjustment. On the job, the workers' labor intensity coefficient was most likely still well below 1 (where 1 indicates optimal assiduity while the worker is at work). My concept of (intrasystemic) adjustment is broadly similar to what others have described as the "technocratic," "administrative," or "engineer-

ing" option: "the retention of a 'directed society,' but one in which coercion has given way to new managerial expertise and the use of systems analysis to 'steer' the society in a predetermined direction" (Paul M. Cocks, "Retooling the Directed Society: Administrative Modernization and Developed Socialism," in Jan F. Triska and Paul M. Cocks, *Political Development in Eastern Europe* [New York: Praeger, 1977], pp. 53–92; Ronald Amann, "Technical Progress and Political Change in the Soviet Union," in NATO Economic Directorate, *The CMEA Five-Year Plans (1981–1985) in a New Perspective* [Brussels: NATO, 1982], pp. 155–57).

11. In other words, adjustments are policies designed to make the given system work better. Adjustments might include resort to environmental variables, for example, the importation of advanced technologies or exchanges of scholars and experts designed to change the pattern of skills within the system.

12. Also required for each product is equality of quantities demanded and supplied. This may be achieved through the general equilibrium mechanism of a market price system or through iteration procedures (including "bureaucratic iteration") in a system that allocates resources by nonprice methods.

13. The term *supplemented market* originates with Józef Wilczynski, *The Economics of Socialism*, 4th ed. (London: Allen & Unwin, 1982), pp. 5–6.

14. Robert W. Campbell, *The Soviet-Type Economies: Performance and Evolution*, 3rd ed. (Boston: Houghton Mifflin, 1974), pp. 190–99; Wilczynski, *Economics of Socialism*, pp. 137–39; Pryor, *Comparative Study of Economic Systems*, chap. 5.

15. Michael Ellman, *Planning Problems in the U.S.S.R.* (Cambridge, Eng.: Cambridge University Press, 1973); S. E. Goodman, "Computing and the Development of the Soviet Economy," in U.S. Congress Joint Economic Committee, *Soviet Economy in a Time of Change*, 2 vols. (Washington, D.C.: U.S. Government Printing Office, 1979), 1: 524–53; Janice Griffen, "The Allocation of Investment in the Soviet Union: Criteria for the Efficiency of Investment," *Soviet Studies* 33, no. 4 (1981): 593–609; Frank A. Durgin, Jr., "The Third Soviet Standard Methodology for Determining the Effectiveness of Capital Investment (SM-80 Provisional)," *The ACES Bulletin* 24, no. 3 (Fall 1982): 45–62; Alec Nove, "Socialism and the Soviet Experience," in idem, *The Economics of Feasible Socialism* (London: Allen & Unwin, 1983), pp. 103–5 ("Mathematical Methods and Programming").

16. Aron Katsenelinboigen, *Studies in Soviet Economic Planning* (White Plains, N.Y.: M. E. Sharpe, 1978), p. 41.

17. Oskar Lange and Fred M. Taylor, *On the Economic Theory of Socialism* (Minneapolis: University of Minnesota Press, 1938). Compare with Abba P. Lerner, *The Economics of Control* (New York: Macmillan, 1944) for a more passive role of government in a competitive market model with social property.

18. Nove, *Economics of Feasible Socialism*, pp. 119–20.

19. Alec Nove, *The Soviet Economic System* (London: Allen & Unwin, 1977), p. 289.

20. Jaroslav Vanek, *The General Theory of Labor-Managed Market Economies*

(Ithaca, N.Y.: Cornell University Press, 1970); idem, *The Participatory Economy* (Ithaca, N.Y.: Cornell University Press, 1971). All subsequent quotations not marked with a footnote are from the latter volume; page numbers will be cited in the text.

21. This point is made by Vaclav Holesovsky in his review of Vanek's *The Participatory Economy*, in *Journal of Economic Issues* 7, no. 1 (March 1973): 100.

22. Richard L. Carson, *Comparative Economic Systems* (New York: Macmillan, 1973), pp. 623–28.

23. Vanek, *The Participatory Economy*, p. 12.

24. Benjamin Ward, review of Vanek's *The Participatory Economy*, in *Journal of Economic Issues* 7, no. 1 (March 1973): 97.

25. Paul E. Koefod, review of Vanek's *The Participatory Economy*, in *Journal of Economic Literature* 10, no. 4 (1972): 1222.

26. See chap. 9. By 1984, there were signs that Chinese adjustments would go more in a liberal direction

27. See chap. 10 ("Hungary").

28. It was also disdainful of X-efficiency; that is, it was X-inefficient. "X-inefficiency means that firms and economies operate below their theoretical potential," that "for a variety of reasons people and organizations normally work neither as hard nor as effectively as they could" (Harvey Leibenstein, "Allocative vs. 'X-Efficiency,' " *American Economic Review* 56, no. 3 [1966]: 392–415). For critical appraisals of the concept, see George J. Stigler, "The Existence of X-Efficiency," *American Economic Review* 66, no. 1 (1976): 213–16, and Louis De Alessi, "Property Rights, Transaction Costs, and X-Efficiency: An Essay in Economic Theory," *American Economic Review* 73, no. 1 (1983): 64–81.

29. "The central objective of economic reforms in Eastern Europe has been to generate political legitimacy in the postmobilization period" (Rudolf L. Tökés, "Hungarian Reform Imperatives," *Problems of Communism* 33, no. 5 [September–October 1984]: 3).

Chapter 2

1. The classical plan in the USSR regulated labor both through state-set wages and administrative control. At the peak of Stalinism in Russia, there were an estimated 9 million slave laborers (Stanislaw Swianiewicz, *Forced Labour and Economic Development: An Enquiry Into the Experience of Soviet Industrialization* [New York: Oxford University Press, 1965], pp. 31, 50). This is a low estimate. Other estimates include: Anton Antonov-Ovseyenko, *The Time of Stalin: Portrait of a Tyranny* (New York: Harper & Row, 1981), p. 212 (with a high estimate of 18.84 million between 1935 and 1940); Jerry F. Hough and Merle Fainsod, *How the Soviet Union Is Governed* (Cambridge, Mass.: Harvard University Press, 1979), pp. 176–77; Robert Conquest, *The Great Terror: Stalin's Purge of the Thirties*, rev. ed. (London: Macmillan, 1973), pp. 708–9. Party

members are supposed to go where they are ordered, but (at the higher echelons) they can usually bend the orders to make them better conform with personal job and locational preferences.

2. The presumed allocative neutrality of prices ("commodity relations") was never realized in practice, not even in the allocation by the material-technical supply network of those goods subject to strict physical rationing. This was recognized by some Chinese economists at a time when the Soviet classical plan was being faithfully copied in China. See, for example, Ch'en Hsi-jun in *Chi-hua Ching-chi* [Economic Planning], no. 7 (1956), cited in Nicholas R. Lardy, ed., *Chinese Economic Planning* (White Plains, N.Y.: M. E. Sharpe, 1978), p. 91. For a discussion of classical plan pricing, see Naum Jasny, "The Soviet Price System," *American Economic Review* 40, no. 9 (December 1950): 845–63.

3. János Kornai, "Comments on the Present State and the Prospects of the Hungarian Economic Reform," *Journal of Comparative Economics* 7, no. 3 (September 1983): 232.

4. In the classical Soviet-type plan and in its neoclassical version as practiced today in the USSR, the adaptation through price of demand to planner-determined supply is carried out by varying the turnover tax per unit of product. In addition to its revenue generating and demand-supply equilibrating functions, the turnover tax acts to insulate the firm from the consumers of the firm's products, as seen in the following diagram:

How a Consumer Goods Producer Is Insulated from Consumer Demand by the Turnover Tax

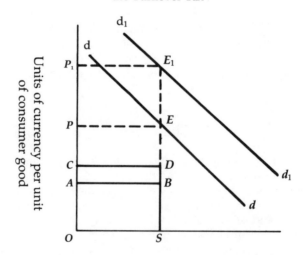

Units of consumer good per year

NOTE: There are two steps. For step 1, *dd* = actual consumer demand for the good; *OS* = planned supply of the good; *SE* or *OP* = equilibrium retail price

(*OSEP* = expected total revenue from retail sales of the good); *SB* or *OA* = planned average cost of production and distribution per unit (*OSBA* = planned total cost of production and distribution); *BD* or *AC* = planned profit per unit (*ABDC* = planned total profit from the good); *DE* or *CP* = turnover tax per unit (*CDEP* = planned turnover tax from the good). The producing firm under the plan must fulfill the following indicators: *OS*; *SB* = *OA*(*OSBA*); *BD* = *AC*(ABDC). The firm is *not* concerned with *dd* or *SE* = *OP*(*OSEP*). In other words, it is not concerned (and, in fact, is not allowed to be concerned) with any price per unit situation above *SD* = *OC*.

For step 2, $d_1 d_1$ = increased consumer demand for the good; EE_1 or PP_1 = additional turnover tax per unit of good ($CDE_1 P_1$ = new planned total tax revenue from the good). The firm remains concerned, as in step 1, with the old planned indicators—*OS*; *SB* = *OA*(*OSBA*); *BD* = *AC*(*ABDC*)—until (and if) these are changed by the planners. The additional tax revenue ($PEE_1 P_{1)}$ is appropriated by the state.

Another way of viewing this is that money made in consumer goods transactions cannot be used to buy producer goods. See Aron Katsenelinboigen and Herbert S. Levine, "Some Observations on the Plan-Market Relationship in Centrally Planned Economies," *Annals of the American Academy of Political and Social Science* 434 (November 1977): 193. The classical Hungarian plan before 1968 had more than two thousand rates of tax separating producer from consumer prices—some positive, some negative (subsidies). For a comprehensive treatment of taxation, see Franklyn D. Holzman, *Soviet Taxation* (Cambridge, Mass.: Harvard University Press, 1962).

5. Firm managers hoard not only labor, but raw materials, capital, spare parts, and "connections" as a hedge against increases in their output plan and the uncertainties of the plan's delivery system. The persistence of "hidden reserves" is a systemic phenomenon that involves considerable factor underemployment.

6. Aron Katsenelinboigen and Herbert S. Levine, "Market and Plan, Plan and Market: The Soviet Case," *American Economic Review* 57, no. 1 (1977): 61–66; Aron Katsenelinboigen, "Coloured Markets in the Soviet Union," *Soviet Studies* 29, no. 1 (1977): 62–85.

7. Allen S. Whiting, *Siberian Development and East Asia* (Stanford: Stanford University Press, 1981), p. 203. When Hungary joined the World Bank and the International Monetary Fund in 1982, it revised its arbitrarily computed exchange rates. The result was that per capita gross national product, which in 1981 (prior to Hungary's admission to the two world bodies) was given as $4,180 per head, fell to $2,100—a huge accounting recession. Now, $2,100 gross national product per capita makes Hungary eligible for low-interest developmental loans (the cut-off level being $2,650). J. Lewis, "World Bank Courts Eastern Europe," *The Wall Street Journal*, September 26, 1984, p. 28.

8. Jan S. Prybyla, "The Economic Crisis of State Socialism: Its Philosophical and Institutional Foundations," *Orbis* 26, no. 4 (Winter 1983): 869–88. There is, parallel to the underground market in goods, a market for information—

some of it factual, the rest rumor. The social interest as formulated by the planners can be called "planners' preferences." Since there are many planners not all of like mind (not even under Stalin), they must arrive through negotiation (or purge) at a unitary preference function. This process, too, involves sizable costs.

9. Chu-yuan Cheng, *China's Economic Development: Growth and Structural Change* (Boulder, Colo.: Westview Press, 1982), pp. 231–35. Figures are from Jasny, "The Soviet Price System," p. 849.

10. On administrative organization of the plan, see Nove, *The Soviet Economic System*, pp. 31–84; Eugene Zaleski, *Stalinist Planning for Economic Growth, 1933–1952* (Chapel Hill: University of North Carolina Press, 1980), pp. 9–82; Abram Bergson, *The Economics of Soviet Planning* (New Haven, Conn.: Yale University Press, 1964), pp. 26–48; R. W. Davies, "The Soviet Planning Process for Rapid Industrialization," and "Planning a Mature Economy in the USSR," in Morris Bornstein, ed., *The Soviet Economy: Continuity and Change* (Boulder, Colo.: Westview Press, 1981), pp. 7–38.

11. Compare these behavioral characteristics with those that define the market entrepreneur (see above, chap. 1, n. 1). However, some of the classical plan's administrators, especially those at the lower levels of the hierarchy, are forced to take risks (in the underground economy) by the tautness of the output plan (Bogdan Mieczkowski, "Bureaucracy, Politics, and Economics in Command Economies" [Working Paper no. 4, Department of Economics, Ithaca College, December 1984]).

12. For discussions of the balances method, see I. A. Evenko, *Planning in the USSR* (Moscow: Foreign Languages House, 1961); Howard J. Sherman, *The Soviet Economy* (Boston: Little, Brown, 1969), pp. 232–60; John Michael Montias, "Planning with Material Balances in Soviet-Type Economies," *American Economic Review* 49, no. 4 (1959): 968–85; Joyce E. Pickersgill and Gary M. Pickersgill, *Contemporary Economic Systems* (Englewod Cliffs, N.J.: Prentice-Hall, 1974), pp. 210–14, 259–62). For discussion of more advanced methods of coordination, see Michael Ellman, *Soviet Planning Today: Proposals for an Optimally Functioning Economic System* (Cambridge, Eng.: Cambridge University Press, 1971), p. 72; Alfred Zauberman, *Mathematical Theory in Soviet Planning* (New York: Oxford University Press, 1976).

13. Martin Spechler, *The Economics of Product Quality in Soviet Industry* (Ph.D. diss., Harvard University, 1971).

14. Támás Bauer, "The Hungarian Alternative to Soviet-Type Planning," *Journal of Comparative Economics* 7, no. 3 (September 1983): 308.

15. Tight labor supply is due to two main interacting causes: (a) high output targets mandated by the plan; and (b) the already-mentioned propensity of firm managements to overstate their labor (especially skilled labor) requirements, that is, labor hoarding in anticipation of increases in the firms' output targets ordered by the planners (without notice) in the course of plan execution. Hoarding of labor, capital, raw materials, and spare parts goes in Soviet technical literature by the name of *hidden reserves*. The reserves can be

used for (illegal) lateral barter deals when plan fulfillment problems arise. The fall in Soviet urban real living standards during the First Five-Year Stalinplan was less than the fall in real wages because of a large increase in the urban labor participation rate (Michael Ellman, *Socialist Planning* [Cambridge, Eng.: Cambridge University Press, 1979], p. 96. Compare with my discussion of China in chap. 9).

16. Nove, *The Soviet Economic System*, p. 212.

17. Xinhua [New China News Agency], Beijing, November 17, 1981.

18. James R. Millar, *The ABCs of Soviet Socialism* (Urbana: University of Illinois Press, 1981), p. 28. See also my discussion in chap. 7.

19. Figure cited by Nove, *The Soviet Economic System*, p. 209, based on explorations by Peter Wiles and Janet Chapman. Compare with Janet Chapman, *Real Wages in Soviet Russia Since 1928* (Cambridge, Mass.: Harvard University Press, 1963); Geoffrey R. Barker, *Some Problems of Incentives and Labour Productivity in Soviet Industry* (Oxford: Basil Blackwell, 1956); Arvid Brodersen, *The Soviet Worker* (New York: Random House, 1966).

20. Joseph S. Berliner, "Managing the USSR Economy: Alternative Models," *Problems of Communism* 32 (January–February 1983): 45. This work originally appeared in Abram Bergson and Herbert S. Levine, eds., *The Soviet Economy: Toward the Year 2000* (Winchester, Mass.: Allen and Unwin, 1983).

21. Holesovsky, *Economic Systems*, p. 299, table 12-3.

22. This is accompanied by what may be euphemistically described as bureaucratic curtness (all-embracing *nekul'turnyi* boorishness of manners). See Herbert S. Levine, "Pressure and Planning in the Soviet Economy," in Henry Rosovsky, ed., *Industrialization in Two Systems: Essays in Honor of Alexander Gerschenkron* (New York: Wiley, 1966), pp. 266–86; János Kornai, "Resource-Constrained vs. Demand-Constrained Systems," *Econometrica* 47, no. 4 (July 1979): 801–19; idem, *Economics of Shortage* (Amsterdam: North Holland, 1980); Michael Keren, "The Ministry, Plan Changes, and the Ratchet in Planning," *Journal of Comparative Economics* 6 (1982): 327–42.

23. For a "revisionist" approach to the thesis of net transfer of resources from agriculture to (heavy) industry under the Stalinplan, see James R. Millar and Alec Nove, "Was Stalin Really Necessary? A Debate," *Problems of Communism* 25, no. 4 (July–August 1976): 49–66, and James R. Millar, n. 7, chap. 7, below.

24. The economic reasoning underlying this ranking of priorities is that heavy industry will act as the locomotive of growth, pulling the lower priority sectors out of their predicament and alleviating the initial intersectoral disproportions. The classical plan is summed up well as the maximization of "the output of a limited range of high priority products under centralized direction by known methods" (Holland Hunter, "Soviet Economic Problems and Alternative Policy Responses," in U.S. Congress Joint Economic Committee, *Soviet Economy in a Time of Change*, 2 vols. [Washington, D.C.: U.S. Government Printing Office, 1979], 1: 23–37).

25. George J. Staller, "Fluctuations in Economic Activity: Planned and Free Market Economies, 1950–1960," *American Economic Review* 54, no. 4, (June 1964): 385–95.

26. Yuan-li Wu, "Foreign Exchange Supply and Planning Under Uncertainty" (unpublished paper).

27. Testimony to the persistence of this classical plan trait is given by the complaint about vertical integration in Chinese industry published by *Remin Ribao* [People's Daily], November 5, 1984, p. 2: "In our mechanical manufacturing enterprises, 69 percent of the total number of enterprises have casting processes, 50 percent have forging processes, 54 percent have welding processes, and over 80 percent have complete facilities covering all the principal processes." This propensity to secure firm self-sufficiency was further encouraged during periods of the radical Maoplan for ideologically rooted reasons.

28. Franklyn D. Holzman, "Soviet Inflationary Pressures, 1928–1957: Causes and Cures," *Quarterly Journal of Economics* 74, no. 2 (May 1960): 167–88; Lynn Turgeon, *The Contrasting Economies: A Study of Modern Economic Systems*, 2nd ed. (Boston: Allyn & Bacon, 1969), pp. 213–35.

Chapter 3

1. See chap. 10.

2. Joseph S. Berliner, "Economic Measures and Reforms Under Andropov," in *The Soviet Economy After Brezhnev: Colloquium 1984* (Brussels: NATO Economic Directorate, 1984), pp. 57–58.

3. Cited by James V. Ogle in "Will Computers Destroy the Soviet System?" *The Washington Post*, November 1, 1981, p. C5.

4. Allocatively rational (scarcity) prices may be expressed as follows:

$$\frac{MSC_a}{MSC_b} = \frac{P_a}{P_b} = \frac{MSU_a}{MSU_b}$$

where *MSC* is marginal social cost, *MSU* is marginal social utility (use value), *P* is price, and *a* and *b* are commodities. The notion of social cost and use value covers private and external costs and use values. Prices are allocatively irrational where either the cost or the use value side of the equation does not hold. Where allocatively irrational prices exercise any allocative influence at all (as they do in all countries of the plan), resource allocation will tend to be wasteful. Prices determined administratively in the plan by reference to the Marxist theory of value will be, by definition, allocatively irrational because (a) Marxist labor value theory does not take into consideration the opportunity cost of land and capital (that is, it is flawed on the cost side of the equation), and (b) it takes no account of utility (that is, it does not hold on the use value side).

5. Claude Aubert, "Chine rurale: la révolution silencieuse," *Projet*, September–October 1982; Jan S. Prybyla, "Where Is China's Economy Headed? A Systems Analysis," *Journal of Northeast Asian Studies* 1, no. 4 (December 1982): 1–24; idem, "China: Economic Development and Political Power," *SAIS Review* 4, no. 1 (1984): 45–59; idem, "Decollectivizing the Collective: Rural Labor in Communist China," *Workers Under Communism*, no. 5 (Spring 1984), pp. 31–36. See also chap. 9.

6. Berliner, "Managing the USSR Economy," p. 46.

7. Morris Bornstein, "Economic Reform in Eastern Europe," in U.S. Congress Joint Economic Committee, *East European Economies Post-Helsinki* (Washington, D.C.: U.S. Government Printing Office, 1977), pp. 102–34.

8. In 1967, wholesale oil prices in the USSR were raised by 130 percent and the price of coal by 78 percent. By 1965, after several increases in quota procurement prices, most Soviet collective farms were breaking even on their quota sales to the state. Taking 1965 average procurement prices for grain, potatoes, pigs, and cattle as 100, the indexes of average prices on collective farm sales in the USSR in 1952 were: grain: 8; potatoes: 7; pigs: 5; cattle: 4. (Morris Bornstein, "Soviet Price Policy in the 1970s," in U.S. Congress Joint Economic Committee, *Soviet Economy in a New Perspective* [Washington, D.C.: U.S. Government Printing Office, 1976], p. 35.) In China, agricultural procurement prices rose by about 30 percent in 1979–80. Steep increases in many consumer goods prices were ordered in Poland, Hungary, and Romania in 1981–82.

9. Morris Bornstein, "The Soviet Price System," *American Economic Review* 52, no. 1 (1962): 64–103; idem, "Soviet Price Theory and Policy," in U.S. Congress Joint Economic Committee, *New Directions in the Soviet Economy* (Washington, D.C.: U.S. Government Printing Office, 1966), pp. 63–98; idem, "Soviet Price Policy," pp. 17–67; idem, "The Administration of the Soviet Price System," *Soviet Studies* 30, no. 4 (October 1978): 466–90; Gertrude E. Schroeder, "The 1966–67 Soviet Industrial Price Reform: A Study in Complications," *Soviet Studies* 20, no. 4 (April 1969): 462–77; Jan S. Prybyla, "Soviet Economic Reforms in Industry," *Weltwirtschaftliches Archiv* [Review of World Economy] 107, no. 2 (1971): 272–316; idem, "Role and Determination of Prices in Mainland China," *Proceedings of the 5th Sino-American Conference on Mainland China* (Taipei: Institute of International Relations, 1976), pp. 505–37; Jean Marczewski, "The Role of Prices in a Command Economy," *Soviet Studies* 23, no. 1 (July 1971): 109–19; Tong-eng Wang, *Economic Policies and Price Stability in China*, University of California Center for Chinese Studies China Research Monograph, no. 16 (Berkeley, 1980); Alan Abouchar, ed., *The Socialist Price Mechanism* (Durham, N.C.: Duke University Press, 1977); Alec Nove, *The Soviet Economic System*, 2nd ed. (London: Allen & Unwin, 1980), chap. 7.

10. The capital charge has been dropped in Bulgaria. Increasingly the tendency is to replace it with a progressive tax on the firm's planned profits. The capital charge, differential rent, and interest on bank loans (for fixed and circulating capital) are deductions from the firms' gross profits payable to the

state. The profits tax is being introduced by China. It will replace the past practice of the state's appropriating the quasi-totality of the firms' gross profits.

11. Nove, *The Soviet Economic System*, p. 175.

12. Béla Csikós-Nagy, "Price Planning—Content of the Price Plan," *Soviet Studies* 37, no. 3 (July 1975): 443–59. Continued state control over many prices is justified by East European spokesmen for the neoclassical plan in terms of the small number of firms in the economy and the monopolistic pricing opportunities this provides.

13. There is a large and growing literature on this subject. See, for example, Gregory Grossman, "The 'Second Economy' of the USSR," *Problems of Communism* 26, no. 5 (September–October 1977): 25–40. (See also n. 21, below.)

14. Vaclav Holesovsky, "Czechoslovakia: Economic Reforms," in NATO Economic Directorate, *Economic Reforms in Eastern Europe and Prospects for the 1980s* (New York: Pergamon Press, 1980), p. 63. "The production associations . . . resemble the vast scale of enterprise characteristic of Stalin's time. One of the virtues of this organizational form is that it reduces the task of central planning by 'internalizing' within the super-enterprise a certain number of transactions that were formerly inter-enterprise transactions and hence required the attention of the central planners" (Berliner, "Managing the USSR Economy," p. 44). See also Manfred Melzer, "Combine Formation in the GDR," *Soviet Studies* 33, no. 1 (January 1981): 88–106. In the USSR, the associations are known as *proizvodstvennye ob'edineniia*; in East Germany, as *Vereinigungen Volskeigener Betriebe*; in Bulgaria, as *Durzhavno Stopanstvo Obedinenie*; in Poland, as *Wielkie Organizacje Gospodarcze*; and in Romania, as *Centrale*. China is experimenting with similar formations.

15. This important problem of conflict between party and state in economic matters cannot be discussed here at any length. It is dealt with by Katsenelinboigen and Levine, "The Plan-Market Relationship," pp. 194–97.

16. Between the emergence of the Solidarity movement and mid-1983 (when the military was in full command), the Polish Communist Party lost 25 percent of its members. In late 1983, it was still losing members at the rate of five thousand a month (*The New York Times*, September 18, 1983, p. 3).

17. Input-output tables were first constructed in Hungary and Poland retroactively for the year 1957 (38 interbranch balances in Poland; 20 in Hungary). The technique has been improved and extended since. In the late 1960s, the number of interbranch balances was 144 in Poland, 80 in Hungary, 70 in Bulgaria, and 125 in the USSR. See Wilczynski, *Economics of Socialism*, p. 21; Herbert S. Levine, "Input-Output Analysis and Soviet Planning," *American Economic Review* 52, no. 3 (1962): 127–37; Albina Tretyakova and Igor Birman, "Input-Output Analysis in the USSR," *Soviet Studies* 28, no. 2 (April 1976): 157–86; Vladimir G. Treml et al., "The Soviet 1966 and 1972 Input-Output Tables," in *Soviet Economy in a New Perspective* (Washington, D.C.: U.S. Government Printing Office, 1976), pp. 332–76.

18. See chap. 8.

19. Benjamin Ward, "Kantorovich on Economic Calculation," *Journal of Political Economy* 48, no. 6 (December 1960): 545–56; Maria Augustinovics, "Integration of Mathematical and Traditional Methods of Planning," in Morris Bornstein, ed., *Economic Planning East and West* (Cambridge, Mass.: Ballinger, 1975); Zauberman, *Mathematical Theory in Soviet Planning*; János Kornai, *Mathematical Planning of Structural Decisions* (Amsterdam: North Holland, 1967); Lev M. Dudkin, ed., *Iterativnoe agregirovanie i ego primenenie v planirovani* [Iterative aggregation and its application in planning] (Moscow: Ekonomika, 1978); Arthur E. King, "Econometric Models of Czechoslovakia: A Survey," *ACES Bulletin* 21, no. 2 (1979): 71–84; N. P. Lebedinskii, ed., *Automatizirovannaia Sistema Planovykh Raschetov* [The automated system of plan calculations] (Moscow: Ekonomika, 1980); Martin Cave, Alastair McAuley, and Judith Thornton, eds., *New Trends in Soviet Economics* (Armonk, N.Y.: Sharpe, 1982).

20. Bauer, "The Hungarian Alternative," p. 314.

21. Istvan Kemény, "The Unregistered Economy in Hungary," *Soviet Studies* 34, no. 3 (July 1982): 349–66; Dennis O'Hearn, "The Consumer Second Economy," *Soviet Studies* 32, no. 2 (April 1980): 218–34; Gregory Grossman, "The 'Shadow Economy' in the Socialist Sector of the USSR," in *The CMEA Five-Year Plans (1981–1985) in a New Perspective* (Brussels: NATO Economic and Information Directorates, 1982), pp. 99–115; Anita Chan and Jonathan Unger, "Grey and Black: The Hidden Economy of Rural China," *Pacific Affairs* 55, no. 3 (Fall 1982): 452–71.

22. Alexander Bajt, "Property in Capital and in the Means of Production in Socialist Economies," *Journal of Law and Economics* 6, no. 1 (April 1968): 1–4. For a good discussion of the economics of property, see Pryor, *Comparative Study of Economic Systems*, chap. 9.

23. "What Khrushchev and Brezhnev sought, each in his own way, was to end the excesses of Stalinism without dismantling the system that gave rise to them. To do so they were willing to pay off blue-collar workers with more money as long as greater income did not mean greater power" (Blair A. Ruble, *Soviet Trade Unions: Their Development in the 1970s* [Cambridge, Eng., and New York: Cambridge University Press, 1981], p. 5). The motivational effect of this new "social compact" between the single-party state and the workers (which includes lifelong employment and subsidized prices for necessities) is summed up by the often-heard comment, "We pretend to work, and they pretend to pay us." See Leonard Schapiro and Joseph Godson, eds., *The Soviet Worker: Illusion and Realities* (London: Macmillan, 1982); Jan F. Triska and Charles Gati, eds., *Blue-Collar Workers in Eastern Europe* (London: Allen & Unwin, 1981); Miklos Haraszti, *A Worker in a Worker's State*, trans. Michael Wright (New York: Universe Books, 1978). The overall conclusion emerging from these diverse studies is that the neoclassical plan's money wages hikes have been insufficient in real terms (that is, in terms of what the extra money could buy) to lift the workers' work motivation out of what I would call the "loafer" range. Absenteeism, stealing social on-the-job time for personal purposes (not job-related—for example, to line up for cabbage), and across-the-board worker alienation

from the system are much in evidence from China to Cuba. Compare with Paul Craig Roberts, *Alienation and the Soviet Economy* (Albuquerque: University, of New Mexico Press, 1971). Chou Yang, chairman of the China Federation of Literary and Art Circles, admitted in March 1983 that alienation could exist in Marxist as well as capitalist systems. In November, he was made to recant publicly (*The New York Times*, November 7, 1983, p. A3). For a discussion of the East European neoclassical plans' wage determination systems, see Jan Adam, "Systems of Wage Regulation in the Soviet Bloc,' *Soviet Studies* 28, no. 1 (January 1976): 91–110.

24. The émigré Soviet economist Igor Birman estimates that individual savings in the USSR come to about 255 billion rubles (170 billion in savings deposits, and 85 billion "under the mattress"). This sum is approaching the Soviet annual wage bill and is higher than the retail trade level. The savings, euphemistically called *otlozhennyi spros* ("deferred demand"), are in fact forced by the absence of quality goods desired by citizens. In the past few years (early 1980s), individual savings deposits have been rising faster than the rate of increase in retail trade. A similar phenomenon can be observed in China and most other state socialist economies of the conservative neoclassical plan (*The Wall Street Journal*, March 21, 1983, p. 20).

25. Martin L. Weitzman, "The New Soviet Incentive Model," *Bell Journal of Economics* 7, no. 1 (Spring 1976): 251–57; Vinson Snowberger, "Comment" on above, *Bell Journal of Economics* 8, no. 2 (Autumn 1977): 591–600; William G. Rosenberg, "Observations on the Soviet Incentive System," *ACES Bulletin* 19, nos. 3–4 (1977): 27–43.

26. Sharp changes in relative consumer, agricultural procurement, and producer (transfer) prices, carried out infrequently, illustrate the continued inflexibility of the system's institutions of information, coordination, and motivation, and represent a violation of one of the four institutional attributes discussed in chap. 1. Such uneven adjustments in the structure of relative prices also work against the neoclassical plan's goal of stability.

27. For more on inflation, see upcoming section, "Goal Priorities."

28. Marianna Graham, "Principal Laws Governing Foreign Investment in China," *The China Business Review* 9, no. 5 (September–October 1982): 22–23.

29. Konstantin Sims, *USSR: The Corrupt Society* (New York: Simon & Schuster, 1982); idem, "The Machinery of Corruption in the Soviet Union," *Survey* 23, no. 4 (Fall 1977): 35–55; Steven J. Staats, "Corruption in the Soviet System," *Problems of Communism* 21, no. 1 (January–February 1972): 40–47; Hedrick Smith, *The Russians* (New York: Ballantine Books, 1976), chap. 3 ("Corruption"); Rafael Bakhmatov, "Bribery in the USSR," *Freedom At Issue*, no. 65 (March–April 1982), pp. 12–15 ("In a world where everyone is stealing, it's even more dangerous to be a misfit."); Alan P. Liu, "The Politics of Corruption in the People's Republic of China," *American Political Science Review* 77, no. 3 (September 1983): 602–23.

30. Lawrence Minard, "The Problem with Socialist Economies: An Inter-

view with Hungary's János Kornai," *Forbes*, August 1, 1983, pp. 64–67, especially p. 67.

31. Katsenelinboigen and Levine, "The Plan-Market Relationship," pp. 193–94. Andrew Gyorgi and James A. Kuhlman, eds., *Innovation in Communist Systems* (Boulder, Colo.: Westview Press, 1978). Ronald Amann, Julian M. Cooper, and R. W. Davies, *The Technological Level of Soviet Industry* (New Haven, Conn.: Yale University Press, 1977); R. Amann and J. M. Cooper, *Industrial Innovation in the Soviet Union* (New Haven, Conn.: Yale University Press, 1982).

32. Amann, "Technical Progress and Political Change," p. 143.

33. "Technological innovation," says János Kornai, "is one of the most crucial problems now facing the socialist economies. Maybe it is the most important. My feeling is we will go through this [technological transformation] but with serious lags and very significant delays. The most important reason for this, in my evaluation, is that the socialist economies are shortage economies. I find an absolutely strong causal relationship between shortage and slow technological innovation." Socialist economies are sellers' markets with scant incentive for producers to innovate. Kornai continues: "Let's take a car like the Trabant, an East German car that is the most common in Hungary because it is the cheapest. Today in Hungary there is a five-year queue for Trabants. In East Germany the queue is eight to ten years. In Hungary you have to pay half the price when you join the queue. It is forced savings in effect. Now the Trabant is a car of the 1950s. Not just the body style, the whole car is thirty years old. Why should the Trabant company produce a modern car if the old one is sold out for a whole decade in advance?" (Minard, "An Interview with Hungary's János Kornai," p. 66). Reprinted by permission of *Forbes Magazine*, © Forbes Inc. 1983. In such a systemic setup, what happens is the exponential duplication of antiques. See also Bruce Parrott, "Technology and the Soviet System," *Current History* 82, no. 485 (October 1983): 326–29, 339.

34. Antoni Chawluk, "The Scope for System Remodeling," *Soviet Studies* 31, no. 1 (January 1979): 99–111.

35. Holland Hunter, "Optimal Tautness in Developmental Planning," *Economic Development and Cultural Change* 9, no. 4 (July 1961): 561–72.

36. Robert W. Campbell, "Management Spillovers from Soviet Space and Military Programmes," *Soviet Studies* 23, no. 4 (April 1972): 590–602. See also two articles by Frederick Kempe on Soviet acquisitions of state-of-the-art Western technology (*The Wall Street Journal*, July 24, 1984, pp. 1, 10; ibid., July 25, 1984, pp. 1, 17).

37. In Czechoslovakia, the proportion of inputs in total gross output was 57 percent in 1970 and 61 percent in 1977. From 1970 to 1978, the capital-labor ratio rose by about 50 percent, rising by about two-thirds in industry. The rate of growth of labor productivity began to fall after 1976 (Holesovsky, "Czechoslovakia: Economic Reforms," p. 63). For China's quality problems under both the radical and conservative neoclassical plans, see Jan S. Prybyla, "Economic

Problems of Communism: A Case Study of China," *Asian Survey* 22, no. 12 (1982): 1207–211; idem, *Readjustment and Reform in the Chinese Economy*, University of Maryland School of Law Occasional Papers/Reprints Series in Contemporary Asian Studies, no. 39 (Baltimore, Md, 1981).

38. The share of investment in the gross national product in Czechoslovakia reached 35.6 percent in 1973, and rose further in the late 1970s (Holesovsky, "Czechoslovakia: Economic Reforms," p. 63). In the classical plan (1951–1955), the share of investment in Romanian national income was 17.6 percent. Under the conservative neoclassical plan (1971–1975), it was 34.1 percent. Heavy industry continues to take the lion's share of investment in Romania (Alan H. Smith, "Rumanian Economic Reforms," in NATO Economic Directorate, *Economic Reforms in Eastern Europe and Prospects for the 1980s* [New York: Pergamon Press, 1980], p. 36). During the classical plan (1953–1957), investment in mainland China averaged 24.2 percent of national income. It jumped to approximately 40 percent during the Great Leap Forward, to 33 percent during much of the Cultural Revolution (the radical plan, 1970–1978), and to about 30 percent in 1980 (conservative plan) (*Beijing Review*, December 21, 1979, p. 10; ibid., September 22, 1980, p. 32). On the continued investment hunger under the neoclassical plan, see Kornai, *Economics of Shortage*, chap. 9.

39. Peter Wiles, "Are There Any Communist Economic Cycles?" *The ACES Bulletin* 24, no. 2 (Summer 1982): 1–20; Xavier Richet, "La réforme economique hongroise," in NATO Economic Directorate, *Economic Reforms in Eastern Europe and Prospects for the 1980s* (New York: Pergamon Press, 1980), pp. 96–97; Barry Ickes, "Cyclical Fluctuation in Centrally Planned Economies" (Working Paper, Pennsylvania State University, 1983).

40. On the coefficient of relative effectiveness and the comparative economic effectiveness of capital investments, see Paul R. Gregory and Robert C. Stuart, *Soviet Economic Structure and Performance*, 2nd ed. (New York: Harper & Row, 1981), pp. 212–19; also see Bergson, *The Economics of Soviet Planning*, pp. 250–65. On the Hungarian g_n index, see Kornai, *Mathematical Planning of Structural Decisions*, pp. 22–27, especially pp. 23–24.

41. For the Soviet cheese example, see Logan Robinson, *An American in Leningrad* (New York: Norton, 1982). The disappearance of lower-priced varieties of a given good from the stores is sometimes traceable to changes in the enterprise success indicators. A switch from *val* to a profit index in the textile industry could mean a change in the assortment to higher-priced dresses (the easiest way to fulfill the profit norm). In this case, the movement toward more "rational economic" control levers results in a new distortion. Sometimes the higher-priced and allegedly higher-quality product is classified (by the maker) as a "new" product. A temporary high price is set by the manufacturer and, in due course, confirmed or changed by the planners. This takes time, often much time, during which the higher price remains valid. As often as not, the "new" product is the old product relabeled or slightly modified.

42. Alec Nove, "When Is a Price Increase Not a Price Increase?" *Soviet Studies* 34, no. 3 (July 1982): 440–43. Also see Steven Rosefielde, "Are Soviet

Industrial-Production Statistics Significantly Distorted by Hidden Inflation?" *Journal of Comparative Economics* 5, no. 2 (June 1981): 185–99; the ensuing "Rejoinder" by James Steiner, *Journal of Comparative Economics* 6, no. 3 (September 1982): 278–87; and Rosenfielde's "Reply," *Journal of Comparative Economics* 7, no. 1 (March 1983): 71–76. See too Robert E. Leggett, "Measuring Inflation in the Soviet Machinebuilding Sector," *Journal of Comparative Economics* 5, no. 2 (June 1981): 169–84; Barry Ickes, "Explaining Soviet Stagflation" (Working Paper, Pennsylvania State University, November 1983); Richard Portes, "The Control of Inflation: Lessons from East European Experience," *Economica* 44, no. 174 (May 1977): 109–30. In his article "Inflation Soviet Style" (*Problems of Communism* 33, no. 1 [January–February 1984]: 48), Fyodor I. Kushnirsky recounts that when he participated in Soviet planning calculation, "the aggregate index of the cost of living was set, *by normative considerations,* to equal 99 percent of the base year level; i.e., its actual values were never computed."

43. The political system of the conservative neoclassical plan uses unemployment as a weapon against dissidents. In the Soviet Union, to apply for an exit visa to Israel is to lose one's (and one's wife's) job. Political undesirables are also barred from better-paid, white-collar employment.

44. In the Hungarian, relatively liberal plan (circa 1979), 200 of the largest industrial firms making final goods also designed and produced 90 percent of their tools (Bela A. Balassa, *Reforming the New Economic Mechanism in Hungary,* World Bank Staff Working Papers, no. 534 [Washington, D.C., 1982], p. 30). Admittedly, around 1979 the liberal plan in Hungary was in temporary remission. Compare with chap. 2, n. 27, above.

45. In bankrupt Poland (with a foreign hard-currency debt of 25–26 billion dollars) net material product in 1979 fell by 2.3 percent, while military expenditures rose 7.5 percent. In 1980, net material product fell by 6 percent and military expenditure went up 0.3 percent. Michael Checinski, "Poland's Military Burden," *Problems of Communism* 32, no. 3 (May–June 1983): 37.

46. Zbigniew Fallenbuchl, *Planning, Market, and Integration in Eastern Europe,* University of Windsor Department of Economics Reprint Series, no. 50 (Windsor, Canada: April 1978); NATO Directorate of Economic Affairs, *COMECON: Progress and Prospects* (Brussels: NATO, 1977).

47. Franklyn D. Holzman, *Foreign Trade Under Central Planning* (Cambridge, Mass.: Harvard University Press, 1974); idem, "Foreign Trade Behavior of Centrally Planned Economies," in Rosovsky, *Industrialization in Two Systems,* pp. 237–65 (also in Bornstein, *Comparative Economic Systems,* pp. 261–78); V. P. Gruzinov, *The USSR's Management of Foreign Trade* (White Plains, N.Y.: M. E. Sharpe, 1979); Wang Lingsheng, "On the Role of Foreign Trade Under Socialism," *Guoji Muyi* [International Trade], no. 2 (1982), pp. 13–20, in *Chinese Economic Studies* 16, no. 3 (Spring 1983): 48–64; Marie Lavigne, "The Soviet Union Inside COMECON," *Soviet Studies* 35, no. 2 (October 1983): 135–53.

48. B. Askanas, G. Fink, F. Levcik, "East-West Trade and Indebtedness of the Individual CMEA Countries Up to 1990," *Perspektiven-Berichte-Analysen der*

Zentralsparkasse und Kommerzialbank (October 1980) [reprinted in The Vienna Institute for Comparative Economic Studies Reprint Series, no. 50 (November 1980)]; George D. Holliday, *Technology Transfer to the USSR, 1928–1937 and 1966–1975* (Boulder, Colo.: Westview Press, 1979); Jan Svejnar and Stephen C. Smith, "The Economics of Joint Ventures in Centrally Planned and Labor-Managed Economies," *Journal of Comparative Economics* 6, no. 2 (June 1982): 148–72; Alan A. Brown and Paul Marer, "Foreign Trade in the East European Reforms," in Morris Bornstein, ed., *Plan and Market* (New Haven, Conn.: Yale University Press, 1973), pp. 153–207; Jan S. Prybyla, "China's Special Economic Zones," *The ACES Bulletin* 26, no. 4 (Winter 1984): 1–23.

49. Nove, *Economics of Feasible Socialism*, pp. 131–32; P. G. Hare and P. T. Wanless, "Polish and Hungarian Economic Reforms—A Comparison," *Soviet Studies* 33, no. 4 (October 1981): 491–517. For a succinct definition by Soviet economists of the Soviet neoclassical conservative plan ("The Novosibirsk Document," 1983), see Appendix B.

Chapter 4

1. Shigeru Ishikawa, "China's Economic Growth Since 1949—An Assessment," *The China Quarterly*, no. 94 (June 1983), p. 248.

2. Miriam London and Ta-ling Lee, "Neomissionary Romancing of China," *The Wall Street Journal*, September 15, 1983, p. 30.

3. *The Wall Street Journal*, December 22, 1981, p. 24; *The New York Times*, April 25, 1982, p. 4.

4. Complimentary accounts of Maoist economics are to be found, among others, in E. L. Wheelwright and Bruce McFarlane, *The Chinese Road to Socialism: Economics of the Cultural Revolution* (New York: Monthly Review Press, 1970); Charles Bettelheim, *Cultural Revolution and Industrial Organization in China* (New York: Monthly Review Press, 1974); John G. Gurley, "Maoist Economic Development: The New Man in New China," *The Center Magazine* 3, no. 3 (1970): 25–33; idem, *China's Economy and The Maoist Strategy* (New York: Monthly Review Press, 1976); Paul Sweezy, "Theory and Practice in the Mao Period," *Monthly Review* 28, no. 9 (February 1977): 1–12; Committee of Concerned Asian Scholars, *China! Inside the People's Republic* (New York: Bantam Books, 1972). On the corollary problem of some Western intellectuals' fascination with communism, see Paul Hollander, *Political Pilgrims: Travels of Western Intellectuals to the Soviet Union, China, and Cuba, 1928–1978* (New York: Oxford University Press, 1981), and review of that book by Peter W. Rodman in *Problems of Communism* 31, no. 3 (May–June 1982): 78–80. Also see Arnold Beichman, "The Spell of Marxism," *Policy Review*, no. 21 (Summer 1982), pp. 109–18.

5. "Mao hit on the idea of muzzling the elite both in and out of the party, thus strengthening workers and farmers in [the] decision-making process . . . Yes, it also messed up the gathering of economic data! A small price to pay"

(O. Robertson, "What's With China's Uninterrupted Revolution?" *Monthly Review* 32, no. 1 [May 1980]: 53). Copyright © 1980 by Monthly Review Inc. Reprinted by permission of Monthly Review Press.

6. Ishikawa, "China's Economic Growth Since 1949," pp. 247–48.

7. On the concept of mass mobilization campaigns, see Gordon Bennett, *Yundong: Mass Campaigns in Chinese Communist Leadership* (Berkeley: University of California Center for Chinese Studies, 1976); Mark Selden, *The People's Republic of China: A Documentary History of Revolutionary Change* (New York: Monthly Review Press, 1979), especially pp. 16–20. Otto Ulč defines *mobilization* as "persuasion fortified by coercion" (Otto Ulč, "Czechoslovakia in 1984," *Current History* 83, no. 496 [November 1984]: 369).

8. Michel Oksenberg, "China's Economic Bureaucracy," *The China Business Review* 9, no. 3 (May–June 1982): 27.

9. Here is a sample of Maoplan planning, borrowed from Audrey Donnithorne's *China's Economic System* (New York: Praeger, 1967), p. 494: "In July 1958 a *hsiang* in Guangdong Province with 20,000 inhabitants drew up a three-year construction plan which called for the setting up of a farm with 10,000 pigs, another with 10,000 chickens, a third with 10,000 ducks, another with 10,000 head of cattle, the opening of 10,000 *mow* of orchards and tea gardens, 10,000 *mow* of fish ponds, a bee farm of 10,000 hives, and new villages for 10,000 people." In colloquial Chinese, *10,000* means simply "a very large number." The State Economic Planning Commission laid down the rules of scientific planning: "If the target demands the fulfillment of 10 points, measures should be taken to fulfill 12 points, with working enthusiasm sufficient to fulfill 24 points" (*Great Leap Forward?* [Bangkok: SEATO, n.d. (1960?)], p. 1). For a more general appraisal of the Maoplan in its Great Leap Forward manifestation, see Roderick McFarquhar, *The Origins of the Cultural Revolution* (New York: Columbia University Press, 1974–), vol. 2, *The Great Leap Forward 1958–1960* (1983).

10. For example, "Agriculture is the foundation, and industry the leading factor of socialist economic development" (*Jen-min Jih-pao* [People's Daily], March 31, 1960, p. 1).

11. Wheelwright and McFarlane, *The Chinese Road to Socialism*, pp. 139, 140. "The Chinese economists we spoke to did not know of any wide application of linear programming techniques" (ibid., p. 140). Copyright © 1970 by E. L. Wheelwright and Bruce McFarlane. Reprinted by permission of Monthly Review Press.

12. Michel Oksenberg and Richard Bush, "China's Political Evolution: 1972–82," *Problems of Communism* 31, no 5 (September–October 1982): 4. The authors identify four major "bureaucratic clusters" into which power is organized in China: (1) the personnel (*nomenklatura*) system; (2) the apparatus governing allocation of material goods, energy, and capital (that is, the central planning system); (3) the propaganda network; and (4) the coercive apparatus of the military and the public security forces. In the radical Maoplan, according

to this view, (1) and (2) were engulfed by mass movements, and lost their coordination functions. The formal personnel system, (1), was replaced by *guanxi* ("personal relationships" and "interconnections"). The other two coordinating power clusters of the radical periods were (3) and (4) (ibid., pp. 3–7).

13. Indeed, in Marxist terms, under the Maoplan changes in the relations of production (including property relations) precede, not follow, changes in the material productive forces. This amounts to a rather far-reaching rewriting of the Marxist scriptures. A careful reading of Marx suggests, on the contrary, that it is the material productive forces (labor, means of production, technology) that are the motor force, the independent variable at the economic "base" of society, not who owns the production means and who does the work (relations of production). The attempt to create urban communes never really got off the ground.

14. In her personal account of the Cultural Revolution, Ruth Earnshaw Lo relates the tribulations that, during the Cultural Revolution, descended on the family's long-time employee, a woman of solid class background (lower-middle peasants), resulting from her ownership of a walnut tree in her native village. Such ownership could have shifted her into the fatal category of rich peasants. To compound the felony, the tree was acquired as legacy from a deceased relative; that is, it was "unearned" wealth (Ruth Earnshaw Lo and Katharine Kindermann, *In the Eye of the Typhoon* [New York: Harcourt Brace Jovanovich, 1980]).

15. The fall of the Gang of Four was followed by revelations and accusations centering on the contradiction between the gang's teachings on abstinence from bourgeois consumption and their luxurious everyday lives. A hint of this scandalous discrepancy between word and deed is found in Roxanne Witke's *Comrade Chiang Ch'ing* (Boston: Little, Brown, 1977).

16. Under the Maoplan, graduates of institutions of higher learning get the same base pay whatever job they are assigned to.

17. *Beijing Review,* December 21, 1979, p. 11. In the 1953–1957 period (the classical plan) the gross output value of heavy industry was 47 percent that of light industry. In 1960 (the end of the Maoplan Leap), it was 66.6 percent (*Beijing Review,* January 26, 1981, pp. 7–8; July 27, 1981, p. 6).

18. *Beijing Review,* March 23, 1981, p. 25; September 22, 1980, p. 32.

19. Liu Shao-ch'i, "Report on the Work of the Central Committee of the Communist Party of China to the Second Session of the Eighth National Congress (May 5, 1958)," in *Second Session of the Eighth National Congress of the Communist Party of China* (Peking: Foreign Languages Press, 1958), p. 64.

20. Jan S. Prybyla, *The Political Economy of Communist China* (Scranton, Pa.: International Textbook Company, 1970), p. 327, table 8-8. One of China's leading reform economists, Jiang Yiwei, put the U-shaped development concept in the context of recurrent administrative centralization and decentralization in the following way: "Centralization leads to rigidity, rigidity leads to complaints, complaints lead to decentralization, decentralization leads to disorder,

and disorder leads back to centralization" (Jiang Yiwei, "The Theory of an Enterprise-Based Economy," *Social Sciences in China* 1, no. 1 (1980): 55. The U theory fits nicely into traditional Chinese concepts of the cyclical, rather than linear, movement of history. Compare with Suzanne Paine, "Balanced Development: Maoist Conception and Chinese Practice," *World Development* 4, no. 4 (1976): 277–304; L. F. Goodstadt, "The Great Divide," *Far Eastern Economic Review*, February 2, 1967, p. 162.

21. But see Christopher Howe and Kenneth R. Walker, "The Economist," in Dick Wilson, ed., *Mao Tse-tung in the Scales of History* (Cambridge, Eng.: Cambridge University Press, 1977); Charles Bettelheim, "The Great Leap Backward," *Monthly Review* 30, no. 3 (July–August 1978): 37–130.

22. This point is made eloquently by Thierry Pairault, *Politique industrielle et industrialisation en Chine* (Paris: La Documentation française, Notes et Etudes documentaires, nos. 4735–736, October 12, 1983), p. 20.

23. China's security forces were reportedly ordered (during the summer of 1983) to round up fifty thousand people considered "antisocial" and punish them to the limit of the newly found socialist law. Most were sent to labor camps in the Tsinghai province; others were executed. In a one-month period (August–September, 1983), about one thousand people were executed for their involvement in crime (economic crime included) (*The New York Times*, September 13, 1983, p. A2).

24. Amanda Bennett, "On a Farm in China Life Is Still Difficult, But Rewards Increase," *The Wall Street Journal*, July 23, 1984, p. 10. "Every family's courtyard has a loudspeaker, connected to the village office. They [the farm officials] used to broadcast political messages. Now they bark out practical commands. 'Time to use fertilizer. Time to spray your crops' " (ibid.).

Chapter 5

1. Cited by Jahangir Amuzegar, *Comparative Economics* (Cambridge, Mass.: Winthrop Publishers, 1981), p. 347. Milovan Djilas, long-standing dissident, thinks that Yugoslav worker self-management is completely artificial, a part of the ruling structure— of the party's political activity (see Thomas J. Bray, "A Conversation with Milovan Djilas," *The Wall Street Journal*, October 20, 1982, p. 33). This view is not shared by others. Compare with Jaroslav Vanek, *Self-Management: Economic Liberation of Man* (Harmondsworth, Eng.: Penguin, 1975).

2. Nove, *Economics of Feasible Socialism*, p. 137.

3. Ljubo Sirc, "The Yugoslav Debt and Socialist 'Self-Management,' " *The Wall Street Journal*, October 13, 1982, p. 31.

4. Some of the problems are raised by Ljubo Sirc in *The Yugoslav Economy Under Self-Management* (London: Macmillan, 1975). Others are discussed in Jan S. Prybyla, *Issues in Socialist Economic Modernization* (New York: Praeger, 1980), pp. 88–108; and in Josip Obradovic, "Workers' Participation: Who Participates?" *Industrial Relations* 14, no. 1 (1975): 32–44.

5. *The Associated Labour Act* (Belgrade: Secretariat of Information of the Socialist Federal Republic of Yugoslavia Assembly, 1977); *The Constitution of the Socialist Federal Republic of Yugoslavia* (Merrick, N.Y.: Cross-Cultural Communications, 1976); Josip Obradovic, *Workers' Participation in Yugoslavia: Theory and Research*, University of South Carolina Institute of International Studies Occasional Papers (Columbia, S.C., n.d. [1974?]).

6. The following account of the Yugoslav firm draws on, among others, Amuzegar, *Comparative Economics*, pp. 327–52; Martin C. Schnitzer and James W. Nordyke, *Comparative Economic Systems*, 3rd ed. (Cincinnati, Ohio: South-Western Publishing Co., 1983), pp. 370–94; Holesovsky, *Economic Systems*, pp. 451–57; and Wayne A. Leeman, *Centralized and Decentralized Economic Systems* (Chicago: Rand McNally, 1977), pp. 159–75.

7. Amuzegar, *Comparative Economics*, pp. 334–35.

8. Ibid., p. 340.

9. Nove, *Economics of Feasible Socialism*, p. 136.

10. The theoretical model of an income-per-employee maximizing firm is to be found in Benjamin Ward, "The Firm in Illyria: Market Syndicalism," *American Economic Review* 43, no. 4 (1958): 566–89. See also chap. 1 of this book.

11. Nove, *Economics of Feasible Socialism*, p. 137.

Chapter 6

1. Morris Bornstein, "The Comparison of Economic Systems: An Integration," in idem, *Comparative Economic Systems*, pp. 15–16.

2. "Kenneth Boulding once remarked that the bus from capitalism to socialism runs only during the early stage of capitalism. If a nation misses the bus, capitalism is there to stay. The same may be said of the bus from central planning to socialist markets. The Hungarians caught it in time, but central planning has endured so long in the USSR that the Soviets may have missed the bus" (Berliner, "Managing the USSR Economy," p. 49). The implication here is not just of level of income, but of duration and complexity of (respectively) market and plan.

3. Alfred G. Meyer, "Theories of Convergence," in Chalmers Johnson, ed., *Change in Communist Systems* (Stanford: Stanford University Press, 1970), pp. 314–42; Jan S. Prybyla, "The Convergence of Western and Communist Economic Systems: A Critical Estimate," *The Russian Review* 23, no. 1 (January 1964): 3–17.

4. This point and the capital replacement problem are developed by Ickes, "Explaining Soviet Stagflation," pp. 6–12.

5. Richard Baum, "Science and Culture in Contemporary China: The Roots of Retarded Modernization," *Asian Survey* 22, no. 12 (December 1982): 1166–1186; Peter Zwick, *National Communism* (Boulder, Colo.: Westview Press, 1983). Baum makes the useful distinction between *bureaucracy*, which is a struc-

tural phenomenon linked to the system of economic organization, and *bureaucratism*, which flows from cultural sources. He makes a parallel distinction between *science*, which requires an ethos of rational skepticism, and *scientism*, which rests on cognitive formalism, thrives on ritualistic obeisance to authority, and fails to separate symbol from substance.

6. Joseph A. Schumpeter, *The Theory of Economic Development* (Cambridge, Mass.: Harvard University Press, 1949), p. 75.

7. "Review and Outlook," *The Wall Street Journal*, January 27, 1984, p. 30. In oligarchic Peru, "after actually going through the required 310 legal steps to set up a small clothing enterprise, . . . someone without experience or political connections would have to work 40 hours a week for more than six months, and pay eight unavoidable bribes, merely to register to do business . . . The equivalent process in Florida [takes] four hours" (Claudia Rosett, "How Peru Got a Free Market Without Really Trying," *The Wall Street Journal*, January 27, 1984, p. 31). In a planned economy, opposition to the removal of institutional and legal barriers to private entrepreneurship comes primarily from the privileged state bureaucracy. In Peru, and places like it, it comes from the "privileged, traditional private sector which depends heavily on state favoritism and wields political clout" (ibid.).

8. "Slow economic growth, should it become a permanent feature, cannot be the foundation for the maintenance of social stability here and now in Eastern Europe—at least outside the Soviet Union. Yet, this is the only possibility in a system of centrally planned economies. At the same time, under the present social, political, and ideological conditions in most countries of the area there is no evidence that the necessary changes in their economic mechanisms will be carried out. It is in this sense that we can talk about the general crisis of East European centrally planned economies" (Támás Bauer, *Mozgo Villág* [Moving World], November 1982, cited by Tökés, "Hungarian Reform Imperatives," p. 11.

9. Berliner, "Managing the USSR Economy," pp. 54–56.

10. *The New York Times*, December 16, 1983, p. A15. "The economic cost of snooping must be enormous; not just the huge financial cost or the wasted time and efforts of all those snoopers but, even more important, the inhibiting of the imagination and expression of ideas of all those people who are conscious of being overheard, who have to be careful about what they say, and to whom, and where. How can one operate a modern and dynamic economy that way?" (Leonard Silk, "Hard-to-Repair Soviet System," *The New York Times*, June 15, 1983, p. D2).

11. The Czechoslovak government commissioned an inquiry into environmental destruction in the country, which is monumental. The findings were reported by the Czechoslovak Academy of Sciences, and promptly declared to be a state secret (Otto Ulč, "Czechoslovakia in 1984," p. 368).

12. Robert Delfs, "Swords into Bicycles," *Far Eastern Economic Review*, August 25, 1983, pp. 91–92.

13. In 1984, even in the relatively liberal Hungarian plan, legally sanctioned private investment opportunities were minimal. A private investor could acquire up to five kinds of utility and construction bonds at six to eight years' maturity and at an annual yield of 7–11 percent. However, the total value of the bonds so available was under 380 million forints, or less than 0.04 percent of recorded savings deposits in Hungary (Tökés, "Hungarian Reform Imperatives," p. 7). See also chap. 10 in this book.

14. Michael Ellman, "Changing Views on Central Economic Planning: 1958–1983," *ACES Bulletin* 25, no. 1 (Spring 1983): 14.

15. "It is utterly and totally impossible to collect information at the centre about micro-requirements and then convey the necessary orders to thousands of executant managers. No serious mathematical economist in the USSR pretends otherwise" (Nove, *The Soviet Economic System*, 2nd ed., p. 55).

Chapter 7

1. Alexander Erlich, *The Soviet Industrialization Debate, 1924–1928* (Cambridge, Mass.: Harvard University Press, 1960); Nicolas Spulber, *Soviet Strategy for Economic Growth* (Bloomington: Indiana University Press, 1964), and idem, *Foundations of Soviet Strategy for Economic Growth* (Bloomington: Indiana University Press, 1964); Alec Nove, *An Economic History of the USSR* (London: Penguin, 1965); Moshe Lewin, *Russian Peasants and Soviet Power* (London: Allen & Unwin, 1968). Extraction of a surplus from the peasants for industrialization (especially heavy industrialization) was a left-wing prescription during the debate (the Preobrazhenskii position). This prescription included replacement of the market as an information and coordination device by central physical planning and state price fixing, the relative industrial and agricultural prices being discriminatory against the peasants; comprehensive socialization of property in the means of production and distribution, and an inward orientation in matters of foreign economic relations; not autarky, but resort to foreign trade only to support the big heavy industrialization push. There was disagreement on the last point between Preobrazhenskii and Trotsky, the latter advocating the internationalization of the socialist revolution. Economist Lev Shanin, representing the far right wing of the intraparty debate, argued for an "agriculture first" approach, for continued use of markets in the short term, for continued use of private property in agriculture and retail trade, and for an outward-oriented position on foreign trade and finance. His argument was based on both agriculture's low capital-output ratio as compared with industry, resulting in large short-term additions to real output from an additional increment of investment, and on agriculture's presumed high propensity to save (higher than for industry). In some respects, Shanin's position resembles the contemporary neoclassical liberal approach to economic development. Economist Nikolai I. Bukharin's right-wing proposals during the debate were essentially a theoreti-

cal rationalization of NEP policies: moderate investment rates; balanced investment, as between agriculture, industry, and other sectors (balanced growth); private property in agriculture and retail trade for the time being; a state price policy that would provide incentives to the peasants and compel state industry to reduce costs; state ownership of the economy's "strategic heights" (most industry, banking, transportation, communications, wholesale trade, foreign trade); and an outward orientation in matters of foreign trade and finance in the short run, the long-run objective being independence from capitalist world trade and finance. In some of its aspects, this position resembles the contemporary neoclassical conservative plan. See Gregory and Stuart, *Soviet Economic Structure and Performance*, chap. 3. The main methodological differences between the left and right approaches to the problem of economic development turn on (a) the use of administrative methods as opposed to "economic" ones, and (b) reliance on direct force (teleological command) versus resort to indirect suasion (a leaning toward more indicative planning).

2. Robert Payne, *The Life and Death of Lenin* (New York: Simon & Schuster, 1964).

3. In addition to surplus extraction and political control, there were other reasons behind Stalin's decision to collectivize Russia's agriculture: (a) dissatisfaction with the class implications of the NEP's *smychka* ("alliance" between the Soviet state and the peasantry), which was seen as working against the urban proletariat or, at least, in favor of the peasantry's richer strata (something that now troubles China's post-Mao rural strategies); (b) the probably sham grain procurement crisis of 1926–27, cited by Stalin in May, 1928, as indicative of a *kulak* ("rich peasant") conspiracy to deny the state grain; and (c) Lenin's insistence on the economies of scale (to the disregard of managerial diseconomies of scale) that could be derived from resort to large farming units. See Alec Nove, "The Decision to Collectivize," in W. A. Douglas Jackson, ed., *Agrarian Policies and Problems in Communist and Non-Communist Countries* (Seattle: University of Washington Press, 1971), pp. 69–97; Jerzy F. Karcz, "Thoughts on the Grain Problem," *Soviet Studies* 18, no. 4 (April 1967): 339–434; R. W. Davies, "A Note on Grain Statistics," *Soviet Studies* 21, no. 3 (January 1970): 314–29; S. G. Wheatcroft, "The Reliability of Russian Prewar Grain Output Statistics," *Soviet Studies* 26, no. 2 (April 1974): 157–80; James R. Millar and Corinne A. Guntzel, "The Economics and Politics of Mass Collectivization Reconsidered: A Review Article," *Explorations in Economic History* 8, no. 1 (Fall 1970): 103–16; Moshe Lewin, " 'Taking Grain': Soviet Policies of Agricultural Procurements Before the War," in Chimen Abramsky and Beryl J. Williams, eds., *Essays in Honour of E. H. Carr* (London: Macmillan, 1974; Hamden, Conn.: Archon Books, 1974), pp. 281–323. Stalin's admission to Churchill that collectivization was worse than fighting World War II is found in Winston Churchill, *The Hinge of Fate* (Boston: Houghton Mifflin, 1950), p. 498.

4. For a comparison of Soviet and Chinese collectivizations, see Prybyla, *Political Economy of Communist China*, pp. 148–67. The 4.5–7 million Ukrainian

victims of famine estimate is cited by Adrian Karatnycky, "Forced Famine in the Ukraine: A Holocaust the West Forgot," *The Wall Street Journal*, July 7, 1983, p. 22.

5. Nove, *The Soviet Economic System*, 2nd ed., p. 125.

6. Ibid., p. 132.

7. James R. Millar, "Mass Collectivization and the Contribution of Soviet Agriculture to the First Five Year Plan: A Review Article," *Slavic Review* 33, no. 4 (December 1974): 750–66; idem, "Soviet Rapid Development and the Agricultural Surplus Hypothesis," *Soviet Studies* 22, no. 1 (July 1970); 77–93. See also his *ABCs of Soviet Socialism*, pp. 21–33. Millar's thesis is based on data supplied by A. A. Barsov, *Balans stoimostnykh obmenov mezhdu gorodom i derevnei* [Terms of trade in exchanges between cities and villages] (Moscow: Nauka, 1969).

8. Robert C. Stuart, "Russian and Soviet Agriculture: The Western Perspective," *The ACES Bulletin* 25, no. 3 (Fall 1983): 46; Ellman, *Socialist Planning*, pp. 94–96, esp. table 4.2, p. 95.

9. See Alec Nove, *The Soviet Economy: An Introduction*, rev. ed. (New York: Praeger, 1965), pp. 47–52.

10. Nove, *The Soviet Economic System*, 2nd ed., p. 198.

11. Nove, *The Soviet Economy*, p. 47.

12. Ibid., pp. 49–50.

13. On different variants of the work-point system, see Jan S. Prybyla, *The Chinese Economy: Problems and Policies*, 2nd ed. (Columbia: University of South Carolina Press, 1981), pp. 82–83.

14. Nove, *The Soviet Economy*, p. 128.

15. Gregory and Stuart, *Soviet Economic Structure and Performance*, p. 230.

16. Ibid., p. 244.

17. Nove, *The Soviet Economic System*, 2nd ed., p. 127.

18. Ibid., p. 143. The ploughman citation is from P. Rebrin, "Glavnoe zveno" [The main link], *Novyi Mir* 45, no. 4 (1969).

19. Gregory and Stuart, *Soviet Economic Structure and Performance*, pp. 338–46, especially table 31, p. 340. Also, for more recent data, see Marshall I. Goldman, *USSR in Crisis: The Failure of An Economic System* (New York: Norton, 1983), p. 47, table II-2.

20. Gregory and Stuart, *Soviet Economic Structure and Performance*, p. 342.

21. Dimitry Pospielowski, "The 'Link System' in Soviet Agriculture," *Soviet Studies* 21, no. 4 (April 1970): 411–35.

22. Nove, *The Soviet Economic System*, 2nd ed., p. 196.

23. Ibid., p. 197.

24. Ibid., pp. 199, 203.

25. Roy D. Laird and Betty A. Laird, "The Zveno and Collective Contracts: The End of Soviet Collectivization?" (Mimeographed paper presented at

the Seventh International Conference on Soviet and East European Agriculture, Grignon, France, July 9–13, 1984), pp. 7–8.

26. Ibid., p. 152; Gregory and Stuart, *Soviet Economic Structure and Performance*, p. 252; Goldman, *USSR in Crisis*, pp. 65, 81; Boris Rumer, "Structural Imbalance in the Soviet Economy," *Problems of Communism* 33, no. 4 (July–August 1984): 29–30; Folke Dovring, "Soviet Agriculture: A State Secret," *Current History* 83, no. 495 (October 1984): 323–26, 338.

27. Seth Mydans, "Soviet Is Facing Another Poor Harvest," *The New York Times*, August 28, 1984, pp. D1, D17.

28. The same is true of many other communist countries. For example, according to the International Monetary Fund, 20–25 percent of Vietnam's rice crop is lost every year directly due to spoilage and damage in transportation, but indirectly (and more fundamentally) due to the system of economic organization (*The Wall Street Journal*, September 19, 1984, p. 34).

29. Ihor Stebelsky, "Food Consumption Patterns in the Soviet Union" (mimeographed paper presented at the Seventh International Conference on Soviet and East European Agriculture, Grignon, France, July 9–13, 1984).

30. Roy D. Laird, review of Karl-Eugen Wädekin's *Agrarian Policies in Communist Europe*, vol. 1, in *Journal of Comparative Economics* 8, no. 1 (March 1984): 109.

31. Alec Nove, "Labor Incentives in Soviet *Kolkhozy*" (Mimeographed paper presented at the Seventh International Conference on Soviet and East European Agriculture, Grignon, France, July 9–13, 1984).

32. Cited by Laird and Laird, "The Zveno and Collective Contracts," p. 12, from a Soviet source.

33. See mimeographed papers from the Seventh International Conference on Soviet and East European Agriculture, Grignon, France, July 9–13, 1984: Michael J. Ellman, "Contract Brigades and Normless Teams in Soviet Agriculture"; Karl-Eugen Wädekin, "Agrarian Structures and Policies in the USSR, China, and Hungary: A Comparative View," especially pp. 15–16; and Nove, "Labor Incentives in Soviet *Kolkhozy*," especially p. 10. A contrary interpretation of the collective contracts movement is given in Alain Pouliquen's mimeographed paper from the conference, "Le Zveno et les Contrats Collectifs: Le Début d'une Recollectivisation du Travail Agricole en USSR?" On Gorbachev's attitude toward the *zveno* and other liberalizing economic changes, see Archie Brown, "Gorbachëv: New Man in the Kremlin," *Problems of Communism* 34, no. 3 (May–June 1985): 1–23, especially pp. 17–23.

Chapter 8

1. Fyodor I. Kushnirsky, "The Limits of Soviet Economic Reform," *Problems of Communism* 33, no. 4 (July–August 1984): 37. See also Nove, *The Soviet*

Economic System, 2nd ed., pp. 121–23 for late developments on the indicator front.

2. V. Sitnin, "Optovye tseny: Itogi i zadachi" [Wholesale prices: results and tasks], *Ekonomicheskaia gazeta,* no. 6, 1968, p. 10. A "normally functioning" enterprise is one whose technical-economic indices correspond to the modern level of national economy's development. This is interpreted to mean enterprises producing the bulk of output in any given branch or region.

3. The only departure from the average planned cost rule was the pricing of petroleum and natural gas, where a variant of marginal cost pricing was introduced. Regional (or zonal) average planned prices were inaugurated for coal, iron ore, and some other metals, and in the oil fields of Azerbaijan. In these cases, accounting prices were used to supplement the procedure.

4. A similar reasoning was behind the increases in agricultural procurement prices; that is, the intent was to make "normally" operating collective farms adequately profitable "on the average." By *adequately* was meant that these farms could cover their costs out of current revenue and make enough profit to pay incentive bonuses and make the planned investments. See Bornstein, "Soviet Price Policy," p. 38.

5. Gertrude E. Schroeder, "The 'Reform' of the Supply System in Soviet Industry," *Soviet Studies* 24, no. 1 (July 1972): 97–119.

6. Nove, *The Soviet Economic System,* 2nd ed., pp. 81–87. See also Alice C. Gorlin, "Industrial Reorganization: The Association," in U.S. Congress Joint Economic Committee, *Soviet Economy in a New Perspective* (Washington, D.C.: U.S. Government Printing Office, 1976), pp. 162–68.

7. Kushnirsky, "Limits of Soviet Economic Reform," pp. 37–39.

8. See Heinz Köhler, *Welfare and Planning: An Analysis of Capitalism Versus Socialism* (New York: Wiley, 1966), pp. 82–105.

9. Herbert S. Levine, "The Centralized Planning of Supply in Soviet Industry," in U.S. Congress Joint Economic Committee, *Comparison of the United States and Soviet Economies* (Washington, D.C.: U.S. Government Printing Office, 1959), pp. 68–85; Montias, "Planning with Material Balances," 963–85; Vladimir G. Treml, ed., *Studies in Soviet Input-Output Analysis* (New York: Praeger, 1977); Ellman, *Soviet Planning Today,* pp. 70–74; Michael Manove and Martin L. Weitzman, "Aggregation for Material Balances," *Journal of Comparative Economics* 2, no. 1 (March 1978): 1–11; Massaki Kuboniwa, "Stepwise Aggregation for Material Balances," *Journal of Comparative Economics* 8, no. 1 (March 1984): 41–53; Gregory and Stuart, *Soviet Economic Structure and Performance,* pp. 122–28; Nove, *The Soviet Economic System,* 2nd ed., pp. 40–48; Harry Schwartz, *Russia's Soviet Economy,* 2nd ed. (Englewood Cliffs, N.J.: Prentice-Hall, 1958) pp. 171–74; Nicolas Spulber, *The Soviet Economy: Structure, Principles, Problems,* rev. ed. (New York: Norton, 1962), pp. 22–26.

10. *The New York Times,* August 6, 1983, p. A4.

11. Kushnirsky, "Limits of Soviet Economic Reform," pp. 37–39. Notice, however, the announcement made in the summer of 1983 designating five

ministries (including the All-Union Ministry of Heavy and Transport Machinery and the All-Union Ministry of Electro-technical Industry) as experimental grounds for enlarging (once again) the decison-making power of enterprises and associations through "wide introduction of self-support systems" (*The Wall Street Journal*, July 27, 1983, p. 27).

12. Nove, *The Soviet Economic System*, 2nd ed., p. 41; Gregory and Stuart, *Soviet Economic Structure and Performance*, p. 123.

13. Ellman, *Soviet Planning Today*, p. 74. For other criticisms of physical planning, see Köhler, *Welfare and Planning*, p. 102–5.

14. For a symbolic treatment of the material balances problem, see Gregory and Stuart, *Soviet Economic Structure and Performance*, pp. 125–28.

15. Jerry F. Hough, *The Soviet Prefects*, (Cambridge, Mass.: Harvard University Press, 1969).

16. Cited in *The New York Times*, June 12, 1983, p. 12.

17. Nove, *Economics of Feasible Socialism*, p. 105.

18. Tretyakova and Birman, "Input-Output Analysis," pp. 157–86. On the "technocratic illusion" (that problems of centrally planned economies are due to inadequate techniques and can be eliminated by the application of new, more adequate techniques), see Ellman, "Changing Views on Central Economic Planning," pp. 14–16.

19. Millar, *ABCs of Soviet Socialism*, p. 74.

20. The basic problem in reaching a balance between total money payments to the population (net of voluntary savings) and the aggregate retail value of goods and services sold to the population at both state-determined and free market prices (financial macro balance) is that a significant part of money payments is made in the form of wages and bonuses to people employed in producer goods industries, in the military, and in social services. Thus, there is a gap between the cost prices of consumer goods and the population's monetary demand for those goods. This gap has widened in the 1950s, 1960s, and 1970s because of increases in workers' wages brought about by wage adjustments (beginning in 1956), by the 1965 inclusion of collective farmers and their families in the state old-age pensions system (jointly financed by the state and collective farms), by the broadening of coverage and raising of money benefits for workers and employees under the social security system (1956), by the abolition of compulsory bond purchases (1958), by partial abolition of personal income taxes (1960–61), and by a rise in the share of cash income in the total income of collective farmers (late 1950s, early 1960s). The macro gap is supposed to be bridged by the turnover tax. The financial micro balance problem is due to shortages of consumer goods.

21. For most goods, the tax is set at a specific ruble amount. For some goods of local importance, it is calculated as a percentage of the enterprise wholesale price. For social reasons, the tax is sometimes differentiated by type of product.

22. Interestingly, between 1933 and 1955 there was no top-level body re-

sponsible for labor and wage policy in the USSR. This did not mean that the wage-setting function was delegated to lower-level organs. It simply meant neglect of the planned wage, increasing departure of the wage from the underlying realities of labor supply and demand, and multiplication of discreet wage adjustments made by industrial and other state enterprises within the official wage structure. See Nove, *The Soviet Economic System*, 2nd ed., chap. 8.

23. Ideological forces also play a part in making the labor market imperfect. Thus, labor is regarded as an obligation of citizens of socialist countries. The citizen's choice between work and leisure is circumscribed not only by economic need, but by socialist moral obligation. His mobility is also restricted by the pervasive housing shortage. Since most housing goes with the job, one thinks twice before quitting one's job.

24. Nove, *The Soviet Economic System*, 2nd ed., p. 212.

25. Smith, *The Russians*, pp. 32–35. For the Chinese variant of special stores, see Fox Butterfield, *China: Alive in the Bitter Sea* (New York: Times Books, 1982).

26. In Soviet theory, labor has six dimensions, which are reflected in the wage scale: length of time worked; degree of skill; region, industry, and enterprise in which work is done; and working conditions. (Gregory and Stuart, *Soviet Economic Structure and Performance*, p. 190).

27. *The Economist*, April 10, 1982, p. 59.

28. Rumer, "Structural Imbalance in the Soviet Economy," pp. 25–26.

29. However, both the central planners and the ministries have been known to reduce by administrative order the share of amortization deductions that the neoclassical adjustment allows enterprises to pay into the production development funds.

30. Berliner, "Economic Measures and Reforms Under Andropov," p. 60.

31. Ibid., p. 61.

32. Kushnirsky, "Limits of Soviet Economic Reform," p. 43.

Chapter 9

1. Ishikawa, "China's Economic Growth Since 1949," p. 245; Cheng, *China's Economic Development*, p. 260, table 9.1.

2. *Beijing Review*, January 2, 1984, pp. 21–22.

3. State Statistical Bureau, *Ten Great Years: Statistics of the Economic and Cultural Achievements of the People's Republic of China* (Peking: Foreign Languages Press, 1960), title of introduction to chap. 2.

4. These are examined in Prybyla, *Political Economy of Communist China*, pp. 60–79, 146–90, and in Cheng, *China's Economic Development*, pp. 77–82, 137–55.

5. On economic activity cycles in China, see Ishikawa, "China's Economic Growth Since 1949," pp. 246–48, 271–72, p. 247 (fig. 1); Cheng, *China's Economic Development*, chap. 10.

6. Lardy, *Chinese Economic Planning*. For the Soviet antecedents, compare this with Zaleski, *Stalinist Planning for Economic Growth*.

7. Village (and urban) fair prices were (and are), in fact, controlled in various ways by local authorities to prevent "profiteering."

8. Ishikawa, "China's Economic Growth Since 1949," p. 256, table 5.

9. *Beijing Review*, December 21, 1979, p. 11.

10. *Beijing Review*, February 28, 1983, p. 13.

11. In agriculture, these arrangements between private and state ownership included mutual aid teams (seasonal and permanent), lower-level cooperatives (where income distribution was according to both labor and the contribution by the households of capital shares), and advanced collectives (payment by labor contribution only). In industry and commerce, the transitional arrangements included "free sale" of part of the output by the private firm (the rest going to the state at state-set prices), elementary state capitalism (in trade, cooperative groups), and advanced state capitalism (joint state-private enterprise), in trade, cooperative stores. In handicrafts, there were supply and marketing groups and cooperatives, lower-level producers' co-ops, and higher-level producers' cooperatives (Prybyla, *Political Economy of Communist China*, p. 175, table 5-11).

12. Xiaogang production team, Liyuan commune, Fengyang county, Anhwei province: "From 1966 to 1976 [during the second leftward adjustment] the peasants here had to depend on grain and relief funds from the state for six months of every year. The collective income was so low that each person got an average of only 25.8 yuan a year as his share [one-quarter of a U.S. cent a day]" (*Beijing Review*, August 24, 1981, p. 22).

13. *Kuang-ming Jih-pao* [Illumination Daily], July 24, 1979, p. 5.

14. Shi Zhongquan, "The 'Cultural Revolution' and the Struggle Against Bureaucracy," *Beijing Review*, December 7, 1981, pp. 17–20. Contrary to evidence and historical experience, the author concludes that "bureaucracy is not an incurable disease inherent in the socialist system."

15. "The national economy can be developed in proportion [in a balanced way] only if the enthusiasm and initiative of an enterprise is aroused according to the demand of the unified state plan" (Sun Xiaoliang, "An Inquiry into the Reform of the Economic Management System," *Renmin Ribao* [People's Daily], March 18, 1983, p. 5, in *Foreign Broadcast Information Service*, March 25, 1983).

16. This problem was recognized in the early 1960s by Sun Yefang, who prescribed a number of mildly market-related measures for its solution. For this he was imprisoned for seven years when "the 'left' mistakes ran amuck" during the Cultural Revolution. See "A Brief Introduction to Sun Yefang's Economic Theory," *Beijing Review*, June 13, 1983, pp. 16–19, and "Sun Yefang's Economic Theory Evaluated," ibid., January 2, 1984, pp. 27–31.

17. Yu Yunyao, "Commenting on 'The Results are Gratifying, the Direction is Worrisome,' " *Renmin Ribao* [People's Daily], April 4, 1983, p. 5, in *Foreign Broadcast Information Service*, April 7, 1983.

18. Thomas G. Rawski, *Economic Growth and Employment in China* (New York: Oxford University Press, 1979), p. 121. Ishikawa, in "China's Economic Growth Since 1949" (pp. 262 [table 7], 263), detects a fall in agricultural labor productivity in three benchmark years as compared with 1957: 1965, 1970, and 1975, with falls of respectively 12.3, 12.2, and 4.5 percent (measured in terms of food grain output per employed person). It should be pointed out that income distribution was not the only factor involved in the poor performance of industrial labor productivity in the 1957–1978 period.

19. Barry M. Richman, *Industrial Society in Communist China* (New York: Vintage Books, 1969), p. 629; Cheng, *China's Economic Development* p. 355.

20. Liang Wen, "Holding an Unbreakable Rice Bowl and Eating from the Common Pot," *Jilin Ribao* [Jilin Daily], May 19, 1979, in *Foreign Broadcast Information Service*, May 22, 1979.

21. Ishikawa, "China's Economic Growth Since 1949," p. 254, table 4.

22. Ibid.; Du Runsheng, "Good Beginning for Reform of Rural Economic System," *Beijing Review*, November 30, 1981, p. 16. Du, vice-minister in charge of the State Agricultural Commission, put the subsistence level rural income (in 1980–81) at 120 yuan. The cost of living index in the countryside rose by 22 percent between 1976 and 1980 (according to Ishikawa).

23. This was known as the "policy of readjustment, consolidation, filling-out, and raising standards." It was adopted by the Ninth Plenary Session of the Eighth Party Central Committee in 1961. See Prybyla, *Political Economy of Communist China*, chap. 9.

24. See, for example, Zhang Gong, "Mao Zedong's Thought on Socialist Economic Construction," *Beijing Review*, December 19, 1983, pp. 14–17, 23; Wang Qi, "Inheriting and Developing Mao Zedong Thought," ibid., December 26, 1983, pp. 20–26; Stuart R. Schram, " 'Economics in Command?' Ideology and Policy Since the Third Plenum, 1978–84," *The China Quarterly*, no. 99 (September 1984), pp. 417–61. If the chairman could see what is being done to his thought, he would surely protest, "I am not a Maoist!"

25. Some of the old-time party regulars of the First Five-Year Plan (1953–1957) and the first rightward adjustment (1961–1965) have, by 1985, apparently fallen by the wayside. Teng Hsiao-p'ing's experiments with what looks like a neoclassical liberal plan (or perhaps more), the promise of similar things to come in industry and commerce (October 20, 1984, Central Committee decision—see below), and the party rectification are resented by these people, some of whom are still very powerful. They include not a few People's Liberation Army commanders, Chen Yün and his bird-cage economics are apparently of this faction; its leaders include Wei Guoging, Xu Qiuli, Peng Zhen, Wong Zhen, and Wang En-mao (*The Nineties Monthly*, September 1984, cited in *Inside China Mainland*, November 1984, pp. 1–3).

26. *Beijing Review*, May 11, 1979, p. 16. "Prices in China today are very much out of joint with reality. While the entire price system must be reformed in a fundamental way, it is hard to do so at present. In the next few years, only the very unreasonable prices of consumer goods will be revised up or down, if the general level of prices can be maintained basically stable on the market. Where capital goods are concerned, adjustments of unreasonable prices will be speeded up if this does not affect the retail prices of consumer goods" (Ren Tao, "Reform Holds Key to Success," *Beijing Review*, May 16, 1983, p. 17). The longer price reform is postponed, the less likely it will ever be carried out.

27. I disregard, as for the time being technically impossible, the solution of perfect electronic centralization. But the mathematicians, economists, and engineers are working on it; flawless centralization may yet come to pass, at least on the conceptual level.

28. Jan S. Prybyla, "The Chinese Economy: Adjustment of the System or Systemic Reform?" *Asian Survey* 25, no. 5 (May 1985): 553–86.

29. *Beijing Review*, December 19, 1983, p. 17.

30. Jan S. Prybyla, "China's New Economic Strategy: Defining the U.S. Role," in The Heritage Foundation Asian Studies Center, *Backgrounder*, no. 24, April 8, 1984.

31. See, for example, Aubert, "Chine rurale," pp. 955–71; idem, "The New Economic Policy in the Chinese Countryside" (Mimeographed paper presented at the Seventh International Conference on Soviet and East European Agriculture, Grignon, France, July 9–13, 1984). Donald Zagoria, "China's Quiet Revolution," *Foreign Affairs* 62, no. 4 (Spring 1984): 879–904.

32. The account of the three contract types draws on Aubert, "The New Economic Policy," pp. 3–4.

33. *China Daily*, March 10, 1983, p. 4.

34. "Party Central Document No. 1," in *Inside China Mainland*, May 1984, pp. 1–8. See also Frederick W. Crook, "The Baogan Daohu Incentive System: Translation and Analysis of a Model Contract," *The China Quarterly*, no. 102 (June 1985), pp. 291–303.

35. *Beijing Review*, November 19, 1984, pp. 20–22; and ibid., July 2, 1984, pp. 8–9: "The machines are well maintained and costs are falling."

36. "Some comrades think that grasping economics is parasitism . . . and they look on the development of commodity production as capitalism . . . In the eyes of these comrades . . . for farmers to participate in commodity circulation activities and engage in commerce—especially in long haul transport and sales—is heterodoxy and opportunism" ("Party Central Document No. 1," p. 5). "Although there are no national statistics on what proportion of families use their tractors or trucks solely for transportation, some counties do keep records. In Hsin-tu County in Szechwan Province, there are 2,000 families offering tractor, truck, and other machine services. About 11 percent use their machines only for transportation, while 53.5 percent use them for farming and transportation, 27.1 percent only offer farming services, 5.9 percent process

farm produce, 1.7 percent do machine repairs, and 0.7 percent provide irrigation services" (*Beijing Review*, November 19, 1984, p. 22).

37. Aubert, "The New Economic Policy," p. 10.

38. Ibid., p. 23.

39. Ibid.

40. *Inside China Mainland*, May 1984, pp. 2, 7.

41. "It is essential to stress ideals and discipline in implementing the open policies. Some thought we were restricting our principles [of neoclassical liberalism] when I spoke of ideals at the national science and technology conference. We were not. They are being continuously expanded further yet, *but our minds are perfectly clear on whether they will be expanded beyond the point of control* [emphasis added]" ("Deng: Reform is 'Second Revolution'," *Beijing Review*, April 8, 1985, p. 6). The reference to "restricting our principles" is to Teng's anti–spiritual pollution speech of March 7, 1985, which apparently sent shock waves through the economy. See "Deng Says China Sticks to Socialism," *Beijing Review*, March 18, 1985, pp. 15–16, and Amanda Bennett, "China Tightens Grip on Its Economy, But Foreign Trade Appears Unaffected," *The Wall Street Journal*, March 20, 1985, p. 33.

42. Such a turn in the terms of trade (that is, in favor of agriculture) cannot be taken at face value. See Nicholas Lardy, "Consumption and Living Standards in China, 1978–83," *The China Quarterly*, no. 100 (December 1984), p. 862.

Chapter 10

1. "Hungary: The Quiet Revolution," *The Economist*, September 20, 1980, p. 51. There was a brief (1953–54) neoclassical conservative interlude during the first premiership of Imre Nagy.

2. In 1954–55, G. Peter circulated his ideas on the subject, which eventually found their way into print in 1956 in the form of a book on the significance of efficiency and profitability in the planned economy. János Kornai's *Overcentralization in Economic Administration*, published in 1959 (see Bibliography), was circulating in mimeographed form in 1955–56. A government-appointed committee headed by Stephen Varga recommended comprehensive changes in the Hungarian Stalinplan in 1957. Apart from agriculture, not much was done with these various proposals until 1968. During his first premiership, beginning in 1953, Nagy tried to adjust Rákosi's Stalinplan in a neoclassical conservative direction (the "New Course"). He was accused of "rightism" and removed in April 1955, then was shot.

3. Prior to 1968, adjustments of the Stalinplan were limited to agriculture (see below).

4. János Kornai, "The Dilemmas of a Socialist Economy: The Hungarian Experience," *Cambridge Journal of Economics* 4, no. 2 (June 1980): 147–57. Kor-

nai's five conditions for efficiency are: proper incentive system, cost-benefit calculation, fast and flexible adjustment mechanism, entrepreneurship, and personal responsibility. The four ethical principles of socialism are: socialist wage-setting ("to each according to his work"), solidarity, security, and priority of the general interest (see ibid., pp. 148–49).

5. Istvan Szavay, *Heti Vilaggazdaság* [Weekly world economy], (Budapest), November 20, 1982, pp. 51–52, in *Foreign Broadcast Information Service*, Hungary, no. 6691 (1982), p. 35.

6. Although until recently the USSR, Hungary's chief supplier of oil, raised its oil price with a lag (compared to the world price), the marginal cost of oil for Hungary is the world market price (Bela A. Balassa, *The Hungarian Economic Reform, 1968–81*, World Bank Staff Working Papers, no. 506 [Washington, D.C., February 1982], p. 15).

7. Ibid., p. 11.

8. Ibid., p. 14, table 1.

9. This nefarious material-technical supply network (to which reference has been made in earlier chapters) truly conforms to English lexicologist Samuel Johnson's 1755 *Dictionary* definition of *net*: "Anything reticulated or decussated at equal distances, with interstices between the intersections."

10. Rezsö Nyers, "Interrelations Between Policy and the Economic Reform in Hungary," *Journal of Comparative Economics* 7, no. 3 (September 1983): 223.

11. Kornai, "The Prospects of the Hungarian Economic Reform," p. 250.

12. Some of these imaginative combinations of private and social property harking back to the prenationalization, precollectivization period of United Front economics include the "intermediate" joint state-cooperative-private property arrangements and the several gradations of cooperative property used in China at one time (before 1952 in industry and commerce; before 1956 in agriculture). In the service trades and a few other areas, vestiges of mixed property forms survived until the Cultural Revolution (1966) (Prybyla, *Political Economy of Communist China*, chaps. 3 and 5, especially p. 175, table 5-11).

13. Kemény, "The Unregistered Economy in Hungary," p. 351.

14. Kornai, "The Prospects of the Hungarian Economic Reform," p. 251. The Chinese version of "trickle-down" theory was given by Teng Hsiao-p'ing: "Our government promotes the policy that some people get rich first. Then we'll have the other people get rich. Our final purpose is to have all the people get rich."

15. Nyers, "Interrelations Between Policy and the Economic Reform," p. 217.

16. Kornai, "The Prospects of the Hungarian Economic Reform," p. 245.

17. Nyers, "Interrelations Between Policy and the Economic Reform," p. 222.

18. Kornai, "The Prospects of the Hungarian Economic Reform," p. 229. And, Kornai adds, "with little success."

19. Exporters received the price obtained in convertible currency trade times the exchange rate, plus a rebate for imputed indirect taxes set at 10 percent of export value except for light industrial products, iron, and steel. Processed food exports were not subject to these regulations. Production taxes for individual firms have been abolished. Subsidies for firms from the state budget are seen as temporary. But, as Balassa points out, in 1981 various subsidies came to 42 percent of the profits of industrial firms (Bela A. Balassa, *Reforming the New Economic Mechanism in Hungary*, World Bank Staff Working Papers, no. 534 [Washington, D.C., 1982], pp. 1–11). See also László Rácy, "On the New Price System," *East European Economics* 12, no. 1 (Fall 1981): 49–69.

20. Balassa, *Reforming the New Economics Mechanism*, p. 3.

21. Michael Marrese, "Agricultural Policy and Performance in Hungary," *Journal of Comparative Economics* 7, no. 3 (September 1983): 330; Csaba Csaki, "Economic Management and Organization in Agriculture," ibid., pp. 326–27.

22. Edward Hewett, "The Hungarian Economy: Lessons of the 1970s and Prospects for the 1980s," U.S. Congress Joint Economic Committee, *East European Economic Assessment, Part I, Country Studies, 1980* (Washington, D.C.: U.S. Government Printing Office, 1981), pp. 484–523.

23. József Berényi and Sándorné Holé, *Figyelö* [Observer], November 18, 1981, pp. 1–4, cited by Balassa, *Reforming the New Economic Mechanism*, p. 8.

24. Bauer, "The Hungarian Alternative," p. 314.

25. Kornai, "The Prospects of the Hungarian Economic Reform," pp. 228–29, 231. Kornai notes (p. 230) that now firms can legally increase their domestic prices even if the profitability of exported goods does not rise, provided that the profits on exports meet the numerical targets judged acceptable by the planners. A number of other legal-administrative exceptions to the competitive pricing principle have been introduced.

26. Marrese, "Agricultural Policy and Performance in Hungary," p. 330.

27. These issues are raised by James Mulick, "The New Economic Mechanism in Hungary: A True Reform?" (M.A. paper, Department of Economics, Pennsylvania State University, 1984).

28. Kornai, "The Prospects of the Hungarian Economic Reform"; Bauer, "The Hungarian Alternative"; Balassa, *Reforming the New Economic Mechanism*.

29. "Even if the price is uncontrolled it is risky for an enterprise to change it" (Bauer, "The Hungarian Alternative," p. 308).

30. Kornai, "The Prospects of the Hungarian Economic Reform," p. 231.

31. Kornai, "Dilemmas of a Socialist Economy," p. 151.

32. Ivan Volgyes, "Kadar's Hungary in the Twilight Era," *Current History* 83, no. 496 (November 1984): 361–62.

33. Bauer, "The Hungarian Alternative," p. 305.

34. Ibid., p. 312. "The 'commanding heights of industry' . . . retained their central organizational structure; even with the 'reform' orientation, the

centralized areas of the economy (some 275 production units) still account for more than two-thirds of the total production, and in these areas 'decentralization,' local initiatives and local management really mean very little" (Volgyes, "Kadar's Hungary," p. 362).

35. Kornai, "The Prospects of the Hungarian Economic Reform," p. 244.

36. Marrese, "Agricultural Policy and Performance in Hungary," pp. 336–37; Ivan Volgyes, "Dynamic Changes: Rural Transformation, 1945–1975," in Joseph Held, ed., *The Modernization of Agriculture: Rural Transformation in Hungary, 1848–1975* (New York: Columbia University Press, 1980), pp. 351–500; Balassa, *The Hungarian Economic Reform*, pp. 24–29.

37. Mulick, "The New Economic Mechanism," p. 27.

38. The success of Hungarian agriculture—in output, productivity, and quality of products—cannot be attributed exclusively to the private sector. It is also due to making the cooperative sector more truly voluntary, to generous state investment in agriculture, and to the establishment of organizations known as technically operated production systems that diffuse up-to-date technology and "agribusiness mentality" among receptive (properly motivated and [less than elsewhere] coerced) farmers. Nevertheless, the contribution of the private sector is important. Work done on private plots is said to be equivalent to 750–800 thousand man-years. See Balassa, *The Hungarian Economic Reform*, p. 28; Mulick, "The New Economic Mechanism," p. 29. On the technically operated production systems, see Patricia Giles Winpenny, "The Impact of Western Technology on the Hungarian Feed-Livestock Economy: A Case Study of the Babolna Agriculture Combinate" (M.A. dissertation, Institute of Soviet and East European Studies, Carleton University, 1981).

39. József Mocsáry, "Centralization of the Hungarian Enterprise System and Its Impact on the Efficiency of Production Control and the Regulatory System," *Eastern European Economics* 21, no. 2 (Winter 1982–83): 76–103; Csongor Horváth, "On the Size of the Firm," *Eastern European Economics* 18, no. 3 (Spring 1980): 34–61; Márton Tardos, "The Increasing Role and Ambivalent Reception of Small Enterprises in Hungary," *Journal of Comparative Economics* 7, no. 3 (September 1983): 277–87.

40. Mulick, "The New Economic Mechanism," pp. 35–36, and Tökés, "Hungarian Reform Imperatives," p. 6. As of early 1984, there were 121,000 people in 11,000 teams working for their state factories or cooperatives on a contractual basis (*The Economist*, April 14, 1984, p. 57).

41. Mulick, "The New Economic Mechanism," p. 35. In early 1984, there were 4,900 such units with 28,000 members. There were also 130,000 licensed private craftsmen (electricians, builders, dressmakers) (*The Economist*, April 14, 1984, p. 57).

42. Volgyes, "Kadar's Hungary," p. 364.

43. Bela A. Balassa, "Reforming the New Economic Mechanism in Hungary," *Journal of Comparative Economics* 7, no. 3 (September 1983): 264–67.

44. Ibid., p. 266.

45. Kornai, "The Prospects of the Hungarian Economic Reform," p. 232. A statement from Poland's Solidarity Union released on February 25, 1985, puts the matter this way: "Profit, ostensibly one of the objectives of [Poland's 1985] price increases, is an artificial category devoid of any economic significance in our system. What is profitable today can become unprofitable tomorrow, and vice versa, because of the government's manipulation of prices" (*The Wall Street Journal*, April 17, 1985, p. 29).

46. The 1967 labor code gives the unions the right to veto management decisions with which they are in basic disaccord. Although not publicized, this right is reportedly used regularly ("Hungary: The Quiet Revolution," *The Economist*, September 20, 1980, p. 70).

47. Tökés, "Hungarian Reform Imperatives," p. 18.

48. Ibid., p. 12.

49. Ibid., p. 17.

50. Bauer, "The Hungarian Alternative," p. 312.

51. On the theory of overlapping preference zones, see Jan Drewnowski, "The Economic Theory of Socialism: A Suggestion for Reconsideration," *Journal of Political Economy* 69, no. 4 (August 1961): 341–54.

52. Peter Murrell, "Hungary's Hidden Economic Handicaps," *The Wall Street Journal*, October 22, 1984.

53. *The Economist*, September 20, 1980, p. 68.

54. In 1975, when the government hardened its line on private plots, the result was wholesale slaughtering of pigs. Since then, the threshold of taxable income derived from private agriculture has been raised threefold, investment in the private sector has been increased, and land not suitable for cooperative farming has been leased to families for private farming. The private sector supplies more than half the pigs, poultry, wine grapes, and fruit; two-thirds of Hungary's eggs; and four-fifths of early vegetables (Balassa, *The Hungarian Economic Reform*, p. 26).

55. Ancillary industrial and service activities of the collective farms were discouraged before 1968. A sample survey of eighty-six agricultural co-ops (1979) shows that these activities are more profitable than farming proper. The surveyed cooperatives obtained more than 90 percent of their profits from ancillary activities (Balassa, *The Hungarian Economic Reform*, p. 26).

56. *The Economist*, October 13, 1984, p. 53: "If you hack in cabs or on computers, and if you have to work in a centrally-planned economy, then almost everybody knows that Hungary is the place to be."

Chapter 11

1. The inventor of the model of market socialism, Oskar Lange, was an ardent practitioner of classical Stalinist planning after he returned to Poland

from Chicago. Shortly before Stalin's death, he published an article praising the dictator's exceptional intellectual endowments in the field of economic theory and practice.

2. A. Ross Johnson, *Yugoslavia's Significance for the West* (Santa Monica, Calif.: Rand Corporation, 1984).

3. Deborah D. Milenkovitch, *Plan and Market in Yugoslav Economic Thought* (New Haven, Conn.: Yale University Press, 1971), p. 294.

4. David Granick, *Enterprise Guidance in Eastern Europe: A Comparison of Four Socialist Economies* (Princeton, N.J.: Princeton University Press, 1975), p. 333.

5. Robin Alison Remington, "The Politics of Scarcity in Yugoslavia," *Current History* 83, no. 496 (November 1984): 374, 392.

6. Theories of labor management predating Yugoslav practice include those of the Italian Marxist Antonio Gramsci (labor management and plan) and French journalist and economist Pierre-Joseph Proudhon (labor management and market).

7. Granick, *Enterprise Guidance in Eastern Europe*, p. 334.

8. Ellen T. Comisso, in her *Workers' Control Under Plan and Market: Implications of Yugoslav Self-Management* (New Haven, Conn.: Yale University Press, 1979), argues that the Yugoslav centralizing-decentralizing cycles are not due to special Yugoslav peculiarities, but to inevitable pressures within the self-management system in which market and plan are inherently unstable. Self-managed firms are dissatisfied with the irrationalities and inefficiencies of the plan and press for market decentralization. When they obtain it, they become dissatisfied with the income differentiation, inflation, and fluctuations, and press for plan centralization.

9. Remington, "Politics of Scarcity in Yugoslavia," p. 370.

10. The importance of informal pressures in the Yugoslav institutional setting is stressed by Granick, *Enterprise Guidance in Eastern Europe*, pp. 349–50. Moral suasion is present in both market and plan systems (recall Hungary), but it is especially significant in the currently decentralized, defederalized Yugoslav economy. Social pressure, including publicity, is put on enterprises by government bodies (especially the commune, which is interested in a fairly equitable pattern of income distribution among enterprises within its jurisdiction) and by social organizations of all kinds. Leading personnel of enterprises rotate horizontally among organizations; such rotation (as Granick notes) is primarily confined to the same commune, and almost certainly to the same republic. In anticipation of such moves, managers and other responsible officials of enterprises and BOALs give attentive hearing to the wishes of commune and republican authorities.

11. See, for example, John H. Moore, "Self-Management in Yugoslavia," in U.S. Congress Joint Economic Committee, *East European Economic Assessment, Part 1* (Washington, D.C.: U.S. Government Printing Office, 1981), pp. 215–29, and idem, *Growth with Self-Management: Yugoslav Industrialization, 1952–1975*

(Stanford: Hoover Institution Press, 1980). "Worker self-management is completely artificial; it is really part of the ruling structure, part of the party's political activity. Self-management cannot be efficient because it's part of the ruling structure" (Milovan Djilas, in Thomas J. Bray, "A Conversation with Milovan Djilas," *The Wall Street Journal*, October 20, 1982, p. 33). The power of the party is not negligible, even if fractured. Since his expulsion from the party in 1954, Djilas has spent nine years in prison. He is not allowed to travel abroad or to publish in Yugoslavia. The Yugoslav periodical *Ekonomska Politika* (January 18, 1982) has this to say: "How could we talk of the responsibility of a working organization for investment, for instance, if the consent or support of the commune committee of the League of Communists is the crucial point in an investment decision?" (Sirc, "The Yugoslav Debt," p. 31).

12. See, for example, Laura d'Andrea Tyson in her various writings, including *The Yugoslav Economic System and Its Performance in the 1970s* (Berkeley: University of California Institute of International Studies, 1980), pp. 27–30.

13. Michael T. Kaufman, "Decentralized Decision-Making Plagues Yugoslav Economy," citing Oskar Kovacs, Economics Faculty Dean, Belgrade University (*The New York Times*, October 29, 1984, p. D8).

14. *The Wall Street Journal*, July 5, 1983, p. 50. In Montenegro, a steel mill was built despite the fact that the region has hardly any raw materials and is short on roads and railways. There are six electric power grids, one for each republic. Shortages of electricity in one area cannot be relieved by surpluses elsewhere. The Feni nickel mine in Macedonia was expanded at the cost of tens of millions of borrowed dollars precisely at a time when prices of nickel fell drastically on world markets (*The New York Times*, October 29, 1984, p. D8).

15. A "community of interest" is yet another vapid term in the Yugoslav self-management lexicon, this one referring to an organization that is comprised of both users and suppliers of given services, the users and suppliers in most cases being organizations themselves. Communities of interest are mandatory for education, health, science, and culture, but also exist for railways, electric power, and public utilities (Martin Schrenk, Cyrus Ardalan, and Nawal A. El Tatawy, *Yugoslavia: Self-Management Socialism and the Challenge of Development* [Baltimore, Md.: Johns Hopkins University Press, 1979], p. 371).

16. Howard Wachtel, *Workers' Management and Wages in Yugoslavia* (Ithaca, N.Y.: Cornell University Press, 1973).

17. Tyson, *The Yugoslav Economic System*, p. 4.

18. Ljubo Sirc, "What Yugoslavia Needs, the IMF Can't Offer," *The Wall Street Journal*, August 10, 1983, p. 25.

19. Amuzegar, *Comparative Economics*, p. 341.

20. Tyson, *The Yugoslav Economic System*, p. 5.

21. Granick, *Enterprise Guidance in Eastern Europe*, p. 332.

22. *The New York Times*, September 25, 1984, p. A2.

23. When the national bank started negotiating a rescue package with

Western bankers, it did not even know how much was owed (*The Wall Street Journal*, July 5, 1983, p. 50).

24. Cited in *The Wall Street Journal*, October 28, 1982, p. 35.

Chapter 12

1. Charles Gati puts this nicely with reference to Poland: "The people believe Poland is their country; the rulers believe in 'people's Poland' " ("Polish Futures, Western Options," *Foreign Affairs* 61, no. 2 [Winter 1982/83]: 298).

2. On quantitative performance of the neoclassical plan and the Yugoplan, see Paul R. Gregory and Robert C. Stuart, *Comparative Economic Systems*, 2nd ed. (Boston: Houghton Mifflin, 1984), chap. 12.

3. Prybyla, "The Chinese Economy," pp. 562, 567, 569–70, 571–72.

Appendix A

1. See Köhler, *Welfare and Planning*, pp. 82–122; Wassily Leontief, "The Structure of Development," *Scientific American*, September 1963, pp. 148–66. Also in Wassily Leontief, *Input-Output Economics* (New York: Oxford University Press, 1966), pp. 41–67.

2. Campbell, *Soviet-Type Economies*, pp. 186–87.

3. Ibid., p. 187.

Appendix B

1. John F. Burns, "Soviet Study Urges Relaxing of Controls to Revive Economy," *The New York Times*, August 5, 1983. Copyright © 1983 by The New York Times Company. Reprinted by permission.

2. Kushnirsky, "Limits of Soviet Economic Reform," p. 37.

BIBLIOGRAPHY

Abouchar, Alan. *Economic Evaluation of Soviet Socialism*. New York: Pergamon Press, 1979.

Abramov, Fyodor. *The New Life: A Day on a Collective Farm*. New York: Grove Press, 1963.

Adam, Jan. *Wage Control and Inflation in the Soviet Bloc Countries*. London: Macmillan, 1979.

Adizes, Ichak. *Industrial Democracy Yugoslav Style*. New York: Free Press, 1971.

Akademiia Nauk SSSR, Institut Ekonomiki. *Sovetskaia sotsialisticheskaia ekonomika 1917–1957 gd.* [Soviet socialist economy 1917–1957]. Moscow: 1957.

Amin, Samir. *The Future of Maoism*. New York: Monthly Review Press, 1983.

Andors, Stephen. *China's Industry, Revolution, Politics, Planning, and Management, 1949 to Present*. New York: Pantheon Books, 1977.

Antal, László. "Development with Some Digression—The Hungarian Economic Mechanism in the Seventies." *Acta Oeconomica* 23 (1979): 257–74.

Arrow, Kenneth. *Social Choice and Individual Values*. 2nd ed. New York: Wiley, 1963.

The Associated Labour Act. Ljubljana: Dopisna Delavska Univerza, 1977.

Balassa, Bela A. "The Economic Reform in Hungary, Ten Years After." *European Economic Review* (1978): 245–68. [Republished in: Balassa, Bela A. *The Newly Industrializing Countries in the World Economy*. New York: Pergamon Press, 1981.]

——. *The Hungarian Experience in Economic Planning*. New Haven, Conn.: Yale University Press, 1959.

Balinky, Alexander et al. *Planning and the Market in the USSR: The 1960s*. New Brunswick, N.J.: Rutgers University Press, 1967.

Barsov, A. A. *Balans stoimostnykh obmenov mezhdu gorodom i derevnei* [Terms of trade in exchanges between cities and villages]. Moscow: Nauka, 1969.

Bauer, Támás. "Investment Cycles in Planned Economies." *Acta Oeconomica* 21 (1978): 243–60.

———. "The Second Economic Reform and Ownership Relations: Some Considerations for the Further Development of the New Economic Mechanism." *Eastern European Economics* 22, nos. 3–4 (1984): 33–87.

Baum, Richard. *Prelude to Revolution: Mao, the Party and the Peasant Question, 1962–66.* New York: Columbia University Press, 1975.

Baum, Richard, and Teiwes, Frederick C. *Ssu-Ch'ing: The Socialist Education Movement, 1962–1966.* Berkeley: University of California Institute of East Asian Studies, 1968.

Belov, Fedor. *The History of a Soviet Collective Farm.* New York: Praeger, 1955.

Berend, Ivan, and Ranki, Gyorgÿ. *Hungary: A Century of Economic Development.* New York: Barnes & Noble, 1984.

Bergman, T. *Farm Policies in Socialist Countries.* Translated by Lux Furtmuller. Lexington, Mass.: Lexington Books, 1975.

Bergson, Abram. *The Economics of Soviet Planning.* New Haven, Conn.: Yale University Press, 1964.

———. "Toward a New Growth Model." *Problems of Communism* 22 (1973): 1–9.

———. "Toward a New Growth Model: Comment." *The ACES Bulletin* 24 (1982): 89–92.

Bergson, Abram, and Levine, Herbert S., eds. *The Soviet Economy: Towards the Year 2000.* London: Allen & Unwin, 1983.

Bernstein, Thomas P. "Stalinism, Famine, and the Chinese Peasants: Grain Procurements During the Great Leap Forward." *Theory and Society* [Amsterdam], May 1984, pp. 339, 397.

Bettelheim, Charles. *Cultural Revolution and Industrial Organization in China: Changes in Management and the Division of Labor.* New York: Monthly Review Press, 1974.

Bigler, Robert M. "The Role of Bureaucracies and Experts in the Planning and Implementation of Hungary's New Economic Mechanism." *East European Quarterly* 18 (1984): 93–112.

Birman, Igor. "From the Achieved Level." *Soviet Studies* 30 (1978): 153–72.

———. *Secret Incomes of the Soviet State Budget.* The Hague, Neth.: Martinus Nijhoff, 1981.

Bliss, C. "Prices, Markets, and Planning." *Economic Journal* 82 (1972): 87–100.

Böhn, Antai, and Kolosi, Támás, eds. *Structure and Stratification in Hungary.* Budapest: Institute for Social Sciences, 1982.

Bombelles, Joseph T. *Economic Development of Communist Yugoslavia, 1947–1964.* Stanford: Hoover Institution Publications [73], 1968.

Bornstein, Morris. "Improving the Soviet Economic Mechanism." *Soviet Studies* 37 (1985): 1–30.

———, ed. *Plan and Market: Economic Reform in Eastern Europe.* New Haven, Conn.: Yale University Press, 1973.

Brown, Archie. "Political Science in the Soviet Union: A New Stage of Development?" *Soviet Studies* 36 (1984): 317–44.

Brugger, Bill. *China: Radicalism to Revisionism, 1962–1979.* New York: Barnes & Noble, 1981.

Brus, W. *The Market in a Socialist Economy.* London and Boston: Routledge and Kegan Paul, 1972.

———. *Socialist Ownership and Political Systems.* London: Routledge and Kegan Paul, 1975.

Bukharin, Nikolai I., and Preobrazhenskii, Evgenii A. *The ABCs of Communism.* London: Penguin, 1969. [Introduction by E. H. Carr; book originally published in 1920.]

Burg, Steven L. *Conflict and Cohesion in Socialist Yugoslavia: Political Decision-Making Since 1966.* Princeton, N.J.: Princeton University Press, 1983.

Burks, R. V. "The Coming Crisis in the Soviet Union." *East European Quarterly* 18 (1984): 61–71.

Byrd, William. "Enterprise-Level Reforms in Chinese State-Owned Industry." *American Economic Review* 73 (1983): 329–32.

Byrd, William; Tidrick, Gene; Jiyuan, Chen; Lu, Xu; Zongkun, Tang; and Lanton, Chen. *Recent Chinese Economics Reforms: Studies of Two Industrial Enterprises.* Washington, D.C.: World Bank, 1984.

Cannock, Michael. "The Effects of Self-Management in Yugoslav Industrial Growth." *Soviet Studies* 34 (1982): 69–85.

Carr, E. H. *Foundations of a Planned Economy, 1926–1929.* 3 vols. London: Macmillan, 1969–1978.

———. *History of Soviet Russia.* Vol. 2. London: Macmillan, 1978.

Cave, Martin. *Computers and Economic Planning: The Soviet Experience.* Cambridge, Eng.: Cambridge University Press, 1980.

Cave, Martin and Hare, Paul. *Alternative Approaches to Economic Planning.* London: Macmillan, 1981.

Chang, King-yuh, ed. *Perspectives on Development in the PRC.* Boulder, Colo.: Westview Press, 1984.

Chapman, Janet G. "Soviet Wages Under Socialism." In *The Socialist Price Mechanism,* edited by Alan Abouchar, pp. 246–81. Durham, N.C.: Duke University Press, 1977.

Ch'en, Jerome, ed. *Mao Papers: Anthology and Bibliography.* London: Oxford University Press, 1970.

Cheng, Chu-yuan. "Economic Development in Taiwan and Mainland China: A Comparison of Strategies and Performance." *Asian Affairs: An American Review* 10 (1983): 60–86.

Cherevik, E., and Shvyrkov, Y. *An ABC of Planning: Fundamentals of the Theory and Methodology of Economic Planning.* Translated by Peter Greenwood. Moscow: Progress 1982. [Distributed in the United States by Imported Publications (Chicago).]

China's Search for Economic Growth: The Chinese Economy Since 1949. Beijing: New World Press, 1982.

Clayton, Elizabeth. "Notes on the Productivity of Soviet Private Agriculture." *The ACES Bulletin* 21 (1979): 85–91.

Cockburn, Andrew. *Threat: Inside the Soviet War Machine.* New York: Vintage Books, 1984.

Cohen, Stephen. *Bukharin and the Bolshevik Revolution: A Political Biography.* New York: Knopf, 1973.

Comisso, Ellen Turkish. *Workers' Control Under Plan and Market: Implications of Yugoslav Self-Management.* New Haven, Conn., and London: Yale University Press, 1979.

———. "Yugoslavia in the 1970s: Self-Management and Bargaining." *Journal of Comparative Economics* 4 (1980): 192–208.

Conquest, Robert, ed. *Agricultural Workers in the USSR.* London: Bodley Head, 1968.

———. *The Great Terror: Stalin's Purge of the Thirties.* New York: Macmillan, 1968.

The Constitution of the Socialist Federal Republic of Yugoslavia. Merrick, N.Y.: Cross-Cultural Communications, 1976.

Conyngham, William J. *The Modernization of Soviet Industrial Management.* Cambridge, Eng.: Cambridge University Press, 1982.

Croll, Elizabeth; Davin, Delia; and Kane, Penny, eds. *China's One-Child Family Policy.* London: Macmillan, 1985.

Csaba, László. "New Features of the New Hungarian Economic Mechanism in the Mid-Eighties." *The New Hungarian Quarterly,* no. 90 (1983): 44–63.

Davies, Robert W. *The Industrialization of Soviet Russia.* 2 vols. Cambridge, Mass.: Harvard University Press, 1980.

Deng, Liqun. *Tantan Jihua Tiaojie he Shichang* [A discussion on planning regulation and market regulation]. Beijing: People's Publishers, 1979.

Desai, Padma, ed. *Marxism, Central Planning and the Soviet Economy.* Cambridge, Mass.: M.I.T. Press, 1983.

Deutscher, Isaac. *Stalin: A Political Biography.* New York: Vintage Books, 1960.

DeWulf, Luc. "Economic Reform in China." *Finance & Development,* March 1985, pp. 8–11.

Dirlam, Joel, and Plummer, J. L. *An Introduction to the Yugoslav Economy.* Columbus, Ohio: Merrill, 1975.

Dittmer, Lowell. *Ethics and Rhetorics of the Chinese Cultural Revolution.* Berkeley: University of California Institute of East Asian Studies, 1981.

Djilas, Milovan. *Tito: The Story from Inside.* New York: Harcourt Brace Jovanovich, 1980.

Doder, Dusko. *The Yugoslavs.* New York: Random House, 1978.

Doenges, Byron. "Soviet Resource Allocation: Military vs. Civilian." In *The Soviet Economy After Brezhnev,* pp. 171–89. Brussels: NATO Economic Directorate, 1984.

Domar, Evsey. "The Soviet Collective Farm." *American Economic Review* 16 (1966): 734–57.

Donáth, F. *Reform and Revolution—Transformation of Hungary's Agriculture, 1945–1975.* Budapest: Corvina, 1980.

Drewnowski, Jan, ed. *Crisis in the East European Economy.* New York: St. Martin's Press, 1982.

Du, Runsheng. "China's Countryside Under Reform." *Beijing Review,* August 13, 1984, pp. 16–21.

————. "Explaining China's Rural Economic Policy." *Beijing Review,* April 30, 1984, pp. 16–21.

Dubey, Vinod, coord. *Yugoslav Development with Decentralization.* Baltimore, Md.: Johns Hopkins University Press [for the World Bank], 1975. [Report of a World Bank mission to Yugoslavia.]

Dunmore, Timothy. *The Soviet War Economy.* London: Macmillan, 1984.

Dyker, David A. "Decentralization and the Command Principle—Some Lessons from Soviet Experience." *Journal of Comparative Economics* 5 (1981): 121–48.

Ekstein, Alexander. *China's Economic Revolution.* New York: Cambridge University Press, 1977.

Ellman, Michael. "Aggregation as a Cause of Inconsistent Plans." *Economica* 36 (1969): 69–74.

————. "Agricultural Productivity Under Socialism." *World Development* 9 (1981): 979–90.

————. "Changing Views on Central Economic Planning: 1958–1983." *The ACES Bulletin* 25 (1983): 11–29.

————. *Collectivisation, Convergence and Capitalism: Political Economy in a Divided World.* Orlando, Fla.: Academic Press, 1984.

————. "Did the Agricultural Surplus Provide the Resources for the Increase of Investment in the USSR During the First Five Year Plan?" *Economic Journal* 85 (1975): 844–63.

————. "On a Mistake of Preobrazhensky and Stalin." *Journal of Development Studies* 14 (1978): 353–56.

————. *Planning Problems in the USSR.* Cambridge, Eng.: Cambridge University Press, 1973.

Erlich, Alexander. "Stalin's Views on Economic Development." In *Continuity and Change in Russian and Soviet Thought,* edited by Ernest J. Simmons, pp. 81–99. Cambridge, Mass.: Harvard University Press, 1955.

Estrin, Saul. *Self-Management: Economic Theory and Yugoslav Practice.* Cambridge, Eng.: Cambridge University Press, 1983.

Fainsod, Merle. *Smolensk Under Soviet Rule.* New York: Vintage Books, 1958.

Falkierski, Henryk. "Economic Reform and Income Distribution in Hungary." *Cambridge Journal of Economics* 3 (1979): 15–32.

Fallenbuchl, Zbigniew M. "Collectivization and Economic Development." *The Canadian Journal of Economics and Political Science* 3 (1967): 1–15.

Farkas, Richard P. *Yugoslav Economic Development and Political Change: The Relationship Between Economic Managers and Policy-Making Elites.* New York: Praeger, 1975.

Fedorenko, N., and Shatlin, S. "The Problem of Optimal Planning of the Socialist Economy." *Problems of Economics* 7 (1968): 3–29.

Feiwel, George P. *The Soviet Quest for Economic Efficiency.* New York: Praeger, 1972.

Feuchtwang, Stephan, and Hussain, Athar. *The Chinese Economic Reforms.* New York: St. Martin's Press, 1983.

Fisher, Lewis A., and Uren, Philip E. *The New Hungarian Agriculture.* Montreal: McGill-Queen's University Press, 1973.

Friedländer, Michael. *Die ungarische Wirtschaftsreform.* Forschungsberichte, no. 99. Vienna: Wiener Institut für Internationale Wirtschaftsvergleiche, 1984.

Friss, István. "Planning and Economic Reform in Hungary." In *Progress and Planning in Industry: Proceedings of the International Conference on Industrial Economics* [April 1970], edited by Z. Roman, pp. 61–64. Budapest: Akadémiai Kiadó, 1972.

———, ed. *Reform of the Economic Mechanism in Hungary.* Budapest: Akadémiai Kiadó, 1971.

Furubotn, Erik, and Pejovich, Svetozar. "Property Rights and Economic Theory: A Survey of Recent Literature." *Journal of Economic Literature* 10 (1972): 1137–162.

Gadó, Ottó, ed. *Reform of the Economic Mechanism in Hungary.* Budapest: Akadémiai Kiadó, 1972.

Gilder, George. *The Spirit of Enterprise.* New York: Simon & Schuster, 1984.

Gintis, Robert. "Consumer Behavior and the Concept of Sovereignty: Explanations of Social Decay." *American Economic Review* 62 (1972): 267–78.

Goldman, Marshall I. "Gorbachev and Economic Reform." *Foreign Affairs* 64 (1985): 56–73.

———. *USSR in Crisis: The Failure of an Economic System.* New York: Norton, 1983.

Goodman, S. E. "Computers and the Development of the Soviet Economy." In *Soviet Economy in a Time of Change,* by the U.S. Congress Joint Economic Committee, pp. 524–53. Washington, D.C.: U.S. Government Printing Office, 1979.

Granick, David. *Enterprise Guidance in Eastern Europe: A Comparison of Four Socialist Economies.* Princeton, N.J.: Princeton University Press, 1975.

Gray, Jack, and Cavendish, Patrick. *Chinese Communism in Crisis: Maoism and the Cultural Revolution.* New York: Praeger, 1968.

Gregory, Paul R., and Stuart, Robert C. *Comparative Economic Systems.* 2nd ed. Boston: Houghton Mifflin, 1985.

———. *Soviet Economic Structure and Performance*. 3rd ed. New York: Harper & Row, 1986.

Griffin, Keith, ed. *Institutional Reform and Economic Development in the Chinese Countryside*. London: Macmillan, 1984.

Grossman, Gregory. "Notes for a Theory of the Command Economy." *Soviet Studies* 15 (1963): 101–23.

———. "Scarce Capital and Soviet Doctrine." *Quarterly Journal of Economics* 67 (1953): 311–43.

———, ed. *Value and Plan*. Berkeley: University of California Press, 1960.

Gumpel, Werner. " 'Sozialistische Marktwirtschaft' Zur Theoretischen Legitimation eines wirtschaftlichen Konzepts." *Osteuropa Wirtschaft* 261 (1981): 79–87.

Gurley, John G. *China's Economy and the Maoist Strategy*. New York: Monthly Review Press, 1976.

———. "Maoist Economic Development: The New Man in New China." *The Center Magazine* 3 (1970): 25–33.

Gutmann, Gernot, and Klein, Werner. "Wirtschaftspolitische Konzeptionen sozialistischer Planwirtschaften." In *Wirtschaftspolitik im Systemvergleich*, by Dieter Cassel, pp. 93–116. Munich: Verlag Franz Vohlen, 1984.

Hahn, Werner G. *The Politics of Soviet Agriculture, 1960–1970*. Baltimore, Md.: Johns Hopkins University Press, 1972.

Hanson, Phillip. "Success Indicators Revisited: The July 1979 Decree on Planning and Management." *Soviet Studies* 35 (1983): 1–14.

Harasymiw, Bohdan. *Political Elite Recruitment in the Soviet Union*. St. Antony's/Macmillan Series, edited by Archie Brown. London: Macmillan, 1984.

Hare, Paul G. "The Beginnings of Institutional Reform in Hungary." *Soviet Studies* 35 (1983): 313–30.

———. "Economics of Shortage and Non-Price Control: A Review Article." *Journal of Comparative Economics* 6 (1982): 406–25.

———. "Industrial Prices in Hungary, Part I." *Soviet Studies* 28 (1976): 362–90.

Hare, Paul G.; Radice, Hugo; and Swain, Nigel, eds. *Hungary: A Decade of Economic Reform*. London: Allen & Unwin, 1981.

Hayek, Friedrich A. *Collectivist Economic Planning*. London: Routledge and Kegan Paul, 1963.

———. *The Road to Serfdom*. Chicago: University of Chicago Press, 1944.

———. "The Use of Knowledge in Society." *American Economic Review* 35 (1945): 519–30.

Hedlund, Stefan. *Crisis in Soviet Agriculture*. New York: St. Martin's Press, 1984.

Held, Joseph, ed. *The Modernization of Agriculture: Rural Transformation in Hungary, 1848–1975*. New York: Columbia University Press, 1980.

Herlemann, Horst G., ed. *Quality of Life in the Soviet Union*. Boulder, Colo.: Westview Press, 1985.

Herod, Charles. *The Nation in the History of Marxian Thought: The Concept of Nations with History and Nations Without History*. The Hague, Neth.: Martinus Nijhoff, 1977.

Ho, Samuel P. S., and Huenemann, Ralph W. *China's Open Door Policy: The Quest for Foreign Technology and Capital*. Vancouver: University of British Columbia Press, 1984.

Hoffman, Erik P., and Laird, Robin F. *The Politics of Economic Modernization in the Soviet Union*. Ithaca, N.Y.: Cornell University Press, 1982.

Holzman, Franklyn D. *Foreign Trade Under Central Planning*. Cambridge, Mass.: Harvard University Press, 1974.

Hook, Sidney. *The Hero in History: A Study in Limitation and Possibility*. Boston: Beacon Press, 1962.

Horchler, Gabriel Francis. *Hungarian Economic Reforms: A Selective, Partially Annotated Bibliography*. New Brunswick, N.J.: American Hungarian Foundation, 1977.

Horvat, Branko. *The Political Economy of Socialism: A Marxist Social Theory*. Armonk, N.Y.: M. E. Sharpe, 1982.

―――. *The Yugoslav Economic System: The First Labor-Managed Economy in the Making*. White Plains, N.Y.: International Arts and Sciences Press, 1976.

Horváth, Csongor. "On the Size of the Firm." *Eastern European Economics* 18 (1980): 34–62.

Hough, Jerry F., and Fainsod, Merle. *How the Soviet Union Is Governed*. Cambridge, Mass.: Harvard University Press, 1979.

"The Hungarian Economy: Considerations of Reform." *Eastern European Economics* 22, nos. 3–4 (1984).

Imfeld, Al. *China as a Model of Development*. Translated by Matthew J. O'Connell. Maryknoll, N.Y.: Orbis Books, 1976.

Ishikawa, Shigeru. "China's Economic System Reform: Underlying Factors and Prospects." *World Development* 11 (1983): 647–58.

Jasny, Naum. *Essays on the Soviet Economy*. New York: Praeger, 1962.

―――. *The Socialized Agriculture of the USSR*. Stanford: Stanford University Press, 1949.

―――. *The Soviet Economy During the Plan Era*. Stanford: Food Research Institute, 1951.

―――. *Soviet Industrialization, 1928–1952*. Chicago: University of Chicago Press, 1961.

Johnson, Chalmers A. *Peasant Nationalism and Communist Power: The Emergence of Revolutionary China, 1937–1945*. Stanford: Stanford University Press, 1962.

Johnson, D. Gale. *Progress of Economic Reform in the People's Republic of China*.

American Enterprise Institute Studies, no. 367. Washington, D.C.: American Enterprise Institute for Public Policy Research, 1982.

Jones, Ellen. *The Red Army and Society: A Sociology of the Soviet Military*. Winchester, Mass.: Allen & Unwin, 1985.

Joseph, William A. *The Critique of Ultra-Leftism in China, 1958–1981*. Stanford: Stanford University Press, 1984.

Jurkovic, Pero. "Content and Characteristics of the Public Financing System." *East European Economics* 21 (1982–83): 3–49.

Kaachaturov, Tigran Sergeevich. *The Economy of the Soviet Union Today*. Moscow: Progress Publishers, 1977.

Kahan, Arcadius, and Ruble, Blair A., eds. *Industrial Labor in the USSR*. New York: Pergamon Press, 1979.

Kalecki, Michal. *Introduction to the Theory of Growth in a Socialist Economy*. Oxford: Oxford University Press, 1979.

Kantorovich, Leonid V. *Ekonomicheskii raschet nailuchsheskogo ispol'zovaniia resursov*. Moscow: 1959. [On perfectly centralized planning based on an optimizing mathematical model. In English, *The Best Use of Economic Resources*, edited by G. Morton and translated by P. K. Knightsfield. Cambridge, Mass.: Harvard University Press, 1965.]

Karcz, Jerzy, ed. *Soviet and East European Agriculture*. Berkeley: University of California Press, 1967.

Katsenelinboigen, Aron. *Soviet Economic Thought and Political Power in the USSR*. New York: Pergamon Press, 1980.

———. *Studies in Soviet Economic Planning*. White Plains, N.Y.: M. E. Sharpe, 1978.

Kaufman, Michael. "Hungarians Have Tips for Soviet Farmers." *The New York Times*, April 14, 1985, p. 2E.

Kempe, Frederick. "Hungary Takes a Flier in Private Ownership of Business Enterprises." *The Wall Street Journal*, March 26, 1982, pp. 1, 16.

Khan, Azizur Rohman, and Lee, Eddy. *Agrarian Policies and Institutions in China After Mao*. Bangkok: International Labour Organization, 1983.

King, Charles D., and van DeVall, Mark. *Models of Industrial Democracy: Consultation, Co-Determination, and Workers' Management*. The Hague, Neth.: Mouton, 1978.

Kir'ian, M. M., ed. *Voenno-tekhnicheskii progress i vooruzhennye sily SSSR* [Military-technological progress and the armed forces of the USSR]. Moscow: Voenizdat, 1982.

Kirsch, Leonard J. *Soviet Wages: Changes in Structure and Administration Since 1956*. Cambridge, Mass.: M.I.T. Press, 1972.

Knight, Peter T. *Economic Decisionmaking Structures and Processes in Hungary*. Staff Working Paper, no. 648. Washington, D.C.: World Bank, 1984.

———. *Economic Reform in Socialist Countries: The Experiences of China, Hungary,*

Romania, and Yugoslavia. Staff Working Paper, no. 579. Washington, D.C.: World Bank, 1983.

Köhler, Heinz. *Welfare and Planning: An Analysis of Capitalism Versus Socialism.* New York: Wiley, 1966.

Kolaja, Jiri. *Workers' Councils: The Yugoslav Experience.* New York: Praeger, 1965.

Kornai, János. *Economics of Shortage.* Amsterdam: North-Holland, 1980.

———. *Overcentralization in Economic Administration.* Oxford: Oxford University Press, 1959.

———. "Resource-Constrained versus Demand-Constrained Systems." *Econometrica* 47 (1979): 801–19.

Kovrig, Bennett. *Communism in Hungary from Kun to Kadar.* Stanford: Hoover Institution Press, 1979.

Kramanics, Gabriel. "Hungary." *Eastern European Economics* 19 (1981): 47–53.

Krylov, Constanin A. *The Soviet Economy: How It Really Works.* Lexington, Mass.: Lexington Books, 1979.

Kueh, Y. Y. "China's New Agricultural Policy Program: Major Economic Consequences, 1979–1983." *Journal of Comparative Economics* 8 (1984): 353–75.

———. *Economic Planning and Local Mobilization in Post-Mao China.* Research Notes and Studies, no. 7. London: Contemporary China Institute, 1985.

———. "Economic Reform in China at the *Xian* Level." *The China Quarterly,* no. 96 (1983), pp. 665–68.

Kushnirsky, Fyodor I. *Soviet Economic Planning 1965–1980.* Boulder, Colo.: Westview Press, 1982.

Laird, Roy D.; Hajda, Joseph; and Laird, Betty A., eds. *The Future of Soviet Agriculture in the Soviet Union and Eastern Europe.* Boulder, Colo.: Westview Press, 1977.

Lampert, Nicholas, and Davies, R. W. *Whistleblowing in the Soviet Union: A Study of Complaints and Abuses Under State Socialism.* Studies in Soviet History and Society, edited by R. W. Davies. London: Macmillan, 1984.

Lane, David. *The End of Social Inequality? Class Status and Power Under State Socialism.* Winchester, Mass.: Allen & Unwin, 1982.

Lange, Oskar. "The Computer and the Market." In *Socialism, Capitalism, and Economic Growth,* edited by Charles Feinstein, pp. 158–61. Cambridge, Eng.: Cambridge University Press, 1965.

Lardy, Nicholas, ed. *Chinese Economic Planning.* White Plains, N.Y.: M. E. Sharpe, 1978.

Lavigne, Marie. *The Socialist Economies.* White Plains, N.Y.: International Arts and Sciences Press, 1974.

Leites, Nathan. *Soviet Style Management.* Santa Monica, Calif.: Rand Corporation, 1984.

Lerner, Abba P. "The Economics and Politics of Consumer Sovereignty." *American Economic Review* 62 (1972): 258–66.

————. *The Economics of Control.* New York: Macmillan, 1944.

Levytsky, Borys. *The Soviet Political Elite: Brief Biographies.* Stanford: Hoover Institution Press, 1970.

Lewin, Moshe. *Political Undercurrents in Soviet Economic Debates: From Bukharin to the Modern Reformers.* Princeton, N.J.: Princeton University Press, 1974.

————. *Russian Peasants and Soviet Power.* London: Allen & Unwin, 1968.

Lewis, Paul. "Hungary Builds Lively Economy on West's Ideas." *The New York Times,* December 3, 1981, pp. A1, D5.

Li, Chengrui. "Are the 1967–76 Statistics on China's Economy Reliable?" *Beijing Review,* March 19, 1984, pp. 21–28.

Liang, Heng, and Shapiro, Judith. *Son of the Revolution.* New York: Knopf, 1983.

Liberman, Y. G. *Economic Methods and the Effectiveness of Production.* New York: International Arts and Sciences Press, 1971.

Lin, Wei, and Chao, Arnold, eds. *China's Economic Reforms.* Philadelphia: University of Pennsylvania Press, 1982.

Lin, Zili. "On the Contract System of Responsibility Linked to Production—A New Form of Cooperative Economy in China's Socialist Agriculture." *Social Sciences in China* 4 (1983): 53–104.

Linz, Susan J., ed. *The Impact of World War II on the Soviet Union.* Totowa, N.J.: Rowman & Allanheld, 1984.

Liu, Guonguang, and Zhao, Renwei. "Relationship Between Planning and Market Under Socialism." In *Economic Reform in the PRC,* edited by George C. Wang, pp. 89–104. Boulder, Colo.: Westview Press, 1982.

Lo, Ruth Earnshaw, and Kindermann, Katherine. *In the Eye of the Typhoon.* New York: Harcourt Brace Jovanovich, 1980.

Lockett, M., and Littler, C. "Trends in Chinese Industrial Management, 1972–1982." *World Development* 11 (1983): 683–704.

Low, Alfred. *Lenin on the Question of Nationality.* New York: Bookman Associates, 1958.

Lu, Baifu. "The Way for Agriculture." *Beijing Review,* January 24, 1983, pp. 14–17.

Mace, James E. "Famine and Nationalism in Soviet Ukraine." *Problems of Communism* 33 (1984): 37–50.

Macesich, George. *Yugoslavia: The Theory and Practice of Development Planning.* Charlottesville: University Press of Virginia, 1964.

Mao Tse-tung. *A Critique of Soviet Political Economy.* Translated by Moss Roberts. New York: Monthly Review Press, 1977.

————. *Mao Tse-tung and the Political Economy of the Border Region.* Translated by Andrew Watson. New York: Cambridge University Press, 1980. [Translation of Mao's *Economic and Financial Problems.*]

————. *On Khrushchev's Phony Communism.* Peking: Foreign Languages Press, 1964.

———. "Reading Notes on the Soviet Union's Political Economy." In *Miscellany of Mao Tse-tung's Thought*. Joint Publications Research Service, no. 61269-2. Washington, D.C.: U.S. Technical Information Service, 1974.

Marer, Paul. "Economic Performance and Prospects in Eastern Europe: Analytical Summary and Interpretation of Findings." In *East European Economic Assessment, Part 2*, by the U.S. Congress Joint Economic Committee, pp. 19–95. Washington, D.C.: U.S. Government Printing Office, 1981.

———. "Exchange Rates and Convertibility in Hungary's NEM." In *East European Assessment, Part I*, by the U.S. Congress Joint Economic Committee, pp. 525–48. Washington, D.C.: U.S. Government Printing Office, 1981.

———. "Economic Reform in Hungary: From Central Planning to Regulated Market." In *East European Economies: Slow Growth in the 1980s*, by the U.S. Congress Joint Economic Committee, pp. 223–297. Washington, D.C.: U.S. Government Printing Office, 1986.

Mark, Gregory A. "Hungarian Consumers and the New Economic Mechanism." *East European Quarterly* 16 (1982): 84–104.

Markish, Huri, and Malish, Anton F. "The Soviet Food Program: Prospects for the 1980s." *The ACES Bulletin* 25 (1983): 47–65.

Marshak, T. A. "Centralized Versus Decentralized Resource Allocation: The Yugoslav Laboratory." *Quarterly Journal of Economics* 82 (1968): 561–87.

Matthews, Mervyn. *Privilege in the Soviet Union*. London: Allen & Unwin, 1978.

Maxwell, Neville. *China—Changed Road to Development*. Elmsford, N.Y.: Pergamon Press, 1984.

McAuley, Alastair. *Economic Welfare in the Soviet Union*. Madison: University of Wisconsin Press, 1979.

McFarlane, Bruce. "Political Economy of Class Struggle and Economic Growth in China, 1950–1982." *World Development* 11 (1983): 659–72.

McFarquhar, Roderick. *The Origins of the Cultural Revolution*. 2 vols. Oxford: Oxford University Press; New York: Columbia University Press, 1983.

McNeal, Robert H. *Stalin's Works: An Annotated Bibliography*. Stanford: Hoover Institution Press, 1967.

Meade, James. "The Theory of Labor-Managed Firms and of Profit-Sharing." *Economic Journal* 82 (1972): 402–28.

Medvedev, Roy A. *Let History Judge: The Origins and Consequences of Stalinism*. New York: Vintage Books, 1973.

———. *On Socialist Democracy*. New York: Knopf, 1975.

Meisner, Maurice. *Marxism, Maoism, and Utopianism*. Madison: University of Wisconsin Press, 1982.

Mesa-Lago, Carmelo, and Beck, Carl, eds. *Comparative Socialist Systems*. Pittsburgh, Pa.: University of Pittsburgh Press, 1975.

Milenkovitch, Deborah D. *Plan and Market in Yugoslav Economic Thought*. New Haven, Conn.: Yale University Press, 1971.

Millar, James R. "Mass Collectivization and the Contribution of Soviet Agriculture to the First Five-Year Plan." *Slavic Review* 33 (1974): 750–66.

———. "Soviet Agriculture Since Stalin." In *The Soviet Union Since Stalin*, edited by Stephen F. Cohen, A. Rabinowitch, and R. Sharlet, pp. 135–54. Bloomington: Indiana University Press, 1980.

Montias, John Michael. *The Structure of Economic Systems.* New Haven, Conn.: Yale University Press, 1976.

———. "Types of Communist Economic Systems." In *Change in Communist Systems*, edited by Chalmers Johnson, pp. 117–34. Stanford: Stanford University Press, 1970.

Moore, John H. *Growth with Self-Management: Yugoslav Industrialization, 1952–1975.* Stanford: Hoover Institution Press, 1980.

———. "Self-Management in Yugoslavia." In *East European Economic Assessment, Part 1,* by the U.S. Congress Joint Economic Committee, pp. 215–29. Washington, D.C.: U.S. Government Printing Office, 1981.

Murrell, Peter. "An Evaluation of the Success of the Hungarian Economic Reform: An Analysis Using International Trade Data." *Journal of Comparative Economics* 5 (1981): 352–67.

Myers, Ramon H. *The Chinese Economy Past and Present.* Belmont, Calif.: Wadsworth, 1980.

Myrdal, Jan, and Kessle, Gun. *China: The Revolution Continued.* New York: Pantheon Books, 1970.

Neal, Fred Warner. "Yugoslav Approaches to the Nationalities Problem: The Politics of Circumvention." *East European Quarterly* 18 (1984): 327–34.

Nemchinov, V., ed. *The Use of Mathematics in Economics.* Edinburgh: Oliver and Boyd, 1964.

Neuberger, Egon, and Duffy, William J. *Comparative Economic Systems: A Decision-Making Approach.* Boston: Allyn and Bacon, 1976.

Nishiyama, Chiaki, and Leube, Kurt R., eds. *The Essence of Hayek.* Stanford: Hoover Institution Press, 1984.

Nove, Alec. *Political Economy and Soviet Socialism.* Winchester, Mass.: Allen & Unwin, 1978.

———. *Stalinism and After.* London: Allen & Unwin, 1978.

———. *Was Stalin Really Necessary?* London and New York: Praeger, 1964.

Obradovic, Josip. *Worker's Participation in Yugoslavia: Theory and Research.* Occasional Paper, no. 4. University of South Carolina Institute of International Studies, 1975 [?].

Olcott, Martha Brill. "The Collectivization Drive in Kazakhstan." *Russian Review* 40 (1981): 122–42.

O'Relley, Z. Edward. "Hungarian Agricultural Performance and Policy During the NEM." In *East European Economies Post-Helsinki,* by the U.S. Congress Joint Economic Committee, pp. 365–78. Washington, D.C.: U.S. Government Printing Office, 1977.

Organization for European Economic Development. *Yugoslavia*. Paris: Organization for European Economic Development, 1982.

Ovseynko, Anton Antonov. *The Time of Stalin: Portrait of a Tyranny*. New York: Harper & Row, 1981.

Pairault, Thierry. "Chinese Market Mechanism: A Controversial Debate." *World Development* 11 (1983): 639–45.

Pasic, Nojdan; Grozdanic, S.; and Radevic, M., eds. *Workers' Management in Yugoslavia: Recent Developments and Trends*. Geneva: International Labour Office, 1982.

Peebles, Gavin. "Inflation in the People's Republic of China." *The Three Banks Review*, no. 142 (1984), pp. 37–57.

Pejovich, Svetozar, and Furubotn, Eirik G. "Property Rights, Economic Decentralization, and the Evolution of the Yugoslav Firm, 1965–1972." *Journal of Law and Economics* 16 (1973): 275–302.

Pepper, Roy. *Romania: The Industrialization of an Agrarian Economy under Socialist Planning*. Baltimore, Md.: Johns Hopkins University Press, 1979.

Perkins, Dwight. *China's Economic Policy and Performance During the Cultural Revolution and Its Aftermath*. Development Discussion Paper, no. 161. Cambridge, Mass.: Harvard Institute for International Development, 1984.

Perrolle, Pierre M., and Ginsburg, Phillip E., eds. "Mao Tse-tung's Speeches at the Chengchow Conference," *Chinese Law and Government* 9 (1976–77): 3–92.

Piskotkin, Mikhail. *Sotsializm i gosudarstvennoe upravlenie* [Socialism and state administration]. Moscow: Nauka, 1984.

Portes, Richard. "Hungary: Economic Performance, Policy, and Prospects." In *East European Economies Post-Helsinki*, by the U.S. Congress Joint Economic Committee, pp. 766–815. Washington, D.C.: U.S. Government Printing Office, 1977.

Powell, Raymond. "Plan Execution and the Workability of Soviet Planning." *Journal of Comparative Economics* 1 (1977): 51–76.

Prasnikar, Janez. "The Yugoslav Self-Managed Firm." *East European Economics* 22 (1983–84): 3–79.

Preobrazhenskii, Evgenii A. *The Crisis of Soviet Industrialization*. Edited by Donald A. Filtzer. London: Macmillan, 1980.

———. *Novaia ekonomika: Opyt teoreticheskogo analiza sovetskogo khoziaistva* [New economics: Attempt at a theoretical analysis of the Soviet economy]. 2nd ed. Moscow: Komokadizdat, 1926.

Prybyla, Jan S. *The Chinese Economy: Problems and Policies*. 2nd ed. Columbia: University of South Carolina, 1981.

———. *Issues in Socialist Economic Modernization*. New York: Praeger, 1980.

———. "Man and Society in China: Some Reflections for Our Times." *Vital Speeches of the Day* 41 (1975): 551–54.

——. *The Political Economy of Communist China.* Scranton, Pa.: International Textbook Company, 1970.

Pryor, Frederic L. "The Impact of Social and Economic Institutions on the Size Distribution of Income and Wealth." *American Economic Review* 57 (1973): 50–73.

——. *Property and Industrial Organization in Communist and Capitalist Nations.* Bloomington: Indiana University Press, 1973.

——. "Some Costs and Benefits of Markets: An Empirical Study." *Quarterly Journal of Economics* 91 (1977): 81–102.

Rakowska-Harmstone, Teresa, ed. *Perspectives for Change in Communist Societies.* 2nd ed. Bloomington: Indiana University Press, 1984.

Ramet, Pedro, ed. *Yugoslavia in the 1980s.* Boulder, Colo.: Westview Press, 1985.

"Resolution on Questions in Party History Since 1949, Adopted by the 6th Plenum of the 11th Central Committee of the Communist Party of China on June 29, 1981." *Beijing Review*, July 6, 1981, pp. 10–39.

Rigby, T. H., and Harasymiw, Bohdan, eds. *Leadership Selection and Patron-Client Relations in the USSR and Yugoslavia.* Winchester, Mass.: Allen & Unwin, 1983.

Robinson, Joan. *The Cultural Revolution in China.* London and Baltimore, Md.: Penguin, 1969.

Rocca, Raymond, and Dziak, John. *Bibliography on Soviet Intelligence and Security Services.* Boulder, Colo.: Westview Press, 1985.

Rosefielde, Steven, ed. *Economic Welfare and the Economics of Soviet Socialism.* New York: Cambridge University Press, 1981.

Rupp, Kalman. *Entrepreneurs in Red: Structure and Organizational Innovation in the Centrally Planned Economy.* Albany: State University of New York Press, 1983.

Rusinow, Dennison. *The Yugoslav Experiment: 1948–1974.* Berkeley: University of California Press, 1977.

Rydenfelt, Sven. *A Pattern for Failure.* New York: Harcourt Brace Jovanovich, 1984.

Sacks, Stephen R. "Divisionalization in Large Yugoslav Enterprises." *Journal of Comparative Economics* 4 (1980): 209–25.

Schapiro, Leonard, and Godson, Joseph. *The Soviet Worker.* 2nd ed. London: Macmillan, 1984.

Schnytzer, Adi. *Stalinist Economic Strategy in Practice: The Case of Albania.* Economies of the World Series. Oxford: Oxford University Press, 1982.

Schram, Stuart R. " 'Economics in Command?' Ideology and Policy Since the Third Plenum, 1978–84." *The China Quarterly*, no. 99 (1984), pp. 417–61.

——. *Mao Zedong: A Preliminary Reassessment.* Hong Kong: Chinese University Press, 1984.

————, ed. *Chairman Mao Talks to the People, Talks and Letters: 1956–1971.* New York: Pantheon Books, 1974.

Schrenk, Martin; Ardalan, Cyrus; and El Totany, Nawal A. *Yugoslavia: Self-Management, Socialism and the Challenges of Development.* Baltimore, Md.: Johns Hopkins University Press [for the World Bank], 1979. [Report of a World Bank mission to Yugoslavia.]

Schroeder, Gertrude E. "The Soviet Economy on a Treadmill of 'Reforms.' " In *Soviet Economy in a Time of Change,* by the U.S. Congress Joint Economic Committee, pp. 312–40. Washington, D.C.: U.S. Government Printing Office, 1979.

Schumpeter, Joseph A. *Capitalism, Socialism, and Democracy.* 3rd ed. New York: Harper, 1950.

Schwartz, Benjamin. "Modernization and the Maoist Vision: Some Reflections on Chinese Communist Goals." *The China Quarterly,* no. 21 (1965), pp. 3–19.

Scott, Harriet Fast, and Scott, William F. *The Armed Forces of the USSR.* 3rd rev. ed. Boulder, Colo.: Westview Press, 1984.

Selected Readings from the Works of Mao Tse-tung. Beijing: Foreign Languages Press, 1976.

Selected Works of Deng Xiaoping (1975–1982). Beijing: Foreign Languages Press, 1984.

Seroka, James H. "Local Political Structures and Policy Outposts in the Yugoslav Commune." *Studies in Comparative Communism* 17 (1979): 63–74.

Sharpe, Myron E., ed. *Planning, Profit and Incentives in the USSR.* Vol. 1. White Plains, N.Y.: International Arts and Sciences Press, 1966.

Sik, Ota. *Plan and Market Under Socialism.* Translated by Eleanor Wheeler. White Plains, N.Y.: International Arts and Sciences Press, 1967.

Simes, Dimitri K. "The Soviet Parallel Market." *Survey* 21 (1975): 42–52.

Sirc, Ljubo. *The Yugoslav Economy Under Self-Management.* London: Macmillan, 1979.

————. "The Yugoslav Economy Under Self-Management: A Postscript." *South Slav Journal* 2 (1979): 9–11.

Smolinski, Leon, ed. *L. V. Kantorovich: Essays in Optimal Planning.* White Plains, N.Y.: International Arts and Sciences Press, 1976.

Soós, Károly A. "Causes of Investment Fluctuations." *Eastern European Economics* 14 (1975–76): 25–36.

Spulber, Nicholas. *Soviet Strategy for Economic Growth.* Bloomington: Indiana University Press, 1964.

————, ed. *Foundations of Soviet Strategy for Economic Growth.* Bloomington: Indiana University Press, 1964.

Stalin, J. *Economic Problems of Socialism in the U.S.S.R.* New York: International Publishers, 1952.

Staller, George. "Fluctuations in Economic Activity: Planned and Free-Market Economies." *American Economic Review* 54 (1964): 385–95.

Starr, John Bryan. *Continuing the Revolution: The Political Thought of Mao.* Princeton, N.J.: Princeton University Press, 1979.

Starr, John Bryan, and Dyer, Nancy Anne. *Post-Liberation Works of Mao Zedong: A Bibliography and Index.* Berkeley: University of California Institute of East Asian Studies, 1976.

Stojanović, Radmila. *The Functioning of the Yugoslav Economy.* Armonk, N.Y.: M. E. Sharpe, 1982. [Published simultaneously in *Eastern European Economics* 20 (1981–82): 3–274.]

Stuart, Robert C. *The Collective Farm in Soviet Agriculture.* Lexington, Mass.: Heath, 1972.

———. "Russian and Soviet Agriculture: The Western Perspective." *The ACES Bulletin* 25 (1983): 43–52.

———, ed. *The Soviet Rural Economy.* Totowa, N.J.: Rowman & Allanheld, 1983.

Su, Wenming, ed. *Economic Readjustment and Reform.* China Today [*Beijing Review* special feature series]. Beijing: Beijing Review, 1982.

Sugar, Peter, and Lederer, Ivo, eds. *Nationalism in Eastern Europe.* Seattle: University of Washington Press, 1969.

Sun, Yefang. *Social Needs Versus Economic Efficiency in China: Sun Yefang's Critique of Socialist Economics.* Edited and translated by K. K. Fung. Armonk, N.Y.: M. E. Sharpe, 1982.

Tardos, Márton. "The Role of Money: Economic Relations Between the State and the Enterprise in Hungary." *Acta Oeconomica* 25 (1980): 19–36.

Timar, Matyas. *Reflections on the Economic Development of Hungary, 1967–73.* Budapest: Akadémiai Kiadó, 1975.

Travers, Lee. "Post-1978 Rural Economic Policy and Peasant Income in China." *The China Quarterly,* no. 98 (1984), pp. 241–59.

Tretyakova, Albina, and Birman, Igor. "Input-Output Analysis in the USSR." *Soviet Studies* 28 (1976): 157–86.

Triska, Jan F., and Gati, Charles, eds. *Blue Collar Workers in Eastern Europe.* Winchester, Mass.: Allen & Unwin, 1981.

Tucker, Robert C., ed. *Stalinism: Essays in Historical Interpretation.* New York: Norton, 1977.

Tyson, Laura D'Andrea. "Incentives, Income-Sharing, and Institutional Innovation in the Yugoslav Self-Managed Firm." *Journal of Comparative Economics* 3 (1979): 285–300.

———. *The Yugoslav Economic System and Its Performance in the 1970s.* Berkeley: University of California Institute of International Studies, 1980.

Ulam, Adam B. *Stalin: The Man and His Era.* New York: Viking, 1973.

U.S. Congress Joint Economic Committee. *Soviet Economy in a Time of Change.* Vol. 1. Washington, D.C.: U.S. Government Printing Office, 1979.

―――. *Soviet Economy in the 1980s: Problems and Prospects, Part 1 and Part 2.* Washington, D.C.: U.S. Government Printing Office, 1983.

Vanek, Jaroslav. *The General Theory of Labor-Managed Market Economies.* Ithaca, N.Y.: Cornell University Press, 1970.

―――. *The Labor-Managed Economy.* Ithaca, N.Y.: Cornell University Press, 1977.

―――. *The Participatory Economy: An Evolutionary Hypothesis and a Strategy for Development.* Ithaca, N.Y.: Cornell University Press, 1971.

―――, ed. *Self-Management: Economic Liberation of Man.* Ithaca, N.Y.: Cornell University Press, 1975.

Varga, Werner. "Yugoslavia's Battle for Economic Stability." *East European Economics* 19 (1981): 58–74.

Volin, Lazar. *A Century of Russian Agriculture.* Cambridge, Mass.: Harvard University Press, 1970.

von Mises, Ludwig. *Human Action: A Treatise on Economics.* 3rd rev. ed. Chicago: H. Regnery, 1966.

Voslensky, Michael. *Nomenklatura.* New York: Doubleday, 1984.

Wachtel, Howard. *Workers' Management and Workers' Wages in Yugoslavia.* Ithaca, N.Y.: Cornell University Press, 1973.

Wädekin, Karl-Eugen. *Agrarian Policies in Communist Europe.* Studies in East European and Soviet Agrarian Policy, edited by Alec Nove, vol. 1. The Hague, Neth., and London: Martinus Nijhoff; Totowa, N.J.: N. J. Allanheld Osmun, 1982.

―――. *The Private Sector in Soviet Agriculture.* Berkeley: University of California Press, 1973.

Wakeman, Frederic, Jr. *History and Will: Philosophical Perspectives of Mao Tsetung's Thought.* Berkeley and Los Angeles: University of California Press, 1973.

Walker, Kenneth R. *Food Grain Procurement and Consumption in China.* New York: Cambridge University Press, 1984.

Wang, George C., ed. and trans. *Economic Reform in the PRC: In Which China's Economists Make Known What Went Wrong, Why, and What Should Be Done About It.* Boulder, Colo.: Westview Press, 1982.

Wang, Tong-eng. *Economic Policies and Price Stability in China.* Berkeley: University of California Institute of East Asian Studies, 1980.

Ward, Benjamin. "The Firm in Illyria: Market Syndicalism." *American Economic Review* 48 (1968): 566–89.

―――. "Marxism-Horvatism: A Yugoslav Theory of Socialism." *American Economic Review* 62 (1967): 509–23.

Wiles, Peter. *Economic Institutions Compared.* New York: Wiley, 1977.

Wilhelm, John. "Does the Soviet Union Have a Planned Economy?" *Soviet Studies* 31 (1979): 268–74.

Witke, Roxanne. *Comrade Chiang Ch'ing*. Boston: Little, Brown, 1977.

Wu, Tien-wei. *Lin Biao and the Gang of Four: Contra-Confucianism in Historical and Intellectual Perspective*. Carbondale: Southern Illinois University Press, 1983.

Wyzan, Michael L., and Utter, Andrew M. "The Yugoslav Inflation." *Journal of Comparative Economics* 6 (1982): 396–405.

Xue, Muqiao. *China's Socialist Economy*. Beijing: Foreign Languages Press, 1982.

————. *Current Economic Problems in China*. Edited, translated, and with an introduction by K. K. Fung. Boulder, Colo.: Westview Press, 1982.

————, ed. *Almanac of China's Economy*. Hong Kong: Modern Cultural Company Ltd., 1984.

Yanowitch, Murray. *Social and Economic Inequality in the USSR*. White Plains, N.Y.: M. E. Sharpe, 1977.

————. *Work in the Soviet Union: Attitudes and Issues*. Armonk, N.Y.: M. E. Sharpe, 1985.

Yu, Guangyuan, ed. *China's Socialist Modernization*. Beijing: Foreign Languages Press, 1984.

Zaleski, Eugène. *Planning Reforms in the Soviet Union, 1962–1966*. Chapel Hill: University of North Carolina Press, 1967.

————. *Stalinist Planning for Economic Growth, 1933–1952*. Chapel Hill: University of North Carolina Press, 1980.

Zauberman, Alfred. *The Mathematical Revolution in Soviet Economics*. Oxford: Oxford University Press, 1975.

————. *Mathematical Theory in Soviet Planning: Concepts, Methods, Techniques*. Oxford: Oxford University Press, 1976.

Zhiping, Cheng. "Price Reform Key to Increasing Production." *Beijing Review*, April 22, 1985, pp. 15–16, 21.

Ziyang, Zhao. "The Current Economic Situation and the Reform of the Economic Structure." *Beijing Review*, April 22, 1985, pp. 1–15. [Report on the work of the government (March 27, 1985) to the third session of the Sixth National People's Congress.]

Zwass, Adam. *The Economies of Eastern Europe in a Time of Change*. London: Macmillan, 1984.

INDEX